Willow
Creek
Seeker
Services

This is the definitive study of the most influential church in North America.

Lyle E. Schaller
Author
One of America's leading church consultants

Willow Creek Seeker Services is a penetrating critique of the most talked about church in America. I found the first two-thirds of this study to be eminently fair in presenting Willow Creek's program and the last third to be devastating in its critique.

James Montgomery Boice
Author and senior pastor
Tenth Presbyterian Church
Philadelphia

Willow Creek Seeker Services

Evaluating a New Way of Doing Church

G. A. Pritchard

BakerBooks
A Division of Baker Book House Co
Grand Rapids, Michigan 49516

Published by Baker Book
a division of Baker Book House Company
P.O. Box 6287, Grand Rapids, MI 49516-6287

Fourth printing, January 2001

Printed in the United States of America

Library of Congress Cataloging-in-Publication Data

Pritchard, Gregory A., 1957-
Willow Creek seeker services : evaluating a new way of doing church / Gregory A. Pritchard.
p. cm.
Revision of author's thesis (Ph.D.—Northwestern University, 1994).
Includes bibliographical references.
ISBN 0-8010-5274-2 (pbk.)
1. Evangelistic work—Illinois—South Barrington—History—20th century. 2. Willow Creek Community Church (South Barrington, Ill.). 3. Non church-affiliated people—United States—Religious life. I. Title
BV3775.S68P75 1995
280—dc20 95-21487

For information about academic books, resources for Christian leaders, and all new releases available from Baker Book House, visit our web site:
http://www.bakerbooks.com/

To Skipp and Bob Pritchard

Mom and Dad,
Thank you for your love and wisdom;
By your words and deeds,
Your children have seen how to live.

To honor you.

Contents

Contents

Preface

Why are you reading this book?

As I researched and wrote this volume, I wondered about those who would eventually read it. What made them interested in the strategy of a church that they would probably never attend? What was their motivation and objective?

I realized that the majority of readers would be my fellow evangelicals: A book about an evangelical church, even a fast-growing and influential church like Willow Creek, would have less appeal to those without an evangelical commitment. The majority of these readers are probably coming to the topic with some preconceived ideas and opinions; in effect, they are already Willow Creek advocates or critics. A word should probably be said to each.

I also recognized that there would probably be a significant group of readers who are interested observers outside of the evangelical community. These individuals may be curious about the Willow Creek phenomenon, interested in church growth generally, or be my colleagues in the academic study of religion. I will also make a brief comment to this group of readers.

To evangelicals who agree with Willow Creek:

If you agree with Willow Creek, you may be reading this book to gain useful principles and ideas to apply to your local situation. I believe that you will be able to sift through this material and collect some helpful ideas.

And, yet, this is a rare opportunity for you to take a long, honest look at what you are doing and why you are doing it. The writer of Proverbs counsels us that wisdom comes to those who "search for it" (2:4). I would encourage you to have the attitude that I found in a Willow Creek staff member: When I began this study, he responded that this type of inquiry was "very important," as it was an opportunity to get an outside perspective. "We're not going to like everything people say about us," he said, "but if we stop listening, that's a dangerous sign."

To evangelicals who disagree with Willow Creek:

If you disagree with Willow Creek, you may be reading this to gain a critical perspective of Willow Creek. I believe that you will be able to sift through this material and find some ways to criticize Willow Creek.

And, yet, if you are an evangelical, you realize that our human hearts are "deceitful above all things" (Jer. 17:9). As Bible believers, you believe that human beings are innately prone to lie to themselves in order to justify their behavior. Genesis records Adam's attempt at this dishonesty as he simultaneously blamed his failure on both Eve and God: "The woman you put here with me—" (Gen. 3:12). The first step of an evangelical critical of Willow Creek should be to question his or her own motivation. The second step should be to be willing to learn whatever he or she can from Willow Creek.

To interested observers:

As should already be clear, Willow Creek, at present, is a highly contentious topic in the evangelical community. And yet this dispute pales in comparison to the cultural wars that America is currently in the throes of. There are few political topics that will get a more heated response than asking what someone thinks of the "religious right." Thus it is likely that you are not a merely neutral interested observer.

A temptation of individuals who are involved in political disputes is to vilify their opponents and uncritically praise their allies. For example, it is very difficult to find anyone involved in politics who describes Clarence Thomas and Anita Hill with anything other than admiration or condemnation. Yet this politicizing distorts how one sees reality. Complexity and a myriad of colors become black and white cartoonish characters.

A normal human response in political conflict is to ridicule one's opponents. One should be wary of the temptation to mock others. It is true that anyone who is a student of human nature often finds himself tickled by the absurdities of other people's behavior. And we evangelicals are often a particularly humorous bunch. But there is significance to sarcasm's root meaning, "eating flesh." For embedded in a scornful smirk is the tooth decay of a rancid pride. The cynicism of a superior attitude is blind to simple truths, as when Jesus said, "Unless you change and become like little children, you will never enter the kingdom of heaven" (Matt. 18:3).

It seems I do not have a different thing to say to each group. In fact, I am merely repeating what I have been saying to myself as I worked on this study. As human beings, each of us is tempted to see that which reinforces our own beliefs and lifestyles. We need to be wary of our pride and biases and commit ourselves to search for the truth in humility and honesty. The doorway to truth is very low. We must humbly bend our necks to enter.

Introduction

Why Study Willow Creek?

Willow Creek is leading a worldwide movement. Attending a recent Willow Creek training conference in South Barrington, Illinois, were over 2,300 church leaders from Australia, the Bahamas, Canada, England, Holland, Honduras, India, Japan, Korea, Mexico, Norway, Scotland, Sweden, the United States, and Venezuela. Since 1988 Willow Creek has sponsored Christian Leadership conferences in the United States, England, Wales, France, Australia, and New Zealand with an attendance of more than 50,000 individuals. Willow Creek is currently shaping how church is "done" for thousands of churches.

In a recent interview, Willow Creek's senior pastor, Bill Hybels, explained that he does not think denominations are "the wave of the future." This raises the obvious question, What *is* the wave of the future? Hybels and Willow Creek's answer is found in the logo of the Willow Creek Association (the organization that Hybels founded to spread the Willow Creek vision), a picture of a series of waves. We can understand Willow Creek's influence on the worldwide evangelical church through these waves of the future.[1]

The First Wave

Willow Creek's first wave of influence is through the basic operation of its ministries and size of the church itself. Willow Creek has more than two hundred seventy full and part-time staff members who run the church's programs and ministries. The Willow Creek Association has nineteen staff members. All of these individuals are committed to the Willow Creek understanding of how "to do" church. More than 280,000 Willow Creek audiotapes are sold yearly in its "Seeds Ministry," and more than a million people attend church functions annually.

The Second Wave

The second wave is made up of hundreds of churches that have adopted a Willow Creek style seeker service designed for the unchurched. *Christianity Today* has described Willow Creek as the "undisputed prototype" of this new way of doing church. Bill Hybels has been the most persuasive advocate in making "seeker-targeted" churches a viable option for evangelicals.[2]

As a result of this influence, Willow Creek has hatched a large and growing brood of baby "Creeker" churches. Most of these Willow Creek style churches are new congregations being planted around the country and world.

The Third Wave

The third wave of influence is the thousands of churches and pastors who have altered their music, programming, and preaching to be "seeker friendly" or "seeker sensitive." An advertisement for another church's leadership conference in *Christianity Today* explained, "This is especially for fairly traditional churches like ours that can't go the excellent Willow Creek way but still want to change for growth with balance." These churches want to be "seeker friendly" or "seeker sensitive" without having a service for the unchurched. By the time of publication, there will be close to one thousand churches that have joined the Willow Creek Association, "an international Network of Churches Ministering to the Unchurched." These are primarily churches in the second or third wave.[3]

The Fourth Wave

In the fourth wave of influence are the thousands of churches and individuals around the world who have been influenced by the Willow Creek programs, principles, books, and tools that the church has produced. An example of this influence is the "Network" training program that was developed at Willow Creek. This program clarifies a number of Willow Creek ideas concerning spiritual gifts and places them in an easily transferable program.[4]

The well-known church consultant Lyle Schaller has described Willow Creek as the most influential church in North America and perhaps the world. At the least, Willow Creek is spearheading a worldwide movement that is revolutionizing churches. If we can understand the church leading this revolution, our discussion may be helpful to those churches and individuals who are a part of this growing movement as well as to those that are outside of it.[5]

How to Study Willow Creek

One of the great strengths—and weaknesses—of those of us who are evangelicals is a willingness to quickly proclaim what we believe. In the midst of our culture, which is flooded by relativism, we are willing and often eager to proclaim that we have found the truth in Jesus. Yet a problem often arises in how we as evangelicals deal with each other.

We are often zealous to lower our theological cannons and blast away at those in the evangelical family with whom we may disagree, before we really know what they are saying and doing. I need to be clear here. We need to be willing to do battle for the truth. As evangelical patriarch Ken Kantzer has written, "Theological battles are not alien to evangelicalism. They never have been." But before we critique our evangelical family, we need to make sure we understand them.[6]

This is especially true when the issue under consideration is a controversial one. One *Christianity Today* senior editor commented on how evangelicals are bitterly quarreling about the use of marketing tools:

> This consumer-oriented approach is enthusiastically embraced by some and passionately denounced as "pragmatism" by others. (To raise the issue in a representative group of pastors is sure to provoke an argument reminiscent of the Arminian/Calvinist or eschatological debates of yore.)[7]

Many have invested years, even decades, in defending their understanding of how the church should operate. This is no casual conversation over tea and crumpets.

In the midst of such a rhetorical battle, often one's first motivation is to win, rather than to truly understand one's opponents. Each side tends to talk past the other. As a result, neither side truly understands the other, and polemic points are won at the expense of the facts. Arguments are advanced, but truth is a casualty. Defenders react against what they feel are inaccurate or distorted critiques but often don't listen to legitimate questions from their evangelical brethren. Sometimes critics have targeted what they believe is a compromise of the faith but have not adequately studied those who adhere to what they are critiquing.

Imagine this evangelical conflict as a deeply embedded marital dispute. This is a marriage in trouble. Both sides feel misunderstood and accused. Both feel threatened and thus angry. Each is tempted to lash out at the other.

The foundational step toward the healing of this marriage is to really listen to each other and establish a common description that both can agree with. Until this common description is established, opposing analyses are merely thrown back and forth as accusations. The first section of this book (chapters 1–13) is my attempt to establish a common description of this new way of doing church. I used sociological tools to do this. Chapters 14–20 then provide my analysis of the strengths and weaknesses of this new strategy.

Sociological Method

Much of this problem in communication is because we as evangelicals are not seeing ourselves clearly. Before we proclaim what should be, we need to ask, What is? There is a great need to study empirical reality rigorously. This book attempts, using the best methods and tools of sociology, to understand empirical reality. This sociological method leads to the emphasis of several issues.

Limited Topic

Part of the current communication problem among evangelicals is that debaters on both sides of the church-marketing issue have argued over too large a canvas with too wide a brush. To speak of all the churches influenced by church growth and marketing is neither credible nor helpful. There needs to be a commitment to the highest standards of accuracy. Until the topic of a study is more limited, little accurate description can take place. Our topic is, thankfully, more confined. This book is a description and analysis of Willow Creek's seeker service. By using a sociological microscope to study Willow Creek, we can hope to understand the core of this growing movement.

Research History

The next step of a proper sociological method is to give a research history. In May of 1989, I was involved in a Ph.D. program at Northwestern University. My proposal for my doctoral dissertation had just been turned down. I had wanted to do a large cultural study of evangelicalism, but I was told that it was too broad a topic for a dissertation.

I was meeting with my advisors in a few weeks and needed to find an alternate, smaller subject for my dissertation. I pondered the question, "What limited topic within evangelicalism would they let me research and write about?" I decided to study Willow Creek because of its proximity to where

I lived and I prepared my proposal, which they accepted. I eventually wrote my dissertation, and this book is drawn from that research.

The point behind this history? I did not want to write this book. I did not come to the study of Willow Creek with a strong motivation to defend or attack Willow Creek. Although I am an evangelical, I did not come to my study of Willow Creek primarily as an advocate or critic, but as a researcher. This may have been my greatest advantage. My lack of an agenda has helped me describe the church more fairly.[8]

The Description

Approximately two-thirds of this book is a description of what Willow Creek is doing and why. The major question of this study was, "How is Willow Creek seeking to help unchurched individuals convert to the gospel?" My research methods flowed from this question.

A strong emphasis of what is often called qualitative sociology is to listen to the individuals who are being studied. I listened to the people of Willow Creek. When I met with Willow Creek staff, I told them that I wanted to be fair and accurate. I interviewed about seventy Willow Creek staff, lay leaders, and attenders and had conversations with hundreds of other participants. I studied the internal research that the church made available to me. I attended the church and its various programs for about two and a half years. I transcribed a year of weekend messages from June 1989 to May 1990 and did a content analysis of these talks. A part of this content analysis was a computer concordance of how many times every word was used during that year of messages.[9]

In my efforts to be fair and accurate I asked church staff members and others who were interviewed to read this book to see if they agreed with my descriptions. Generally, they did.

After reading several chapters, teaching pastor Lee Strobel commented that he believed I was "trying to be fair and complete and honest." Evangelism director Mark Mittelberg called the chapters on truth and gospel "accurate" and explained, "I think you do a really good job of synthesizing." Programming director Nancy Beach, after reading the chapters on programming, remarked that she felt I was "fair" and had done a "good job." Former church leader Dave Holmbo called a draft of the majority of the history chapter "amazingly accurate." After reading the section describing his influence on Willow Creek, television evangelist Robert Schuller responded, "I don't think anybody has ever understood me or interpreted me the way the truth really is—like you have." Willow Creek theologian

Gilbert Bilezikian commented after reading a draft of the first thirteen chapters of the book.

> I think you are doing a super work that will be very useful—like a course in modern ecclesiology. Your approach is fair and objective. You have done a lot of research in related areas to be able to proceed with an evaluation of WCCC. Great Job!

I don't list these comments to pat myself on the back. The point is that those I have described generally believe I have succeeded in accurately representing them. When they haven't agreed with my understanding, I have often put their responses in the text or endnotes to give an alternative perspective. This openness to others' feedback is an acknowledgment that Willow Creek is very complicated. Teaching pastor Lee Strobel admits, "I've been on staff for three years and going to church for ten and I don't understand it all. I think very few people do." The best sociologists acknowledge that empirical reality is very messy. It is not easy to describe a church with fifteen thousand weekly attenders.[10]

The Limitation of Sociology

Sociology, like every academic discipline, has potential biases. One of these is the empirical atheism that many sociologists bring to their work. As sociologist Nancy Ammerman describes, "Sociology explains things 'as if' there were only human causes."[11]

A Christian sociologist ultimately must view that sort of empirical study rather skeptically. Much can be learned from a rigorous study of empirical data, yet a Christian understands sociological study as a description of a soccer match in which only half the players are visible. A Christian sociologist knows the empirical data represents only part of the truth. He affirms a belief in a spiritual, invisible reality that profoundly impacts the visible. This is not to dismiss the value of a rigorous empirical sociological analysis. It merely notes that from a Christian point of view, this is only half the reality.

Evaluation

What can be learned from Willow Creek? What questions need to be asked? What critiques need to be made? The last part of this book addresses these issues. At that point the discussion moves from a sociological description to a theological evaluation.

To raise the topic of evaluation, I need to underline again the need we all have for humility. If I were to study any church (or person) as closely as I examined Willow Creek, I would find many flaws. We live in the shadow of the fall and are all sinful creatures. Sin is the one empirically verifiable biblical doctrine. So before we pick up a stone, we should look very closely at ourselves.

Purpose

The purpose of this book is to describe and analyze what *is*. Both sides of the debate over marketing within evangelicalism will be able to use my research in their arguments. But I hope that both will truly seek to learn and listen. Although this book represents years of study, I do not have all truth. Neither do you. We need to stop acting as if we do. The tone of our family feud has not been particularly pleasant. We need to listen and learn from one another.

Ultimately, history will record the influence of the Willow Creek movement. Will it be significant and long-lasting, or is Willow Creek another evangelical fad? One hundred years from now, our descendants will be able to see the strengths and weaknesses of the Willow Creek movement rather more easily. In the midst of the trees of history, it is often difficult to see the forest. Yet we must try. Whether you are an advocate or a critic, it is important to try to understand Willow Creek to know how to be faithful to our Lord. We must all be humble and honest and willing to learn.[12]

Part 1

Understanding the Willow Creek Way of Doing Church

1

A New Way of Doing Church

Willow Creek is different.

I will sketch a couple of verbal pictures of this new way of doing church.

Fall 1983. I first heard of Willow Creek after moving to the Chicago area to attend graduate school. After a few weeks in the area, a friend suggested that we go to a church she had occasionally attended, and I reluctantly agreed. I, probably like most Americans, don't enjoy visiting new churches.

Upon approaching the church, I suspected that it was unique. It had a graceful, curving entrance road that stretched beside a beautiful lake filled with Canada geese. There were hundreds of cars being guided by dozens of parking attendants—similar to the traffic control at a professional sporting event.

From the enormous parking lot, we walked with hundreds of others toward a massive but attractive concrete, steel, and glass edifice. We entered a wall of glass doors. I felt like I was going to a rock concert.

We stepped into a huge four-star-hotel-like atrium and followed a flow of people traffic toward the auditorium. We passed smiling ushers who were handing out programs at the doors. We were not otherwise approached or greeted and seated ourselves wherever we wanted in the individual, well-cushioned "movie theater" seats. The entire audience was white and casually well-dressed. I would have chosen a seat at the back and the side, but my friend chose the front and center. I followed.

As we entered the auditorium, a group of musicians was on the stage playing professional-quality light jazz. After a few minutes, a stylishly dressed man in his late twenties came onto the stage, smiled brightly, and said, "Good Morning! Welcome to Willow Creek!" He asked us to stand, and we sang a short praise chorus. That was the full extent of our participation in the service.

The rest of the program included a drama dealing with the topic of the day, an offering in which visitors were asked not to participate, a few musical numbers involving both singers and a backup band, and a thirty-minute talk that was very humorous and had the crowd laughing uproariously at several points.

In my previous work as a Christian educator, I had opportunity to travel around the United States and Europe and experience a wide variety of Christian organizations and churches. I thought I had seen everything. Willow Creek was different.

Fall 1990. The audience was dazed. They had just been through an hour-long kaleidoscope of drama, multi-media, and rock and roll music. It was the Willow Creek production "What a Ride!" which celebrated the fifteen years of the church's existence. This extravaganza had deftly touched the emotional chords of those attending, and they had felt at different times sad, mirthful, pensive, and happy. A slender man smartly dressed in coat and tie strolled with a microphone to the center of the platform. It was Bill Hybels. He said:

> You know, we're into fifteen years now as a church, and yet many of us are still asked, quite often these days, "What is Willow Creek all about?" And at this occasion I just want to summarize it to you. Willow Creek is about God. We really believe in him. Not as a remote deity who is unconcerned, but a God who is alive, powerful, and concerned and eager to intervene in lives like our lives. Willow Creek is about God.
>
> And Willow Creek is about people, people who have discovered along the path of life that life without purpose is not much of a life.
>
> And life spent just piling up resources, shooting for positions of power, trying to experience pleasure—it's not all that much of a life. And life apart from being related to God is not much of a life; it's pretty shallow.

More than twenty-six thousand individuals saw this show and heard this explanation. Perhaps half were visitors to the church. The explanation is typical of how Hybels and Willow Creek staff and volunteers present to unchurched individuals what they are doing.

These two brief descriptions provide a quick picture of Willow Creek's weekend services. Willow Creek attracts thousands of unchurched people to its seeker services. It presents professionally staged programs that skillfully address the real-life issues and needs of its audience, often in a stirring way. Speakers then suggest that a life with God is the best way to satisfy these needs.

At the same time, the speakers endeavor to refute Christianity's alternatives. They argue that those who choose a life of pursuing possessions, power, or pleasure will ultimately find life unsatisfying. Their explanation of God's nature emphasizes God's love and desire to be involved in people's lives. They argue that human fulfillment comes only as individuals respond to and build a relationship with God.

Willow Creek's Strategy

Willow Creek's method of presenting the gospel to unchurched individuals is unique. There is a need to understand what Willow Creek is doing. But before we seek to comprehend Willow Creek's seeker service we need to understand why Willow Creek believes it is necessary. We need to understand Willow Creek's overall strategy.

In a talk on the philosophy of Willow Creek, Hybels declared:

> We are like many other churches when it comes to our purpose. Almost every Bible-believing, Christ-honoring church believes in a biblical purpose . . . a church that is exalting, edifying, evangelistic, and [involved in] social action.

But after stating this purpose, Hybels clarified how Willow Creek perceives its distinctiveness: "We are very different when it comes to the strategy of how we achieve those purposes. That is where Willow Creek is unique."[1]

The heart of Willow Creek's strategy centers on unchurched Harry (or Mary), the "typical" unmotivated, unchurched individual. Hybels says:

> Nonchurched Harry is this composite man. He is this person, right now, who is in his family room—feet upon the footstool, reading the paper, watching TV, a can of beer in hand.

The strategy of Willow Creek is a response to Hybels's next words: "How in the world are you going to get that guy out of his chair all the way to a place of spiritual maturity?" The Willow Creek answer is the "Seven Step Strategy":

1. A friendship develops between Harry and a Willow Creek attender;
2. The attender shares a verbal witness with Harry;

3. Harry visits a Willow Creek weekend meeting, which is designed for unchurched individuals;
4. Harry begins attending "New Community," a midweek worship and teaching meeting;
5. Harry joins a small group;
6. Harry uses his gifts in serving;
7. Harry becomes a good steward of his finances.

Here is a brief review of this seven step strategy.

Step 1: A friendship develops between Harry and a Willow Creek attender. Hybels believes that if Harry is ever going to come to church, it will be because of a relationship with a good friend. "Some believer in this church is going to have to build a relationship with nonchurched Harry," he says. He describes this relationship as "probably the only bridge we can build to him that's going to touch his life for Christ." Hybels encourages Willow Creek attenders to develop "relationships of integrity" with unchurched Harrys and Marys.

Hybels regularly shares with the congregation stories of his relationships with non-Christian friends. In all of Hybels's anecdotes there is a strong sense of his affection for, and intimacy with, these nonbelievers. Hybels encourages Willow Creek staff and attenders to cultivate relationships with non-Christians. Hybels teaches them that as they care for these individuals, they are showing them God's love.[2]

Step 2: The Willow Creek attender shares a verbal witness with Harry. Hybels encourages church attenders to share their faith in Christ with their friends. He asks them, "How many of you have enough of a grasp of God's plan of salvation that (a) you can understand it and (b) you can communicate it to others?" A four-week Impact evangelism seminar is designed to help attenders learn how to do this.

This seminar assures Christians that they don't have to be rude or obnoxious in sharing their faith. It teaches that a regular believer can and should give a natural verbal witness of how he or she came to faith and then teaches attenders a simple method of how to communicate the gospel to their friends. After someone is trained at an Impact seminar, he or she is then encouraged to take the step of sharing a verbal witness to an unchurched Harry and inviting him to a weekend seeker service.[3]

Step 3: Harry visits a Willow Creek weekend meeting, which is designed for unchurched individuals. The weekend services are devised to support and supplement the personal witness of Willow Creek Christians. From the music and drama to the message at the end, the entire service is designed to present a simple "Christianity 101" to visiting unchurched Harrys and

Marys. Hybels seeks to build credibility and identify with unchurched Harry. Hybels also teaches "Christianity 101" to these visiting Harrys to show them that Christianity is relevant and works. The ultimate goal of this service is to have Harry respond to the gospel in faith.

Step 4: Harry begins attending New Community, a midweek worship and teaching meeting. The church staff recognizes that the weekend service is not a worship service. They believe that Christians need to worship God and get more substantial teaching if they are going to grow to spiritual maturity. This midweek service is where these elements of Willow Creek's purpose (exalting and edifying) are satisfied. Besides regular biblical teaching and worship this is the time when communion is served once a month.

Hybels exhorts Christians in the weekend services to attend the New Community services: "I think all of you, personally, who call yourselves Christians, this Wednesday or Thursday night ought to drive in the direction of obedience [and attend]." Hybels asserts that the result of this faithfulness in attending New Community services will be an increase in spiritual growth.

Step 5: Harry joins a small group. Hybels regularly encourages believers to join a small group of other believers. "I can't believe every serious Christian isn't involved in a little platoon." The Willow Creek handbook explains, "Small-group involvement provides fellowship for the believer as well as a group for accountability, discipleship, encouragement, and support." This is also the environment where Harrys begin to learn basic disciplines of the Christian life and systematically learn about their responsibilities to the church.

Step 6: Harry uses his gifts in serving. The next stage in the seven step strategy is for Harry to attend the four-week Network seminar, to learn about his spiritual gifts, and then begin serving in the church. Hybels encourages attenders to stop being merely a part of an audience and begin serving. When they do, he says, "They're not just spectators in the stands, but they're coming up to the plate with a bat in their hands, and they're saying, 'I want to be a player.'"

Step 7: Harry becomes a good steward of his finances. Only at this point in Harry's process of maturing can the sensitive topic of finances be raised. "Stewardship" refers to money management and glorifying God with one's resources. Hybels explains, "We learned in just the past years . . . that somehow we have to try to bring about a second conversion, and that is to convert a consumer into a contributor."

Hybels teaches that a 10 percent tithe is the foundational amount that a believer should give to the work of the church. Although regular teaching takes place at New Community concerning finances, Hybels decided that the issue was important enough to be singled out as a separate step of the strategy.

He tells Christians:

> It's time for more of you to step to the plate who are a part of this church and ask yourself the question, "If everyone else in the church supported this church the way . . . my family supports it, would this church exist?"[4]

Hybels believes that Willow Creek's uniqueness lies in this specific seven step strategy to bring unchurched Harry to spiritual maturity:

> I contend most churches understand their purpose to some extent, but they don't have a clue as to what kind of strategy they need to put into effect to take Harry out of his armchair and eventually to bring him to a place of spiritual maturity in the body of Christ.

This seven step strategy is at the heart of Willow Creek. Hybels sees life as a grand mission to communicate God's message of salvation to unbelievers and help believers become fruitful in this cause.

Willow Creek's Seeker Service

The one unique element about Willow Creek's strategy is their weekend church service, which is designed for non-Christians. All other elements of Willow Creek's strategy (personal evangelism, Bible teaching, small groups, volunteer training, worship, and others) are common in evangelical churches. Thousands of church leaders attend Willow Creek's leadership conferences to understand this seeker service. It influences thousands of churches across the country and world; those most strongly influenced have adopted the seeker service model. Why do Willow Creekers design a church service for unchurched individuals?[5]

Hybels explains to a group of pastors, "[The] passage you need to understand if you're going to understand who we are is Luke 15." Hybels sees Luke 15 as a series of three parables with "a common thread."

> [The] common thread is that something of great value winds up missing: the sheep is missing, the coin is missing, the son is missing. And that which is missing really matters to somebody.

Hybels explains that Jesus is teaching these parables to show God's love toward the lost: "Jesus is saying, 'Would you please understand this, that lost, wayward, irreligious people, in spite of their sin, really matter to my Father.'"[6]

The impact of this passage on Willow Creek is profound. Hybels continues, "In two of the three stories Jesus says, 'And that which is missing matters enough to launch an all-out search.' And in all three of the stories, retrieval brings rejoicing." Willow Creek sees itself as a church that is conducting an "all-out search" for lost people. Hybels admits, "We are lock, stock, and barrel sold out to the concept that 'lost people matter to God.' It's not a cliché around here. We use it a lot. It's a creed."

This church creed gives the church its guiding vision for what it does. In response to many of my questions on why the church did or did not do something, staff members and volunteers would repeat to me the church's motto: "Lost people matter to God." In practice, Willow Creek's commitment to reach the unchurched is the axis of its ministry. In particular, the weekend seeker service is the central and dominating activity at Willow Creek. More time and energy goes into the weekend service than any of the other activities at Willow Creek.[7]

Why do Willow Creekers believe a seeker service is necessary for evangelism? Creekers argue that there is a need for a neutral place for unchurched Harrys to investigate Christianity. They contend that the gap between the normal unchurched Harry and the traditional evangelical church is too wide to be easily bridged. Hybels explains to a group of pastors:

> What does the seeker walk into in ninety-nine out of one hundred churches across this land? He walks into a service that has been designed from stem to stern for the already convinced.
>
> It's a worship service. It's designed all the way through for someone who has a long background in church involvement, who understands the lingo, who has all the prerequisite knowledge.

To communicate with an unchurched Harry, Hybels argues, you need to start where he is. Evangelism director Mark Mittelberg explains this idea in the light of his own experience:

> Even though I think I probably have had a gift of evangelism, I found it very difficult on my own
>
> - to bridge the cultural gap,
> - make the message clear,
> - break down stereotypes that people had against evangelism, and
> - lead them to Christ.

This is the primary goal of Willow Creek weekend services—to convert unchurched Harrys and Marys to Christ. One staff member described Willow Creek's theology as permanent and its methods flexible:

Willow Creek is amazingly able to take the two-thousand-year-old gospel and retain it, not try to alter the gospel, but be radical with allowing it to be preached in a variety of ways. The methods of how Willow Creek seeks to achieve this goal of evangelism are what make the weekend services distinctive.

The Methods of the Seeker Service

During the weekend meetings Hybels is primarily attempting to persuade unchurched Harry to become a believer. His role is that of a motivator and agent of change. Hybels intuitively uses many time-proven principles of how to persuade an audience.

There are several steps to this process of persuasion. The following outline of how Hybels seeks to persuade individuals shows the unique communication strategy of Willow Creek's seeker services.

Understanding

Before attempting to persuade someone to adopt a new point of view one must first try to understand where that person is. Hybels and his colleagues seek to understand unchurched Harrys. This is described in chapters 3 and 4 of this book.

Programming

The programming of the weekend service is designed to prepare Harry for Hybels's message. In chapters 5, 6, and 7, I describe the physical environment and programming that help guide this process of persuasion.

Credibility

Hybels seeks to be a reliable and trusted friend to a visiting unchurched Harry. He wants to be honest and sincere and show genuine affection for Harry. See chapter 8.

Identification

Hybels believes that a cultural chasm exists between Willow Creek and the unchurched. Hybels seeks to bridge this chasm and affirm to Harry that "we are the same." Hybels desires to move as close as possible to Harry and identify with him. See chapter 9.

Relevance

Hybels addresses Harry's real life needs. He argues that Christianity is the best means to satisfy these felt needs and provide personal fulfillment. See chapter 10.

Christianity 101

Hybels asserts that Christian teaching can help unchurched Harry in his daily life. Christianity 101 is presented through Scripture, illustrations, practical how-to's, and psychology. See chapter 11.

The Truth of Christianity

Hybels seeks to remove Harry's roadblocks to faith and argues against competitors to Christianity. He affirms that Christianity is true and reasonable. See chapter 12.

The Gospel

Hybels explains the central truths of the gospel. He teaches Harry about God, human nature, Christ, and how to trust Christ for salvation. See chapter 13.

Commitment

Hybels challenges Harry to decide to receive Christ's forgiveness. Hybels argues that either Harry decides for Christ or, by neglect, he rejects him. See chapter 13.

Before we try to understand Willow Creek in the present, however, we need to understand Willow Creek in the past.

2

Willow Creek's History

It has become commonplace to note that to truly understand someone, one needs to understand his or her history. The same is true with organizations. What are the major historical influences that have shaped Willow Creek?

Whenever Willow Creek staff were asked to clarify their beliefs, they would quickly associate themselves with the broader evangelical church and its theology. I asked Dr. Gilbert Bilezikian, Hybels's mentor and the church's theologian, "What is Willow Creek's relationship to the broader evangelical world?" He responded, "If we were to join any kind of organization, it would be the National Association of Evangelicals. That's where our kinship is, and we feel at home among them."

Sociologist James Hunter defines American evangelicalism as "the North American expression of theologically conservative Protestantism." As such, its primary identifying characteristics are its theological beliefs. According to Hunter these are "the standard tenets of Christian orthodoxy, . . . the centrality of the Bible as the infallible and inerrant Word of God," and the necessity of preaching the gospel to all mankind. Evangelicalism defined in this way includes perhaps thirty to fifty million Americans.[1]

Under this broad umbrella are a variety of evangelicals including charismatics, fundamentalists, Pentecostals, conservative evangelicals, progressive evangelicals, and all sorts of denominational types.

Evangelicals come in many shapes, sizes, and flavors. Within the doctrinal framework described by Hunter, evangelicalism is made up of conflicting and competing ideas and methods. In a sense, evangelicalism operates as a marketplace where ideas and methods are marketed and bought into.[2]

Willow Creek was born into this religious marketplace and received most of its ideas and methods from others. As it has matured into a large and growing church, it has become an influential leader within evangelicalism. This chapter is a short historical review of some of the dominant influences on Willow Creek: the youth group Son City, cofounder of the church Dave Holmbo, the 1979 "train wreck," church theologian Dr. Gilbert Bilezikian, and church-growth mentor Robert Schuller.

Son City

One day, when I was attempting to set up a meeting with Hybels, I was asked to sit in the waiting room of his office. On the wall was a copy of an article from the *Chicago Tribune* describing an audience: "All white and neatly dressed, they were switched from mood to mood by Bill Hybels, a young man exuding control in word and gesture." The article could have been written during the previous week. However, it was a description of the youth group "Son City" in 1974, a year before Hybels even began Willow Creek.[3]

In this seed form we see much that would later grow into the fully grown plant of Willow Creek. Hybels is still firmly in command; the church is still predominantly white, neatly dressed, and middle class; the youth group strategy is still being used successfully; and the church is still attracting the interest of the media.

Hybels and his senior staff are often asked, "Where did the distinctives of Willow Creek come from?" They usually refer to the Son City days. Former associate pastor Don Cousins explains, "The vast majority of our philosophy was developed during the Son City days. All we have done since then is put handles on what we did by instinct then." One primary Son City leader and church staff member called Son City "the prototype" for Willow Creek. He explained that in many ways Willow Creek was merely "an adult Son City." What was Son City?[4]

In August of 1972, Bill Hybels began leading a group of thirty high school students in South Park Church in Park Ridge, Illinois. Over the course of the next nine months, the group "Son Life" grew to include seventy-five students. At this point the group desired to reach out to nonbelieving friends, but there were several objections. Some of the kids felt that the meeting environment (the church basement), the music ("Kumbaya,"

"Pass It On," etc.), and the teaching (Hybels's long, Scripture-filled sermons) would not communicate to their friends.[5]

For this reason, in May of 1973, "Son City" was begun as an outreach to nonbelieving youth. The environment, music, and messages were adapted to the audience. During the next two years the group grew to approximately one thousand young people. Don Cousins wrote in 1979 that in 1975 the leadership of Son City "answered God's call to implement these same biblical principles on an adult level by starting a church." Thus, at least in part, Willow Creek based its beginning philosophy and methods on an evangelistic youth ministry. We see this influence of the youth group on the church in a variety of ways: leadership being raised up from within, the importance of a seeker service, volunteers' zealous commitment, an emphasis on spiritual gifts, the significance of teams, and the influence of entertainment.[6]

Leadership

Virtually all the staff of the church in its early days were veterans of the youth group. They had proven their giftedness in Son City and were quickly hired on to transplant their methods to the adult ministry of the church. From the very beginning Willow Creek preferred to hire staff members from within. This is still true, as over 90 percent of Willow Creek ministry staff are hired from within the church.[7]

In the Willow Creek model, the requirements of leadership include character and spiritual authenticity. These qualities can only be seen over time, as Don Cousins explains: "It is extremely difficult to judge a person's character or spiritual authenticity in an interview. You have to see them at work for some time." Willow Creek does not like to hire individuals who haven't demonstrated their character in the ministry there.[8]

Son City leaders believed they had a unique ministry with a unique strategy and that individuals needed to learn this strategy before they could become leaders. As a result, the leadership of Son City was entirely homegrown. When Hybels started Willow Creek, he raised his disciple Don Cousins up to be the new Son City director. Willow Creek leaders feel that anyone who is hired from the outside will spend a great deal of his or her first year of ministry learning and will make only a limited contribution.

During most of my study, Hybels supervised three individuals in a management team who in turn managed the rest of the staff. Two of these three were students in the original thirty-member youth group. It is fascinating that after fifteen years and twenty thousand regular attenders, the central leadership of virtually all the church's work has remained firmly in the hands of people who shared the common experience of the youth group.[9]

The Importance of a Seeker Service

As I noted above, when Hybels first proposed to the youth group that they could invite nonbelievers for an evangelistic meeting, the kids were hesitant. After Hybels agreed to changes that would meet their concerns, two other suggestions were made. One individual recommended that the meeting have drama to make Hybels's teaching "come alive." Another proposed that multi-media could be used to communicate effectively.[10]

What ultimately sold these programming changes to Hybels and the others was that they worked. At their first meeting for seekers fifty to sixty kids made a commitment to Christ. It was near midnight that night by the time each had prayed with a Son City leader to receive Christ. Hybels records his response:

> When it was all over, I went out to the back of the church and sat on the sidewalk alone, leaning back against a red brick wall. I shook my head. This is absolutely unbelievable. Where would all those seekers be if we hadn't designed a service for them?[11]

The Willow Creek seeker service is merely a continuation of the Son City seeker service.

Commitment and Hard Work

Many of the leaders of Son City were raised in the late 1960s, when any cause to change the world was very popular. They, and many others who were a part of the Jesus movement in the early 1970s, found a receptive audience for the message about a bearded rebel from two thousand years ago. As Lynne Hybels explains, "We were young people looking for a cause, and we'd found one—to reach unchurched high school students and draw them to Jesus Christ."[12]

The result of this youthful idealism being unleashed was an enormous commitment and a willingness to sacrifice. As one adult observer commented, "Total involvement was the expected norm." The popular phrase that the students used to express this was "Whatever it takes." This kind of commitment resulted in tremendous numerical increases in the youth group. The root below this flourishing growth was the conviction that they had the truth. One Son City leader explained, "We were so convinced that we were doing what God wanted us to do and that this was right. It was just right!"[13]

Various stories circulate throughout the church that describe this commitment in the early days. One individual began offering rides from his home in a distant suburb to the church in Park Ridge. This eventually turned into a ten-car caravan, and then the renting of a bus, and then later the renting of four buses. As one student later expressed it, "Sometimes, we choose to be obsessed." This ideal of commitment and hard work continued into the church. An ironic Willow Creek proverb expresses this same idea: "Exhaustion is next to godliness."[14]

Spiritual Gifts

Early in the history of Son City the concept of spiritual gifts began to be emphasized. As the ministry became increasingly larger, individuals were expected to pitch in. At the same time, as they felt like they were a part of a movement, they desired to contribute.[15]

The leaders of Son City put people into specialized groups that could accomplish different projects. One Son City leader explains:

> We called them modules. We had different gift groups that broke out of this large group called "Son City." There would be an art module. There would be a drama module. There would be a photography module.

The members of these modules were the Christian students who continued to meet together in Son Village, the youth group's Bible study. They joined modules relating to their interests and abilities.

Whenever a Son Village project was scheduled, the work would be divided within the various modules. A leader explains:

> If we were going to do some kind of big event on Wednesday night:
>
> - The art module would be involved in all the decorating, all the posters, and all the stuff that was going to go up.
> - The photography module would be planning on how they were going to shoot pictures of the event.
> - The drama module would obviously be working on the drama for the evening.
> - An AV module would be thinking about the screen.
> - A production module would be thinking about the sound system and the lighting stuff.

Using one's gifts to help the ministry naturally emerged as the means to get the work done. Hybels began to teach about the importance of clarifying and using one's spiritual gifts. A leader remembers:

> These different modules would all have their roles in really . . . helping people use their gifts. Helping people identify their gifts and helping people use them: That started almost right at the beginning.

This belief eventually evolved into the church's present-day emphasis on the importance of a believer knowing and confidently using his or her gifts in the work of the church. This teaching is stressed in the New Community messages and is spelled out in the church's Network seminar.

The Significance of Teams

Another characteristic of Son City that has helped shape the church is the importance of teams. Don Cousins explains:

> Bill got the youth group to about eighty kids [and] realized very quickly that he, relationally, was as far as he could go. And so at that point . . . he and a few others put their heads together and said, "You know, if we just broke this thing down and divided into some teams."
>
> So he appointed four teams, took the eighty kids, made them twenty kids each. Each of those teams in the first year grew to about eighty.

Each of these teams was led by a group of four student leaders—captain, co-captain, secretary, and assistant secretary. These teams became virtual mini youth groups in themselves. One Son City leader explained that teams "provided an internal structure to what became a very large group of kids. There was a lot of ownership, a lot of loyalty, a lot of feeling of belonging that came from these teams."

Son City's use of teams to achieve goals has made teams very influential in Willow Creek. For example, the church's programming team plans each weekend service. The team reviews and critiques a videotape of a previous week's service. They then hammer out a detailed program for the coming week. Staff work together in teams throughout the church.

The Influence of Entertainment

In order to attract the attention of high school students, the topics and activities of Son City naturally drifted toward high school level entertainment. Son City was not unique in this focus on entertainment in youth ministry. Evangelical para-church youth groups like Young Life and Campus Life had made entertainment a major part of their ministry for decades. The strategy of Young Life is summarized in the famous saying of its founder, Jim Rayburn: "It's a sin to bore a kid with the gospel."[16]

Yet Son City seemed to stretch the boundaries of youth ministry. One of Son City's leaders explained:

> We are in that auditorium and the windows are open and the music is howling at ear-splitting decibels. There are flashing lights going all over the place with these big ambulance lights. There are kids literally bouncing off the walls screaming at the top of their lungs. Everything that you would not think would be happening in a church sanctuary, is definitely happening in a church sanctuary.

Son City had the "Hallowed Queen" competition, where guys came in drag. At one point the sanctuary of the church was decorated as a jail. When fake lightning exploded, someone was blown off a ledge because too much gunpowder was used. There were full-scale gymnastics routines done down the aisles of the church. The motto of Son City was "Anything bigger, better, and more bizarre." This emphasis on entertainment naturally flowed into the programming of the church. To comprehend the church's emphasis on programming, we need to understand Dave Holmbo's influence on the church.[17]

Dave Holmbo

To explain Dave Holmbo's influence on the church, I need to refer back to the plaque of the *Chicago Tribune* article I saw on the wall of Hybels's waiting room. The plaque was entitled "To Dave and Bill who made it all possible for the glory of God." When I first saw the plaque, I asked myself, *Who is this mysterious Dave who received top billing over Bill?* I discovered over time that it was Dave Holmbo, the leader of the music group that had originally asked Hybels to lead the Bible studies for the youth group. Holmbo had co-led Son City and then cofounded Willow Creek with Hybels.

Dave Holmbo grew up in a "very fundamentalist" church as a quiet rebel. He never rejected the church or the gospel, but he and his friends enjoyed breaking a few rules. And in his church there were many rules to break.[18]

The fact that Holmbo was a silent dissident is one of the crucial characteristics of his life. He, like many young fundamentalists, lived two lives. On the one hand, he lived in his church world and had a circle of Christian friends and activities, including working at a Christian camp in the summers and participating in music in his home church. On the other hand, Holmbo developed interests and friends in the "real" world. He loved contemporary rock music, had many non-Christian friends, and eventually attended secular Northeastern Illinois University. As Holmbo says, "I felt like I was living in two different worlds," and there was a growing strain between them.

In his college years, Holmbo began to move away from the fundamentalism of his youth. He and his friends began saying to themselves, "Some of this stuff just doesn't ring true. And there are all these rules and stupid stuff about this and that." Holmbo came to a point where he said, "I've got to throw this stuff out." Yet he never completely threw away the faith. He was left in a quandary, as he didn't see how he could bring his two worlds together.

Music eventually became the cord that he used to tie the two worlds together. In both his "real" world and his church world, music was a large part of his life. His parents had him taking piano lessons when he was eight. However, instead of hymns, he enjoyed playing Beach Boys tunes. This love of contemporary music continued to grow in his college years.[19]

At the very time he was moving away from fundamentalism, Holmbo was asked to help with South Park, an evangelical church that wanted to use contemporary music. He eagerly accepted. Holmbo observes that South Park was considered liberal by the fundamentalist churches of his past. In fact, it was solidly evangelical but had discarded fundamentalism's separatism. As Holmbo explains, South Park was a "little more open-minded." South Park's pastor was interested in starting a contemporary, more informal type of morning service. The music Holmbo used for this service included singable choruses, and there was a pop feel to it.[20]

Holmbo's gifts in music and creativity flourished in this new setting. He started Son Company, a singing group made of all the members of South Park's youth group. He needed an acoustic guitarist. When a group of long-haired young men attended the church looking for a church home, there happened to be an acoustic guitarist—of sorts—among them. His name was Bill Hybels. Holmbo fondly remembers, "He was a hack acoustic guitarist; he sort of banged on the guitar." This was the inauspicious beginning of the future Willow Creek team.[21]

After leading the music group a while, Holmbo realized that the young people needed more teaching: "There was not enough [spiritual] feeding going on for the kids. . . . In tandem with the rehearsal on Wednesday nights, we decided we would do a Bible study." Holmbo asked Hybels to teach the Bible study and comments, "That was phenomenally successful as well." Son City was off and running.

Holmbo's influence on the youth group and the church can be understood from this brief review. He was the rebel who was frustrated with the traditional church. Instead of being satisfied with normal youth group music and programming, he enjoyed being radical. He was fascinated with contemporary forms of music and was in touch with what communicated to students and his peers.

Holmbo was a dreamer who created a new artistic direction for the youth group and then the church. The story of Son City—Willow Creek—is a story, in part, of how Holmbo's "real" world and church world came together: He integrated the music and artistic ideas of his "real" world with the basic theology of his church world.

Holmbo's programming strategy in the youth group evolved over time. There was a pragmatic relationship between his programming and the students' response. As students responded positively to some programming change or musical innovation, this response registered with the leaders and shaped future programs. Yet this programming approach wasn't so much market analysis in the early days. Holmbo explains that "there was a part of it that I was just saying, What would really turn me on?" He used Beach Boys stylings and arrangements because he "just loved them." Holmbo brought his gifts, interests, and creativity and intuitively shaped a new way to think about youth programming.

While Hybels provided the teaching and practical emphasis, Holmbo provided the creative music, drama, and programming. While Hybels tended toward a business-oriented bottom line, Holmbo tended to be ethereal. As one friend described him, "Dave's feet didn't touch ground often; he landed annually and that was just to relaunch."[22]

In fact, Holmbo's contrast with Hybels provided some of the original strength of the group. It provided a mix of direction and fun that was attractive to students. It was neither Bill's nor Dave's youth group or church. Yet their mutual leadership provided an environment where students, and then adults, could develop a sense of ownership. What united this mix of gifts and personality was a common passion. As Lynne Hybels explains, "They shared a mutual frustration with how it (church) had been done in their past; and a mutual yearning to do it another way."[23]

Holmbo's mix of gifts and personality had a profound effect on the church. People I interviewed said that even over a decade after he left, Holmbo's personality could still be seen in the programming and creativity of the church. What caused him to leave was the next major influence on the church.

The 1979 "Train Wreck"

During my interviews with people, I occasionally came across information that I could tell was important but that I did not initially understand.

This was the case with the 1979 "train wreck." One individual often referred to this mysterious time as an important landmark for the church. Others marked their involvement in the church in relation to the events of the train wreck. The church's magazine, *Willow Creek,* reviewed the fifteen years of the church's history and spent six pages describing the train wreck and only four pages describing the following ten years of the church. The "train wreck" was a crucial time for the church.[24]

When the church began, it experienced great success, having one thousand weekend attenders at the end of the first year. Hybels, Holmbo, and the fast-growing staff were incredibly busy in the large and growing church. Eighty-hour weeks became the norm instead of the exception. Hybels and Holmbo were newly married but were teased that they were spending more time together than they were with their wives. Holmbo explains, "From the time I woke up until the time I went to bed, I just thought and did everything in terms of the church."

The result of this breakneck speed was a strain on relationships. Holmbo later confessed that he neglected his wife, as she was only "getting the leftovers" of his time and energy. Friendships were also under the strain of a lack of time as each staff member went about doing his own ministry. Don Cousins recalls, "The mindset was: You go your way and do your ministry, and I'll go mine and do my ministry." The pace was fast and furious. The staff at one point went nearly six months without a staff meeting. The fabric of the church was becoming frayed.

In early 1978, in response to the ambiguities and problems of this open-ended arrangement, Hybels called together the staff and proposed a change in the structure:

> We can have any kind of structure you want, but there has got to be a person with whom the buck stops. Let's not do this by personality; let's do it by giftedness. Who among us do you think has the strongest leadership gifts?

Everyone was quiet. You could have heard a pin drop. Hybels finally had to nominate himself: "Well, I think that I probably do."

Willow Creek magazine commented over a decade later, "Clearly lacking a mandate, Bill Hybels became 'senior pastor' of Willow Creek Community Church." In essence, Hybels successfully placed a hierarchical authority structure, with himself at the top, into what was once a more informal organization. This precipitated a series of events.

Over the next few months, Holmbo felt his relationship with Hybels had changed. Where once he was coleader, now he was reporting to Hybels as supervisor. He felt that there was a growing feeling, in light of Willow

Creek's success, that "there were things at stake bigger than friendship." As a result, he admits, "We were starting to retreat into ourselves. . . . We were protecting ourselves."

The relationships that were the fabric of his life began to unravel. Holmbo reveals:

> There was a feeling of a decline in ownership. The pronoun "we" became less evident. The idea of "this is ours" started to deteriorate. It started to happen in very subtle and insignificant ways.

The dream was beginning to dissipate; the adventure wasn't as exciting as it once was.

As a result, Holmbo began "not to discount" other means to relieve the pain that he was feeling. He later confessed that during this time, he made "critical errors" in his "personal moral life and integrity." *Willow Creek* magazine explains that "he became enmeshed in sin," which in this context is an evangelical synonym for adultery.

Eventually Hybels became aware of Holmbo's sin. Hybels later confessed that he should have confronted the sin earlier. However, in the fall of 1978, he realized that he needed to do something. He created a board of elders, in part, to deal with the crisis. At the first meeting, elder Laurie Pederson remembers, "Bill unloaded and unveiled the whole ugly mess."

The elders had no idea what they had gotten themselves into. Besides seeking to solve the obvious problem of Holmbo's sin, there were relational tangles and some underlying philosophical conflicts that were difficult to unravel. The situation demanded a full year of meetings with many "tragic moments" and much weeping.

This first stage of the crisis concluded in the fall of 1979, when Holmbo submitted his resignation because of "philosophical differences." The next Sunday morning Hybels made an incidental announcement that Holmbo, the cofounder of the church, was leaving:

> By the way, Dave Holmbo resigned yesterday. He felt like he was going in a little different direction with his life than we were going as a church, and so we wished the best for him.

The result was nothing less than explosive. As Hybels recalls, "People just went nuts."

Hybels and the elders had decided not to reveal Holmbo's sin in the hope that his marriage could be salvaged. But they were unprepared for the backlash. Many accused Hybels of making a power play and the elders as his accomplices in the process. People immediately took sides. One individual explained to me that depending on whom someone was close to, Hybels or Holmbo, he or she viewed the situation differently. Some people left immediately and others dribbled out over the next two years.[25]

There was deep hurt in the congregation and suspicion of Hybels's motives. It was a hard time for Hybels: "For almost a year I felt like I was in a war. . . . I felt every single time I stepped up to preach, I was on trial. . . . We were always just one New Community away from extinction." There were no easy solutions, and the tensions did not easily dissipate. As elder Laurie Pederson describes it, "There was wave after wave after wave of conflict."

This turmoil involved the very core of the church. Eventually one-fourth of the staff and one-third of the lay leadership left, about two hundred people in all. Those who stayed were close to Hybels and identified with him. Hybels came to describe this time as "the 1979 train wreck."

Eventually the church emerged from the crisis. Part of the reason it survived was that despite the problems, the church was still attracting large groups of people on the weekends. The weekend crowd was virtually unaware of the turmoil. And many of these individuals quickly got involved in the growing vacancies in the church's leadership. One person described to me that the first week he attended, there was an announcement that they needed a piano player. The next week he was playing up on stage.

As a result of the "train wreck," there were several important changes in the church:

- The content of what was taught at the church was changed.
- There was a fundamental shift in the structure and management of the church.
- The attitude and approach of individuals toward relationships, particularly the leadership's, was clearly shifted.

Theology

Hybels was convicted there had been too great an emphasis in the church on the grace of God. *Willow Creek* magazine records that the word *sin* was "almost never heard in the early days of the church." So Hybels began to emphasize the holiness of God and human sinfulness. One person described to me what he heard when he first began attending at this time:

> One of the first messages I heard Bill give was when he was saying, "We're gonna preach the gospel right out. We're not gonna hedge on it. We're not gonna tickle people's ears any more. And if you don't like it, leave."

The assumption of this statement was that the church had in fact been "tickling people's ears." But no longer. Hybels began a new series on the holiness of God.[26]

This new emphasis, along with the fact that the creative core of the church had been gutted, created a new environment. Where before the atmosphere was one of celebration, now it was one of somber assessment. Lynne Hybels explains, "For many people the tone was hard to take. It was such a departure from the first three years when it had been so warm, open and no-questions-asked unconditional love."

However, this change was a relatively short-term shift. Hybels admitted that for a period of time "the pendulum swung a little too far to the other side." Soon the church began to reemphasize its celebration and acceptance mode. The next two shifts were more permanent in nature.

Management

The church had been burned and learned its lesson. Where once there had been a more open-ended management style, the church began to emphasize strict lines of authority, accountability, and business management. One staff member from this time explained that "the church became more institutional." *Willow Creek* magazine reports, "There were crucial changes.... The staff took on a well-defined reporting structure to make accountability possible." Management guru Peter Drucker's books began to circulate among the staff. Even to this day Drucker's book *The Effective Executive* is used almost as a managerial Bible for some staff.

Many of the creative people who hadn't left immediately felt uncomfortable as the church became more institutional. One said, "Creative people don't feel comfortable in institutions." It was a couple of years before a new creative core was developed in the church.

Other resources were used to manage the church effectively. *Leadership and the One Minute Manager* by Kenneth Blanchard eventually became required reading for all new staff. This book provides an outline of how managers can structure the work of the individuals they are supervising. It teaches how to organize effective and productive business relationships. The youth group's atmosphere of a spiritual party became a spiritual business.[27]

Relationships and Loyalty

The last change brought about by the "train wreck" was the result of the pain of the conflict. As these idealistic kids had sought to take on the world, they had been open and vulnerable. In the "train wreck" of conflict, failure, and deep disappointment, everyone was hurt. As one person described it, "People were shook." Individuals naturally became cautious. The relationships that became most important were the ones that survived this experience. Trust was not easily given again.

Loyalty and longevity became the distinguishing characteristics of the people who could be trusted. One of Bill's closest friends was hired in the midst of the turmoil. He explains:

> Everything was in limbo. Everybody was shaky. And they hired me because they were at a point where they said . . . "We have to have control, stability; we have to make sure that we're ready to go."

The staff and leaders who stayed became the new core of the church. More accurately, the new core were those who had remained loyal to Bill during the crisis. One staff member described the staff that left: "They identified with Dave and the others. Maybe a better way to put it is they identified less with Bill." This loyal-to-Bill core is still present in the church. One staff member I interviewed had been on staff for four years and felt like he had just arrived. He was not a part of this more permanent core. A good friend had teased him that he would not feel a part of the church until he had been on staff ten years.

Loyalty became the most prized virtue in the church and disloyalty one of the greatest vices. One staff member explained to me that the central unspoken question that the leadership have toward a newcomer is, "Do you really care about the church and this ministry?" When I probed this issue, one central leader admitted, "You're right; the need for loyalty" is "very high."[28]

I discovered during my interviews with staff members a deep fear of being labeled disloyal. Virtually any time staff members told me something about the church that could be interpreted negatively, they would quickly try to qualify their remarks, ask me not to use their comments, or request that I not identify them as the source. They wanted to avoid the earmark of disloyalty. One of these individuals admitted, "I don't want to be seen as a curmudgeon." The only dissatisfied staff member I found remarked, "They [church leadership] value loyalty more than honesty."[29]

There is no question that the "train wreck" had a profound effect on the church.

Dr. Bilezikian

When any staff member told me about the history of the church, he or she invariably would cite the powerful influence of professor Gilbert Bilezikian on the young and impressionable college student Bill Hybels.

To understand Bilezikian and his effect on the church, we need to look briefly at his history. While Bilezikian was growing up in France, he attended a conservative Reformed church. However, the church had little impact on his life, and as a young man he drifted away. When he went to college he majored in philosophy and felt drawn to existentialism. The questions of loneliness and the meaning of life were very real to a young man whose mother had died when he was four and who as a teenager had experienced the brutal Nazi occupation of Paris.[30]

When Bilezikian was twenty, he went with some friends on vacation to the mountains. While there they decided to attend a Salvation Army tent meeting in a small village in order to heckle. The odd nineteenth-century uniforms and format were humorous to these modern and educated young men. In the midst of their snickers, Bilezikian suddenly dropped to his knees. His friends, assuming he was mocking the service, exclaimed "Good one, Gil," and "That's really funny."

But he wasn't mocking. He refers to this experience now as a "private transaction with God." He explains that his life was fundamentally changed from that point on:

> I had this overpowering sense of the presence of God. It was like God was saying, "I have done so much for you, and this is how you treat me?"
>
> I went to my knees and immediately I felt this sense of love and acceptance. I knew right then that I was a new person. I knew that I couldn't do anything else but to go into God's service.

This service would take him to the United States to an evangelical seminary and then to Ph.D. studies. He then pastored or taught in many places, ending up teaching at Trinity College in Deerfield, Illinois, for two years and then for the next nearly twenty years at Wheaton College.

It was at Trinity College in 1972–74 where he taught Hybels. Hybels attended Trinity College for two years and registered for two of Bilezikian's classes, Christian Doctrine and 1 Corinthians. Hybels recalls sitting in Bilezikian's college classes and being inspired by his teaching:

> Dr. B. would say, "I don't see many churches like this in America in the '70s. I mean, I see buildings and I see programs, I see budgets and I see a lot of activity." He said, "I just don't see the life of what the Scriptures is talking about. I

> don't see that kind of life being breathed out in a vital way in a fellowship called a church."
>
> And he would just look off into the distance, and he would say, "Someday, someday the mold will be broken. Somebody will get serious about doing church God's way and they're gonna take all the risks and endure all the attacks. Someday, somebody will start a church, and it will be a lot like this; it will rock the world."

This verbal dreaming had a powerful effect on young Hybels. He began dreaming about the possibility of a new kind of church, saying to himself, *I'm not sure there's anything I could devote my life to that would have greater significance than that.* And he concluded, *That seems to be about the most worthwhile objective in the world.* During these years Hybels was teaching and coleading the Son City youth group, so much of what he was learning from Bilezikian he was able to put into practice and teach to the kids that same week.

Hybels felt that in Bilezikian he had found a mentor who echoed his frustration with the traditional church. Bilezikian records that during this time in Chicago he was angry about the traditional church:

> Attending church on Sundays became a torment from which I would return home livid with anger. . . . It was as if the ideals that were assiduously pursued were tedium, inertia, mediocrity, rigidity, and closed-mindedness—and all in the name of Christ.[31]

Bilezikian would express in his classroom his frustration with the traditional church and would, with his theological brush, paint a picture of what could be. He records Hybels's response:

> In class he was very attentive. I felt his cold, steel-blue gaze fixed on me, watching me as if I had been secretly placed under his surveillance.
>
> But I soon discovered that he was intently internalizing the teaching, and that, under the appearance of critical scrutiny, he was actually absorbing and processing the content of the courses into his own thinking.[32]

Hybels began to ask questions after class and a relationship soon developed.

Don Cousins describes the influence of this relationship: "Dr. B. became the transformer and Bill Hybels became the transformee." Coleader Dave Holmbo puts it, "He [Hybels] was profoundly affected by Gilbert's teaching." Hybels later writes in the acknowledgments of his book *Seven Wonders of the Spiritual World*: "To my spiritual mentor, Dr. Bilezikian, whose contribution to my life has been incalculable."[33]

A large part of this "incalculable" influence is the theological framework and ideas that Professor Bilezikian taught young Bill. Bilezikian says,

> I'm a theologian so I must admit that a lot of my understanding of the Bible has been built into the community church through the teaching, either direct or mediated through others, especially Bill.[34]

To understand Bilezikian's theology we need to view it against the broader backdrop of evangelicalism. A curious feature of evangelicalism is that there is no official creed. Beyond the most basic theological framework of affirming the Bible, gospel, and creeds of the early church, there is no set way to clearly delineate one's theological convictions. By default, individuals' descriptions of their beliefs are often influenced by the theological division in evangelicalism between Calvinism and Arminianism.[35]

Frequently people use what are called the five points of Calvinism to clarify what they believe. This is true even if, like Bilezikian, they fundamentally disagree with Calvinism. Dirk Jellema briefly explains the five points of Calvinism:

> - *total depravity* (i.e., man after the Fall, cannot choose to serve God)
> - *unconditional election* (God's choice of the elect is not conditioned on any action by them)
> - *limited atonement* (Christ died for the elect only, since those He died for are saved)
> - *irresistible grace* (divine grace cannot be rejected by the elect)
> - *perseverance of the saints* (once elect, always elect) [italics added][36]

Bilezikian calls himself a "one-and-one-half-point Calvinist." Bilezikian agrees with point five, the perseverance of the saints: "I just cannot think that once God has made a commitment, our redemption is ever in doubt." He also believes a part of the first point, total depravity. However, he qualifies this belief:

> The Calvinists carry it too far, as the hymn that says "such a wretched worm as I." Humans are not worms. Even in the most broken person, there is something of the *imago dei* [i.e. the image of God]. But there is no doubt that from birth. . . . we have a propensity for sin, but I wouldn't define it in such somber terms as the Calvinists do.

Rather than the Calvinist's pessimistic understanding of humans as totally depraved, Bilezikian would emphasize a more optimistic understanding of their value and ability. In contrast to the Calvinistic points two and four that affirm the unconditional choice of God in a salvation that cannot be resisted, Bilezikian believes that humankind has a freedom of the will that either receives salvation or resists God. Lastly, in opposition to the Calvinistic doctrine that Christ died only for the elect, Bilezikian believes that he died for all humankind. In sum, what we find in Bilezikian is a rather cheerful Arminianism. Several aspects of Bilezikian's theology were particularly influential on Hybels.

Warm Relationship with Jesus

Hybels's background was Calvinistic as he describes:

> I was raised in a denomination that stresses God's transcendence. We thought of God in lofty and exalted terms. . . . I knew what it meant to fear God, and I understood the importance of serving him. I expected to one day stand under his judgment, and I believed it was my duty to obey his commandments.[37]

Through his relationship with Bilezikian, Hybels began to wrestle with the idea of an intimate relationship with God. Hybels confesses, "One thing . . . was lacking in my Christian experience: any real understanding of the close relationship God wishes to have with his children." Hybels explains the profound effect that Bilezikian's example and teaching had on him:

> In college I met a professor who amazed me. He would sometimes talk about his relationship with Jesus Christ as though he had just had lunch with him. I couldn't understand that kind of relationship with the "immortal, invisible, God only wise, in light inaccessible hid from our eyes"—but I wanted it.
>
> And so I started hanging around the professor after class until one day I got up the courage to ask, "How do you seem to know Christ in a way that I don't?"

Bilezikian said in response, "Maybe you understand Jesus only as the forgiver of your sins." He began encouraging Bill to relate to Jesus as a friend. Bilezikian recalls teaching him about "Jesus the Friend" and "Jesus the Person," with the result that it "overwhelmed Bill." In contrast to the Calvinist Reformed emphasis of relating to a holy and transcendent God, Bill heard the Arminian/pietistic message that emphasized the immanence of God's presence. In particular, he learned about a warm relationship with Jesus. Dave Holmbo explains, "The idea of an intimate friendship or relationship with Christ was something that Gilbert brought to us." Thus a very strong pietistic influence came into Bill's understanding and practice and soon his teaching.[38]

Importance of the Church

Hybels remembers Bilezikian lecturing in his college classroom:

> He would say, "Some of you young, bright, potential students need to throw your life away. You need to not count your life as dear anymore. . . .
>
> "You've got to die to everything that allures you, and you've got to live for Christ. And you've got to live for the kingdom. And you've got to live for the church."[39]

Bilezikian recalls two aspects of his teaching about the church that were particularly influential on Hybels:

> He resonated with the concept of the church as community—rather than as institution or organization—as body, as community, as organism.
>
> And then the second thing was the mission of the church, not to be just self-sustaining or self-perpetuating, but to reach weekly into the society and claim it for Christ.[40]

The Church as Community

We can understand the impact of this teaching by comprehending Hybels's background in the Christian Reformed Church, which was supported by a very strong Dutch ethnic heritage. In the Dutch subculture, individuals were expected to grow up, get married to other Dutch kids, and attend a Dutch Christian Reformed Church. The popular saying and bumper sticker that summarized this ethnic pride was "If you're not Dutch, you're not much."

These Christian Reformed Dutch had a tradition of stubborn pride and a commitment to independence and self-reliance. They were skeptical of raw emotion in relationships and displayed a tough stoicism. But during his college days in the early 1970s, Hybels began experiencing the counterculture emphasis on the importance of intimacy and authenticity. He found this emphasis on honesty attractive. Bilezikian's emphasis on the church as community gave Hybels a means to understand his experience. What Hybels received from Bilezikian was a theological justification for the "authentic" relationships that were so popular in the early 1970s. Intimacy and the emotions are pivotal to this new approach toward life. Authentic relationships became an integral part of this vision of the church.[41]

The Mission of the Church

The Christian Reformed Church, as an organization, downplayed outward vision and evangelism and encouraged continuity. As a result, evangelism was not emphasized and the natural gravity of the institution led it toward being resistant to change. Self-sustaining churches within this framework were, by definition, successful.[42]

In contrast, Hybels listened to an angry Bilezikian, who taught that the church was not an institution to maintain the status quo. Bilezikian argued that the church is a community of people who were to turn the "world upside down." Instead of maintaining the internal focus of his home church, Hybels turned his vision outward.[43]

Hybels thus accepted a new definition of spiritual success where the goal of the church was to a large extent to affect those outside the church. As Hybels recalls Bilezikian's teaching, "You've got to live for the lost. And you've got to live with one eye on eternity from here on out." In a sense, the criteria of business could now be applied to the spiritual realm. The standard of success naturally became the number of those who were affected, and evangelism became the driving force of the church. Hybels had a new understanding of what the church should be and do, but he didn't have a model of how the church could implement this vision. Then he began to read a book by Robert Schuller.

Robert Schuller

Hybels was frustrated with the traditional church. He chose a mentor in Bilezikian who also was angry with the church. Yet besides his own experience with the Son City youth group, he did not have any models for how church could be done differently. Then he discovered the writings of Robert Schuller.[44]

While still coleading Son City, Hybels began to read *Your Church Has Real Possibilities* by Schuller. He was attracted to Schuller's message of the "unlimited potential" of the church. In 1975, before he started Willow Creek, he attended The Robert Schuller Institute for Successful Church Leadership, a yearly conference that Schuller sponsors at his Crystal Cathedral in California. This experience solidified a profound influence that Schuller was to have on Hybels and Willow Creek.[45]

What most interested me about Schuller's influence on the church was how staff members I interviewed neglected to mention it in their histories of the church. I first discovered it while at lunch with a staff member, Steve. We were having a warm and friendly discussion, and Steve described to me how Bill was influenced to buy a large tract of land for the church campus. But curiously, he left out who had encouraged him to do this. I asked who this mystery person was. Steve, rather reluctantly and hesitantly, told me it was Robert Schuller.

As a rule, staff members were frank and open in their responses to my questions. Yet it was clear from other staff members' lack of forthrightness about Schuller, and the uneasiness of those whom I did ask about Schuller's influence, that the staff seemed to be embarrassed about Schuller's impact on the church. Many of the staff who were hired in more recent years were entirely unaware of Schuller's influence on Hybels and the church.[46]

To understand Schuller's influence on the church, we need to take a brief look at him. In 1955 Schuller was an ambitious twenty-eight-year-old minister in the Reformed Church in America. He was called by his denomination to start a new church in Orange County, California. Yet there were virtually no families in this area that had a history in his denomination. Schuller explained that this attempt at church planting was "a totally new change in Church extension philosophy. Normally a denomination didn't start a branch church in a suburban community unless they had a lot of their people there."

Schuller was left in a quandary: How could he have a church with no members? As Schuller thought and prayed about his situation he came up with a strategy:

> I prayed for guidance and I had a real answer to prayer. And the answer I got was that one-half of the people who move into this community have turned all the other churches off.

He decided to reach out to this unchurched portion of the community: "My calling was to try to make the connections with, win the confidence . . . of the non-religious crowd."

How did Schuller do this? He first rang doorbells at thirty-five hundred homes and asked, "Are you an active member of a local church?" Schuller explains, "If they said no, I said, 'Great! I'm glad to meet you.'" He then asked them, "Why don't you go to church?" After listening to their answers, he then inquired, "What can I do for you? How can I help you? I'm here to start a new church. What would make you come to a church?" Individuals then expressed various reasons why they might come to church—if the church didn't preach about politics—if the church had a counseling program for teenagers—if the church had a singles program. Schuller's strategy was a response to these comments. "I listened to their answers," he says. Schuller concluded that to reach his Garden Grove neighbors, he had "to throw the kind of bait out that they would like."[47]

He started Garden Grove Community Church—with two fundamental changes: He modified the method of how he communicated and he modified the content of what he communicated.

Methods

Schuller asks, "What kind of a worship service would you conduct if to the best of your knowledge all the people that were in your church that Sunday morning weren't even Christians? Would you praise God? Of course not. Could you serve communion? Obviously, no."

Schuller claims that his shift in methodology has started a significant trend in Christianity: "An undisputed historical fact is that I am the founder, really, of the church-growth movement in this country." The central core of his shift in method is the application of marketing ideas for the church. He claims, "I advocated and launched what has become known as the marketing approach in Christianity."[48]

He argues, "If you want to succeed in marketing a church, you cannot ignore the retailing principles." In his book *Your Church Has Real Possibilities,* Schuller claims that there are proven "Principles of Successful Retailing":

> 1. *Accessibility.* "They've got to get to you without a big hassle."
> 2. *Surplus parking.* "If a church were to grow, it must have surplus parking."
> 3. *Inventory.* "You have to have what they want. . . . Find what their needs are. You have to study psychology to know what the deep emotional needs of human beings are before you open your mouth and start talking to them. . . . There enters self esteem psychology and theology."
> 4. *Service.* "You've got to have people that will welcome them in. 'Hello, I'm glad you've come in. How are you today?' . . . You don't have a consumer until they come back."
> 5. *Visibility.* "They've got to know you're there, know what you are and know that you have what they need and want. . . . You have to advertise."
> 6. *Good cash flow.* "Before you borrow money to expand, build up your income to the point where you can afford to borrow the funds."[49]

What were the results of applying these principles to Schuller's church? The major strategy of Schuller's ministry became to impress the unchurched individuals in Garden Grove: "The secret of winning unchurched people into the church is really quite simple. Find out what would impress the nonchurched people in your community." Schuller selected speakers, topics for his talks, and music that he believed would do so. Schuller explains, "Inviting Dr. Peale was my attempt to impress unchurched people in my community." Schuller gave optimistic, inspirational talks on topics helpful to the unchurched. Entertainment became a major part of his church services. He sought to create a pleasurable and relaxing environment for the unchurched, building a multi-million dollar Crystal Cathedral, which became famous around the world for its extravagance.[50]

Schuller elevated the importance of convenience for his religious consumers. He comments, "I found people would drive twenty miles one way . . . for an inspirational message. I have no doubt that accessibility was the biggest thing I had going for me." He maintains that the size of the parking lot helps determine the ultimate size of the church; as a result, he created what he claimed was the "largest paved church parking lot in the world." He developed the world's first drive-in church, where individuals could watch the service while sitting in their cars.[51]

Schuller argued that serving the customers of the church requires a trained laity. The church staff trains this work force. Schuller says, "The job description of our key staff men is *to recruit, train and motivate the lay people*" (author's emphasis). He developed various ministries within the church that would respond to various needs of the people. In order to be effective, Schuller believes that pastors should model themselves after business leaders and learn how to plan strategically—"If you fail to plan you're planning to fail."[52]

Schuller also was on the forefront of the use of technology for religious communication. Because his church is so large, he had a huge video screen installed behind the pulpit so that everyone in the congregation could see him clearly. He also became one of the most prominent television evangelists, utilizing the latest and best in technology.[53]

Message

Schuller explains that adopting this new orientation to church has profound effects on his message. He believes that pastors should not "try to preach heavy theology" on Sunday mornings:

> Don't even try to preach the Bible in expository sermons, if the crowd of people you've got would be turned off by all of that. You have got to win them and build relationships with them.

Instead, Schuller adopted a variation of Norman Vincent Peale's "positive thinking" in a gospel of "possibility thinking." Soon after Schuller had first arrived in Garden Grove, he invited Peale to speak at his new drive-in church. Schuller recalls Peale's message that morning:

"What would Jesus Christ have to say to you if he could stand here and talk to you through me?" He boomed out that tremendous question, waited until his voice had moved out into the surrounding orange groves, and then he continued, "Would he tell you what miserable sinners you are?"

He paused again and then continued, "No, I don't think so. . . . I think he would immediately begin telling you what great people you can become if you will only let His Holy Spirit of faith, hope and love fill every ounce and fibre of your being!"[54]

Peale's success, as one of the most popular writers and preachers in America, was very attractive to this young ambitious minister. Peale had a powerful influence on Schuller: "That sermon by Dr. Peale changed my [speaking] style from 'preaching' to 'witnessing.'" Schuller, imitating Peale, began to communicate a message of Christianity that focused on meeting the emotional and psychological needs of people. He then published these reworked sermons in a series of self-help books, *Your Future Is Your Friend*, *Success Is Never Ending*, and *Failure Is Never Final*. His message focused on the advantages of Christian faith for the problems of daily living.

In 1982 he explained his strategy in his book *Self Esteem: The New Reformation:*

I have seen my calling as one that communicates spiritual reality to the unchurched who may not be ready to believe in God. I have been trying to carry on a dialogue with persons who are not at all prepared to listen to "someone with God-talk."

As a missionary, I find the hope of respectful contact is based on a "human-need" approach rather than a theological attack.

From Schuller's perspective, one shouldn't emphasize theology when talking to unchurched individuals: "Don't try to sell them your theology when they haven't even decided yet if they want to be Christian."[55]

Schuller believes that there is a need for a new reformation to move from a "theocentric" focus to this "human needs approach." Without this radical change he believes there will be a "failure in mission." The unchurched "will spurn, reject, or simply ignore" the pastor who merely speaks the biblical message. Schuller believes that the unchurched will "take notice" only when one focuses on "their needs" and "their human hurts."[56]

Schuller then summarizes the effect of this radical shift on the church's task, saying, "This means that the most important question facing the church is: What are the deepest needs felt by human beings? Schuller's answer to this question is—self-esteem. "I contend that this unfulfilled need for self-esteem underlies every human act, both negative and positive," he says. The rest of Schuller's book is an attempt to reframe Christian theology with self-esteem at the hub. For example, he redefines sin: "Sin is any act or thought that robs myself or another human being of his or her self-esteem."[57]

For many in the evangelical community this was nothing less than heresy. Schuller acknowledges that his reputation in the evangelical community has suffered from his approach to theology: "I've been controversial . . . I don't use the typical evangelical language of 'You're a sinner. You got to admit you're a sinner.'" It was one thing to chuckle at Schuller's drive-in church, but many evangelicals viewed his reworking of theology as a pagan syncretism where psychology had swallowed up theology. Schuller's attempt at theology was met by many evangelical theologians with anger or condescension. It was this condemnation and disrespect of Schuller's message within the evangelical community that probably caused Willow Creek staffers to hesitate to acknowledge his influence.[58]

Schuller's Influence

As I have noted, Hybels was only dreaming of starting a church when he attended Schuller's institute on church leadership in 1975. After returning he recruited individuals to join him in starting a church that was rooted in this new strategy. After Willow Creek had been operating for a while, Hybels took approximately twenty-five members of Willow Creek's leadership core out to Schuller's leadership conference to be trained in Schuller's strategy. Holmbo explains what a great encouragement this was for these young Willow Creekers:

> Even at the conference, Bill was recognized. As people were all sitting at the church, Schuller pointed Bill out and just asked Bill to stand up and said, "I want you to know that this man right here is doing something out in Chicago which is actually what we are talking about at this conference." That was real affirming to us.

Hybels also had a personal relationship with Schuller and even asked Schuller to be the speaker at a major fundraising dinner at Willow Creek in 1979. Hybels followed Schuller's advice to buy a large tract of land for the church campus. Hybels eventually hired away one of Schuller's staff to serve as the director of Willow Creek's student ministry. After Willow Creek became successful, Schuller asked Hybels to come back and speak at The Robert Schuller Institute for Successful Church Leadership.[59]

Dave Holmbo explains that Schuller had a profound effect on Hybels and the Willow Creek core:

> Schuller came along and said, "Yeah, that really is a God-given thing. I believe it can happen and you should believe it could happen." It was coming from someone who had a certain level of credibility of his own.

Methods

When Willow Creek leaders tell the history of the church, they invariably emphasize the importance of a community survey that Hybels and a few others took in 1975:

> For four weeks, a group of four people asked the following question: "Do you go to church?" If the person said yes, the survey was over. If no, there was a follow-up question: "Why not?"[60]

The most common answer to "Why not?" was that "the church was always asking for money." Other answers were:

- I am unable to relate to the music.
- I am unable to relate to the message.
- The church does not meet my needs.
- The services are predictable and boring.
- The church makes me feel guilty.

The answers gave guidelines as to what Willow Creek would teach and do in the future. Based on this information, the church formulated its strategy by specifically requesting visitors in the weekend services not to participate in the offering at the church; developing music that these visitors could enjoy; crafting messages that related to the audience and met their needs; creating services that were exciting; and seeking to avoid making participants feel guilty.[61]

The history of the survey is well known to church members. What is not understood is that much of this strategy is the result of Schuller's influence. Schuller argues:

> Those "churches" that are willing to become "missions" will succeed. Churches that are incapable of understanding what it means to become a mission, or are unwilling to pay the high price of dying as a church and being born again as a mission, will disappear entirely or will perpetuate themselves as fringe elements that are largely ignored.[62]

The first step to becoming a mission in Schuller's system is to understand the audience, or market, that one is addressing. Schuller writes in *Your Church Has Real Possibilities* that a pastor needs to develop an "inventory" of his community. Schuller urges pastors, "You should establish a goal of canvassing door to door, all of the homes in your community." Now we can understand young Hybels's enthusiasm for taking a survey. His new mentor told him he should.[63]

Much of the strategy that resulted from this survey and marketing focus closely resembled Schuller's own church strategy. Curiously, from Schuller's perspective, Hybels was able to be more Schullerian than Schuller:

> I was the first person to introduce real church growth to the American Church. . . . He [Hybels] became the first guy to take these principles, refine them, maximize them to the ultimate length of their potential.

"Hybels," Schuller adds, "took it the whole shot, a lot farther than Schuller ever took it."

Schuller believes that Hybels was able to do this because:

> He wasn't a member of a denomination. He didn't belong to a denomination that says that you have to follow a certain church order on Sunday morning. You have to open with a hymn, you have to have the Scripture reading, you have to have a congregational prayer, you have to serve communion once in a while. The Dutch Reformed in my denomination didn't allow me to just break loose and do anything I wanted to do.

From Schuller's perspective, Hybels is the son who has become a success. "I am so proud of him. . . . I think of him as a son," he says. "I think of him as one of the greatest things to happen in Christianity in our time." Schuller cheers, "Scholars that outrun the masters are great people," and "Bill Hybels is doing the best job of anybody I know!"

Message

The result of Schuller's focus on understanding and meeting the needs of his audience eventually led him to emphasize self-esteem. Self-esteem is but one psychological category of his teaching. He believes that theology has stumbled by not recognizing the truths that psychology has been discovering: "Theology has failed to accommodate and apply proven insights in human behavior as revealed by twentieth-century psychologists." This dependence on psychology led him to frame the Christian life in psychological categories: "I was the first theologian to write a theology of self-esteem." As I noted above, this theological message emphasized God's love and obscured mankind's sin.[64]

Hybels's commitment, adopted from Schuller, to be relevant and meet human needs brought with it much of this same theological content. In the early years of the church Hybels preached Schuller's message of God's unconditional love with an emphasis on psychological ideas. One staff member described Hybels's teaching in the first four years:

> Lots of stuff on self-image and real helpful stuff, but it wasn't real clear scriptural stuff. I don't think it was by design; I think it was just by accident.

Cousins, writing in 1979, teaches other youth leaders that messages "must be positive, uplifting, non-threatening, non-judgmental, inspirational, helpful, and joyous experiences." This cheerful Christianity is very Schullerian.[65]

As I already noted, part of the fallout from the 1979 "train wreck" was that Hybels began emphasizing sin and the holiness of God. Hybels acknowledges about this time:

> I was guilty of imbalanced teaching. I made continual references to God's unconditional acceptance of who we are, regardless of what we do, what we say, how we live. . . . Consequently, some people of the church just didn't care about the holiness of God. How could they? They didn't hear about the seriousness of sin and the scars it leaves. Nor did they hear much about justice. They just heard a lot about acceptance and grace.

After the "train wreck" Hybels attempted to keep Schuller's method of being a mission to the unchurched and yet discard or radically modify Schuller's message or theology. Looking back he confesses:

> I had failed God by representing him inaccurately before people, and I felt deep pangs of guilt. Not only did I feel foolish, I felt remorseful and embarrassed.
>
> Frequently I broke down before the Lord and said, "You're absolutely right. It's my fault. I was more concerned about people liking this church and becoming a part of it than I was about their understanding the true identity of God. I distorted who You are to make You more acceptable to them."[66]

Hybels's repentance from Schuller's message is apparent in the evangelical gospel that Hybels preaches. He is now willing to confront unchurched Harry with the blunt words of the gospel in a way that Schuller doesn't. Hybels commented in an interview that he has told Schuller, "At Willow Creek I preach about sin. I use the *S* word, Bob." All of the Creekers that read this section made some comment to the effect, "We don't agree with Schuller's theology." Evangelism director Mittelberg responded that he didn't want "people to think what we're doing squares with what he [Schuller] calls a positive message." And to be fair, I never found at Willow Creek the avoidance of biblical terminology like "sin" that one finds with Schuller.

However, Willow Creek's teaching during the weekend services still emphasizes a strong psychological element. Hybels's and Willow Creek's reliance on psychology, although not as strong as Schuller's, is still very real. While Schuller has emphasized "self-esteem," Hybels has stressed "personal fulfillment." While Schuller uses the category of meeting "human needs," Hybels uses the idea of "Christianity 101" or "user-friendly doctrine."

The young Hybels was captivated by Schuller's vision of a different way of doing church. Hybels read in one of Schuller's books:

> Believe you can build a Twenty-First Century church now! You can be the founder and leader of such a great new inspirational center.
>
> Some reader of this book will build the greatest church ever built in America—a walk-in, drive-in church in blizzard country! With seven-days-a-week activity! It will be a sensation for Christ![67]

All of the preceding influences on Willow Creek had one thing in common—a connection with Bill Hybels. Son City provided the initial strategy and people that Hybels then led to start Willow Creek. Dave Holmbo was influential in helping Hybels shape the youth group and the early direction of the church. The "train wreck" was important as it pared down the staff to those who were loyal to Hybels and caused Hybels to reorganize the church as a spiritual business. Bilezikian was significant as he both inspired Hybels on his quest for a better church and gave him his basic theology. Schuller was influential in providing Hybels with a model of how the church should adopt both new methods and a new message. Yet Bill Hybels is the central cord of Willow Creek's history around which all these other threads wrap. The importance and influence of Bill Hybels on Willow Creek has, if anything, increased during the history of the church.

These individuals and situations provided central ideas that Hybels then used to shape Willow Creek and its new way of doing church. The first step in this new strategy is understanding Willow Creek's target audience: unchurched Harry.

3

Understanding Unchurched Harry

Willow Creek bases all it does on a thorough understanding of its chosen primary audience, unchurched Harry. This strategy originated in Son City, when Son City met high school students "where they were," on their own ground. Hybels and coleader Holmbo crafted all of the programming and teaching toward this end. The idea, Hybels explained, "was predicated on the fact that a seeker is fundamentally different in composition than someone who is already convinced and a part of the Christian family."[1]

From this perspective, reaching non-Christians involves gathering information about them, learning all about who they are, their background, their environment, their tastes and beliefs. Only when these elements are known, explained evangelism director Mark Mittelberg, can Willow Creek begin to move unchurched Harrys: "That is the nature of persuasion—bringing a person from where they are to where they need to be."[2]

Finding out about unchurched Harry involves researching and creating a full profile of who Harry is. This chapter focuses on Willow Creek's means of gathering information—marketing research. The next chapter gives the results—a full profile of who unchurched Harry is.

Marketing Research

Hybels employs marketing categories and tools in collecting information to understand his audience. In popular understanding, *marketing* is a synonym of *advertising*. In reality, marketing is much more. In fact, many experts have come to see marketing as a large part of the creative genius of a business. Tom Peters and Bob Waterman studied the most successful companies in America and wrote *In Search of Excellence*, the best-selling business book of all time. Philip Kotler, professor at Northwestern University and one of the leading authorities on marketing, summarizes their findings concerning marketing:

> What they found was that all of these companies shared a set of basic operating principles, among them
>
> - a keen sense of customer ("stay close to the customer")
> - a keen sense of the market ("stick to your knitting")
> - and a high ability to motivate their employees to produce high quality and high value for the customers.

Marketing views business from the perspective of the consumer and has been summarized in the famous marketing proverb, "The customer is king."[3]

Kotler defines marketing:

> *Marketing* is the business function that
> *identifies* unfulfilled needs and wants
> *defines* and measures their magnitude
> *determines* which target markets the organization can best serve
> *decides* on appropriate products, services and
> *programs* to serve these markets [emphasis added].

Marketing has become a highly sophisticated means of understanding potential markets and designing products to service these markets. One can apply this marketing perspective on needs, research, target markets, market share, target-audience profile, product to virtually any human endeavor.[4]

The marketing approach has, through the church-growth movement, deeply influenced the evangelical church in the last twenty-five years. The leading advocate of this evangelical use of marketing is pollster George Barna. *Christianity Today* has described Barna as "the church's guru of growth." In his book *Marketing the Church* he condemns the evangelical church:

> My contention, based on careful study of data and the activities of American churches, is that the major problem plaguing the Church is its failure to embrace a marketing orientation in what has become a marketing-driven environment.[5]

It is important to observe where Barna gained his insights and enthusiasm for marketing. He writes in the acknowledgments of *Marketing the Church:*

> I am indebted to Bill Hybels, pastor of Willow Creek Community Church near Chicago, for his vision and relentless quest to see that vision become a reality for the glory of God.
>
> It was during my time in Wheaton, Illinois, while attending the Rev. Hybels' church that I first had my eyes opened to the meaning of evangelism and church growth.

> If I had my way, there would be 100,000 Willow Creek Churches in this country. With God's blessing, perhaps we can make some headway toward that goal.[6]

Now Barna comes into perspective. He is seeking to distill many of the working marketing principles of Willow Creek, add his polling savvy and data, and evangelize the rest of the evangelical church with the result. He has sought to further this agenda by publishing the quarterly *Christian Marketing Perspective*, creating special marketing church-growth seminars, and writing a wide assortment of books.[7]

Barna has received a very positive reception by much of the evangelical community, and several of his books have become evangelical best-sellers. But in many ways, Barna is merely a publicist. He was excited by his experience with Willow Creek and he wants to spread the word. Willow Creek is the source of much of the inspiration and information behind the evangelical enthusiasm for marketing.[8]

Willow Creek has so enthusiastically adopted and applied the principles of marketing that it has received growing attention from business schools and publications. Harvard Business School, for instance, selected Willow Creek as the subject of one of its famous case studies. Its author, who was eventually hired as the president of the Willow Creek Association, explains that the staff of Willow Creek "attribute much of their success to the simple concept of *knowing your customers and meeting their needs*" (author's emphasis).[9]

Willow Creek's strategy has also been discussed in the pages of *Fortune* magazine and the *Wall Street Journal*. In the latter, Peter Drucker explains that Willow Creek and its imitators are employing simple marketing ideas: "None of these marketing lessons are new. Anyone who has taken a marketing course these past 30 years or who has read a marketing text should know them."[10]

Marketing Ideas Used by Willow Creek

Two of the marketing ideas that Willow Creek currently employs are defining a target audience and research.

Target Audience

Willow Creek places a great emphasis on defining a target audience, the individuals for whom it wants primarily to aim its services. Hybels states that everything that happens in a weekend service is a direct response to the target audience that Willow Creek has selected. For example, Hybels chooses humor that his target audience likes. He describes a "private pet peeve" that he has about how pastors use Charlie Brown and Lucy humor:

> A lot of *target audience* men find that just a little bit effeminate and elementary. I mean that's not a real high level. Your cosmopolitan businessmen don't really get their chuckles from Lucy, okay? [emphasis added].

This comment reveals that Hybels's target audience is "cosmopolitan businessmen." To personalize and simplify the idea of a target audience, Hybels has given the typical target person a name—"unchurched Harry." Nancy Beach, the programming director, describes unchurched Harry as "a person who lives out here in the suburbs. . . . He probably has some church experience but most likely he left it for various reasons: it became irrelevant; he became too busy and decided it wasn't important to his life." Hybels says that Harry is between the ages of twenty-five and forty-five, college educated, white collar, and an independent thinker. Harry is also married and has kids.

Willow Creek has obviously focused on reaching men. Hybels elaborates:

> We shoot unashamedly for the male, and that's somewhat controversial. But our feeling is that it's tougher to reach men than it is women. Men seekers are real tough to reach.
>
> So if we set our standards at reaching unchurched males, we'll probably in so doing reach larger numbers of females.

Why this particular target audience for weekend services was chosen by Hybels is further revealed by his remark, "Generally a pastor can define his appropriate target audience by determining with whom he would like to spend a vacation or an afternoon of recreation." Hybels explains that a pastor often has a "passion for a particular people group. The example I always turn to is the apostle Paul, who had a passion for planting churches among the Gentiles." This common affinity of the audience with the personality of the pastor enhances the pastor's abilities to persuade Harry.[11]

The staff isn't particularly concerned with the individuals who don't fit unchurched Harry's profile. Hybels explains:

> We don't ask . . . how do we please believing Bob at our weekend services, because he's not our *target audience*. It's unchurched Harry—he's the person we're after. And so we orient that whole thing toward him [emphasis added].

Research for Understanding Unchurched Harry

Once Hybels and Willow Creek have chosen unchurched Harry as the target audience for the weekend service, the next step in the process is to find out more about Harry. Marketing guru Kotler argues that once a business's mission is established, the next step is "external analysis." Willow Creek wants to start where unchurched Harry is, to understand what he thinks, what he likes, what he doesn't like, what he needs.[12]

Pollster Barna argues, "Research is a critical step for marketing the church. Often we attempt to minister to needs that do not exist while ignoring needs that scream for attention." Barna believes that marketing research is an effort to be faithful stewards of resources and time. He believes that research will ultimately determine one's effectiveness:

> Unless we take the time and make the effort to discover—objectively and factually—what people care about, how they hurt, and what service they look to the church to offer, we run a serious risk of being irrelevant and of little value to the people who need what we have to offer.[13]

This commitment to research comes directly out of marketing. Kotler explains, "*Marketing research* is the systematic design, collection, analysis, and reporting of data and findings relevant to a specific marketing situation facing the company" (author's emphasis).[14]

An example of a company that is committed to research is the Hallmark card company. In a society that is rapidly changing, Hallmark believes that research is essential. The *Wall Street Journal* comments:

> It might seem that all this change threatens Hallmark and its Norman Rockwell world. In fact just the opposite is true. The more society atomizes—the more divorces, latchkey kids. . . . the more niches are created for greeting cards and greeting card sales. . . .
>
> Hallmark relies heavily on research, some of it computer-age scientific. The company uses focus groups and panel tests. It can take every card made in the last five years and analyze whether it sold and why or why not.[15]

Thus Hallmark has attempted to stay on the cutting edge of society's changes and address the needs of its audience. Hallmark has created divorce announcements, sympathy notes because a pet has died, and a variety of other exotic cards to fit its changing audience.

Willow Creek is also committed to doing such research. It uses four different types of research: relationships with unchurched Harrys, research retreats, professional research, and Hybels's own research.

Relationships with Unchurched Harrys

Business marketing research strategies often try to harvest the understanding of those directly involved in the sales of a business. Typically, the salespeople who see the customers every day are more aware of their needs and concerns. Marketer Kotler describes this strategy as a "Composite of Sales-Force Opinions." Likewise Willow Creek staff and lay leaders are specifically instructed to try to understand their unchurched friends, family, neighbors, and acquaintances. In fact, the first step of the church's seven step strategy is to develop relationships with unchurched Harrys and Marys. Hybels recommends that his staff develop a lifestyle of interacting with nonbelievers:

> I have suggested for many years that our pastors at Willow Creek find authentic interest areas in their lives—tennis, golf, jogging, sailing, mechanical work, whatever—and pursue these in a totally secular realm. Instead of joining a church league softball team, why not join a park district team?[16]

Programming director Nancy Beach explains, "We all try to cultivate relationships, strategically, with target audience kinds of people. . . . We're trying to progressively stay in the world." This commitment—to develop relationships with unchurched individuals—gives the staff and lay leadership first-hand knowledge of what makes them tick. Teaching pastor Strobel reveals:

> I have constant contact with unchurched people and maintain a lot of relationships with people who are unchurched in an effort to understand where they're coming from.

Research Retreats

Business research is business specific. Each business adopts or develops various research techniques to discover the information that it wants. We mentioned above how Hallmark creates panel groups for research in choosing appropriate cards. Willow Creek, applying their idea of teams, has developed the unique technique of research retreats.

Hybels recruits a team of people each spring to go on a retreat to discuss proposals for what subjects should be addressed on the weekends during the next ministry year. According to Lee Strobel, teams include "some on staff, some lay people, some real involved people, some just average people who attend the church."

Hybels asks each individual to talk to both seekers and Christians to come up with a list of fifteen possible series of talks. For two to three days this group of approximately ten individuals discusses each idea. They select the series that they believe are the most relevant to unchurched Harry. The final list of proposed topics and titles is entirely subject to Hybels's discretion.[17]

Following this initial research retreat, another retreat is scheduled for August. A group of six to eight key staff and elders joins Hybels while he is on his study break in Michigan to discuss the proposed series one more time. They whittle down the list. Yet again the final list is subject to Hybels's revisions.

Individual ministries in the church may also do research together. For example, the programming team goes to plays, musicals, concerts, and movies to understand the culture of unchurched Harry. The entire programming team went to the musical *Les Miserables* and to a Janet Jackson concert. Nancy Beach explains:

> We stay on very close track with what is working artistically outside of the church. We're very aggressive at going after the movies and the TV shows and the plays and all this kind of thing so that we know what's moving people outside of our sphere.

They believe if they can learn what communicates with Harry, they can utilize these same methods and ideas in their programming.[18]

Professional Research

Business believes in expert research of its external environment. Kotler states, "The key to organizational survival and growth is the firm's ability to adapt its strategies to a rapidly changing environment." Barna echoes this: "An effective marketer must base his plans and tactics on *recent and accurate information*" (author's emphasis). Thus, in Barna's view the first step of effectively marketing a church "is to conduct research that focuses on the consumers' attitudes and behavior."[19]

After Barna was inspired by Hybels's marketing at Willow Creek, he began focusing much of his research on how the American church can more effectively market the gospel. He has produced a series of marketing reports and books toward this end. Willow Creek and Hybels have now returned Barna's compliment by referring to Barna's research. I regularly heard staff members quote one of Barna's conclusions. Hybels himself writes a blurb on the cover of Barna's book *The Frog in the Kettle:* "I try to read everything George Barna writes . . . not only because I *want* to—but because I feel I *have* to!" (author's emphasis).[20]

Willow Creek has also used quantitative research to gain a specific understanding of their audience. Nancy Beach describes a church survey in the mid 1980s: "Maybe six years ago there was a major survey that they did, but it still wasn't scientifically done. . . . The way they sampled it was like, 'Whoever wants, please fill it out.'" In the intervening years—since Barna has popularized professional research for marketing the church—Willow Creek has tried to do more credible research. They hired Barna's company to do a major research project on Willow Creek. Approximately six thousand four hundred individuals from the weekend service returned the survey. Willow Creek has been increasingly utilizing the results of Barna and other researchers to map out the characteristics of unchurched Harry. Teaching pastor Lee Strobel writes, "Researchers have been working hard to come up with a composite portrait of the average unchurched American."[21]

Bill Hybels's Research

Like most of Willow Creek's strategy, Willow Creek's marketing research finds its root in Bill Hybels. Hybels led the original survey research team. Hybels encourages church participants to understand their unchurched friends. Hybels leads the church's major research retreats. Hybels assesses the conclusions of these retreats. Hybels sees all this research as helpful and necessary.

Yet probably a more important source of information for Hybels is his informal rubbing of shoulders with rank-and-file unchurched Harrys and Marys. As Beach explains, Hybels "just socializes with a lot of unchurched people." Through relating to Harrys and Marys, he determines how to communicate relevantly to them. Beach describes Hybels in this way:

> I guess there's nobody who has a better [unchurched Harry] profile, at least personally. . . . He knows their reactions when they do eventually come and visit and communicates those to us.
>
> But he also just has gotten to know them so well that his instincts for how to speak to that particular audience tend to be very accurate.

The key idea in this description is the word *instincts*. Bill Hybels is intuitive in his approach to determining the topics for the weekend meetings. As one staff member explained, Hybels is "in touch with lots of people and kind of gets the feel of 'Are you getting what you need to grow?'" One staff member described how the various weekend messages are chosen: "The process of how those are arrived at is largely intuitive, but it's an informed intuition." Hybels utilizes the information from the other sources of research, but the final judgment comes down to his gut instincts and what he thinks the Holy Spirit wants him to do.[22]

4

Profile of Unchurched Harry

Marketing theory and research demand as many details as possible about the target audience. Barna argues:

> To successfully market your product, you have to identify its prospective market. The key to market identification—sometimes referred to as "target marketing"—is to be as specific as possible.[1]

This task has been made easier because of a book that Willow Creek teaching pastor Lee Strobel has recently written, *Inside the Mind of Unchurched Harry and Mary*. Harry is more than just a twenty-five- to forty-five-year-old suburban, college educated, white collar professional, who is married with kids. To fill in the profile, this chapter examines Harry's lifestyle, needs, and attitude toward Christianity.[2]

Harry's Lifestyle

When businesses chart their target audience they inevitably focus on distinctive lifestyle characteristics. Similarly Willow Creek has a clear idea of Harry's age, marital status, education, and work.

Age. Strobel argues that "churches that are successful in reaching unchurched people focus on particular age groups." Willow Creek's target audience is the twenty-five to forty-five age group. According to Barna's survey, nearly 60 percent of Willow Creek's weekend audience are these baby boomers—ages twenty-seven to forty-five. Another 14 percent are baby busters ages fourteen to twenty-six. Thus nearly 75 percent of the Willow Creek weekend audience are between ages fourteen and forty-five. The average age of a weekend attender is thirty-six.[3]

Marital status. About 60 percent of Willow Creek's weekend audience are married, and most have children. Only 25 percent of the audience are single and 12 percent are divorced. This reality of family relationships will determine many of the needs that this population group has.

Education. Considering Willow Creek's location in Chicago's northwest suburbs, it is not surprising that the majority of weekend attenders are well educated. Barna's study concludes that those who have graduated from college comprise about 50 percent. Another 25 percent are either currently enrolled in college or have attended some college.[4]

The factor of education is vitally important. People who have a college education and are living in comfortable, middle-class suburbs tend to be politically conservative. Barna discovered that 59 percent of Willow Creek attenders described themselves as conservative and only 12 percent as liberal. The audience Willow Creek is seeking to reach is sophisticated. As Hybels said, "Almost the whole church considered themselves to be deep thinkers." These factors influence the language and style used in public programs and the selection of appropriate topics.

Jobs. The kind of jobs people have is in direct relation to education. The great majority of Willow Creek attenders are professionals. They also actually have jobs. While the national unemployment rate tends to be around 7 to 8 percent, according to the Network survey, Willow Creek's is only 3.7 percent. The statistics also show a very high percentage (12 percent) of individuals who are self-employed. Individuals who attend Willow Creek are using their educations in well-paying professional jobs. They earn enough that they are able to purchase homes in middle- to upper-middle-class neighborhoods.[5]

Even though Harry is making an income that allows him to live in one of these middle-class neighborhoods, he still is financially stretched. The Barna study showed that of those who attend Willow Creek only once a month, 58 percent don't pay off their credit cards on a monthly basis. Harry is living close to the financial edge and has little excess cash.

Needs as the Key to Sales

Marketing theory spotlights the needs of individuals in order to market to them. Kotler explains:

> The marketing concept holds that the key to achieving organizational goals consists in *determining the needs and wants of target markets* and delivering the desired satisfactions more effectively and efficiently than competitors [author's emphasis].[6]

Thus, needs, from the vantage point of marketing, are the motivators for new sales. Kotler explains, "Needs and wants create a state of discomfort in people, which is resolved through acquiring products to satisfy these needs and wants." Marketers have the job of determining what these needs are and then providing products that will satisfy them.[7]

Kotler explains that an "extremely important responsibility" of a business is to "identify new market needs and opportunities and respond to them with appropriate and effective product solutions." If one wants new sales, one focuses on the buyer's needs. For example, a newsletter for Allstate Insurance teaches that successful salesmen make "sales presentations with the needs and preferences of their prospects in mind."[8]

Barna has applied this marketing framework to Christianity. When he teaches how to market the church, he merely identifies the church as the marketer, the product as the gospel, and the audience (those with needs) as the consumers. "This is what marketing the church is all about: providing our product (relationships) as a solution to people's felt need."[9]

Needs in this view are the key to open new doors of sales. Barna explains:

> New people are attracted to a church because it meets their personal needs. The more successful a church is at fulfilling people's needs, the greater are its chances for growth.[10]

Don Cousins taught the staff about "the old business axiom, Find a need and meet it." He asked, "Any business that identifies a need in a consumer out there . . . [and meets] the need is going to have what kind of business?" He answers his rhetorical question, "A thriving business."

From this perspective, a felt need is like a warning light in a car's dashboard that the car is low in oil. It alerts the driver to a serious problem and spurs him to find a solution. Thus to address the felt needs of the audience is to focus on those issues that the audience is already concerned about. Lee Strobel affirms this strategy: "The most effective messages for seekers are those that address their felt needs."[11]

What is the source of these felt needs? Marketer Kotler teaches:

> Culture is the most fundamental determinant of a person's wants and behavior. Whereas lower creatures are largely governed by instinct, human behavior is largely learned.

> The child growing up in a society learns a basic set of values, perceptions, preferences, and behaviors through a process of socialization involving the family and other key institutions.

Thus, from a marketing standpoint, to comprehend someone's needs you must understand their culture.[12]

Harry's Felt Needs

Willow Creek wants to understand unchurched Harry's culture. Hybels writes, "We've tried to crack our cultural code." What are some of unchurched Harry's felt needs?[13]

Personal Fulfillment

In the last three decades there has been a fundamental shift in how Americans view and live life. Pollster Daniel Yankelovich observes that many Americans' fundamental life goal has become personal fulfillment:

> Cross-section studies of Americans show unmistakably that the search for self-fulfillment is . . . an authentic grass-roots phenomenon involving, in one way or another, perhaps as many as 80 percent of all adult Americans.[14]

Americans are pursuing their own happiness. Yankelovich observed, "My firm's studies showed more than seven out of ten Americans (72 percent) spending a great deal of time thinking about themselves." The felt need of fulfillment involves many other particular felt needs, all of which determine whether or not Harry is fulfilled. If Willow Creek can present its message so that it resonates with Americans' felt need for fulfillment, we can expect that Harrys will listen.[15]

Identity

Americans used to be content with achieving and faithfully executing adult roles and responsibilities. Adult roles, and the web of relationships in which they are involved, once provided a clear understanding of self and identity.

Roles are now, however, less important in American culture. Joseph Veroff conducted a major study of Americans' attitudes toward themselves. He concludes, "Meaning and self-definition no longer derive primarily from the accession to adult status and the adequate or outstanding performance of adult roles."[16]

Veroff writes that modern Americans are dubious of roles: "Role and status designations have become objects of suspicion, as though they were different from—and even contradictory to—the core self, the essential person." Personal identity has become a much more self-created and thus rather tenuous affair. A psychological worldview has been popularized to provide this subjective framework. As Veroff explains, "It is clear from the data that men and women have become much more psychological in their thinking about themselves and understanding their own lives."[17]

Companionship

Many Americans are lonely. George Gallup Jr. concludes:

> As many as four in ten Americans admit to frequent or occasional feelings of intense loneliness. Americans are, in fact, the loneliest people in the world.[18]

Barna quickly focuses on loneliness as a felt need that the church should address: "The national surveys I have conducted over the past several years indicate that loneliness is one of the major growing problems in America." Barna preaches that loneliness "is the kind of social problem that the Church needs to identify and respond to."[19]

Marriage

In a society where individuals are pursuing fulfillment and feeling lonely, intimacy is greatly prized. Veroff observed a shift in modern America toward an "increased emphasis on interpersonal intimacy as opposed to social organization as a means of integration." He explained there are "many different pieces of data to support the general conclusion that interpersonal intimacy has become a vehicle for personal fulfillment." Marriage is the major means of providing intimacy for most Americans and thus is still very popular.[20]

But it is also very fragile. The search for fulfillment has provided an internal strain within marriages. Many people see their marriage as competing against their personal happiness. The high degree of autonomy that accompanies the search for personal fulfillment has made intimacy more difficult. A symptom of the strain between personal fulfillment and intimacy during the last thirty years has been the skyrocketing American divorce rate. When individuals find marriage conflicts with their search for happiness, they often abandon it.

Many people are thus fearful that their marriages may not withstand the pressures that they face. They don't want their own marriage to become another divorce statistic. This concern is visible in the Willow Creek survey, in which attenders selected which values they most prized. "Close relationships with family" was second, behind a "deep relationship with God." In response to this need, Willow Creek usually has at least one series on relationships each year.

Family

A consequence of the breakup of so many American marriages is the dismantlement of many American families. An increasing percentage of children are growing up in broken or remodeled families. Even if families have stayed together, it is an increasing strain on parents to financially and emotionally care for their children. More and more families have two incomes, and thus the parents have less time for their kids. The parents in these families often realize that they need help in learning how to parent effectively.

To raise children well is a particularly strong desire for unchurched Harry and Mary, as they are in the prime childrearing years (twenty-five to forty-five). The Barna study of Willow Creek pointed out that "an amazing 93 percent over 46 have had children." Harry and Mary see the church as a way to care for their children.

A curious dimension to this need is the fact that even many skeptical unchurched Harrys want their children to receive moral and religious training. Strobel explains that "even if Harry's not spiritually sensitive, he wants his children to get quality moral training." Strobel refers to a polling study that concluded that

> 55% of unchurched baby boomer men said they definitely have no plans to join a church in the next five years—but 73% of them said they want their children to get religious training.[21]

Relief of Stress

Unchurched Harry and Mary are harried. They feel pressures from their jobs, extended families, kids, and marriages. According to one national survey, a full 89 percent of Americans described themselves as "busy"—more than any other characteristic. One individual described to me how he would schedule his church involvement around his job: "I'll make an appointment just before . . . and then right at the very end." Life for unchurched Harry is lived in the pages of a Daytimer schedule.[22]

Added to the furious pace of suburban life for many Americans are the increased desires for intimacy and fulfillment discussed above. As expectations have risen concerning emotional well-being, people generally have felt less happy rather than more satisfied. A result of these broad trends is tremendous emotional stress. A church-wide survey revealed about one-third of those attending Willow Creek feel "totally stressed out."

Meaning and Morality

The discipline of the sociology of religion has generally acknowledged a deep human need for meaning and morality. In most cultures around the world, religion has provided this framework. Many unchurched Harrys do not have a clear purpose or moral code, and they feel this need.[23]

As Lee Strobel writes, "Harry is morally adrift, but he secretly wants an anchor." Strobel argues that Harrys "are beginning to conclude that moral anarchy isn't all that Hugh Hefner once painted it to be." Harry wants a moral map to guide him through the dangerous journey of life.[24]

Yet Harry wants more than merely a moral map. Harry desires a clear sense of purpose and destiny. As Strobel explains, "Harry isn't much of a joiner, but he's hungry for a cause he can connect with." In this regard Harry is open to receiving leadership from those he trusts. As Strobel writes, "Harry may distrust authority, but he's receptive to authentic biblical leadership."[25]

Willow Creek approaches unchurched Harry as a spiritual consumer. Hybels believes "unchurched people today are the ultimate consumers." He explains:

> The 45-and-under generation has a consumer-oriented mindset. They patronize the restaurants and stores they like, and they'll attend a church for the same reason.

When a newcomer attends, Hybels views him as shopping in a new store. At Willow Creek, the customer Harry is king. Although Creekers aim at Harry's needs and expect to hit their targets, there is one large problem. Harry doesn't particularly like Willow Creek's product.[26]

Harry's Attitude toward Christianity

Christianity, particularly what has become known in the media as "fundamentalism," is viewed negatively by many Americans. Evangelism director Mark Mittelberg describes this negative attitude:

> You watch Oprah or watch Donahue or watch Geraldo, and they are dealing with some moral issue and a biblically centered, balanced Christian stands up and states his position, what happens? They laugh him out, right? They shut him off and say, "Get out of here."

I interviewed one newspaper reporter who had written about Willow Creek. He explained to me that the Willow Creek staff "know that their old-fashioned religion's got a real bad rep [reputation]." Strobel referred to a national survey where individuals were asked to rank professions for their level of honesty and integrity. This survey located television evangelists near the bottom of the list—between organized crime bosses and prostitutes.[27]

There is a great deal of skepticism and cynicism in the American public toward organized religion in general and evangelical Christianity in particular. This is especially true of those Willow Creek is trying to reach. In virtually every category, the Willow Creek target audience is more negative toward religion than an average American.

In the Gallup study on Americans' attitudes toward religion, people were asked, "How important would you say religion is in your life?" The following percentages indicate that less than half of Willow Creek's target audience said religion is "very important":

- 48% of the college educated
- 49% of those with over $30,000 income
- 47% of men
- 53% of whites
- 42% of those aged 18–29
- 51% of those aged 30–49

Compare the target audience's percentages to those of their demographic opposites who affirm that religion is "very important":

- 69% of those who didn't have a high school education
- 61% of those who make less than $20,000
- 62% of women
- 72% of non-whites
- 68% of those 50 and older

The Willow Creek target audience (educated, financially well-off, male, white, and young) is a particularly skeptical, or at least unmotivated, bunch.[28]

Americans, nevertheless, like the idea of being spiritual. They even like the idea of God. Consistently in national polls, over 90 percent of all Americans affirm their belief in God. Most Americans (76 percent) even affirm that they "completely agree" (41 percent) or "mostly agree" (35 percent) with the statement, "Prayer is an important part of my daily life." This is extraordinary. By these measurements, Americans are some of the most spiritual people in the world. How are we to put together this odd puzzle of spiritual, yet skeptical, people?[29]

Thus far, this description of unchurched Harry's attitude toward Christianity has put all unchurched individuals into one category. It might be helpful to attempt to clarify this picture with a description of three different kinds of unchurched Harrys.

Hostile Harrys

Strobel describes this group as "people who are hostile or negative toward religion in general." The hard-core portion of this group is atheistic or agnostic in their beliefs. Since over 90 percent of Americans affirm a basic belief in God, this portion of the group is relatively small.

A larger group of "hostile Harrys" affirms a belief in God yet remains negative toward Christianity in general. One might wonder what would lead a hostile Harry to attend Willow Creek. Although a sincere Harry or a curious Harry may be interested in checking out a church in the community, a hostile Harry probably wouldn't. The majority of hostile Harrys are probably asked by a friend or family member to Willow Creek. Yet even with these relationships, these Harrys are hostile toward Willow Creek, as Hybels describes:

> They come in, they sit down, they cross their arms and they say, "Well the first thing you need to know is that I don't necessarily buy the book. I mean the Bible isn't all that compelling to me."

Skepticism is hostile Harry's basic attitude toward Willow Creek.

The classic hostile Harry at Willow Creek, curiously enough, is Lee Strobel, now one of the main speakers at the weekend services. Strobel acknowledges:

> I've been kidded that I was Unchurched Harry, but actually that's too mild a nickname to describe my attitude back then. It sounds like someone who's stuck in spiritual neutral.
>
> A more appropriate description of my mindset would have been "Anti-Church Charlie" because I was so negative toward spiritual matters.[30]

Strobel was trained in journalism and law, and when he first came into contact with the church was the legal editor of the *Chicago Tribune*. Strobel explains his former attitude:

> I was an atheist. I just thought that the idea of God was ridiculous. I'm a very skeptical person. My background is in journalism and law, so you've got to prove it to me, and the idea of God just sounded absurd.[31]

Strobel's first contact with the church came through his wife. She was invited by a neighbor to attend Willow Creek and did. When she returned home, Strobel asked her, "You didn't give those guys any of our money, did you?"[32]

Strobel eventually attended Willow Creek with his wife, but he was not interested in spiritual things, as he reports:

> I wanted to find a scam. You know, that was what I really wanted. Because if I found that this was a scam, then I could not only discount the church, but I could discount its message.

Hostile Harry is not a spiritual seeker.

Curious Harrys

The second group of unchurched individuals is those "curious Harrys" who are spiritually intrigued and are interested in Willow Creek's message. They usually affirm a basic belief in God and often have some background experience with Christianity.

However, most of these individuals do not attend church regularly. It is this group—spiritually minded but rather negative toward organized Christianity—that is probably the bulk of Willow Creek's unchurched audience. Most of these people believe in God, but they don't believe in church. As Lee Strobel explains, "Harry has rejected church, but that doesn't mean he has rejected God."[33]

It may be more accurate to describe curious Harrys as semi-churched rather than unchurched. Most of them affirm some of the central beliefs and practices of Christianity. One of Barna's studies even concluded that 52 percent of the unchurched claim "they have made a personal commitment to Jesus Christ that is important in their life." Several staff members told me in this regard that more than 50 percent of those who are attending and converting at Willow Creek are ex-Roman Catholics. Willow Creek is addressing many who already affirm much of its message.[34]

Sincere Harrys

The third group is "sincere Harrys" who have made a commitment to investigate Christianity to discover if it is really true. Lee Strobel calls this type of person a "sincere seeker":

> They say "I'm going to check this out. I'm going to investigate this. . . . They're going to ask some questions. . . . They're going to take a step to check it out in their own way.

Generally this process, at the very least, involves attendance at the weekend services. Various tapes and books are offered at the church bookstore to facilitate this investigation. People with questions are also invited to a four-week "Foundations" class that deals with Christianity's truthfulness. Occasionally special programs such as a debate on the historicity of Christ's resurrection are offered to interested seekers.

The distinctiveness of this group of Harrys is their sincere search for the truth. Strobel explains that sincere seekers are attempting "to check it out, whether it's very systematically or whether it's more on an ad hoc basis." Seekers are encouraged to ask honest questions, as Strobel describes:

> One way I legitimize the inquiry process is to assure Harry at the outset. "You know, you're doing exactly what God wants you to do. He honors those who honestly check him out.
>
> "The Bible says in Hebrews 11:6 that God 'rewards those who earnestly seek him.' So you should have confidence; you're doing the right thing by asking whatever questions you have on your mind."[35]

Willow Creekers believe that anyone who is sincerely searching for the truth will find it. Mittelberg asserts, "If someone becomes a true seeker and they stick with it, they will become a believer." He bases this on Jesus' statement in John 7:17, "If anyone chooses to do God's will, he will find out whether my teaching comes from God or whether I speak on my own."[36]

The role of seeker is very crucial at Willow Creek. Individuals I interviewed who had not made a commitment to Christianity frequently identified themselves to me by saying, "I am a seeker." Thus, not only is "seeker" the church's designation for unchurched people—but also unchurched Harrys often accept this label for themselves. Sincere seekers also have a certain status around Willow Creek. Those who are not yet seekers often feel pressure to accept this designation and actively investigate Christianity.[37]

The Process of Coming to Faith

Creekers often mention "a process" of how individuals come to faith. As Mittelberg explains, "there are steps previous to even being a seeker at all." In fact, there is a chart—"Stages of Spiritual Growth"—produced by the evangelism department to depict this process. The chart describes those farthest from a commitment as "being hostile to spiritual things" (hostile Harrys). The next group on the chart are those who are "open to spiritual things" (curious Harrys). The last group depicted is "actively investigating spiritual things" (sincere Harrys). Strobel explains, "Evangelism is most often a process, not a sudden event."[38]

In a sense we could say that Harry has a series of conversions, not merely one. Hostile Harrys are converted to curiosity. Curious Harrys are converted to sincerely seeking. Sincere seekers are only then converted to Christianity. Willow Creek has no intention to immediately convert hostile Harrys. They merely want him to take the next step. As a staff member explained at a Good Friday service, "Wherever you are on your spiritual journey, we hope this will be useful as a tool to spur on your spiritual growth."

Generally staff find that it often takes six months for hostile Harrys to eventually go through the "Stages of Spiritual Growth" and make a commitment to Christ. Yet there is no absolute rule or time line in this assessment. Strobel took almost two years to make his decision to follow Christ, and others make a commitment to Christ on their first visit to the church.[39]

The entire weekend service at Willow Creek is designed to meet the needs of unchurched Harry. Hybels explains, "We decided to defer to the customer except where it conflicted with Scripture." Hybels recalls that this idea was present at the original survey: "We tabulated their responses, and from that we shaped our programming plans."[40]

Once again this idea is a transplant from marketing theory. Barna argues:

> By matching the appeal of your product to the interests and needs of specific population segments, you can concentrate on getting your product to your best prospects without wasting resources on people who have no need or interest in your product.[41]

The church's international newsletter explained that a new Willow Creek style church was beginning in Malaga, Spain: "In principle the philosophy remains the same but the final expression will reflect a different culture . . . a different target audience." The selection of a different target audience determines a different strategy. There is, as one Willow Creek advocate argues, "a radicality and flexibility implied in the approach of Willow Creek."[42]

Much of the Willow Creek strategy and ideas make sense as a response to understanding the market of unchurched Harry. As Strobel explains, "unchurched Harry and Mary won't buy what doesn't interest them." To interest Harry, the programming of the church is a direct response to the target-audience profile of unchurched Harry.[43]

5

Weekend Service Programming

Bill Hybels preaches to a group of pastors:

> You can be as pious as you want to be and say, "But at church we are going to give them monotonous and lifeless preaching and expect great things to happen."
>
> Okay, you do it your way. But what I think is the better part of wisdom is to say this creature that I'm trying to reach is different from his daddy. He's different from his mother. He's not going to be content to just come and sit through a lifeless, rather predictable, dull experience.

Hybels argues for good programming that provides an exciting, creative, and interesting experience for unchurched Harrys.

Hybels believes that three of the top "transferable principles" pastors should take away from Willow Creek's leadership conferences are creative programming, effective preaching, and strategic staffing of programming personnel. Hybels, in fact, advocates recruiting programming staff before other staff; he compares church staffing priorities to hiring a farm worker to spread seed before hiring a reaper. Hybels warns, "There ain't nothing to cultivate if you don't have people spreading a lot of seed."[1]

In many ways programming is the creative heart of the Willow Creek weekend (or seeker) service. This chapter first examines the physical environment of Willow Creek, then the general concepts behind the programming, and finally the specific programming events. The next chapter narrows in on the use of the arts. Chapter 7 deals with the principles of persuasion used in programming.

The Physical Environment of Willow Creek

Programming director Nancy Beach describes what Harry finds when he approaches Willow Creek: "The first thing he sees when he's entering the vicinity of the church are flashing lights and police lights and police officers who are trying to ease the traffic congestion." Thousands of cars stream in and out of the Willow Creek parking lot. The experience is similar to attending a professional sporting event or a rock concert. The staff hope Harry's first response is, "Oh, they care enough about the fact that there's congestion out here to do something about it."

"The next thing he notices," Beach explains, "is the property and the grounds. We consider the statement the grounds make to be very, very important, as important as anything else we do." The result of this intensive effort is very attractive grounds. In fact, the church was approached by a Nissan location scout about filming a car commercial on their front drive, which curves around their private lake. Although the scout drove over one thousand five hundred miles looking for "curves, hills and natural beauty," he could find no location more attractive than Willow Creek's front drive.[2]

Harry's first impression of Willow Creek is also shaped by the traffic safety team in their bright orange outfits. Willow Creek purposely places "some of our friendliest people" on the team to welcome Harry. As one visitor noted, "Before you are even in the door you can draw two conclusions: First, if this is a church, it is not like most churches; and second, it is a well-run operation that is prepared for guests."[3]

Hybels believes that Harrys are continuing to make value judgments as they walk into the building, asking, "Are you up to date? Are you contemporary? Or are you locked in antiquity? Are you trying to force an atmosphere on us that's contrived?" In contrast to a churchy atmosphere, there are no Christian symbols. It is purposely designed to be similar to a corporate headquarters. As Hybels explains,

> What we want him to do is just say, "I was just at corporate headquarters for IBM in Atlanta Wednesday, and now I come to church here and it's basically the same." Neutrality, comfort, contemporary, clean: Those are the kinds of values that we want to communicate.

Following the crowd, Harry walks through what could be the atrium of a four star hotel. Harry follows the flow of people toward a wall of doors where ushers are handing out simple brochures. Beach explains that these greeters are instructed "to be friendly but keep their distance a little bit, so that people don't feel overwhelmed." The brochure is very attractive and appears to be professionally printed. The brochure explains what an unchurched Harry can expect during the service and how he can get more involved in the church.

As Harry enters the auditorium, popular music is being played softly through the sound system. Harry chooses his own plush seat in what appears to be a huge movie theater. Until a singer walks onto the stage in a few minutes to begin the service, Harry is able to look over his program, enjoy the music, and gaze through the huge windows that are at the sides of the stage. From any seat in the auditorium, he can see Canada geese floating on Willow Creek's lovely private lake.

Don Cousins taught a group of staff why creating this high quality environment is so important: "What do you think was the number one reason why the average person likes Disney World like they do?" He answered,

> They take care of it. Now, what they're basically saying is it's excellent. They do it right. Okay? That extends to their programming, what they do with their amusement parks, what they do with their hotels, and how they treat their employees and how they want their employees to treat the people.
>
> The more we can create an environment that has that kind of appeal and similarity for Harry, the better off we are. Because, you see, that's what he's attracted to.

Willow Creek has two goals in mind in the creation of this efficient and beautiful environment: to win Harry's respect and to relax Harry.

Win Harry's Respect

Hybels says, "Before you get a guy listening to your message you really have to have a little respect." If the landscaping, facilities, and even the traffic control can be seen to be superior, Hybels believes that Harry will be more open to listen to what he has to say.

Relax Harry

Cousins rhetorically asks a group of staff, "Do you tend to listen effectively when you're on the spot?" He answers, "We tend to listen when we're relaxed." As one management team member explained, "Effective ministry is going to have to put this guy at ease."

How does Willow Creek try to put Harry at ease? By creating a beautiful environment. Hybels believes, "If you have flowers and vegetation . . . [it] can have a kind of peaceful effect. . . . Beauty has a way of affecting all of us, doesn't it?" Another staffer clarifies, "We are trying to make the person off the street feel comfortable." Creekers are trying to create "a safe place" for unchurched people.[4]

Programming Concepts

Having created a beautiful and relaxing atmosphere, Willow Creek then tries to produce a professional program that will help persuade Harry to become a Christian. The goal of programming, Nancy Beach explains, is to "harness the arts or a variety of mediums to sort of pave the way, or prepare the listener, for the message they're going to hear in the latter half of the service." Depending on the day, that message may be helpful principles for how Harry can deal with a felt need or some element of Willow Creek's central message, the evangelical gospel about Jesus Christ. Thus, the program is ultimately a means of pre-evangelism, preparing the audience for the speaker; it can best be described in terms of package and flow.

Package

The Willow Creek staff think of the programming in a weekend service as a whole unit—"a package." Each package has a fundamental goal that shapes what is selected for each section of the program. For example, one weekend service was designed to show unchurched Harrys the inadequacy of moralism as a way of life. All of the programming events (songs, drama, media, Scripture lesson) were chosen with that fundamental goal in mind.

The length of a weekend service is one hour and ten minutes. The speaker's talk is usually about thirty-five to forty minutes. The programming package of music, drama, and Scripture reading is approximately thirty minutes in length. The order of how these events are presented changes from week to week. Nancy Beach says, "We put the order together each week based on the elements that we've prepared."

Flow

Willow Creek's programming package is designed to move people both intellectually and emotionally, as Beach explains:

> We try to take them in the entire hour someplace. . . . We're trying to move them down the field. . . .

> Each week it's different, but sometimes it's trying to wake them up and alert them to the issue and problem or get them thinking in a certain direction, or feeling in a certain direction. So then the speaker can go at it much more directly.

Beach continues, "We try to avoid what we call the slot mentality." A slot mentality "has no flow, and you're not taking someone from point A to point whatever." In contrast, Willow Creek designs their programming to be a fluid transition to the talk.

A subpoint of Willow Creek's idea of "flow" is the concept of "links." The programming staff try to have each element of the package link to the next element in a smooth transition. For example, when the speaker walks onto the stage, the band plays appropriate transition music to prepare the audience for his message. There is no dead time in the program.

One specific type of link is called "turning a corner." After a drama that deals with an emotionally painful topic, Beach believes it wouldn't be appropriate to immediately give announcements in a lighthearted tone. When package elements change from one emotion to another, the programming is designed to guide the audience's emotions—"turning a corner." There is continuity to the programming from the prelude to the closing prayer.

Programming Elements

About thirty minutes before the service begins, the doors open to the auditorium. Unchurched Harry and churched Larry now can enter and find their seats. A tape of instrumental music is playing over the sound system to relax the audience. As Beach explains, "Silence is somewhat awkward and threatening to a person."[5]

Prelude

A prelude of live music begins immediately before the service. It serves as a sort of flag to the audience that the service is about to start and that they should find their seats. The prelude is virtually always an instrumental piece rather than a vocal one. Depending on the morning, the music might be provided by a jazz group, a solo flutist, a thirty-piece orchestra, or a rock or country band.

The choice of music that is selected for the prelude fits the overall program of that morning—the package. As Beach explains:

That choice is based on what else is going to happen musically in the service. It's our chance to balance things out a little bit and give people a taste of something that they may not get at any other spot.

The prelude gives the staff an opportunity to experiment or to use a musical style that is a little risky. Beach says, "The prelude is one place where we can do some things that are appealing to more narrow audiences without hurting our overall effect."

Congregational Song and Greeting

After the prelude, usually a singer with a microphone walks to the center of the stage and welcomes everyone to Willow Creek. He or she asks the audience to stand and open their program, where they will find the words to the congregational song for that morning.

The song is usually a simple chorus that can be sung rather easily. The programming team try to choose songs that have a contemporary style. Even an unchurched Harry who has never attended Willow Creek before can easily follow along. For example, on Sunday, September 16, 1990, the song was "He Is Our Peace":

He is our peace,
Who has broken down every wall,
He is our peace, He is our peace.
(Repeat)

Cast all your cares on Him,
For He cares for you,
He is our peace, He is our peace.
(Repeat)

The choice of what song to use is rather difficult from Willow Creek's point of view. "It's the hardest song to select lyrically," Beach explains, "because we're putting words in the mouths, in a sense, of people who don't believe whatever those words are. And so our list of songs that we feel comfortable with is so short."

After the song, the singer on the platform says, "Say hello to someone sitting near you and then sit down." The programming team realizes that many unchurched Harrys feel uncomfortable with this portion of the service. I interviewed one unchurched Harry who had attended Willow Creek only a few times. He told me, "I hate that part of the service when they ask us to shake hands." When I asked Nancy Beach if all unchurched Harrys feel this way, she responded:

> That, I think, has a lot to do with temperament. Because the extroverted types are fine with it. . . . If we didn't have that at all, some who are more extroverted would say, "That is the most unfriendly church I have ever been in."

This congregational greeting is the last participation of those who are attending that morning. The rest of the service is conducted entirely from the stage.

Vocal Music Performance

A vocal music performance usually comes after the congregational greeting. There is also another vocal music performance some time later in the package. Sometimes a soloist performs these musical numbers alone, but usually a small group of singers joins the main singer. This soloist and backup singers, supported by the band, then perform a song. The pop style of the song fits the tastes of the typical unchurched Harry. The experience is similar to hearing a professional singer and band on Jay Leno's *The Tonight Show.*

The musical performance is excellent. A few of the singers and musicians are professional musicians during the week and see their participation in the church's musical program as a way to serve the church. The majority are amateurs who have a great deal of musical talent and experience and have auditioned and passed demanding tests to join the singing and instrumental teams. Both professionals and amateurs must rehearse repeatedly in preparation for their weekend performance.[6]

On a Tuesday evening, for instance, a full week-and-a-half before the weekend performance, the vocal team comes together to learn a new song. Beach explains, "At that time they're just going through the notes and trying to learn it." By the following Tuesday the vocal team "are expected to have memorized the lyrics and the music and come in ready to work on it more from the sense of communicating and expressing themselves." They again rehearse on the Saturday night just before the first service.

Like all of the programming, the musical numbers start where Harry is—both in style and substance. Creekers have "bookends," or parameters, of what is appropriate music for the target audience. The style may be jazz, pop, rock, classical, or maybe even country, but it stays within these bookends of what is enjoyable for Harry. As Willow Creek's evangelism director expresses it, "We have to ask, What do these people that we want to reach listen to?" The reason Lee Strobel first attended Willow Creek was his wife's encouragement that it played music that was "'hot' and upbeat, the kind I'd listen to on the radio."[7]

Willow Creek's musical lyrics also start where Harry is. Beach believes that many Harrys think that "Christians are simplistic or hypocritical." To fight against this stereotype, Beach occasionally has a singer introduce a song by "talking about what he or she struggles with." She uses songs that avoid clichés and spiritualized and archaic language. The singers don't use "a church tone of voice" or "'happy talk' songs," but normal, everyday language.

A fundamental goal of the musical performance is for the visiting unchurched Harrys and Marys to identify with the singers: "We're humans too." The specific elements of the vocal performances stress Creekers' similarities with Harry. Almost all of the singers are between the ages of twenty-five and forty. They are dressed in clothes that are similar to the typical unchurched Harry and Mary. The songs emphasize the similarities between Creekers and unchurched Harrys.

Scripture

The next section of Willow Creek's program is called "Scripture." In this segment of the program, one of the church's teachers or leaders comes to the center of the platform and gives a short talk to focus the topic for that day. In many ways, it could be argued that this section of the program is mislabeled. It is not a time of merely reading Scripture. It is designed to help define the problem of the day and then to show the relevance of the Bible to the problem.

By using personal illustrations and discussing topics of current affairs, the speaker builds credibility with the audience as he clarifies the problem or issue of the morning. He shows that he knows what is going on in society and stresses his similarities with unchurched Harry. He addresses Harry's concerns in a way that is relevant, interesting, and nonthreatening. As Beach pictures it, "It's almost like a mini four-to-five-minute message, tying in Scripture verses to the issue—whatever it is—that we are discussing." Beach believes that Harry will receive the message:

> We're taking this book that a lot of people have stuffed on their shelf, we're reading from it, and we take it seriously. . . . That's what we base our whole church on, the truth of that book.

The Scripture time is also a good illustration of the importance of the flow that we mentioned before. The speakers who do these mini Scripture talks are given a script of the drama and songs that precede or follow the Scripture time in order to prepare their message. Thus they know where they fit in the service and consciously try to guide the flow of the program. Sometimes they select the verses with this in mind and at other times Hybels (or another main speaker) gives a reference he wants them to use. They then write a transcript of what they plan to say, maintaining the flow of the program. As Beach describes, the Scripture time is a "very important bridge."

Drama

Since the use of drama, the next event in the program, is so important to the Willow Creek weekend service, it will be treated fully by itself in the next chapter.

Announcements and Offertory

Usually after the short drama, there is a brief pause for announcements and the offertory before the speaker's message. The primary purpose of the announcements is to welcome unchurched Harry to Willow Creek. These announcements are usually limited to information that is important for unchurched individuals. This may include explaining a "Foundations" class or some other resource for unchurched Harry.

There is also an announcement each week that the offering is only for those individuals who are regular attenders of Willow Creek. One of unchurched Harry's basic attitudes toward Christianity is, "The church is money hungry." Willow Creek bends over backward trying to dispel this bias. Visitors are told each week that they are viewed as guests and do not need to participate in this part of the service. During the offering the band plays an instrumental piece that fits in the flow of the program. The offertory usually leads to the last and most important element of the program—the message.[8]

As should be clear from the discussion thus far, all of the programming is considered preparation for the speaker's message. The message, to be treated more fully in later chapters, is the culmination and centerpiece of the seeker service.

6

The Use of the Arts

Willow Creekers believe that most traditional churches are dreary for unchurched Harry. Hybels declares that a "misconception that many [unchurched] people hold about Christianity is that it's boring." Willow Creek is attempting in its programming to be the exact opposite of boring. They want to be exciting.[1]

The programming team's mission is to vary musical, dramatic, and visual art forms to get and keep Harry's attention. Hybels explains to a group at a pastors' conference:

> Variety, variety, variety, variety. You'll get sick of hearing that in the next couple days. But friends, in every other environment except church, nonchurched Harry is exposed to variety.

Hybels explains that Harry is saying to himself, "Why does the world put all this energy into creativity and variety, and then the church, who supposedly is peddling this fantastic eternally significant message—why don't they care?"

Willow Creek tries to show how much they care by investing enormous amounts of time and energy into providing enjoyable and interesting programs for visiting Harrys. As Hybels asserts, "This is the generation that grew up on television. You have to present religion to them in a creative and visual way."[2]

Hybels was asked once, "What really were some of the contributing factors to the initial explosion at Willow Creek?"

> After thinking long and hard about it, I now look back and I realize that in one little group of a handful of people was:

- a national-caliber musician,
- a national-caliber media person,
- and a national-caliber drama person—
- and we didn't even know it.

> But that had a lot to do with the perception by the non-churched community that something very exciting was happening at the Willow Creek theater.

A large part of unchurched Harry's positive experience at Willow Creek was that he saw a new, creative, exciting program on the stage every week.

Unchurched Harrys I interviewed enjoyed this experience of creativity. Strobel recalls visiting as an unchurched Harry:

> From week to week, I never knew what was going to happen at those church services, and that unpredictability fostered an atmosphere of anticipation among those in attendance.
>
> It was sort of like the feeling before a big football game or rock concert. Nobody knew exactly what was going to occur, we just knew that we all were going to experience something different and exciting.[3]

This chapter will examine the broad context of communication in American culture, the use and goals of drama at Willow Creek, and the controversy over the use of entertainment in Christian churches.

The Communication Revolution

A fundamental shift in modern communication has shaped how Americans process information. Neil Postman, a professor of communication arts at New York University, believes that "the age of exposition" (based on the printing press and the word-based process of reasoning) has been transformed into "the age of show business" (based on television and the use of images). A revolution has occurred in how people process information and view the world. This revolution can be seen by looking at recent communication methods in general and at Willow Creek's specific use of these innovations.[4]

Television has been the main impetus behind this shift in communication. Fundamental to television is the preeminence of images over ideas. As the modern proverb instructs, "A picture is worth a thousand words." And to keep individuals' attention, these pictures need to be regularly changed. Robert MacNeil, coanchor and executive editor of the *MacNeil-Lehrer News Hour,* explains that television news programs are designed "to keep everything brief, not to strain the attention of anyone but instead to provide constant stimulation through variety, novelty, action, and movement."[5]

One example of this communication revolution is the contrast in presidential debates in the last two centuries. When Abraham Lincoln debated Stephen Douglas, Douglas spoke for one hour, Lincoln rebutted his arguments for one-and-one-half hours, and then Douglas had a half hour for rebuttal. In the 1988 presidential debates, George Bush and Michael Dukakis only answered reporters' questions and were limited to two-minute answers with one-minute rebuttals. The average viewer's attention span would not permit a lengthy format. The result of this communication revolution is that individuals are increasingly unable to follow an argument, think critically, and process information from a single source without visual and auditory stimulation.[6]

Creekers are very aware that unchurched Harry has been profoundly influenced by media, especially television. Strobel explains, "Baby boomers are the first generation to grow up watching television, and it has shaped the way we process the world." This revolution in how individuals receive information is shaping all forms of communication—including Christian communication.[7]

Willow Creek's programming reflects the shift from word-based to image-based communication. If they are going to reach Harry, Creekers believe that they must use his language—the media. Hybels reveals why:

> It's my perception that society has changed so much in the last twenty years; . . . people in my generation are becoming so visually oriented and so event conscious. Everywhere they go their senses are being stimulated. . . . They go to a lounge and there are hundreds of thousands of dollars worth of sound and lights, and they go to a stage show and there is this fantastic presentation.

Willow Creek communicates to unchurched Harrys by using the tools of the modern media.

One of the clearest examples of their adaptation to modern communication is Willow Creek's use of drama. Willow Creek's use of drama has a long history. When Hybels first raised the idea of having an evangelistic outreach to the Son City youth group, a student suggested they use drama. Hybels explains his response: "I honestly didn't know what she was talking about. I mean, I was from Kalamazoo, Michigan. We only got one network channel." Hybels and Son City took the risk, and soon drama became a regular part of the outreach to unchurched students.[8]

Why? Like most of what became the classic Willow Creek program, it obviously worked. Unchurched Harrys enjoyed the moving or humorous skits. When Creekers explain why drama and multi-media are so successful, they often refer to American culture. "We've seen that in our TV generation," evangelism director Mittelberg explains, "drama is an important thing and the way to kind of break through some barriers and communicate a message." In American homes, televisions are turned on an average of more than seven hours a day. Creekers believe that in this context, drama powerfully speaks the language of unchurched Harrys.[9]

The Goals of Drama at Willow Creek

The short dramas presented at the weekend services have very specific goals. They involve

- revealing common human problems,
- enabling Creekers to identify with unchurched Harry,
- providing self-understanding for Harry, and
- lowering Harry's defenses.

Revealing Common Human Problems

Each skit is a five- to eight-minute dramatic performance that introduces or illustrates a problem or issue that will be addressed during the service. In the flow of the Willow Creek program, drama usually comes toward the beginning. As one drama writer explained:

> Drama is the best way we know of to really portray the problem of whatever it is that we're going to talk about. In other words, every service has a theme or a main point. And drama is the way that we can connect people with the problem, not the solution.[10]

The dramas try to depict common human problems. One writer explains that he attempts to understand and describe various human difficulties by "clarifying issues, stating problems, [and] showing emotional struggle." Thus Nancy Beach acknowledges that they must "have people writing scripts who are really in touch with human nature and with what people struggle with."[11]

One Willow Creek drama, "Great Expectations," involves a couple who have been trying to have a baby for years. They try to adopt and are right on the verge of finally receiving a child. At the last minute the adoption falls through and they are crushingly disappointed. The wife explodes in a rage at God. The husband, deeply hurt himself, tries to comfort his wife. The drama closes with the wife weeping in her husband's arms. There were no magical answers at the last minute to solve this painful human problem.

When Willow Creek has attempted to use drama to teach answers to unchurched Harry, the results have been less than satisfying. As Lee Strobel explains, these attempts "ring hollow to Unchurched Harry and Mary, who are demanding more sophisticated and detailed answers than can be presented through a brief, broad-brush dramatic scene." Beach believes, "If it could be better said in a message, then it probably shouldn't be said in a drama. . . . Drama is terrible for trying to preach at people."[12]

Willow Creek dramas usually end unresolved, and the problems they raise are unanswered. As a drama writer explains, "The drama's job is just to open up a can of worms and sort of stick our fingers in there and stir them around. Then it's the speaker's job to deal with the worms." In a sense the drama serves as a way of clarifying the emotional issues that unchurched Harry and Mary are already feeling. By doing this the programming is able to bring "the problem into relief so it can be seen, isolated," and felt.

Enabling Creekers to Identify with Unchurched Harry

In contrast to the musical part of the program, which can depict a relationship with God, drama sketches the human dimension of life. As Beach explains, "Drama scripts end up pointing more towards the horizontal relationships than the vertical." An example of this description of human relationships is the following partial transcript of a drama about a couple's sexual relationship.

M = Male voice F = Female voice

M What time is it?

F 11:15.

M Where are you going?

F To bed. Good night.

M Hey. It's been a while.

F Yeah. Well, after seventeen hours I'm usually ready for a good night's sleep.

M Come on. You know what I'm talking about. Honey, what's wrong?

F I can't catch my breath. It's okay. This always happens when I'm swept off my feet!

M Very funny.

F I'm going to bed.

M I'll be right up.

F I'll be asleep.

M I'll wake you up.

F I'll lock the door.

M I'll break it down.

F Now that I would like to see.

M Hey, what is your problem?

F MY problem?

M Yeah. I want to make love to my wife, and . . .

F Oh, is that it? You want to make love to your wife. Oh, I thought you were looking for something to do during halftime?

M Dear, hockey doesn't have a halftime. Would you stop treating me like this? I'm just getting real tired of it.

F Well, I'm getting real tired of being the last thought of the day. Or a cure for your insomnia!

When this drama was presented, the Willow Creek audience was at times laughing uproariously and at other times so quiet that I could have heard a pin drop. With this drama, Creekers can sketch a problem that most married folks can understand. But even more, the drama team was able to identify with unchurched Harry and Mary and say in effect, *We have problems too; we are very similar to you.* As Beach explains, the "purpose of a drama scene is not to drive home the three points of the sermon message. It's to prepare them . . . to let them know that we understand where they already are."

Providing Self-Understanding for Harry

Dramas are occasionally fashioned to help Harry see himself and thus to feel a bit uncomfortable. Strobel explains that dramas are designed "to raise issues. They're to create discomfort. They're to allow us to see things in our lives that we may not otherwise see or recognize."

The skit continues:

M You are not a cure for my insomnia.

F Oh, but I am the last thought of the day?

M Would you just give me a break?

F Well, it just feels like that. I mean, you come home, you eat dinner, and then you park yourself on the couch for the rest of the night, snoring between headlines. You don't have a meaningful word to say to me all night.

M All right. What do you want me to do?

F You know perfectly well what I want you to do.

M Fine. You want to talk, we'll talk.

F I don't want to talk.

M But you just said . . .

F Doggone it, Steve, I want you to notice me— make me feel important or special.

M Oh. So you want me to woo you? I thought I got all that out of the way when we were dating. I'm sorry. I shouldn't have said that. Come on, Paula.

F No. If you want me, you have to get me.

M Well, I can't if you're gonna be staring at me.

F Well, what do you want? Do you want me to go into the next room?

M Well . . .

F Forget it!

Many unchurched Harrys see themselves in this drama. Their wives don't feel listened to. Their wives feel ignored. Their wives are frustrated by sexual intimacy without emotional intimacy. Harrys are confronted in the drama by the painful awareness that they treat their wives with this same insensitivity. The drama has accomplished its purpose, as unchurched Harry has uncomfortably seen himself.

At times during this drama, Harrys not only see themselves in this husband, but they are able to laugh at him, and themselves, as well. Strobel explains:

> People see themselves through the drama, identify with it, laugh with it, release some tension, and build a sense of anticipation toward the message when they know they're gonna start to get some answers.

Lowering Harry's Defenses

The programming team see the first thirty minutes of the service as a "backdoor" to influence Harry. Beach explains that listeners' "defenses are lower when they are communicated to through artistic forms . . . than when someone is standing up speaking directly at them." Beach believes "they know when someone is speaking, that that person is out to persuade them. The arts are much more effective, coming through the back door in a more subtle way."

When an unchurched Harry—particularly a hostile Harry—walks through Willow Creek's doors, he isn't particularly interested in Willow Creek's message. He is defensive and resistant toward the Christianity he thinks is going to be foisted on him. One way drama can lower Harry's defenses is by getting him to laugh. For example, in the drama from which I have been quoting, the husband is trying to give attention and affection to his wife:

> M Wait, wait—look. Come on. Why don't you come over here? Let's both just sit down, get comfy. Come on. {Long pause.} You look nice tonight. Your shirt is pretty. Your make-up looks good. Your hair smells nice. Your skin is soft. So, how am I doing?
>
> F Fine, if I were a well-dressed cocker spaniel!

The drama up to this point had become increasingly tense. When the skit was performed, the wife's witty comeback here was greeted by loud laughter from the audience. The humor both relieved tension and lowered defensive barriers.

Humorous Drama

Humor is a regular staple for the drama team. Many of the humorous skits are reminiscent of the popular network show *Saturday Night Live.* In fact, several *Saturday Night Live* characters, such as the "church lady" or the muscleheads "Hans and Franz," have regularly appeared on the stage at Willow Creek. One of Willow Creek's publications about drama is even entitled *Sunday Morning Live.* Americans love to laugh. It's not a fluke that the most popular television shows over the last decade were the comedies *The Cosby Show, Roseanne,* and *Home Improvement.* Americans will turn on the TV show, or go to the church, that makes them laugh.

And Willow Creek wants to make Harry laugh; this satisfies the goal of creating enjoyable programming to which Harry will want to return. But the deeper reason for the use of humor, explains psychologist Robert Oliver, is "to disarm the audience, to remove its barriers of suspicion and possible hostility, to make it willing to listen." Oliver instructs:

> Laughter is a gentle and effective means of shaking an audience into a receptive attitude. It creates a bridge of good fellowship over which the later persuasive appeals may march.[13]

Willow Creek's programming successfully elicits laughter from unchurched Harry and prepares him to hear its message. These pleasant emotions have the effect of swamping the previous negative preconceptions that unchurched Harry is bringing to Willow Creek and creating a more positive emotional attitude toward Willow Creek, and thus Christianity.

An illustration may help explain this idea. One Willow Creek drama skit begins with a mother talking to her son at their home. The son is anxious about having to talk to his father about changing his college major to the Russian language. The mom is trying to reassure him that his father is really a sensitive guy deep down and will support him in his decision.

At this point there is a loud sound of whirling helicopter blades overhead. A rope falls to the stage from the rafters up above. Rambo-Dad, dressed in his combat fatigues and carrying a machine gun, rappels down the rope shooting wildly. When the son explains to Rambo-Dad that he wants to begin studying Russian, Rambo-Dad yells something to the effect of, "No son of mine is going to learn a commie language!" while again firing his machine gun wildly. The result? The crowd is laughing with great hilarity at the caricature of an obviously unsupportive and insensitive father. The goal of the humorous skit was achieved—Harry's barriers are lower. The importance of being loving and caring can now be raised in the message later in the program.

By taking a humorous slant to current events, relevant topics, and sensitive issues, Creekers are able to get and then keep Harry's attention. Staff are very conscious of the value of humor in their program, and they are highly skilled at achieving it.

Emotional Drama

Creekers are also highly skilled with emotional drama. Sometimes the drama or media presentation can get Harry to lower his defenses by touching some deep emotional chords. Lee Strobel recalls seeing a Willow Creek media presentation, when he was still a hostile and skeptical Harry, that featured two clay figures:

> One, a grandfatherly God; the other, a man who was trying to please Him. . . . He offered God his money, his hobbies, his house—he even offered to march around with a sign that said, "Repent." . . .
>
> At the end, the man realized that what God really wanted was his heart, and when he offered it, God pulled him onto His lap and embraced him.
>
> There I sat, a street-toughened newspaperman, and I had tears in my eyes! Those goofy little clay figures had succeeded in doing an end-run around my emotional defense system.[14]

Strobel the skeptic saw the beauty of God's love and was touched by it. As one programming team member put it, "The drama is feeling—it's showing, it's not telling." Once the drama helps to clarify the problem of the day, the audience is ready for the next step of the program. This strategy has led to a mini controversy within the evangelical community.

The Entertainment Controversy

The question of whether or not Willow Creek's programming is actually entertainment is a controversial one. As one Willow Creek advocate explains, "Willow Creek has been accused of being in the entertainment business."[15]

Critics describe Willow Creek's use of media methods as entertainment and a compromise of the gospel. Fundamentalist pastor John MacArthur has recently written *Ashamed of the Gospel: When the Church Becomes Like the World* about what he calls the "worldly use of pragmatism." He has chapters on "The User-Friendly Church?" and "Gimme That Show-Time Religion," which attack some of Willow Creek's central ideas.[16]

Hybels is deeply offended when critics charge that Willow Creek is involved in entertainment. A Willow Creek proponent reports that the "leadership of Willow Creek has expressed its deep sense of hurt at the comments of those who have inaccurately accused them of offering entertainment in place of proclamation." Hybels argues that Willow Creek is merely using the arts in order to communicate truth:

> Who was the master composer? Who created the arts? Whose idea was it to communicate the truth through a wide variety of artistic genres? I think it was God. Then why has the church narrowed its options and selected a talking head as its only form of communicating the most important message on the planet?

Creekers feel offended when others describe their work as entertainment. They believe they are merely presenting the gospel creatively.[17]

This controversy is muddled, as there has been very little attempt, on either side, to clarify what is meant by "entertainment." According to the *Oxford English Dictionary,* entertainment is to use the creative arts to provide an "interesting, agreeable," or "amusing" experience for an audience.[18]

Understood in this way, Willow Creek is certainly using entertainment. The programming of the seeker service is designed to provide an interesting, agreeable, and sometimes amusing experience for unchurched Harry—in order to present the gospel to him more effectively.[19]

And yet, there is a difference between using entertainment as a means and having entertainment as the end. To have entertainment as the end or goal of Willow Creek's activity would mean that they are successful if Harry leaves agreeable and amused. Willow Creek's intended use of entertainment as a means is successful only if some Harrys convert to Christianity.[20]

Although Creekers avoid the word *entertainment,* they are seeking to creatively provide an interesting, agreeable, and amusing experience for unchurched Harrys. As Hybels asserts, "My generation expects to have his senses stimulated to some extent." By using the modern means of the media, the church is speaking Harry's language and seeking to present a message about God's love that avoids Harry's negative preconceptions.[21]

Willow Creek is committed to creating programming that stirs human emotions. Not only does the drama get Harry's attention, but it leads him toward Willow Creek's solution. In effect, programming is used as a means of persuasion. To this end, the programming is crafted according to several basic principles, which are dealt with at some length in chapter 7.

7

The Programming Principles of Persuasion

We have examined how Willow Creek implements its programming vision; now we need to ask a more probing question. Why? Why is Willow Creek's programming successful in persuading unchurched Harrys to become Christians? One measure of this success is the number of individuals who are baptized every six months at the church. While I was doing my study, the following number of individuals were baptized.

June	1989	365
December	1989	200
June	1990	661
December	1990	222
June	1991	342

These totals do not include the many people who made a commitment to Christ at Willow Creek but were not baptized there. Yet this short list shows that hundreds, even thousands, of unchurched Harrys and Marys are making commitments to Christ at Willow Creek. Why? What are the principles of persuasion that Willow Creek's programming employs? Willow Creek's programming is relevant and excellent. It gives Harry anonymity and time and it appeals to his emotions.

Relevant

Willow Creek's programming starts where Harry is. It focuses on Harry's "target audience profile." All music, drama, and media fit Harry's interests and tastes. By starting where Harry is, Willow Creek is seeking to gain and keep his attention. Nancy Beach declares:

> You have to get his [Harry's] attention in the first few minutes or you've lost him. Because his life is on such a pace and he is so absorbed in other things, unless we are relevant . . . we are going to lose him.

Harry is concerned with his immediate world and his felt needs. So, often the central issue or problem that is raised in the programming is one that is directly connected to Harry's felt needs. By addressing an issue that Harry is already concerned about, Willow Creek is attempting to guide a moving car, rather than trying to steer a parked one. In a sense, the programming is fashioned to make Harry curious, to create in him a desire to hear the speaker address an important topic.

Excellent

Excellence is a central value at Willow Creek. As Hybels teaches, "Excellence inspires people. It makes you want to do more and do it better." Creekers use the term *excellence* as the evaluative criteria of their work in every area—in this case, their programming. We see this commitment to excellence in the music and drama, lighting and sound systems, and constant evaluation.

Music and Drama

Beach believes, "Nonchurched Harry has been exposed to excellence, through movies, television, theater. . . . He has seen some very excellent things." As a result, he evaluates everything else through this filter of quality.

Willow Creek sees itself as competing with Harry's excellent entertainment. Strobel reports, "*Sesame Street* and Disney World have set high standards in the minds of today's consumers." Willow Creek has attempted to match these standards in their music and drama.[1]

The result of this commitment is that Harry comes to the weekend services knowing that he is going to see a professional production. He won't have to listen to a voice that is breaking while trying to hit a high note or have to see inept actors. Lee Strobel explains from his former perspective as an unchurched Harry, "I didn't have to sit there and worry that somebody was going to sing really bad and I was going to feel really embarrassed for them."[2]

All participants in the service are highly skilled and thoroughly prepared. They also are generally attractive people who are well-dressed. Unchurched visitors "see excellence," as evangelism director Mittelberg explains, "sharp people out there singing and in dramas."

This quality often elicits respect from visiting unchurched Harrys. Strobel reveals his response when he was visiting the church:

> In my profession as a journalist, I strive to be at the top of my profession. I mean that was really my life. . . . And so I was tremendously impressed that these people took this ministry thing just as seriously as I took my own work.

Excellence is a common ground between Harrys and Willow Creek.

Lighting and Sound System

Although Harry isn't aware of it, he is sitting in a dream of a theater auditorium. Willow Creek's lighting and sound systems are top of the line. As Hybels says to visiting church leaders, "To show you how fanatical we are about these things, we have . . . several hundred thousand dollars worth of sound and lights in this auditorium."

This commitment to excellent lighting and sound has been there from the beginning of the church. "In the early days of the church," Beach recalls, "before we had any money, and before any of the staff was paid . . . [we] were willing to invest money in the basic needs that we had for lighting and sound." Every Sunday morning the technical producer and his crew would wake at four o'clock and set up the lighting systems in the local theater where the church was meeting, "because lighting makes a statement."

Over the two-and-one-half years I attended the church, the sound was always warm and had the proper volume. I never once heard the screeching feedback that one associates with microphones. The lighting was also unobtrusive and seemingly perfect. In fact, the very lack of attention the sound and lighting commanded illustrates its excellence. I never witnessed a lighting or sound mistake during any program at Willow Creek.

Like virtually everything else that Willow Creek is committed to, they urge other Christian leaders to adopt the same priority. At the Willow

Creek leadership conference, Hybels exhorts the pastors that lighting is absolutely crucial:

> You could dramatically improve your lighting for less than five hundred dollars. You could hire an electrician to come in, route some of your beams, and I guarantee you, the first Sunday you turn those things on there will be this intangible excitement factor.

Constant Evaluation

When Hybels is trying to emphasize the importance of excellence, he often refers to other churches he has attended:

> Almost everything, from the parking lot to the architecture to the printing materials to starting late to shoddy sound, terrible lighting, really half-baked music, and—shall I go on? You know?—Almost every single thing about that service and the facilities . . . said, "We don't care."

Hybels is attempting with Willow Creek to bring together and train people who do care. A major tool he and his fellow leaders use is evaluation—the same kind of critical judgment that Hybels used to critique the church he described above.

Hybels says, "What we keep saying around here is, 'How can we do the optimum? How can we get everything working for us and nothing working against us?'" This goal for the optimum is realized through a series of regular programming evaluations. Hybels explains:

> We still subject ourselves to weekly evaluations, and we start by saying:
>
> - How do we feel about the prelude?
> - How do we feel about the transition between the prelude and the opening chorus?
> - How do we feel about the chorus?
> - How do we feel about the transition?
>
> And we just go minute by minute by minute by minute all the way through the service—every week.

When the staff run out of ideas of how to fine-tune the program or facilities, they sometimes hire high-powered consultants to tell them how to improve. Hybels reports:

> We brought in the consultant who did the light show for Disney-Epcot, the laser thing. . . . [He] spent the weekend here last weekend. . . . We feel that we've been

> somewhat stagnant at the current level that we're at with our lighting, and we wanted someone to push us and say, "Here's five ways you could do it better."

The result of this scrutiny is a great deal of expertise.

Giving Harry Anonymity

Willow Creek's programming environment and content are a direct response to their understanding of who unchurched Harry is. Creekers believe that Harrys are uncomfortable in the new and strange setting of a church. By creating a situation of anonymity, Creekers hope to put Harry at ease. They have several beliefs concerning what Harry feels and wants in his initial contact with a church.[3]

Harry Is Anxious

Creekers believe that Harry is entering the unknown when he first begins attending church. As a result, Harry is anxious because he doesn't know what is expected of him. Former unchurched Harry Lee Strobel relates, "It would be comparable to the feeling that a Christian would have if he walked into a Moslem mosque for the first time." Strobel believes:

> They're afraid of doing something wrong—staying seated when everybody else responds to an unspoken cue and rises to their feet; being unable to locate a Bible verse that everyone else has quickly found. . . .
>
> They don't want to draw attention to themselves through some inadvertent gaffe.[4]

If Harry finds church particularly strange, he wants to be able to leave quickly. Beach explains, "If he's invited by someone, he'll agree to take separate cars so that he can make a quick getaway if he doesn't like what's happening here." Harry is nervous.

Cousins explains the motivation behind the desire to provide anonymity:

> The only way we're going to get Harry to relax is if we clear up real fast the fact that "Hey Harry, we're not going to ask you to identify yourself. We're gonna make you as comfortable as possible."

By letting Harry remain anonymous, Creekers hope that Harry is able to relax and listen to the program and speaker.

This provision for anonymity doesn't mean that Willow Creek doesn't pay attention to Harry. In fact, the opposite is true. Cousins explains:

> Effective ministry is going to have to put this guy at ease. . . . We've got to hand him a program that's simple to read. We've got to give him directions about where to park, where to walk in, give him a general idea of where to sit, let him see exactly what's coming—so that he's not in fear of "what am I going to have to do next?"

A great deal of thought and effort goes into Willow Creek's attempt to create a safe and anonymous experience for Harry. As a staff member describes it, Harry needs to hear the "unsafe message in a safe place."

Harry Wants to Observe, Not Participate

Creekers believe that Harry wants to see what is going on from a distance. Those who are attending a Willow Creek seeker service presentation are, for the most part, passive observers—an audience.

Willow Creek's programming has been designed with this spectator element built in. As Nancy Beach explains, the church's programming is "built on the premise that we think that they [Harrys] just want to be spectators when they're checking things out." Hybels explains, "Our seekers don't want to say anything, sing anything, sign anything, or give anything."[5]

This anonymity gives Harry the freedom to decide when, or if, to get more information or seek involvement. Strobel says anonymity "preserves their [Harrys'] control. When I first went to church, I wanted to maintain as much control of the situation as I could because this gave me security." By giving Harry control, Willow Creek is trying to get Harry to relax.[6]

Harry Wants Some Social Distance

Outside of his normal web of social relationships, Harry is uncomfortable. Creekers believe that if Harry has to introduce himself to a lot of people when he visits a church, he probably won't come back. Beach explains, Harry "doesn't want any recognition when he gets here." Thus, Willow Creek has created an environment where Harry can enjoy the music and drama and listen to the talk without the messiness of social interaction. Willow Creek trains its ushers to smile and greet people but not to "assault them." As one attender explained, "You don't feel like people are going to come up to you and ask you questions. You can blend in until you feel comfortable."[7]

A characteristic of Willow Creek that allows anonymity is its size. Even in the early days, Willow Creek was attracting a large number of attenders, and thus newcomers felt less conspicuous. They realized that probably no one would know all of the hundreds and even thousands of attenders. As Strobel recalls, "When I first started coming, Willow Creek was already 'in'—attracting quite a few people." The experience is similar to attending a large concert or massive suburban movie theater. Harrys make their own way and no one approaches or questions them. They are anonymous.

Giving Harry Time

Strobel explains, "Anonymity gives *time* to Unchurched Harry and Mary. It creates a safe environment for them to seek after the truth about Christ at their own pace" (author's emphasis).[8]

Evangelism director Mittelberg asserts, "People go through a process in coming to Christ—a process. And I believe in, and respect, that process." As I noted in chapter 4, Creekers believe that hostile Harrys are converted to curiosity; curious Harrys are converted to sincerely seeking; only then are sincere Harrys converted to the gospel.

Creekers emphasize the idea of process in contrast to what they call the "event-oriented" approach. Hybels describes how many evangelicals are "tempted to tell people who've been living for twenty, thirty, or forty years under a totally secular worldview, 'You've got just a couple of minutes at the end of this service to make a decision that's going to determine your eternity.'" Creekers argue that most Harrys won't make a quick decision to follow Christ. Evangelism director Mittelberg recalled what one evangelical said to him, "If your seeker services are to reach . . . people for Christ, do you give them an opportunity every week? You might have only one chance." Mittelberg explained in response:

> That's almost a self-fulfilling prophecy. . . . Because we think we only get one chance, then we try to bring closure to the deal all in one shot. And because we try to do that—we scare the person away.[9]

In contrast, Mittelberg argues that Harry needs the exact opposite. "If we put too much pressure [on Harrys], we don't give them time to go through the process." Creekers believe that Harry needs time to go through a process of discovery at his own pace. Cousins explains what Willow Creek is trying to communicate to Harry:

> Harry, just take your time. We realize that you've had some bad experiences in your background.

> You've gone for a long time thinking that God was not relevant in your life, that he didn't have any answers to the tough issues of life.
>
> So, Harry, this is going to take some time, and that's okay. You come here and sit here, be around here as long as you need to.

The environment of the programming is designed to create this nonthreatening situation.

The freedom to investigate Christianity at one's own pace even gives Harry and Mary freedom to ignore the gospel for a while. For example, one unchurched Mary said at her baptism:

> The first year I almost sat here with my arms folded, daring God to love me. I just didn't want to be involved; I thought it was all show and hype.
>
> And then slowly I began to see my boys changing and my husband changing. And they were growing in their walk. It was probably eight to ten months later that I finally decided that I had better start listening with a different ear.

Hybels explains that the unchurched "want to seek from the shadows, and if we allow that, they'll hang around and sooner or later they're going to be moved."[10]

Creekers believe that they need to communicate at a pre-evangelism level for some time before many Harrys will be ready to respond to the gospel. Willow Creek programming attempts to help Harry take the next step in the process as a spiritual seeker. Part of the process for Harry is reunderstanding who God is. Willow Creek can help by dismantling common misconceptions about who God is or by removing roadblocks to faith.[11]

A large part of the weekend service is designed to help people reunderstand who God is. Beach asserts, "We feel like God is very misunderstood. . . . We're trying to show the different dimensions to the character of God in hopes that ultimately they'll get a more balanced view." Beach believes that a particular strength of music is its ability to reframe how individuals think about God. Music, she argues, can help shape an individual's understanding of God: "And our hope is that over time . . . people would get a more whole view of who he [God] is." Whereas the drama tends to depict the problems of life, more often "the music portrays the answers."

By helping Harry reunderstand who God is, Creekers are also trying to help him see who he is—in relation to this God. Hybels quotes one unchurched Harry who wrote him:

> I came to the church convinced that I was a Christian. At the three-month mark of my involvement at the seeker's service, I came to the startling conclusion that biblically speaking I wasn't a Christian.

> It took a couple months for that to settle in. . . . and that took a few months and then I finally came to a point . . . where I made the decision to trust Christ.

By giving Harry time to investigate Christianity at his own pace, Creekers believe that he will understand the biblical truth about God and then respond to him.

Emotional

For thousands of years, writers have noted the importance of the emotions in the process of persuasion. Aristotle explains that "rhetorical study, in its strict sense, is concerned with the modes of persuasion." One of these modes is the use of emotions to enable persuasion to take place. Aristotle refers to the emotional mode as "putting the audience into a certain frame of mind."[12]

Modern studies have confirmed how the emotions affect persuasion. "Persuasive discourse," psychologist Gerald Miller concludes, is "an amalgam of logic and emotion." Psychologist Kari Edwards observed from her experiments that "affect means of persuasion" were more effective than "cognitive means of persuasion." The most successful forms of persuasion influence the audience's emotions. Willow Creek staff intuitively know the power of emotions to persuade. Thus a major goal of the weekend programming is to move Harry emotionally.[13]

Emotions in American Culture

Americans are perceived in the international community as emotionally expressive. Each year there is an international advertising competition at Cannes, France. *Time* magazine reported after the 1991 contest:

> One U.S. entry met a shocking rebuff. It is a lump-in-the-throat spot about Mike Sewell, a youth born with Down's Syndrome, who found a job and happiness at McDonald's.
>
> The crowd in the giant auditorium at Cannes greeted it with raucous boos and whistles.

Marcio Moreira, creative director at McCann-Erickson Worldwide, commented that international viewers "don't like to have their emotions manipulated." He explained, "Schmaltz is an American idiom. We're a people who cherish wearing our feelings on our sleeve."[14]

Americans love to feel deep emotion. Television encourages an odd sort of emotional vulnerability. It's not unusual on talk shows for the host to ask an intensely personal question and expect the guest to share his most intimate feelings before an audience of millions. An example of this was the much advertised Oprah Winfrey interview of Michael Jackson that delved into how Michael was "beaten" as a child. As Richard Corliss wrote in *Time* magazine, the interview "was at the very least great TV: live, reckless, emotionally naked."[15]

Daytime television is filled with soap operas—because Americans watch them. Soap-like dramas are now found regularly on prime-time television. An advertisement for a particular show says, "You'll laugh. You'll cry. You'll fall in love." The advertisement was selling the show on its ability to elicit strong emotional reactions from its viewers.[16]

Americans' emotional orientation has increased in the last few decades. A part of the 1960s counterculture was an emphasis on authenticity and emotional honesty. This emotional orientation became increasingly true of the wider American population throughout the 1970s.[17]

Hybels affirms this shift: "We've come to acknowledge vulnerability as a sign of strength and the ability to express our true emotions as a needed quality in our stressful society." Although in the past men weren't considered manly if they cried, today it is increasingly acceptable. The role model for American men has shifted from a stoic John Wayne to a sensitive Bill Clinton. As a result, Americans are particularly open to emotional programming. Thus Willow Creek has found it very effective to program to Harry's and Mary's emotions.[18]

The same proclivity toward emotions that we find in American entertainment we also observe in Americans' sentient approach to God. The Gallup organization found that nearly six out of ten Americans believe that God communicates to them through their internal feelings. This total is equal to the number of Americans who believe that God uses the Bible to communicate and is twice the number of Americans who believe that God uses other people to communicate to them. Americans depend on their emotions in their highly individualistic relationships with God. If Willow Creek's programming is able to touch Harry's emotions, it is speaking Harry's spiritual language.[19]

Willow Creek's Use of Emotional Programming

Willow Creek's emotional programming strategy is based on their understanding of the human being. One drama writer explained, "People are people. People have feelings, people have thoughts. You've got to speak to both." One programming staff member quoted his fellow staffers as saying, "You know what? If we take this song and you take this song, and you push these together, these will help people to feel their emotions." Willow Creek's drama, music, and words attempt either to soothe or excite various emotions, depending on the goal of the programming at a particular time.

As I showed above, Willow Creek's dramas are often designed to define a problem or issue so the audience can experience it. As a drama writer explained to me, many skits are devised to "recreate the problem so people feel it. They feel the tension; they feel, 'Hey, this is tough.'"

Willow Creek's music is also structured to spark an emotional response from Harry. Music, by its very nature, triggers more of an emotional response than a rational one. Hybels describes how one of Willow Creek's singers was able to prompt an emotional feeling during the previous weekend's seeker service: "He got done with that song and really there was just this holy kind of aura in this place."

Even short comments by singers and the Scripture readers are crafted to touch or guide listeners' emotions. They provide the links for an entire seeker service that is designed to stir and lead unchurched Harry's emotions.

"Moments" are a key aspect to Willow Creek's emphasis on emotions in programming. Beach explains:

> I think our primary goal in the music and the drama, when we feel we've really arrived, or done something that mattered, is when we can be used by God to create some kind of "moment" for people. And that's a big word around here.

Steve, a program staff member, commented about the TV show *Life Goes On:*

> One of the reasons why we love that show is because almost in every show there's some kind of moment. Now it's not a spiritual moment, but there's some point in those shows where you are glued emotionally. . . . It moves people. . . .
>
> Those kinds of moments need to happen in church. Church should be a place where more of those happen than anywhere else. It's okay to be emotional, because our spirits are being moved, we're in touch with God, and the Holy Spirit is moving.

The staff believe that if they work as hard as they can and select the right songs, music, and scripts, special moments will be the result. Beach explains the effect of these special moments, "We are trying to create moments with music and drama—moments of tears or laughter." "Moments," then, are the times when the staff, and the Holy Spirit, use the church's programming to spark a deep emotional response from the audience.[20]

Emotion as a Means to Understand Truth

Strobel underlines why it is important to program these emotional moments: "Harry doesn't just want to know something; he wants to experience it." Strobel reports that for "many Unchurched Harrys who are on a spiritual journey, experience—not evidence—is their mode of discovery." As noted above, many Americans experience their relationship with God in their emotions, not their rational ideas. With its dramatic programming, Willow Creek is attempting to speak Harry's language—that of his emotions. Thus, Strobel argues, "The objective of evangelism should be to bring Unchurched Harry into a personal encounter *with* God, not just to merely pass on information *about* God" (author's emphasis). By creating moments of deep emotion, Willow Creek is attempting to help Harry re-experience some of the pain of his problems and then show how God wants to meet people in their pain.[21]

By hearing serious questions and feeling the pain of the performers, it is not uncommon for the audience to cry during a particularly emotional drama. As Strobel said about the "Great Expectations" skit, "There was not a dry eye in the house." One new attender explained to me that she got "a lot of warm, fuzzy feelings" when she attended the church. What was the result of this common feeling of another's pain? Strobel believes:

> For somebody who is a hard-hearted individual who is just investigating the claims of faith in Christ . . . to feel that it knocks down a barrier when they can cry amongst all these other people at something they see together.

Through the emotional dramas, Harry becomes more open to hearing Willow Creek's message, and even in some way begins to understand it emotionally.

Emotions as a Back Door to Persuasion

Great military strategists throughout history have always argued against attacking an opponent's reinforced positions. Likewise Willow Creek has designed its program to avoid Harry's conscious defenses. Beach explains:

> If you give them a musical experience or a dramatic experience, you can go through what we call the back door and you can somehow get them to emo-

> tionally and intellectually respond . . . to some things, and they hardly even know it's happening because their resistance is much, much lower.

Creekers seek to communicate through the back door of Harry's emotions.[22]

Psychologist Robert Oliver suggests that there are three basic uses for emotions in the persuasive process. The first is to remove hostility. Chapter 6 described how laughter can remove barriers of hostility and suspicion.

Oliver teaches that "the second function of emotion is to create a general mood which will provide a proper atmosphere for the speaker's plea." After a particularly intense emotional feeling has been created, it tends to persist as an emotional mood.[23]

An illustration may help to flesh out this idea. A Willow Creek drama began with several actors in front of the Vietnam War Memorial. Two Vietnam vets are looking at the name of a close friend from their squad. They chuckle as they remember his humor. They recall how he remained faithful to his wife during his tour. In the midst of their memories, they tear up. Near them is a woman remembering her brother who died so far away. She reminisces about his laughter and how he used to take care of her. She calls him her "knight in shining armor" and whispers through her tears, "I loved you, Danny; I miss you."

Three tourists come boisterously and rudely into the scene and begin snapping pictures. They are ignoring or are insensitive to the others and their pain. They call out loudly, "Cheese!" as one of their party takes pictures. One of the soldiers says angrily, "This isn't Disney World!" A tourist retorts, "We are here to see the monuments." A soldier replies, "We are here to see a friend—a good friend!" The sister says softly, "A brother." The scene closes.

Someone walks to the podium and explains, "We see things like this and we are tenderized. We are offended when we see something important treated as trivial." He then explains that "the things that are not important to you may be most important to us." The poignant moment of the drama is carried on as a mood as Hybels later speaks on the importance of communion and baptism for Christians. The emotional drama created an openness in the listeners to hear what was really important to Hybels.

Oliver believes, "The third function of emotion is to energize the audience's support of the speaker's proposal by linking it with the emotional" desires of the audience.[24]

Hybels describes how the audience responded emotionally during a song about God's faithfulness:

> The lyrics said:
>
> "My Redeemer is faithful and true. . . .
> Everything he has said he will do.

> Every morning his mercies are new,
> My Redeemer is faithful and true."

> And I was looking around the auditorium at a lot of our seekers, and I sensed that what they were saying was, "There's no one in this world who is faithful and true."

The song addressed the fundamental human need to trust another in a relationship. As chapter 4 stated, Harry and Mary are lonely and feel a great deal of alienation and stress. They hurt with the emotional pain of broken relationships and the desire for a stable relationship. The song was presenting God as the only one who is able to be faithful to meet these desires. Hybels explains:

> A lot of them have been married two or three times—spouses aren't faithful. A lot of them had been promised things at work that didn't happen—employers aren't faithful. A lot of them have been deceived by friends. . . .
>
> I just felt seekers were saying, "Could it be there is someone in this crazy, mixed-up, uncertain world . . . who is faithful and true in everything he promises he will do?"

Emotional programming such as this identifies a deep human desire and then presents how Christianity can satisfy this desire.

The Ethics of Emotional Programming

What are the limits of appropriate emotional programming? An image is indelibly burned into the minds of most Americans. During the television evangelists' scandals of the 1980s, the picture of Tammy Faye Bakker's pleading for money was aired dozens of times on network news programs. While tears flowed in streams through her mascara, she pleaded with her viewers to help her husband—television evangelist Jim Bakker—and her out of their financial difficulties. When many think of emotional manipulation in modern America, this is the image that quickly springs to mind.

Willow Creek staff are aware that emotional programming can become manipulative. As one admitted, "There's a fine line between persuasion and manipulation." What is this fine line?

One drama writer explained:

> You become manipulative . . . when you make someone think they've arrived at a decision, but they really didn't. . . . You become manipulative when you sneak around and you get people to feel something in an attempt to sort of supersede . . . their thinking faculties.

In other words, manipulation is when the programming completely supplants the critical thinking of the audience and maneuvers an individual into decisions that he or she does not want to make.

An example of emotional manipulation is detailed in the U.S. Army's manual of *Intelligence Interrogation*. The manual instructs interrogators of enemy captives to "manipulate the source's emotions and weaknesses to gain his willing cooperation." It explains:

> The exploitation of the source's emotion can be either harsh or gentle in application (hand and body movements, actual physical contact such as a hand on the shoulder for reassurance, or even silence are all useful techniques that the interrogator may have to bring into play).[25]

Short of prohibiting physical violence, the manual provides no ethical guideline for interrogators. Their job is to get information and to be willing to "manipulate the source's emotions" to do so. What is it that distinguishes Willow Creek's programming from this sort of manipulation?

Staff members were befuddled when I asked them this question. They have a feel for what is and is not appropriate programming; but they had a difficult time defining either. As Nancy Beach put it, "You *just know* when you're going for the emotions too much" (emphasis added). Willow Creek's ethics are largely based on gut instincts. Nancy Beach argues, "I really do trust our instincts."

It is rare for the programming team to disagree on whether a particularly emotional drama or song should be used. Creekers have a common understanding that has, like much of Willow Creek's mindset, not been deeply analyzed. The staff usually resorted to Willow Creek axioms of truth, integrity, and restraint in answer to my questions about ethics in programming.

Truth. Evangelism director Mittelberg explains that the programming team "probably see opportunities where they could pull people's emotions around, if that's what they wanted to do. [But] it's got to be based on truth and legitimate emotions." He continued, "I have a hard time putting my finger on the exact word or phrase to use, but 'true,' meaning what we're getting people to feel is based on truth. True teachings, true ideas."

If an emotion is going to be the goal of a particular drama, it must be an appropriate emotional response to the truth being addressed; for instance, who God is, who they are. The singers are asked to sing the lyrics, Beach explains, "as if they were talking to a friend and kind of gesture the way they would do it if they were talking." As one staff member revealed, "What we're trying to do is create moments related to what the real agenda is—that are honest."

Integrity. Virtually anytime someone wasn't able to give a clear or definite answer to one of my questions, he or she appealed to "integrity." Creekers want to be guided by integrity. Beach explains, "As long as it's truthful and real I think it will add to the integrity of what we're trying to do." For example, singers have to mean what they sing or talk about. Beach says:

> They can't make up stuff. It's got to be, certainly, out of their life. . . . When one of our singers had a miscarriage . . . she was talking before the song . . . about how it was hard to find comfort during that time. . . . So people can sit out there and say, "Oh, she knows the pain, too."

Thus, from Willow Creek's perspective programming that is emotional needs to be honest to the person's experience. It must have integrity.

Restraint. Like all media professionals, Creekers are aware that emotions can be channeled past rational thinking altogether. Sometimes the programming team purposely eases off the emotional dynamic. Beach explains:

> If we know there's gonna be a real moving moment . . . something in a service, we try to surround it with times when . . . we can give people a break, so to speak, emotionally.

Willow Creek's programming is designed to stir the audience's emotions and yet give them the freedom to choose.

After reading this chapter, Beach responded, "I wish I could have thought it all through more when interviewed. It is *so* important to us that we do not manipulate people through the arts."

Willow Creek employs the persuasive principles of being relevant and excellent, giving anonymity and time, and using emotion in the elements of each service's program. These programming elements persuasively bring Harry to the point of hearing the central message of the service.

8

The Credibility of the Speaker

In a special message to senior pastors at Willow Creek's leadership conference, Hybels shared a secret:

> Now I don't like to say this around the staff; I don't like to say this, you know, around the church or even in public.
>
> But in closed-door sessions with senior pastors I like to say—it would be difficult for you to overestimate the importance of great preaching. It's not much of an exaggeration to say it's about 85 percent of the game.

When one is aware of the thousands of hours that go into each week of the ministry of Willow Creek, it is extraordinary to hear Hybels say that public speaking is "85 percent of the game." He explains, "The way we kind of say it around here is that effective preaching creates the environment, the openness, the atmosphere, where people begin to do spiritual business."[1]

The message is the essential core of Willow Creek's seeker service. There are seven elements to Willow Creek's messages: credibility, identifying, relevance, Christianity 101, truth, the gospel, and commitment. The rest of this chapter is an explanation of the principle of credibility.

The message starts where the rest of the program leaves off. The program is designed to get Harry's attention and prepare him for Hybels's message. For the first few minutes of his message, Hybels virtually dares Harry not to listen. Hybels is very aware of the truth of Robert Oliver's comment,

"The most impressive point in a discourse is its opening statement." Hybels knows that he needs to build credibility with Harry from the very start.[2]

Hybels believes that his ability to influence others is a result of his credibility:

> The people who have the greatest positive impact in the marketplace are those who have established the greatest level of *credibility* in the marketplace. Most people listen only to those whom they have learned to respect [emphasis added].

Hybels says, "When I can use a contemporary illustration, I build credibility." He is attentive to the audience's response to both his message and to himself. With how he presents both, he is self-consciously trying to build credibility.[3]

To a very large extent he is successful. On one occasion, Hybels gave a series of talks on the importance of small groups. Within a few weeks, three hundred new couples had signed up to join small groups. On another occasion, Hybels suggested during a talk that individuals might want to consider therapy. The counseling office was flooded with phone calls as a result. A staff member in the counseling center explained, "He has so much credibility, people do what he suggests." People trust Hybels.

Credibility is crucial in the persuasive process. Modern psychological research has provided evidence supporting this fact. Stuart Oskamp summarizes, "A large body of research indicates that a message from a highly credible source will produce more attitude change than one from a low-credibility source."[4]

Researchers say credibility is created by prestige, expertise, trustworthiness, attractiveness, similarity, familiarity, and power. Hybels ranks high in every one of these categories in the eyes of unchurched Harry: Hybels has status as the founder and leader of Willow Creek, one of the largest churches in the United States; unchurched Harry sees Hybels as an expert on Christianity; Hybels is honest and sincere, and thus Harry sees him as trustworthy; Hybels is athletic and handsome and dresses like any successful businessman; Hybels is a charming speaker whom unchurched Harrys learn to both like and trust; as Willow Creek has become large and increasingly influential, Hybels is seen as an important leader. The result of all these characteristics is that Hybels has a high degree of credibility in Harry's eyes.[5]

There are five elements to Hybels's particular approach to building credibility: authenticity, integrity, intimacy, emotions, and affection.

Authenticity

Hybels says that he doesn't try to spend a lot of time understanding how he communicates; he just does it. "If I can walk out of this building," Hybels explains, "honestly saying that I did the best I could with God's help to serve the people, then I'm happy; but I've never analyzed it farther than that." Hybels probably hasn't done a detailed study of the psychology of persuasion. He believes if he faithfully communicates, God will use him. However, Hybels does have an intuitive grasp of the elements of persuasion. The first of these elements is authenticity.

The words *authentic* and *authenticity* were regularly used by Creekers to explain how Hybels communicates. One staff member reported, "A really good word" to summarize Hybels's speaking style is "authentic." Hybels teaches a group of pastors:

> When you know you're being right before God yourself, then when you teach about it, there's a ring of *authenticity* in your voice and people say, "I'll bet he doesn't just talk about it" [emphasis added].[6]

According to Hybels, genuine authenticity requires integrity.

Integrity

Unchurched Harry is cynical toward the church. He thinks that Christianity is for hypocrites and that churches want him to be involved so that they can get his money. Hybels is trying to convince unchurched Harry that he and Willow Creek can be trusted. Hybels wants Willow Creek to be a place where Harry can come to hear people of integrity speak the truth. He believes that Harry will ultimately be open to truth-filled communication because "secular people are so sick and tired of being lied to."

As an unchurched Harry, Lee Strobel came to Willow Creek expecting to find hypocrisy. In contrast to his cynicism, Strobel claims, he found integrity at Willow Creek. What "really attracted me was integrity," he says. He believes someone has integrity when "there's an integration between a person's beliefs and behavior." Strobel, like many other unchurched Harrys, became convinced that Hybels and the other leaders were actually living what they were teaching: "There seemed to be a personal integrity of the people that I talked with and the people that I saw." Hybels teaches a group of Christian leaders that when a "pastor starts talking about discipleship with a ring of authority in his voice, that shakes people on a real deep level." Hybels came to believe that this is especially true when a pastor is intimate.[7]

Intimacy

When Hybels describes his speaking style, he sometimes uses the word *transparent* to explain how much he shares about his own life and experience:

> It's just very natural for me to say, "And here's how it's working, or not working, in my own life." And if that kind of thing helps you, fine. If it doesn't you can go to someone who is more of a theorist or something else.

As a result, Hybels uses first person pronouns quite liberally in his talks. In the weekend talks of one year he used *I* 6,152 times and *me* and *my* 1,580 and 1,478 times respectively. Hybels used personal pronouns an average 170.55 times during each talk. In effect, Hybels's talks are a one-way intimate conversation containing a lot of personal confession. This kind of personal sharing and confession bypasses the defense mechanisms of unchurched Harry. One Willow Creek counselor explained the effect of this honesty:

> That type of humility . . . goes miles with people. I think it's one of those things that Bill does well. He'll stand up and say, "I really messed up my marriage," or "I really burned out."[8]

A onetime unchurched Harry described the effect of Creekers' self-revelations: "It seemed like they didn't have anything to hide." Another former unchurched Harry said how this confessional style affected him: "It was very disarming when Bill's approach was to be very transparent and to admit his own shortcomings."

One attender said that the result of Hybels's intimacy is that "you kind of feel like he knows you." On the flip side, the attender also feels like he knows Bill. In hundreds of conversations, I heard Hybels called "Pastor Hybels" on only one occasion. People referred to Hybels as "Bill." Individuals felt like they were on a personal, first-name basis with him—even though most had never met him. With this intimacy Hybels can be honest about delicate and difficult topics without offending people. In turn, individuals feel permission, or perhaps a need, to be honest in response. Hybels is aware that he needs to be honest in this transparency. Without this honesty, he would be stiff and artificial.

Emotions

A large part of Hybels's transparency is his revealing of his emotions. As Hybels explains, "I'm a proponent of being real in relationships. You know I am. That's my style. That's my preference. I'm all for taking risks of self-disclosure."

Hybels often describes an issue in his own life with great emotion. One staff member related that Hybels reveals "the more acute emotions." Some staff members think that Hybels has, over the years, become more emotional in his speaking. As one explained, "Bill has become more of a feeler." Through expressing his emotion during his talks, Hybels is able to create an emotionally charged environment.

Affection

Hybels asserts that a "prerequisite to effective preaching to non-Christians is that we *like them.* If we don't, it's going to bleed through our preaching" (author's emphasis). According to Hybels's close friends and associates, Hybels likes unchurched Harrys. We see this affection in his self-chosen epitaph: "Bill Hybels, friend of sinners."[9]

Hybels believes this affection is central in being able to communicate to the unchurched. Hybels argues that many "preachers forfeit their opportunity to speak to non-Christians, because the unchurched person immediately senses, *They don't like me*" (author's emphasis). Left in this situation, Christian and non-Christian are separated by a wall of misunderstanding over which they lob accusations of "pagan" and "zealot." Hybels argues that the non-Christians have a legitimate complaint against the church and identifies with them. "People that don't know me and love me probably are trying to sell me, or proposition me, or hustle me."[10]

Hybels believes that the solution to this problem is theological. If preachers really believed the Willow Creek motto, "Lost people matter to God," Hybels feels that they would reflect God's concern toward the non-Christian: "I find myself wondering whether these preachers are convinced that lost people matter to God."[11]

When Hybels speaks to Christian groups outside the church, he often tries to help them develop this conviction. As a result he regularly uses Luke 15 as his Bible text. As I mentioned in chapter 1, Luke 15 is a series of three parables about the lost sheep, lost coin, and lost son, and focuses on God's love toward those who are lost. Without this motivation of God's love for non-Christians, Hybels believes, "These speakers distance themselves from the non-Christian listener; it's us against them." Instead Hybels believes that Christians should show the same love toward others that God has shown toward them.[12]

At a pastors' conference, Hybels appeared near tears talking about the importance of loving unchurched people: "Just understand them. Identify with them and their problems. They can tell if you like them. Nonchurched people feel it." Hybels reveals his response to seeing his non-Christian friends ruin their lives:

> More and more these days I am finding it difficult to watch people that I know and love—go from bar to bar, toy to toy, fun fix to fun fix, lover to lover, fad to fad, trying and then crashing, and then trying again and then crashing again. . . . I just feel a kind of pity.

This compassion for unchurched Harry causes Hybels to identify with him.

9

Identifying with Harry

To communicate persuasively, Hybels identifies with his audience. Evangelism director Mittelberg explains that "identifying" means "to move as far as we can in a cultural way so that we can get close to the people that we're trying to reach." Why do Hybels and Willow Creek emphasize identifying with Harry?

Once again we find Hybels articulating a persuasion principle that has been confirmed by research. Oliver explains that the more agreement a speaker can build into his speech, the more there will be a "tendency to go along with the speaker—a 'yes response.'" If Hybels can show that he is similar to Harry, he becomes more familiar and attractive, and thus a more credible witness.

Hybels justifies this strategy by arguing that he is merely following the apostle Paul's example in 1 Corinthians 9:22: "I have become all things to all men so that by all possible means I might save some."[1]

The Cultural Chasm

Creekers believe there is a "cultural chasm" between biblical Christianity and modern unchurched Harrys. Mittelberg explains to visiting pastors:

> Our message here, or a big part of it, is that we as a church need to close that *cultural chasm* ourselves so that we can move over to them culturally and bring to them the message of the gospel so that they can hear it, first of all, and then respond to it [emphasis added].

Mittelberg describes missionary training as a model for how Willow Creek seeks to identify with Harry:

> They [missionaries] need to study the language of the people they're going to, and they need to study the culture of the people they're trying to reach.
>
> And yet, we often, naively, assume that we don't need to do the same thing.

Hybels and other Creekers have studied Harry's culture and language in order to identify with him. "We try to communicate that we know what's going on in the world," Hybels explains, so that "a seeker doesn't feel like he's been transplanted from one age and culture into another age and culture."

An illustration of Willow Creek's affirmation of culture is its handling of holidays. In contrast to many churches, which organize their year around the Christian calendar, Willow Creek acknowledges only two Christian holidays, Christmas and Easter. They also have given special services for the cultural holidays of Thanksgiving, New Year's Day, Mother's Day, Father's Day, Memorial Day, and the Fourth of July. As one Willow Creek advocate writes:

> By recognizing the rhythms of the surrounding communities more than denominational traditions, the church wants to remove any possible hindrances to people attending services.[2]

The purpose of identifying with Harry with the cultural holidays, one staff member explained, is to "connect with them in their world to show them they are not outsiders." When "scores and scores" of Creekers nervously asked Hybels how they should respond to Halloween, he answered, "Lighten up a little." Hybels allows his own children to dress up for Halloween as long as they don't have costumes "associated with the demonic." As might be expected, Hybels does not teach Creekers to abstain from these cultural holidays. There is a deep affirmation of the American culture in Willow Creek's principle of identifying.

"We Are the Same"

Hybels identifies with Harry by adopting his language, clothing, customs, and lifestyle. Whenever it is possible, Hybels underlines that he is similar to the unchurched Harry who has just walked in the door.

We see this clearly in how often Hybels uses the pronouns *us, we,* and *our.* During a year's weekend messages Hybels used *we* 2,084 times, *us* 1,062 times, and *our* 1,007 times. This was an average of 76.9 times each message that Hybels created a verbal community with his words. When he was speaking on how to respond to failure, he identified with the visiting Harrys:

> *We're* hurt, *we're* insecure, *we're* angry, *we're* anxious, *we* don't like becoming students of the setback. *We* don't feel like asking God to teach *us* through this trauma or to give *us* perspective or wisdom.
>
> *We* just want to hurt, *we* just want to strike out, *we* want to blame, *we* want to pout [emphasis added].

These pronouns form a bridge of mutuality between Hybels and Harry. Instead of verbally pointing his finger at Harry, Hybels emphasizes how similar he and Harry are.[3]

And there is a great deal of truth in Hybels's claim of similarity with Harry. Hybels in many ways would enjoy being a business executive like Harry. "I'm a lot like nonchurched Harry," he says. In fact, Hybels reveals he has selected Harry as his target audience because he likes him. Yet this identifying with Harry is also purposeful.

By identifying with Harry, Hybels is trying to highlight those aspects of his personality, experience, assumptions, and attitudes that are similar to Harry's. In a sense, Hybels is clarifying the common ground that he and Harry share. Hybels then has opportunity to appeal to these common characteristics in order to persuade Harry.

"But Hybels Is a Pastor"

Before Hybels can underline all the ways he is similar to Harry, he needs to remove one large hurdle. Pastors are viewed by unchurched Harry with a great deal of suspicion. Harry correctly assumes that it is a pastor's job to influence or evangelize him. As a result, his defensive radar mechanisms are on full power. Hybels knows this and realizes that he needs to turn off Harry's radar. He does this by joking about the role of pastor and portraying himself as an unlikely pastor.[4]

Hybels spoke to a weekend crowd about marital problems:

> I'll bet you'll have conflict with the big three: money, sex, and power. I'll lay odds. You know, whenever I say that I think to myself, a decent pastor would say "I prophesy that. . . ." Lay odds is a little . . .

The audience exploded in boisterous laughter. On another occasion, Hybels told about his past in a role they could more easily identify with: "I, the quintessential thinker, the cool, calculated, Harley-riding lifeguard at that camp, ran to a friend and cried, 'God loves me! I see it now, I feel it now!'"

Hybels portrays himself as surprised that he ever ended up as a pastor: "I had no idea he [God] had any plans for me to be a pastor. I still wonder about that." Other times he specifically steps out of his role as a pastor to identify with Harry: "I don't want to talk to you as a pastor now, I just want to talk to you as a fellow sinner who found amazing grace in Christ." By this depiction Hybels shows that he is aware that Harry is defensive about the pastor role. If he can eliminate being labeled a pastor, Hybels will have a better chance of getting Harry to identify with him.[5]

Hybels states that he "can be as 'normal' as anybody else. There is no verse of Scripture to back up the misconception that one has to be strange to be a committed Christian." He declares to visiting Harrys, "I live in the same kind of real world that you do."[6]

Yet occasionally during his talks, Hybels realizes that he is asking Harry to move beyond his comfort zone too much. During one talk, he rhetorically raised Harry's questioning attitude: "I thought Bill was my kind of guy . . . I thought he lived in the real world like the one I live in." By verbalizing this question, Hybels is identifying with Harry. Hybels takes a verbal step back to allow Harry to catch up.

Hybels's Speaking Style

When people come to Willow Creek for the first time, they are often surprised by Hybels's speaking style. One reporter told me that Hybels's message was similar to a David Letterman monologue. Another new attender compared Hybels's presentation to that of a stylish college professor. Hybels has broken the mold of preaching and developed a mode of communication in which he can identify with unchurched Harrys.

A former unchurched Harry who eventually became a believer explains the effect of Bill's identifying with him:

> Bill is up there doing these messages and he looked like a normal person. I mean he dressed like I did; he didn't have robes on, you know. And I thought, well that's interesting.

The result was that Bill could remove what this Harry called his "defensive mechanism." Hybels could sidestep the barricades that this unchurched Harry put up and intimately present his message in a personal conversation.

A Personal Conversation

To even describe Hybels's method of communication as "preaching" is misleading. In many ways his delivery is more that of a personal conversation. This style is in direct contrast to the popular idea of preaching in American culture. Peter Berger describes the evangelistic fervor that many Americans associate with preaching:

> A peculiar mixture of arrogance ("I know the truth") and benevolence ("I want to save you") has always been the chief psychological hallmark of the missionary activity.[7]

"Preaching" in the modern mind implies a self-righteous and judgmental attitude. In contrast, Hybels is seeking to create a level playing field where all are equal in the sight of God. It is no accident there is no preaching pulpit in the auditorium at Willow Creek. Hybels doesn't want to "preach." As one staff member explained to me, his "teaching has a conversational style."

The historical roots of this approach are found in the Son City youth group. Former associate pastor Don Cousins wrote in 1979:

> The spoken word as delivered at Son City is referred to as "speaking." The word "speaking" indicates that there is a *conversation* taking place . . . a *conversation* between the Director and the Son City students.
>
> These *conversations*, or messages as they are called, are directed to the student who is investigating Christianity [emphasis added].[8]

All of this helps to avoid the preaching label. Cousins continues, "Ideally, the speaking should be done without notes. This will add to the feeling of a conversation taking place."[9]

Hybels approaches his talks as if he is having an extended conversation with a good friend. In fact, the term that Hybels most uses in referring to visiting Harrys is "friend" or "friends." The word *friend* was used 107 times and *friends* 321 times, averaging 7.93 times each talk. The use of this word helps shape the style of communication; rarely does one yell at a good friend.

The conversational elements of affirmation and intimacy are present in Hybels's weekend messages. It is not unusual for Hybels and the other speakers to affirm the audience with a compliment of some sort. Cousins said on one occasion, "I believe that all of us have something in common here this morning. . . . We all want to make a positive contribution to the lives of other people." By complimenting the audience, he is emphasizing the common ground they share as friends.

As I have already shown, Hybels frequently shares intimate details of his own life in these conversations. He regularly talks about his relationship with his wife, Lynne, or his children. It was not unusual to find Hybels revealing some personal or family story relating to the topic under consideration. In fact, the longest illustrations I heard him use were personal and family stories.

Hybels teaches Christians to share their testimonies with their friends so that it's "nonpreachy" and "nonaccusatory." He wants to give his messages in the same way. Strobel explains:

> Unchurched people don't like to be talked down to. Sooner or later, they see through leaders who are trying to project a phony image.
>
> They respond best when speakers talk to them as friends and peers, sharing with sincerity and honesty.[10]

Strobel told me that he usually thought of a specific person as he wrote his talks. That way he could imagine how that person would react and Strobel could build that response into his talk.

What is the result of this approach? Strobel describes the impression he as an unchurched Harry had of Hybels:

> He was an unpretentious guy who lives an active and interesting life, who has street smarts, and who was plugged into the same world that I was. In other words, he was the kind of person I'd like to get to know.[11]

Hybels's Language

Hybels uses Harry's language. The first clue to this is the fact that he used the word *gospel* only eighteen times during an entire year of messages. The entire weekend service is designed to communicate the gospel, yet the word itself is rarely mentioned. This curious incident is underlined when we note that the word *evangelism* was used only on one occasion during the same year. Once again, the entire service is designed to do evangelism (present the gospel), yet the word is virtually not used. Why?[12]

Willow Creek provides all participants at their leadership conferences with a "Church Profile" in which the vision of the church is described: "The dream was to build a church that would *speak the language of our modern culture*" (emphasis added). The very heart of Willow Creek is the idea of speaking unchurched Harry's language, as Lee Strobel explains, "translating 'Christianese' into everyday words." Why is this so important?[13]

Willow Creek's use of language, like all else in their program, is a response to their understanding of Harry. Creekers believe that in the last thirty or more years, American culture has become increasingly secular. Hybels and his Creekers believe there is a language gap between Christianity and the typical unchurched Harry. Hybels's solution to this dilemma is fourfold: (1) eliminate Christian clichés; (2) learn Harry's language; (3) simplify his theology; (4) use a normal tone of voice.[14]

Eliminate Christian Clichés

Creekers contend that Harry doesn't understand evangelical clichés. For example, an evangelical sharing how he became a Christian often uses the expression, "I accepted Christ into my heart as my personal Savior." Mittelberg believes that for a visiting Harry, "that sounds like something I could buy in a little gift shop in Tibet, you know, a little personal savior—and I could put it on my dashboard." Mittelberg asserts, "We use these terms, and yet don't realize that in many cases we're speaking a foreign language."

Hybels avoids clichés. When Hybels told a weekend audience that God "promises to be our strength and peace," he almost apologized: "I don't know how to say that without sounding like I'm spouting off clichés." Hybels explains this strategy:

> The death knell of a seeker's service is clichés. The communicator has got to be able to purge himself of the terminology, because if he doesn't, that in and of itself is enough to make people say, "Boy that's Greek to me."[15]

Learn Harry's Language

Mittelberg asserts, "Our target audience has a language of their own. We need to learn to speak it." Willow Creek's target audience of unchurched Harrys speaks the language of the American marketplace and its psychological culture. Hybels and Creekers are committed to learn and use this language in their efforts to persuade Harry and present the gospel.

To communicate, Hybels and the staff want to use the terminology that Harry uses every day. Therefore, Hybels doesn't use *gospel* or *evangelism*. These terms are not part of Harry's normal terminology. The only time unchurched Harry hears the word *evangelism* is when the network news does an exposé of a television evangelist. As a result, the word *evangelism* raises caution flags for Harry. Hybels avoids all words like *evangelism* that could confuse or spook Harry.

The only individuals who are asked to speak on the Willow Creek platform must be able to use Harry's marketplace language. Hybels explains,

"We make sure that the people doing it are so in tune with seekers that they're gonna talk their language and not fall into the cliché deal." The purpose of using Harry's language is to help Harry more clearly understand the gospel.[16]

Simplify the Theology

Hybels does not want to obscure his message with complicated theological terminology: "In a seeker's service all of our language has to be purged. I mean, you really have to purge your whole vocabulary in a seeker's service." Hybels is trying to communicate a simple theology.

We see this simplification in the theological terminology that was avoided in the messages. In a year, many of the basic terms of theology (ecclesiology, soteriology, Christology, anthropology) were never used. Neither were "immanence" and "transcendence" mentioned at all. Does this mean that no theology was taught? Not at all. But it was a simple theology that generally avoided the technical categories of academic theology. When Hybels did use a meaningful theological word like *repentance,* he explained it at length to the visiting Harrys.[17]

The fundamental step to simplifying the theology, according to Strobel, is translation. Strobel adopts the idea of translation from Millard Erickson. Erickson argues that translation means "expressing the message" in a more contemporary form, but retaining "the content, as one does when translating from one language to another." The goal of this process, Strobel says, is to "translate the Gospel into the everyday language . . . of twentieth-century America."[18]

In this respect Hybels resembles the renewal preachers of the nineteenth century. Nathan Hatch notes that these "unschooled preachers . . . honed the sermon into a razor-sharp recruiting device, [and] drummed out theological subtlety and complication." Making theology more simple was a pragmatic means to achieving better communication.[19]

Hybels uses a variety of descriptions to explain the gospel during the messages. Strobel says, "We try to tell it differently every time, the same information, but cast it differently, so that it can be in terms that people understand." With these simple explanations, Willow Creek is attempting to articulate a lay theology. Strobel explained that one of his talks was just "a different way of saying, 'This is a message on grace.'" One unchurched Harry explained the result of this emphasis: "I knew that these services were for me. They were really talking my language."[20]

Use Normal Tone of Voice

The fourth element of using Harry's language is that speakers and singers use a normal tone of voice. When Nancy Beach and Bill Hybels teach visiting pastors about the programming of the weekend services, they regularly comment on the importance of using a normal tone of voice. Beach explains, "It seems like church people, when they're on the stage—they change their voice." Creekers believe that visiting Harrys feel uncomfortable with this shift in tone. In contrast, Beach reveals, "We're just trying to be normal, and talk normal, and not put on a 'church voice.'" The programming staff specifically train anyone who is to speak or pray from the platform on how to use a normal, conversational tone of voice, rather than a "religious" one.

What is the result of this? Strobel recalls that as an unchurched Harry, "I heard everyday language. When the speaker would pray, he wouldn't use a bunch of 'thees' and 'thous,' but he would talk to God as if he actually knew him." Harry identifies with Hybels as he speaks his language in a "normal" way.[21]

Hybels's Humor

After I had analyzed and filed all the messages by subject, there were seven files larger than any others. God, Bible, Bill, and Emotions were four of these massive files. The files on God and Bible were understandably oversized, as Hybels is attempting to explain to unchurched Harrys who God is and often is referring to the Bible to do so. Also, Hybels's messages are structured as personal, intimate conversations that are often emotional; thus the large files on Bill and the emotions. The fifth huge file was Humor.

Humor is a crucial element of a Willow Creek talk. Hybels emphasizes the importance of humor to a group of pastors: "You guys who speak regularly know how good it is to have good humor." Those visiting Willow Creek are often stunned by the amount and quality of humor in one of Hybels's messages. One unchurched Harry told me, "There is a sense of humor that I have never encountered at any church anywhere." This appraisal of Willow Creek's emphasis on humor is probably accurate.

However, we find that preachers have long had an appreciation for the usefulness of laughter to get across their points. J. I. Packer comments, "Every spontaneous giggle yields another five minutes of empathetic listening, and every preacher will agree that is a precious boon."[22]

Yet the level and type of humor that Hybels employs is distinctive. We observed above that the weekend programming has been shaped by the media, especially television. The same is true of Hybels's messages. Marshall McLuhan has shown that television is a "cool medium . . . in which intimate conversation, relaxed discussion, and humor play a more effective role than fiery rhetoric." Thus Hybels's messages follow this pattern of cool, sardonic delivery replacing hot oratory. In short, Hybels is often very funny.[23]

Kind of Humor

Slight cynicism. When I attended Willow Creek for the first time, I felt like I had experienced a Christian Johnny Carson show. I found out later there was good reason why the activities, ambiance, and especially the humor of the service reminded me of Johnny Carson. Carson is Hybels's favorite comedian and a model of the humor he both enjoys and uses. Hybels is fond of Carson's "little quips" that are realistic, and sometimes cynical, about human nature and the world in which we live. One writer describes Carson's humor as a "nondenominational cynicism" that views all of life equally. Hybels gives an example of Carson's humor:

> Remember when they found out that Ferdinand Marcos had like twenty billion Philippine dollars stashed somewhere in the United States and he [Carson] said, "You know, Marcos made his money the old fashioned way—he stole it."[24]

This kind of cynicism highlights Hybels's points with a smile.

Stories. Hybels often tells humorous stories that Harry can identify with. For example, many unchurched Harrys have flown enough to recognize a rude fellow traveler, so Hybels told this story:

> I was sitting in an aisle seat on a commercial flight recently about fifteen rows back. There was a guy who had about five handbags who got on the front of the plane and started walking toward the rear of the plane.
>
> Every seat he passed he was clobbering every aisle seat passenger there as he went down the center aisle. I mean really whacking them with the cameras and handbags and all this.
>
> But he was careful. After he whacked people on either side he would say, "Sorry, sorry." And then he would whack the next, "Sorry, sorry," and then he kept going.
>
> I watched this man, I watched him coming toward me, and I thought, you know, if he passes me and clobbers me and tries to get off the hook by saying "Sorry," I'm gonna grab him by his necktie and pull him down and say, "Look, I don't think you're sorry, buddy, because if you were, you'd stop clobbering additional people."

The crowd roared with laughter. Harry not only enjoys the story but at the end is often more open to Hybels's point: "One of the acid tests of the depth of a person's repentance is how often he repeats the offense."

Askew pictures. At the heart of humor is the ability to portray something as slightly awry. Bob Hope, the dean of American comedians, says:

> You can make people laugh anytime, if you're talking about things they are already thinking about. The straight lines are already in their heads.
>
> And when you come up with a little twist that's funny, they'll laugh. That's the whole trick.[25]

Hybels often takes a topic of the day and then twists it, like a Hope or Carson, to get a chuckle. Occasionally, he tells a story to raise an off-centered picture. Hybels described driving and stopping at a rest area:

> I pulled into the parking area in that rest area right next to a stretch limo, a white limo, a white stretch limo—must have been thirty feet long.
>
> And there were some sort of scantily clad women hanging around that limo and they were loading cases and cases of what I perceived to be alcoholically enhanced beverages into the trunk and the back seat area.

Hybels then went to the men's rest room and observed a group of sailors changing into civilian clothes:

> They were a part of that limo scene and they were espousing to one another their wildest fantasies of how the night would wind up with alcoholically enhanced beverages and with the women. . . .
>
> So while I was overhearing all of this in the men's room I almost laughed out loud at the thought of saying, "Uh, fellas, before you officially start your orgy here, do you have five minutes for a little, you know, just us guys, spend a little time in the Word, see what God would have to say to us from the Bible. How about it fellas?"

After this vivid portrait of the sailors' planning their sex orgy, Hybels placed the contrasting image of a Bible study. The audience bellowed. Hybels revealed the point behind the story:

> I almost burst out laughing thinking about how that would go down. Now obviously they had their mind and heart, and other parts of their anatomy, sort of programmed toward iniquity.
>
> And they would have had a vested interest in saying, "Thanks, but no thanks. I don't really want to hear from the Bible tonight."

By juxtaposing pictures of an orgy—with a Bible study—Hybels not only generated a huge laugh but raised the serious point that the unchurched often have a "vested interest" in not seeking God.

Teasing. Hybels and the other speakers often tease one another or the audience. By teasing one another, they create the environment of a close family who love and care for one another. By teasing the audience, they include the spectators in this affectionate family. The audience, in turn, sometimes groans or hisses in response to a dumb pun or a play on words.

Hybels took a group of fellow leaders from the church ocean sailing and reported on the novice sailors to the congregation when he returned:

> The very first day out was the kind of day a sailor dreams about—twenty-five-knot winds, six- to eight-foot seas, clear skies; we were hiked over so far we had the rail in the water—very exciting, crashing through waves, out in the open ocean. . . .
>
> I was thoroughly enjoying all of what was happening and I began to notice that the other guys . . . some of them were a little green. So I tried to cheer them up by saying, "It doesn't get any better than this, does it fellas?"
>
> No response, just a few groans. Then a couple guys started heading down below toward their bunks. . . . A couple of the other guys got situated by the railings for purposes that I don't need to go into great detail to describe to you, other than to say that our own Lee Strobel experienced an unplanned protein spill over the side.

Hybels and the other speakers tease about balding hair, intellectual ability, the way the Hybels family eats health food, different types of personality quirks, and the romantic nature of young couples. All of this creates a warm, affectionate, family environment.

The Topics of Hybels's Humor

Virtually anything can be the topic of Hybels's humor, but he does have a favorite subject—himself. Hybels and the Willow Creek audience often enjoy a good laugh at his expense.

Self-mockery. Hybels described how people are beginning to share their feelings more freely in American society.

> People will blurt out almost anything to anyone these days. Have you noticed that?
>
> I could tell that a shift was happening in our culture several years ago when an attractive young mother stopped me after a service, and she described the bliss of breast feeding to me in greater detail than was necessary for a guy like me to hear.

> And I kept wondering while she was talking to me, *Why are you telling me this?* I'm still from the old school. I mean, I thought it was personal. But on she went, telling me about all this stuff. I said, *This is a new age we're moving into now.*

On another occasion, Hybels described how he decided not to do a preflight check of the small plane he was piloting. In mid-flight, he heard a clanging sound, and he realized that the fuel caps were loose.

> I was losing fuel at a rapid rate. And I thought, *That was a stupid thing to do to not check those fuel caps.* Dumb not to have used that checklist.
>
> Then I thought, *This is going to be a very embarrassing reason for crashing.* I mean, a fighter pilot can radio back to the base and say, "I just took a missile from a Soviet MIG; I'm going down." That's a classy reason for crashing.
>
> I was gonna have to call in and say, "May Day; I didn't check my fuel caps and I'm sprinkling suburban lawns with airplane fuel." Very embarrassing.

What is the result of this self-mockery? Like many gifted communicators, Hybels establishes a sense of mutuality with the audience. He explains how he feels foolish or embarrassed, and they in turn can identify with him. One unchurched Harry concluded, "I can't spend time poking holes at this guy mentally, because he's poking holes at himself."[26]

Lynne. A regular topic of Hybels's humor is his relationship with his wife, Lynne. Hybels recalls going home one day looking forward to talking to Lynne. Yet Lynne had been frustrated all day as she tried to finish an article she was writing, and she had just gone downstairs to work out. She didn't give Bill the attention he wanted. Hybels began to pout:

> I started to feel my temperature rising. . . . *Yep,* I said to myself as I paged through the magazine, *They don't make wives like they used to make them. Kiss at the door, slippers, smoking jacket, newspaper, glass of milk, "How was your day, honey?"—they don't make wives like they used to make them.*

He sulked, "June Cleaver wouldn't be pumping iron down in her basement if Ward came home and wanted to talk. I mean she'd meet him at the door with a dress and high heels and a glass of milk." By revealing a difficult—yet funny—time in his relationship with Lynne, Hybels enables the audience to laugh and identify with him and then remain attentive as he explained how he dealt with the problem.

Family. Another major source of Hybels's humor is his family. Hybels told a story about Todd, his young, very organized son:

> He got a little crush on a gal. . . . It actually was on one of our female vocalists. . . .
>
> He actually wanted me to take his picture with her. . . . And so I took the picture of this woman and him and she had her arm down on his shoulder and so.

> Well, on the way home we were driving together and he said, "Boy, Dad, I think she's pretty." And I said, "Well, pal, I wouldn't disagree with you there. I think she's a pretty gal."
>
> And then he said, "I'll bet she keeps her stuff real neat." I mean, what do you say? I mean I was, "Yeah, when I was cruising chicks that was high on my priority list too."

This type of humor serves several functions. Hybels identifies with other parents who have stumbled through parenting with their children. A playful reference to Hybels's past removes Hybels's "pastor" image that hinders communication. Lastly, Hybels now has a listening ear from the visiting Harrys, and he can then give Harrys practical parenting tips.

Ongoing jokes. It was not unusual for Hybels and the other speakers to have ongoing jokes with the audience. The audience knows these inside jokes and enjoys being in the know with the speaker.

The Chicago Cubs were a favorite topic of barbed comments. Hybels commented at the end of a talk on intellectual reasons to believe in God, "I was very tempted to add a fifth reason for believing in God, and that is it's September 10 and the Cubs are still in first place."

Another favorite joke around Willow Creek is the Hybels's family tendency to eat health food. Lee Strobel commented on how many of the futuristic predictions from the 1960s turned out to be so foolish: "They said our diets would include algae and ocean seaweed and synthetic protein. Now that came true, but only at Bill Hybels's house." Hybels himself teases his wife about some of her cooking:

> Now for some strange reason my family didn't carry out the custom of the cake and the candles and the wish-making this year.
>
> Probably because the kids and I wouldn't eat the lentil cake that Lynne made last year, and she's still a little hacked about that old thing. I mean, the neighbor dog wouldn't even eat it; so we knew, we knew it was bad.

Because these jokes are ongoing banter, the audience is often willing to laugh when the joke itself is not particularly sharp.

Modern issues. Hybels and his fellow speakers often raise issues from the current news headlines or well-known topics and make a passing joke about them. When Shirley MacLaine got a lot of press about her New Age views, Lee Strobel made the comment,

> You know, Shirley MacLaine can stand on the beach and say, "I am God, I am God" all she wants, but she's never going to be a god named Shirley, if you can imagine a god named Shirley anyway.

The speakers joked about the TV shows *The Simpsons, Roseanne, Thirty Something,* and the growing popularity of frozen yogurt. Unchurched Harry and Mary are familiar with these popular topics and shows.

The speakers also joke about common experiences. Hybels recalls meeting a fellow passenger on an airplane: "We bet on whether or not we'd leave the gate at the appointed time. I won that one; I always win that one—we always leave late." Hybels won a smile of recognition from business travelers who regularly have late flights. The point is that Hybels and his fellow speakers realize that humor needs to be about a world that Harry is familiar with. By joking about current news or modern issues, Hybels is also identifying with Harry.

The Purpose of Hybels's Humor

To identify with Harry. Hybels explains why he likes to use Johnny Carson style humor:

> The reason I like that kind of humor is not only is it kind of consistent with what I appreciate and like and it hits our target audience, but what does it say? . . . It says you're in touch with the world.

More than just being in touch with the world, this kind of humor emphasizes, "We're on the same journey they are." With this type of humor, Hybels can identify with Harry by portraying himself as a realist who understands how the world really works.

To shift Harry's emotional attitude. By making Harry laugh, Hybels can shift his emotional attitude. As Aristotle explained long ago, "Our judgments when we are pleased and friendly are not the same as when we are pained and hostile." Aristotle described that "persuasion may come through the hearers, when the speech stirs their emotions." When the audience becomes more "pleased and friendly," Hybels can more easily influence them.[27]

Hybels's humor satisfies several goals simultaneously. As Hybels explains, "I think it's good to have the kind of humor that communicates on several levels." Hybels can use humor to identify with his audience, take away their defensiveness, and create a positive emotional attitude. Harry then becomes more open to hearing Hybels's message.

10

Christianity Is Relevant

Hybels explains that "almost every weekend" a "target audience seeker guy" will approach him:

> He'll walk up and he'll say, "Boy, I haven't been to church in a long time. What you did right there, kid, what you did right there, was like somebody planned it for me."
>
> I'll say, "Is that right? You really felt that?" "Yeah, it was just like perfect." "Think you'll be coming back?" "Well, of course; who wouldn't come back to something like this?"

This response is what drives Willow Creek. Willow Creekers call this *relevance*.

Hybels began a question and answer period with a group of visiting pastors. "Most of the questions I get in these kinds of seminars have to do with, 'How do you talk *relevantly* to seekers?'" (emphasis added). Vital to Willow Creek's vision is this idea of relevance. I heard or read the words *relevant* or *relevance* hundreds of times during my study of Willow Creek. What is *relevance?* What does it mean to speak relevantly to seekers?

When Creekers discuss the idea of relevance, the original church survey is often mentioned. As I noted in chapter 2, before the church was begun, Hybels and a few others asked hundreds of suburbanites why they didn't go to church. They heard that people didn't relate to churches' music or message. Those polled said church services were boring, irrelevant, and made them feel guilty.

As I stated in chapter 4, the entire programming of the weekend service is designed to respond to these concerns and acts as a funnel to move people into a place where Hybels's message begins. Hybels then attempts to respond to what has been asked during the rest of the program. He explains, "We need to start where they are and then bring them along."[1]

Relevance is starting where Harry is. In terms of the message, Hybels believes that the doorway into the heart of unchurched Harry and Mary is with topics that interest them: "Unchurched people today are the ultimate consumers. . . . For every sermon we preach, they're asking, *Am I interested in that subject or not?*" (author's emphasis).[2]

Felt Needs

What interests Harry the most are his felt needs. Lee Strobel asserts, "Harry is no longer loyal to denominations, but he is attracted to places where his needs will be met." George Barna exhorts pastors to focus on the felt needs of the unchurched:

> The best way to get the unchurched or nonbelievers to consider the Church valid and worthwhile will be by making ourselves *relevant* to their lives. How do we do that? By understanding their most pressing *felt needs* and responding directly to those needs [emphasis added].[3]

What is the result of this focus on Harry's felt needs? As one might expect, attendance increases for series that are particularly focused on them. When Lee Strobel spoke on "The Rewards of Spiritual Risk Taking," the total weekend attendance was only 11,425. When Hybels began a series on relationships the next week, the attendance jumped by nearly 25 percent to 14,048. Harrys responded in droves. Why? Harry is interested in satisfying his felt needs.[4]

Felt needs are the road to relevance. Mittelberg explains this principle:

> We have to learn to be relevant and give messages that are applicable to the people that we're reaching. In other words, they have to relate to their daily life, their relationships, their families, their workplace.

If the message fulfills this criteria, Harry is motivated to attend, to listen, and to act on what he hears.[5]

When Hybels discusses the myths of marital life to introduce his series on relationships, Harry is all ears:

> I'd like to spend a few minutes this morning unmasking three very widely held myths about marriage. Namely, one, that marriage will automatically end your aloneness. Two, that marriage will automatically heal your brokenness. And three, that marriage will insure your happiness.

Hybels connects the series with three things that Harry wants or "needs." Harry doesn't want to be lonely or broken and Harry wants to be happy. Thus Harry wants to learn about this topic and will attend.

An evidence of the focus on felt needs is the number of need-related words that are used during the weekend service. Over the course of the year, the words *need, needs, feel, feeling, feelings, problem, wanted, pain, broken, disappointment,* and *hope* were used regularly during the messages. Hybels uses these and other emotion-related words to describe how people are seeking to be healed by marriage:

> I don't have to remind this congregation about how much *brokenness* there is in today's world.
>
> Record numbers of young people are growing up in homes where there's not a lot of *happiness;* homes affected by *divorce,* homes *devastated by alcoholism, homes where there's been violence, or verbal or emotional abuse,* or even homes where *love didn't flow* freely for one reason or another. . . .
>
> They're *hoping* against *hope* that this person can *heal their brokenness* or at least *make their pain subside* for a time. You see, a *wounded* young person lives with a lot of covered up *pain* and *disappointment* [emphasis added].

Harry and Mary identify with these descriptions of pain and disappointment. Hybels then provides practical teaching on how Harry's felt needs can be satisfied.[6]

These felt needs are often about everyday issues. An example is a series at the church on parenting. Unchurched Harrys felt the need for counsel in parenting and flocked to hear. Most of Hybels's messages are directed at Harry's daily life. As one unchurched Harry told me, "His messages were so well aimed—just bam, where it hits people." All of these felt needs could be summarized in one dominating concern—Harry's personal fulfillment.[7]

Personal Fulfillment

We observed in chapter 4 that the primary motivation of unchurched Harry is his own personal fulfillment. As Barna writes, "What do we want out of life? Our surveys suggest that we have four primary goals, all related to 'being happy.'" Willow Creek, in seeking to be relevant to Harry, teaches a lot about human happiness.[8]

I mentioned in the last chapter that after my research there were seven files that were much larger than any others. I listed five of these files at that time. The sixth huge file was Fulfillment, to which there were hundreds of references over the course of the year. As Lee Strobel writes, "Unchurched Harry is always ready to listen when the topic is how he can benefit."[9]

Hybels gives an annual "It talk" that is entirely on personal fulfillment:

> It strikes me that it may be time for me to give my annual "It talk," which is simply a recount of my own quest for soul satisfaction that began when I had an existential crisis concerning the meaning and purpose of my life when I was about five years old.
>
> I mean after long hours of soul searching in the sandbox of my backyard, I concluded that my soul could be thoroughly and eternally satisfied if only I had a new two-wheeled bike. . . .
>
> I got a two-wheeled bike and in three days I reached the disconcerting conclusion that this bike was nice to pedal around the neighborhood, but it wasn't "It."[10]

Hybels describes how over the course of his life he became convinced how a different "It" would bring fulfillment. In junior high he wanted a starting position on the basketball team, and in high school he longed for a relationship with "Betty Lu."

Hybels reveals that none of these "Its" satisfied him. He explains how people acquire "the right car," "the right college," "the right job," and "the right house" in their pursuit of fulfillment. Then he describes how people searching for soul satisfaction get married and have kids. He argues that none of these ultimately satisfy.

When individuals realize this, Hybels argues, some say, "Maybe I should buy more expensive toys, climb to higher positions in the marketplace, attain more fame, arrange more fun fixes, find younger and sexier Betty Lus." Hybels attempts to show the weakness of this strategy. He portrays King Solomon from the Old Testament as someone who tried "to crack the code of human fulfillment":

> He finally came clean and he said, "You know what it's gonna take to satisfy the human soul? The person is gonna have to fear God and follow him fully. Because when he does that, God assumes the responsibility of providing soul satisfaction.

Hybels explains that Christians often use *filled* or *filled up* to "describe soul satisfaction." Hybels asks the Harrys in attendance, "I wonder how many of you are really feeling filled these days?" Harrys who aren't feeling particularly happy are all ears.[11]

And the message of how Christianity is the source of true fulfillment is what they hear. Hybels teaches about the Christian way of life:

> This loftier kind of dream, if pursued, will not only fulfill you but will lead to spiritual growth and relational warmth and emotional health and physical strength in your life. Anybody interested?[12]

The reason why Christianity is the more fulfilling way of life, according to Hybels, is that God made it that way: "God made us. He made our minds and our taste buds and our nerves and our innermost souls, and *He knows how to make us truly fulfilled and happy*" (author's emphasis). To use marketing terms, Hybels links fulfillment, Harry's need, with Christianity, Hybels's product.[13]

I should clarify at this point that Hybels doesn't teach a health and wealth gospel. He emphasizes at times that the Christian life has great difficulties and that life is not a bed of roses:

> Let's get this straight: God does not guarantee anywhere in the Bible that Christians will live trouble-free lives. . . .
>
> If you're considering Christianity or if you're trying to live it out, don't expect your Christian life to be a life of perfect bliss.[14]

He has even compared evangelists who promise, "You'll never have problems again" to deceitful used-car salesmen. We don't hear from Hybels the simplistic claim, "Jesus can take all your troubles away!"[15]

But we do hear, "God is committed to helping you see the wisdom of exchanging aspirations, trading in the futility of the American Dream for the fulfillment of a higher kind of dream." Hybels teaches that there are three aspects to the fulfillment that comes from Christianity.[16]

An Intimate Relationship with God

Hybels believes that everyone wants to be happy: "You can't lie to me. Every one of you wants that, everyone here." According to Hybels, Harry's search for happiness is a foolish endeavor because Harry is looking in the wrong place. Hybels argues that only when people turn to God will they experience true fulfillment: "Only a trust-filled relationship with God can satisfy those longings." He continues:

> When your soul is filled with the love of God and when your life is achieving the purposes of God, then you will sense the smile of God, which is satisfaction of the soul.

Hybels depicts this relationship with God as something that needs time and attention to grow. And as the relationship grows, so does the fulfillment:

> Either we're on an upward trajectory, we're soaring spiritually, our relationship with God is deepening day after day after day. It's getting more and more fulfilling, or we're spiritually stagnant.

An Adventurous Cause

A central theme at Willow Creek is that the Christian life is an adventure. Strobel describes how many Harrys hesitate to make a commitment to Christ—because they don't want to give up the excitement in their lives:

> They're afraid that if they receive Christ as their forgiver and as their leader that they're gonna lose out on all the excitement in life.
>
> "Say, you know, am I going to be able to go out and party anymore? Am I gonna be able to have fun anymore? Am I gonna be able to be aggressive at work anymore?"[17]

In response, Strobel claims, "The Christian life is uniquely exciting." He asserts, "If you sign up for this kind of spiritual safari . . . it's more exciting than any kind of a safari that a travel agent can book you on." Hybels teaches that once individuals make a commitment to Christianity, they are starting a new adventure, "the adventure of following Christ—which is the thrill that really fulfills."[18]

Strobel portrays the Christian life as an adventure because individuals get to participate in God's mission or cause. "When we enlist in this Christian adventure we have a commander that we can count on. We have a mission that matters. We have equipment that's unequaled." Strobel questions those who are sitting on the spiritual sidelines, "Where's the fulfillment for somebody who just glides through life making himself comfortable?" According to Willow Creek, the joy of victory comes to those who are on the field.

The thrill of victory is given extra voltage because the cause is eternal. Hybels contrasts the self-centered life with a life that is centered on an eternal cause: "I'm living with a keen awareness that my life is counting for something beyond myself." He continues, "When you start using that endowment from God, just watch the fulfillment factor, the thrill factor in your life, go up because then you feel God using you to advance a cause." Hybels teaches that God "doesn't want us to live an aimless and haphazard life but he wants us to be fulfilled and satisfied." This fulfillment comes from being a participant in God's eternal cause.

Serving Other People

Hybels and the other teachers regularly teach the weekend audience that the cause they are signing up for is to serve people. Yet serving is not pictured primarily as sacrificial but as another means of fulfillment. Don Cousins teaches:

> The great psychiatrist Karl Menninger was once asked what a lonely unhappy person should do. His counsel was this: "Lock the door behind you, go across the street, and find someone who is hurting and help them." It's pretty sound advice.

Cousins argues that many have followed the opposite advice with disastrous effect.[19]

Cousins asserts that fulfillment comes only when one begins to serve others:

> From the background of the Scripture, self-gratification will never bring you true fulfillment. It will never inspire you. It will never motivate you. . . .
>
> It will never energize you. No, fulfillment and inspiration come from making a contribution and an investment in the lives of others. That's when you get a return.[20]

Attenders are taught that fulfillment is the natural result of serving in the church: "Personal fulfillment in good part follows after fruitfulness," Hybels says. Strobel teaches attenders to think about the positive effect for themselves when they serve others: "Think about not only the benefit to other people, but think about the benefit to yourself when that transformation begins to take place."[21]

In essence Hybels teaches Harry that Christianity will satisfy his felt needs and make him happy. We see this clearly in the specific felt needs that Hybels addresses.

Hybels addressed twelve different felt needs over the course of the year I studied. He argued that Christianity is the best means to solve these problems and satisfy these desires and help individuals become fulfilled. Hybels taught about the individual felt needs of anxiety, pain, meaning, anger, identity, and self-esteem and the relational felt needs of loneliness, marriage, sex, parenting, and work and success.[22]

Hybels teaches that true fulfillment comes as the result of beginning to live as God has designed us to and that individuals gain fulfillment when they focus on living as God wants them to live. Hybels and the other speakers often use examples of very successful individuals who found fulfillment in the church:

> Around here, we have corporate presidents and executives and they say, "Yeah, I like my career. My career is great, it's wonderful. I really enjoy it.
>
> "But this, this has a special *fulfillment,* what I do around here. This is investing in something that's gonna last. This is something that's going to pay dividends in eternity" [emphasis added].

Willow Creek presents Christianity as the solution to people's felt needs with fulfillment as the result. Hybels calls this kind of teaching "Christianity 101."

11

Christianity 101

Hybels argues that Christianity is the best means for Harry to satisfy his felt needs and be happy. Hybels calls this helpful teaching "Christianity 101" or "User-friendly Doctrine."

The Purpose of Christianity 101

Hybels teaches pastors how to preach relevantly:

> The main thing seekers want is to be touched by a "so what" factor. Their greatest fear in coming to a church service is the fact that the Bible isn't relevant to their life.
>
> So make it relevant. Up the "so what" factor and you'll be doing good preaching.

This "so what" factor is showing Harry that Christianity will help him in his quest for personal happiness.

Evangelism director Mittelberg explains, "We're seeing more and more that Harry relates to a message that shows how Christianity helps his daily life more than how he can make sure he'll get to heaven in thirty or forty years." Mittelberg believes that Harry wants to know:

> Where is the daily cash value now? How does this affect today and tomorrow? And so we want to show not only that knowing Christ will lead us to heaven but we also want to point out that Christianity is the better way to live.

Strobel teaches, "Harry doesn't just ask, 'Is Christianity true?' Often he's asking, 'Does Christianity work?'" Strobel reveals his goal in speaking "is to help this new generation of Unchurched Harrys understand that

Christianity does work." Hybels explains, "The messages must have high user value. When Unchurched Harry comes out here for a service, he's going to be asking, 'What value does my being here have for my life?'"[1]

Hybels's agenda of messages is taken from Harry's priorities. The underlying idea is from marketing theory. Marketing guru Philip Kotler explains, "The guiding concept is *utility*. . . . Utility is the consumer's estimate of the product's capacity to satisfy his or her needs" (author's emphasis). If Hybels can show Christianity's utility as a means to fulfillment, it will correspondingly be more attractive to Harry.[2]

The primary purpose of Hybels's Christianity 101 is to help unchurched Harry. If Hybels can show that Christianity works, that it is helpful in meeting Harry's felt needs and fostering greater personal happiness, Harry will be interested and hang around. Hybels's ultimate goal is to get Harry to understand the gospel and make a commitment to Christ. Christianity 101 is a means to this end.

While the primary goal of a weekend talk is to help the visiting unchurched Harrys, a secondary goal is to feed the Christians who are attending. When I suggested this observation to Lee Strobel, he responded:

> That's a very good observation. Because it's a major misunderstanding about what we do on the weekends. People who hear what we do think that we do a purely evangelistic service.
>
> If you do a purely evangelistic service, only really talking to the seekers every week, your regular attenders are . . . going to start getting dry and they're not going to be motivated to come on the weekends to bring a seeker.

As a result, Willow Creek speakers design their talks to address two different audiences. On the one hand, they are helping the visiting Harrys take the next step in a spiritual search: "If you don't know him this morning. . . ." Secondarily, they are feeding the Christians: "For those of you who know him already . . ." Strobel explains:

> You've got to feed both. And so you intentionally have to build things into your message to satisfy the needs of the Christians to grow spiritually and primarily to meet the needs of the seekers. So in every message you've got to have two tracks.

Yet the content for this second track for Christians is primarily the Christianity 101. Although Christianity 101 contains a substantial amount of helpful, how-to-live teaching, its central purpose is to show Harry how Christianity is relevant. Ultimately Creekers realize that this second track cannot really provide the meat and potatoes edification that Christians need to grow spiritually. As Cousins argues, "Can teachers edify believers and evangelize the lost at the same time? At Willow Creek, we concluded that we couldn't; the two audiences are too different." Christians in the weekend audience are taught the same Christianity 101 that Harry receives.[3]

The Content of Christianity 101

There are four elements in the teaching of Christianity 101: Scripture, illustrations, practical how-tos, and psychology.

Scripture

Scripture is a central element of the weekend services. Hybels and the other speakers referred to specific Scripture verses a total of 169 times over the course of the year I studied. The words *Bible* and *Scripture(s)* were used 328 and 83 times respectively. The point is, Scripture was regularly referred to (an average of 10.74 times each message) during the weekend talks. Yet more important than the question, How much was Scripture used? is the question, How was Scripture used? Scripture was used topically and was paraphrased.

Topically

Hybels teaches topically during the weekend services. He begins his discussion by trying to clarify why Harry should listen to him, and thus he often addresses one of Harry's felt needs. Hybels attempts to get Harry to agree with him before he ever refers to the Bible: "I usually have to start at a point of agreement," he says. Only at this point does Hybels feel comfortable introducing the Scripture:

> And then I go on and say, "The Scriptures also say. . . ." I've taken them from a point of contact that we agree on and I've worked them toward the point where Scripture says . . . the same basic kind of thing.

Hybels often applies a Bible verse to the topic at hand to tack down the outline of his argument. Thus Scripture is raised topically and is not taught verse by verse. As a result, Hybels's use of Scripture tends to reflect the strategy that has already been outlined in this book. Hybels often refers to verses that support his argument that Christianity is a more fulfilling way of life.

Luke 15 was the chapter in the Bible most often mentioned during the weekend messages. On seven different occasions, this passage was used to underline God's love and concern for the lost. Ecclesiastes 2 was used to prove that pleasure and work do not bring fulfillment. John 10:10, "I have come that they may have life, and have it to the full," was used four times to highlight Willow Creek's message that a relationship with Jesus brings fulfillment.

I also organized a topical index of the 169 specific verses that were quoted over the year. The most popular topic (21 references) was how to have better relationships. The second most common topic (13 references) was about human nature and why people were made for a relationship with God. Another topic with 13 references dealt with how people can begin to live the Christian life. All of these topics were related to why Christianity makes individuals more fulfilled (12 references). Willow Creek's canon within the canon is how human beings can be fulfilled.[4]

The evangelistic method of using topical messages is not new. For example, Billy Graham is known for the saying, "The Bible says" as a way of referring to Bible verses topically during his sermons. Hybels often uses this phrase and its equivalent, "Jesus said," as a way of introducing Bible verses. What is distinctive is not Hybels's topical method, but his strong message: Christianity will fulfill unchurched Harry.

Paraphrased

When Hybels referred to the Bible, the actual Scripture verse was often paraphrased, not quoted. For example, Hybels described the story of the woman caught in adultery being brought before Jesus: "'I forgive this sin,' Jesus says, 'but proof that you are deeply repentant is that you are willing to forsake this behavior by the power of the Holy Spirit in your life.'"[5]

While paraphrasing, Hybels often modernizes the language. Hybels once referred to Luke 17:11, in which ten lepers approach Jesus for healing. Hybels said, "They look at each other and they say, I wonder if he does lepers? I mean, he does all other kinds of healings, does he do lepers?" At times this modernizing can be so extreme that Hybels uses it as a joke, as in his paraphrase of 2 Samuel 24: "[King] David looked back at Joab and said, 'Take a hike. I mean, who wears the robe in this palace, you or me?'"

Instead of describing the historical particulars of an ancient Bible story, Hybels often puts the story in modern terms. For example, he relates, "There's a story of a tax collector named Zacchaeus. He was a very wealthy, white-collar, management type of guy." Hybels paraphrases the passage in 2 Samuel 24 where King David orders a count of the fighting men of Israel: "So David barked out the order, 'Number the troops. I want you to count every buck private, every MP, every cook and bottle washer. I want to know the grand total of my military might.'"

The result of this paraphrasing is that sometimes the Bible tales sound like modern stories. For example, Hybels's description of Jesus sounds like civil rights leader Martin Luther King: "Jesus went from city to city essentially saying, 'I have a dream. I have a dream—a dream of establishing the kingdom of God here on this earth.'"

At times Hybels paraphrases by summarizing a larger portion of Scripture. Hybels condenses Romans 1 by saying, "Paul says that 'the entire human race can be divided into two camps; the camp filled with true worshipers and the camp of non-worshipers.'" He summarizes the book of Ecclesiastes: "'I,' Solomon announces, 'did not find soul satisfaction through self-gratification, and I took the pleasure road as far as it could be taken.'"

Hybels's reasoning behind this paraphrasing is clear. He believes Harry is not interested in the Bible. Harry is preoccupied by his own felt needs and in being fulfilled. Hybels by his paraphrasing is attempting to isolate an idea from a particular Bible text and show its relevance for Harry. Hybels is seeking to simplify a biblical concept and translate it into modern terms. The goal behind this translation is to make biblical ideas understandable and helpful.

Illustrations

Hybels reportedly said at a workshop on public speaking that there are three principles to effective communication: "Number one, illustrate; number two, illustrate; number three, illustrate." It is an understatement to say that Hybels regularly uses illustrations to get across his point. The seventh and largest of the huge files I compiled about the weekend service was Illustrations.

Hybels uses illustrations to make his teaching more vivid and palatable for Harry. Illustrations are the language of images that Hybels uses to connect with Harry's memory and imagination. While a dull communication of theological information might bore Harry, stories provide an opportunity to educate with a smile. Hybels uses a variety of illustrations.

Contemporary Illustrations

Hybels regularly uses contemporary illustrations to grab and focus Harry's attention. Hybels explains, "I select 60 to 70 percent of my illustrations from current events." These illustrations could also be about political and popular figures or current books and movies.[6]

When a major issue or topic hits the headlines in American society, Hybels often uses it as an illustration. A best-selling book, *Bonfire of the Vanities,* was made into a feature motion picture. When Hybels was trying to depict the nature of individualism, he described the main character of this book and movie:

> The main character in Tom Wolfe's best-selling novel *Bonfire of the Vanities* is a young investment banking individualist named Sherman McCoy. Now Sherman McCoy psychs himself up for his daily challenge by repeating to himself the words, *I am master of the universe. I am master of the universe.*

Hybels then described how McCoy's life unravels when he and his mistress are involved in a nasty hit-and-run accident. McCoy is left confused and scared. The master of the universe ends up neither being a master nor having a universe. Hybels uses this illustration as a modern parable of the ultimate failure of the search for success and to enflesh Proverbs 14:12, "There is a way that seems right to a man, but in the end it leads to death." By using an example from the previous week's movie screen, Hybels identified with the visiting Harrys. By using the image of a businessman, Hybels told a story that Harry could relate to.

Personal Illustrations

Hybels and his fellow speakers often use personal illustrations to communicate an idea they are discussing. This kind of illustration may be from their own experience or someone else's. Strobel describes how when his daughter was born, she had severe physical problems:

> I saw my little girl in the incubator, just in a diaper and just this blank look in her eyes and all these things hooked up to her and her little heart pounding away. I was soft toward God right then. . . .
>
> I prayed the kind of prayer that atheists pray sometimes that they don't tell you about, which is, *Dear God, I don't know if you're there; I don't believe you're there; but if you are, please help my little girl, because I can't do anything.*

Strobel tells how his daughter eventually got better and how as a result, he continued to ignore God:

> We just let this window of opportunity just sort of slip shut. I mean I didn't even acknowledge that my prayer had been answered, just went back to life as usual. It was the comfort of the status quo.

By describing his own pain, Strobel gets Harry's attention. By acknowledging how he failed to respond to God's overtures, Strobel underlines how he is similar to Harry. Lastly, by depicting the result of ignoring God, Strobel underlines how much he missed out on—by not responding earlier. Harry sees himself in the mirror of Strobel's personal confession.

Biblical Illustrations

Hybels sometimes tells Bible stories as illustrations of a principle that he is already discussing. When Hybels tries to explain what individualism is, he turns to a Bible story:

> The best way to look at individualism is to look at the quintessential individualist in the Bible, the guy in Luke 15. . . .
>
> Here's a young man who apparently grew up in a stable, loving home under the direction of a wise and godly dad. He probably had plenty of friends, a good position in the family business. . . .
>
> That voice in the caverns of his consciousness would whisper to him, *Why do you put up with all the authority and structure in your life?*

By expanding and dramatizing a Bible story, Hybels is trying to make it illustrate an idea. Rather than exegeting the passage, he illustrates his idea with the story. In this instance, Hybels is attempting to describe the internal thoughts of the prodigal son and then show the consequences of these ideas. Hybels is warning Harry through the story to be wary of the same sort of mistake.

Story Illustrations

Hybels frequently tells stories. Some of these stories might only be a few sentences long, a sort of verbal snapshot. Others could only be described as a verbal documentary and go on for a good portion of that day's message.

In some verbal snapshots, Hybels refers to the drama for that day:

> Some of you right now are groaning and thinking, *Now that's not so fun; I mean, I want to do what the couple in the drama did, spend more time necking on the couch than getting all serious about building into the relationship.*
>
> I don't think any of you building relationships want to end up in the therapist's office, like our drama couple did. You don't want to be in that kind of trouble, do you? So I would just urge you to give me a listen for the next few moments.

In this verbal snapshot Hybels describes the problem of young couples not dealing with difficult issues before they get married. Hybels then underlines the proverb by warning that without this process, couples will end up in the therapist's office.

Hybels also regularly has long documentary illustrations that tell a substantial story. When Hybels was speaking on moralism, he told a long story of how he explained Christianity to someone sitting next to him on an air flight the previous week. Two-thirds of that week's talk (a full twenty pages) was Hybels's retelling his conversation with his seatmate. As Hybels told this story, he was also explaining the gospel to the audience.

Because Hybels was telling a story, somehow the audience seemed to be paying better attention. Hybels was able to draw people into the drama of the encounter, and they began to wonder what would happen next. With his stories, Hybels is trying to motivate Harry to accept his practical guidance.

Practical How-tos

Hybels and his colleagues tell Harry what to do and how to do it. As Cousins said one week in a series, "Next week we'll go a step further and talk about the 'how-tos.'"

Many of these how-tos are about relationship issues. Harrys and Marys who are dealing with difficult relationship problems are very open to these helpful suggestions. Hybels and his fellow teachers regularly give practical suggestions on how to build stronger relationships. For example, during one series on bringing out the best in people, Cousins gave numerous practical suggestions:

> I'm gonna kind of give you, in the remainder of our time . . . a grocery list of ideas that I think if you were to apply, you would find that they would indeed help you in bringing out the best in others.

One of Cousins's suggestions was to write short appreciation notes. "Whenever possible, put it in writing. There is something magical about a note."

The messages are structured in such a way that there is potential for application even when the topic may not directly apply. When Hybels taught a series on marriage, he tried to put in a substantial amount of practical principles for singles:

> I did a series some years back called "Fanning the Flames of Marriage." I . . . kept enough user value in the series so that singles could make carry-overs to their own friendships.

Occasionally Hybels gives the audience "homework." Toward the end of a series on relationships, Hybels explained:

> The first homework assignment is to arrange a talk in an unrushed setting, you and your spouse, and find out how many disconnects are caused by your pace of life. . . .
>
> Part B to that first homework assignment is then list three practical ways to declare war on your runaway pace.

Harry is motivated to do these homework assignments, as they are designed to help him with his felt needs.

This pattern of practical suggestions is a regular feature of Willow Creek's messages. Certain practical principles are often repeated. As Hybels teaches, "I've mentioned some of these little tips or rules before, but let me just repeat a few of them in this context."

"How-to" messages are what some Creekers call "horizontal" or "helpful" messages. Instead of dealing with Harry's vertical relationship with God, a horizontal talk is designed to help Harry live with himself and other people. Hybels provides Harry with bite-size pieces of Christianity to understand and apply.

Strobel believes that during this process, "Something that's very subtle is happening on an apologetic level." He explains that when Harry comes to Willow Creek he hears and then begins to apply some of these practical principles:

> They come and they begin to learn some principles that they can apply in their lives that work. They work because they are biblical. Because they are from God.
>
> They don't buy that yet, but they can make their parenting skills sharper and better, based on Bill's series he just did on parenthood, even if they're not Christians.

After Harry goes home and applies these principles, Strobel argues, he is more open to Christianity:

> You can take a lot of these principles and apply them. And as they do that they begin to see that, "Wow, there is some relevance to my life! The Bible seems to have some relevance for me today." I think that establishes a credibility.

Some of these practical principles the speaker has discovered in the Bible. Some he has learned in his own life. Cousins has said, "Let me give you some practical ideas that have worked for me over the years."

Psychology

Another basic source for these practical principles is the psychological worldview of the American culture. To understand the use of psychology in Willow Creek's messages, we first need to sketch the broader role of psychology in American culture.

Psychology in American Culture

Melody Beattie's book *Codependent No More* has sold more than four million copies. *Time* magazine calls Beattie the "queen of codependence" and pictures her as urging "her readers to 'have clear boundaries,' 'let go of the victim belief,' and, most of all, 'take care of yourselves.'" Although Beattie hasn't received academic training in psychology, she has been able to mix together a palatable stew of psychological ideas, "New Age mysticism" and American self-improvement.[7]

Beattie is one author among hundreds who have popularized a psychological worldview in American society. Popular American culture is dominated by the priorities and categories of psychology. In advice columns or on an *Oprah* show, psychological categories dictate how people understand themselves and how they should live. In fact, a talk show isn't complete unless a psychologist is there to decree why one participant is "codependent" and another is "controlling."[8]

We see an illustration of this in television programming. The only difference between the senior staff of the 1960s *Star Trek* crew and the 1980s *Star Trek: Next Generation* is the addition of a counselor. The counselor regularly advises the captain or provides therapy for a crew member. This staff change in an imaginary star ship is actually a reflection of a shift in the popularity of psychological ideas in American society.[9]

Psychological language has become the primary moral vocabulary of Americans. As a result, those who are seeking to communicate with Americans often use this language. An example is the 1992 presidential campaign: Bill Clinton and Al Gore subtly and effectively used psychological language to reach voters. *Time* magazine summarizes Clinton's self-description:

> Clinton led the national show-and-tell with a tour of the stations of his own life—his father's death in a car accident, his stepfather's drunkenness, his half-brother's drug addiction, his mother's breast cancer. . . .
>
> It's like a 12-step program, minus appeals to a Higher Power.[10]

Likewise Al Gore expressed himself in language that speaks to this psychological culture. *Time* magazine describes Gore:

> Poster boy for self-discovery, the Senator has found a voice that resonates with an angst-ridden generation. . . .
>
> The Tennessean can subtly slip into words like "dysfunction" and "inner child" as adroitly as his supporters buckle on their Birkenstocks.
>
> He makes eye contact when someone talks about "letting go." In conversation, Gore offers Zen-like nuggets like, "Sometimes you can only find something by losing it."[11]

Clinton and Gore were attractive candidates to those who use this language and its moral framework.

Psychology in the Weekend Messages

There is similar use of psychological language in the weekend messages at Willow Creek. Hybels and his fellow speakers regularly use psychological terms to describe the Christian life. The leaders of Willow Creek admitted in interviews that a significant amount of weekend messages' content comes from psychology. One management team member explained:

> A large chunk of the teaching . . . has been focused on psychological principles. . . . Dysfunctional problems, realities in families, dealing with issues in terms of self-understanding—all that kind of stuff—rage, relationships, dating, all of them dealing with a lot of psychological categories and concepts.

The following is a brief list of a number of these categories or ideas, followed by a quote or two to show how each was used in a weekend message.

Self-identity. "For most of us who are honest to admit it, our vocations have a lot to do with our sense of self-identity and self-worth." "[King] David was caught in the midst of kind of an identity crisis."[12]

Temperament. "Just as a person is born with either brown hair or blond hair, green eyes or blue eyes, rather tall or rather small, a person is also born with a totally unique temperament type."

Family history. "You discuss family backgrounds because it's the single greatest determiner of personal identity. . . . You discuss family backgrounds because the family is the single greatest cause of deep, personal pain." "My guess is that many of you have some work to do in peeling back some of the layers of your past, so that you can resolve some of the issues."

Importance of emotions. Hybels asks the audience, "Do you understand this first emotion/second emotion concept?" and then exegetes Cain and Abel's emotions in Genesis 4: "If you read between the lines you get the idea—here is the older brother and he sort of got shown up by the younger brother, and he's probably feeling embarrassed and humiliated, outdone; maybe he feels like a loser. But he hates feeling those feelings."

Self-analysis. "One little phrase that the apostle Paul said to young Timothy in 1 Timothy 4:16 is real important to me. It says, 'Pay close attention to yourself.' Pay close attention to yourself. And that phrase has motivated me more than once to try to really pry off the cover and get at the roots of what's really going on in my life." "If your anger quotient is fairly high, what's at the root of it? What's at the root of your anger? Who let you down? Who disappointed you?"

Addiction. "The first hidden danger associated with overactivating the pleasures in your life is . . . the problem of addiction." "The more they hooked into that activation they became addicted. . . . They just couldn't stop after a time."

Self-esteem. "Our self-esteem soars because we realize that the Son of God valued us so much that he was willing to be put to death on the cross to pay for the sins and the wrongs that you and I have committed. I mean, how can anyone's self-esteem suffer when he knows that God cares about him that much?"

Boundaries. "Boundaries are territorial lines that help us define relationships. Boundaries enable us to build close relationships with family members and friends without losing that very critical sense of separateness that defines who we are as individuals." Hybels paraphrases how Jesus responded to Peter after Peter had asked what was going to happen to John. "Boundaries Peter. You deal with what is within your territorial lines and let John deal with what is within his territorial lines. Stay within your boundaries."

Control issues and conflict resolution. "There's a high probability you're gonna have to wrestle with control issues—Who's in charge here?" "Use the time in your courtship phase to come to grips with . . . each other's conflict resolution patterns."

Hybels not only teaches psychological principles, but often uses the psychological principles as interpretative guides for his exegesis of Scripture. We learn in the above quotes that King David had an identity crisis, the apostle Paul encouraged Timothy to do self-analysis, and Peter had a problem with boundary issues. The point is, psychological principles are regularly built into Hybels's teaching.

I heard several reasons given why this use of psychological principles was necessary. One management team member explained, "Sometimes in order for folks to understand . . . how to apply certain biblical principles, they have to understand themselves and others first." A Willow Creek counselor justified this use of psychological terminology and therapy: "The type of emotional issues we're having today, in my mind, are more complex than back then" in New Testament times. Whatever the reasons, there is a regular diet of categories from the modern psychological worldview in Hybels's Christianity 101.

12

Christianity Is True

As I have shown, Hybels's first argument for Christianity is "it works." This argument leads to the second argument in the Willow Creek arsenal: "It's true." Strobel declares:

> Our challenge, then, is to help this new generation of Unchurched Harrys understand that Christianity *does* work. . . . But we need to communicate that the *reason* it works is because it's *true* [author's emphasis].[1]

Strobel explains, "Because the Bible is God's revelation to his people, it contains a kind of practical and effective help that's unmatched by mere human philosophers."[2]

This dual strategy comes from Willow Creek's understanding of Harry. Strobel asserts:

> The nature of Harry's questions is evolving over time. For many, especially the younger generation, truth isn't an issue because they have become convinced that all religious viewpoints are equally valid. It's the old, "You have your truth and I have mine."[3]

As philosopher Allan Bloom has written, most college students believe "that truth is relative." The majority of Willow Creek's college-educated audience have received a strong dose of this philosophical relativism. Proclaiming that Christianity is true is both irrelevant and trite to such a relativist.[4]

This is why Willow Creek starts with Harry's felt needs and uses the pragmatic argument "Christianity works." This process is designed to create interest in Christianity and to show its value to Harry. Mittelberg explains that the goal of being relevant is to get a hostile Harry to become a curious Harry.

Once a hostile Harry is stirred out of his passive apathy to curiosity, he is open to intellectual persuasion. At this point, Hybels argues that Christianity is the true explanation of reality. Hybels's goal with this step of the strategy is to help curious Harrys become sincere Harrys and to help sincere Harrys become Christians. There are two elements to this argument.

On one hand, Hybels argues that there is substantial historical and philosophical evidence that Christianity is the true explanation of reality. On the other hand, Hybels argues that Harry's current belief system is not true. I will call these parallel rationales "foundational arguments" and "destabilizing arguments," respectively. These two arguments are Willow Creek's approach to the Christian discipline of apologetics.[5]

Apologetics is generally considered to be the Christian discipline of historical and philosophical arguments for the truthfulness of Christianity. Understood in this way, apologetics is a defensive discipline providing reasons why Christianity is intellectually credible.

The idea of destabilization is different from this popular understanding of apologetics. Destabilization is not a defensive process, but an offensive one. Mittelberg explains:

> We challenge his [unchurched Harry's] conclusions and work toward the establishment of the intelligibility of the Christian position. We take away his intellectual reasons—and excuses—for rejecting Christ.[6]

This strategy attacks unchurched Harry's beliefs that would resist Christianity's truth claims.

Destabilizing Arguments

A large part of Hybels's argument that Christianity is true is the complementary argument that Harry's view of reality is false. Before Harry will be interested in considering Christianity as an alternative worldview, he must be willing to consider leaving his present worldview. Hybels uses arguments to destabilize Harry's worldview to encourage this process. As evangelism director Mittelberg states, "Our job is to point out their bias, demonstrate how the facts go against any nontheistic conclusions they've made, and then challenge them."[7]

Destabilizing arguments can be used in several ways. A destabilizing argument can be used to shake up a hostile Harry, to help make him curious about Christianity's truth claims. Once a curious Harry begins to show some interest in Christ, a destabilizing argument is a means of motivating him to make a commitment to become a sincere seeker. Lastly, a destabilizing argument is used to show a sincere Harry that his present philosophy is not tenable, to get him to accept Christianity.

Sociological theory describes this process as "nihilation," a procedure by which one worldview seeks to discredit an opposing worldview. The word *nihilation* comes from "nihilism"—the philosophical system that rejects the existence of meaning. In essence, this process of nihilation (discrediting or destabilizing) pushes an individual toward nihilism (the loss of meaning).

Nihilation puts tension on Harry's worldview and causes Harry to feel unable to adequately explain his world. When a person's worldview is discredited, that individual feels a loss of meaning (nihilism). Mittelberg explains, "What we need to do in apologetics is to test the adequacy of" Harry's worldview. "We must point out at what point the nonbeliever's thinking has gone wrong in an effort to turn him or her to Christ." Hybels describes the goal of this strategy:

> Maybe by taking this assault strategy, this frontal approach, we can create enough action and create enough chaos in people's minds that some conversations will flow that will eventually help some of us a little.

Hybels sees this process of creating "chaos," or destabilization, as an integral part of the process of persuasion. Before one can build a new worldview, one must break down the old.[8]

The word that is commonly used to describe the disorienting experience of a lack of meaning in one's experience is *anomie*. Peter Berger defines *anomie* as "a condition of rootlessness, disorientation, of no longer feeling at home in the world." The etymological root of *anomie* is the Greek word for law—*nomos*. To lose one's worldview is to be left lawless or normless. One who experiences anomie feels disoriented and becomes correspondingly more open to considering a new worldview. This process of creating anomie is the goal of destabilizing arguments.[9]

Saying that the process of destabilization is "offensive" and "aggressive" might mislead. This process during the weekend service is not aggressive or offensive in tone. We find in Hybels a smooth, cordial, and often humorous process of considering and rejecting various competitors of or roadblocks to Christianity.

These arguments often take place within the broader framework of arguing for Harry's fulfillment. Alternatives are often discredited because, Hybels argues, they are unable to provide the fulfillment that Harry desires.

Hybels states that the reason they are unable to provide fulfillment is because they are a false understanding of reality.

There are several types of destabilization arguments that I will review here: alternatives to Christianity, roadblocks to Christianity, misconceptions about Christianity, and consequences of rejecting Christianity.

Alternatives to Christianity

Most Harrys are not committed to another religion. As Hybels explains about the original church survey, "The vast majority of people were not staying away from Christian churches because they were converting to Islam, or converting to Buddhism or Hinduism." In fact, many unchurched Harrys actually affirm many of the central beliefs of Christianity: There is a personal God; Jesus is his Son; the Bible is a revelation from God. There is substantial common ground between Willow Creek and the worldview of many Harrys.[10]

Harry's various normative philosophies could be understood as ways of life rather than as clearly thought-through religions or worldviews. The church views itself in competition with these alternative philosophies for unchurched Harry's attention and commitment. Hybels, in a series titled "Christianity's Toughest Competition," presented and critiqued three competitors to Christianity: individualism, adventurism, and moralism. Hybels explains:

> In this ministry season we're going to think through the leading alternative belief systems of our day, and . . . we're going to let you see . . . whether or not they really provide sufficient answers to the searching questions of life.[11]

Individualism

Hybels's main illustration of individualism is the prodigal son of Luke 15. Hybels depicts such an individualist as saying, "I'll bow to nobody. It's my way or the highway; I'll never bow before God. I'll figure out a way. I'll do it all by myself." Hybels suggests that individualism was the original sin of Adam and Eve: "It was Adam and Eve saying, 'I'm tired of bowing down to God. I don't want to obey his rules and program. I want to make my own.'"

Hybels believes that someone on the individualism path is going to bottom out: "The plain fact is, a card carrying individualist is gonna crash. It's not *if*, it's *when*. Next month? Next year? Twenty years?" Hybels warns that the final destination for all individualists is the judgment seat of God: "I'm not sure I'd want to stand before the holy God on the day of judgment and tell him that my life song was 'I did it my way.'" Hybels destabilizes Harry's philosophy of individualism by arguing that it ultimately leads to loneliness and frustration. As Harry begins to question the wisdom of an individualistic lifestyle, he becomes correspondingly more open to Hybels's gospel.

Adventurism

Hybels says that the second great modern competitor to Christianity is adventurism. He believes that many unchurched Harrys are "so wrapped up in the pleasurable experiences of life, they just can't schedule God in between the thrills and the chills that they're buying for themselves."

Hybels highlights the weaknesses of pleasure seeking and pure adventurism. Hybels then redirects this interest in adventure and argues that Christianity is the greatest adventure. Hybels describes the Christian life as a roller coaster ride of excitement. The fifteen-year anniversary of the church celebrated this idea with the show "What a Ride!" Strobel explains, "The purpose of life, it seems to me, is to score a goal; to do something of supreme significance with your life, something that really matters."

Hybels argues that adventurism not only doesn't satisfy, it frustrates. Hybels destabilizes Harry's philosophy of adventurism by arguing that it's counterproductive.

Moralism

Hybels began his third talk on Christianity's competitors with a long description of his experience of recently taking up racquetball. After a couple months of success in beating his friends, he decided to enter a tournament. There were three levels of skill to choose from, A, B, or C.

> I knew all of what the Bible said about humility and so, so I said to myself, "Admit it Bill, you're probably—you know you've only played a few months—you're probably not gonna win the A level. . . ."
>
> One thing was for sure, I had no interest in the C league whatsoever. I was way past this recreational novice business.

Hybels was attempting to decide between A and B levels when he was asked to play by an average C player, "a little pot-bellied guy, short guy, no reach." After being beaten 21 to 0, Hybels confessed, "I had vastly overrated my abilities." The crowd laughed raucously at Hybels's misguided self-perception.

Hybels then applied his lesson to the unchurched Harrys in the audience: "Nowhere does the problem of overrating oneself happen more frequently than in the spiritual realm. Most people vastly overrate how good they are in the eyes of God." Moralism, Hybels argued, is this tendency human beings have to overestimate themselves in the spiritual realm. He then used his foolish overestimation of his racquetball abilities as a parable of this tendency. After holding a mirror up to himself and describing how foolish he looked, Hybels let Harry see himself in the mirror.

When we reexamine the audience of Willow Creek we see why this argument finds such a responsive chord. I noted above that approximately 50 percent of Willow Creek's converts are former Roman Catholics. Roman Catholics would affirm the central Christian theology that Willow Creek is teaching. The distinctive of Hybels's message is that individuals need to reject the idea that their works will achieve enough credit in heaven's bank to insure their entrance. Hybels's destabilizing argument forces these lapsed Catholics to admit that this well-meaning banking of good deeds isn't enough. These former Catholics then become very open to Hybels's gospel.

If Hybels can get Harry to question, or better yet, discard his alternative philosophy, Harry will be more open to his message. At the very least, the process of destabilization pushes Harry toward anomie, or normlessness. To genuinely feel this lack of meaning is to sense a fundamental disorientation. As Berger explains, a philosophy of life "shelters the individual from ultimate terror." When an individual feels this sort of terror or disorientation there is a corresponding openness to conversion. At this point, Hybels seeks to remove any roadblocks that are in Harry's way.[12]

Roadblocks to Christianity

Unchurched Harry often has questions that hinder him from seriously considering Christianity. Strobel says that "almost all" of the seekers he talks with "have some objection that has hung them up." Creekers call these questions or objections "roadblocks." Mittelberg says that roadblocks bar individuals from genuine interest in the gospel:

> Roadblocks are intellectual objections keeping them from seriously considering the gospel message. . . . What we need to do is knock down these roadblocks by giving answers, adequate answers, that can help clear the way. . . . We need to give the answers to break down the roadblocks to get them to the point where they'll give the gospel a hearing.

Mittelberg explains, "Apologetics is the handmaiden to evangelism. Arguments and evidence do not replace the gospel—they clear the way for it and then back it up." Hybels and his colleagues attempt to knock down roadblocks that they think might be holding Harry back.[13]

Thus the first step in destabilizing roadblocks is diagnosis. Strobel acknowledges, "When I talk to Unchurched Harrys and Marys, I try to diagnose what's causing the blockage so I can recommend a way to get them back on track toward God." This strategy attempts to take Harry's concerns seriously. A certain respect for the legitimacy of Harry's questions is built into the strategy. As Mittelberg explains, "We must clear up any genuine intellectual hang-ups the person has accepted as problematic and give positive reasons for adopting Christianity."[14]

The second step of destabilization is to deconstruct Harry's questions that are holding him back from Christianity. Strobel lists several of the common questions that he often hears from unchurched Harry:

- What about people who have never heard of Jesus?
- Aren't all faiths equally valid?
- Why does God allow innocent people to suffer?
- If God is so all-loving, why does he send people to hell?
- I'm basically a good person. Isn't that enough?
- How do you know you can trust the Bible?
- Aren't miracles impossible?
- Doesn't science contradict the biblical account of creation?[15]

Hybels and his colleagues respond to these questions with either destabilizing or foundational arguments. For example, Strobel used destabilizing arguments in a series he presented on creation versus evolution. A large part of his messages in this series was designed to destabilize Harry's assumption that the evolutionary theory completely accounts for the nature of life. Strobel explains:

> All I wanted to do was to give them enough information to say number one, there are major holes with evolution. Major holes! And the basic major hole is, how did life come here in the first place? . . .
>
> I was trying to reassure them that they don't have to throw out their intellect. . . . I was just trying to knock down the barrier.

Strobel specifically suggested there are different ways that Christians can come down on the issue of creation and evolution and yet remain faithful to the biblical message. His goal wasn't to develop a synthesis between scientific evidence and biblical narrative. Rather, he wanted to eliminate Harry's idea that Christianity has been disproved by evolutionary science:

> My intent in that series was to eliminate, as much as possible, the evolutionary objection that so many seekers had. . . .
>
> I wasn't pushing a particular dogma or particular interpretation of Genesis. I didn't care. I honestly don't care which one they have as long as they eliminate the evolutionary objection that a lot of seekers have.

This strategy of attacking an opponent's position is rhetorically effective. Any politician knows that it is easier, and usually more persuasive, to attack the opponent's plan than to present one's own. In this case, this strategy eliminates the roadblock of the worldview of unchurched Harry. If Hybels and his associates can knock down several of these props, we can expect that Harry will be nervously looking for a new worldview.

Misconceptions about Christianity

Hybels argues that Harry often doesn't look at Christianity as a possible new worldview because he has various misconceptions about it. Strobel asserts that the average Harry is "full of misinformation, such as that the Bible says that the earth is 10,000 years old, or that Scripture is chock-full of contradictions." Until Hybels and his colleagues can destabilize and discredit these misconceptions, Harry will not be willing to consider Christianity as a viable alternative. "Harry will never receive Christ," Cousins argues, "until those misconceptions are dealt with."[16]

Creekers believe that they first need to identify these misconceptions and then seek to systematically dismantle them. Thus again, diagnosis precedes demolition. Harry generally has two different kinds of misconceptions: (1) about God and (2) concerning Christianity generally.

Cousins explains some of Harry's misconceptions about God:

> Who does Harry think God is? Does he view him as a loving, gracious, kind, patient God? No. Harry thinks that God is standing up in heaven someplace—wherever that is—holding a club in his hand. And he's got the feeling that any time he steps out of line, God is about one second away from bashing him over the head.

Cousins argues that Harry is not going to respond to the gospel if he thinks "God is going to judge him and condemn him at every fork in the road." Many of the messages could be described as re-educating Harry about God.

> When I go in there, the church is just going to ask for my money—God just wants my money. They're going to beat me over the head with the gospel or ask me to do something right then and there. . . .

As Hybels and the other speakers pull down Harry's misconceptions, they believe Harry can see the gospel more clearly.

Sometimes destabilizing Harry's misconceptions about Christianity is a subtle process. On other occasions the speakers are blunt in their challenge to Harry: "I'm gonna ask you this morning to let go of some of your misconceptions of Christianity." The goal of the speaker is to debunk these misconceptions and re-educate Harry. "If he's going to respond, this image of God is going to have to be changed."

Consequences of Rejecting Christianity

Part of the destabilizing process is Hybels's presentation of the consequences of not trusting Christ. After describing some of the thrills of Christianity's competition, Hybels often shows the consequences of these alternative philosophies further down the road: "That way that seems so right to you is gonna produce destruction, pain, disappointment."

Hybels asserts that individuals who don't live according to God's plan will run up against the results of their own sin. What appears at the beginning as an endless vision of delight becomes, Hybels argues, an empty mirage. What began as pleasure ends in painful vices and addiction.

Cousins cites the consequences of following false philosophies:

> When you live with guilt, when you live with remorse, when you live with shame, when you live with jealousy, when you live with worry, when you live with anxiety—it drains you emotionally like the fever heat of summer.

Hybels and his colleagues argue that the promises of these alternative philosophies never pay off: "There is no joy, there is no strength, there is no energy, only heaviness in a troubled conscience."

Hybels also contends that often the consequence of these alternative philosophies is broken relationships:

> Some of the saddest, most frustrated and isolated people I know are people who had holes in their hearts. They fell in love with someone they thought sure would fill those holes, only to find out after a few years that marriage provided them with a body to be close to, but not necessarily a relationship that would be a cure for all the loneliness that they feel.

Hybels believes that the rejection of Christianity is a recipe for disaster in relationships.

Hybels depicts Harry's willful commitment to reject God as "putting a four-year-old in the captain's seat of an airborne 747. The kid is ill-equipped to handle the complexities of a high-tech jumbo jet." The result of this decision is a crashed life and broken relationships.

In using destabilizing arguments, Hybels is trying to identify and discredit anything that would hinder Harry from making a commitment to Christ. With some, this might mean a series pointing out the weaknesses of evolution as an explanatory scientific model. For others, it might mean identifying the consequences of individualism, adventurism, and moralism. For all, it involves identifying the roadblocks and misconceptions that keep a person from faith and removing those. As Strobel explains, "If I can answer that objection, all of a sudden they'll look at the gospel. But until that objection is answered, they're hung up and they're in a rut."

Foundational Arguments

The second objective of Hybels's apologetic is to provide historical and philosophical arguments for Christianity's truthfulness. The two basic purposes to Willow Creek's foundational arguments are to stabilize Christians' faith with evidence for Christianity and to give evidence to unchurched Harry that Christianity is true so he will become a Christian.[17]

To Stabilize Faith

Hybels explains the first purpose of foundational apologetics at Willow Creek:

> I want to say to those of you who are Christians, you have no reason to be embarrassed or to shrink back from boldly proclaiming that you walk and talk regularly with a God who is there.

The message that Willow Creek Christians hear again and again is that Christianity is true and reasonable. "The evidence for the existence of God is impressive." Attenders are repeatedly instructed and encouraged that Christianity is the true explanation of reality and that there are answers to the questions skeptics may have. Hybels proclaims:

> You have no reason to shrink back, to cower, when someone challenges your faith, because your faith is not based on shifting sand; it has a strong foundation, a rational foundation, a compelling foundation, logically.

An advertising flyer about an upcoming seminar was sent from the ministry that trains young apologists. The flyer ended with the line "BE THERE OR BE SCARED . . . of the next atheist you meet." This fear is what Willow Creek's apologetics are trying to remove. Thousands of Willow Creek Christians have attended New Community classes designed to answer common questions of the unchurched. New Community attenders have received instruction by Willow Creek's specialists in apologetics. Thousands of Creekers have attended special Willow Creek apologetic programs, such as a debate between an atheist and an evangelical scholar. All of these programs provide evidence that undergirds Creekers' faith.

Hybels teaches that the basis of a healthy Christian life is an intellectual understanding of Christianity's truthfulness. The theme of the church during the year of my study was "Becoming a Fully Informed Follower of Christ." The first series that began that year was a five-week study of the evidence of Christianity's truthfulness. Hybels introduced it:

> The reason we're in this series right now entitled "Faith Has Its Reasons" is so that those of you who are already believers, when you come through a time of testing and doubt and when you're surrounded by people who are cynical and say—Oh, you have a blind faith; you took a flying leap of faith one day; what do you really have as evidence? What do you really have that backs up your claim that Christ is who he says he is?—you've got to have some reasons, friends, more than just saying, I think so. I hope so. It feels like it.[18]

Hybels explains that many Christians don't make it through difficult times because they don't have any intellectual foundations: "There must be a concerted effort to establish an intellectual or rational basis for following Christ." He argues that true Christians must be willing "to develop a root structure for their faith, to engage their minds in the intellectual pursuit of the facts that support their Christian faith."

To Persuade Harry

The second way that foundational arguments are used is as a means to persuade unchurched Harry. Hybels regularly seeks to convince Harry that Christianity is true. Hybels and his colleagues argue that if Harry sincerely asks whether Christianity is true, God will show him that it is. "He [God] promises that those who sincerely seek him will find him." Strobel exhorts, "The step that you need to take is to put God on the front burner and be a serious seeker—begin investigating in a serious way the truth about Jesus Christ."

An assumption behind this strategy is that faith is based on evidence. Strobel describes a popular misconception of faith: "Faith is a sort of wishful thinking that runs contrary to common sense." In contrast, Hybels teaches that faith is a reasonable decision to trust Christ based on the evidence: "There are plenty of facts behind our faith."[19]

Legal Analogy

Hybels's approach to presenting evidence is structured by a legal analogy. Hybels suggests that unchurched Harry is serving on a jury that has to determine Christianity's truthfulness. There are five elements to this legal comparison.

The first element is that the evidence for God should be judged "beyond a reasonable doubt":

> It must be understood from the outset that insistence on absolute proof of the existence of God is an unreasonable and unrealistic request for a person to make.
>
> As we have just discussed, life just doesn't operate that way. We don't even place that kind of evidential burden on the judicial system of the United States.

Hybels says, "We all make decisions based on high probability, seldom on absolute certainty. When we're about to board an airliner for L.A., we don't know with absolute certainty that once it leaves O'Hare, it will subsequently land in Los Angeles." Hybels wants to move Harry toward the point where he can say, "I am now convinced beyond a reasonable doubt that there is in fact a God."

The second element of this legal analogy is the idea of a verdict. Strobel explains that the legal analogy is helpful because it emphasizes "the importance of them making a decision." By emphasizing the idea of a verdict, Hybels pushes Christianity from a back burner to the front and turns up the heat.

The third element of this legal analogy is the importance of examining the evidence. Individuals on a jury have the duty to weigh the information and make an honest decision based on the evidence. As Strobel puts it, "the rationality" of the decision before Harry is underlined by the jury analogy. Hybels underscores the idea that Harry as a juror must decide based on the evidence: "I want to say to all of you seekers who are on the outside sort of looking in, trying to figure all of this out, weigh the evidence very carefully, very honestly."

The fourth element of the legal analogy is that the speaker serves as an attorney who is presenting the evidence to the jury. Strobel explains, "You come into the jury and you present the case as compellingly as you can. . . . I believe it's true and I want to paint the case as honestly, but as compellingly, as I can."

The fifth and final element of the legal analogy is that like any good trial lawyer, Hybels starts with the concerns of the jury. I noted above several of the questions that Harrys often ask at Willow Creek. Hybels and his staff consider these questions reasonable. Strobel says, "Harry has legitimate questions about spiritual matters, but he doesn't expect answers from Christians." Cousins asked a group of staff what "an effective ministry is going to have to do with all of those questions." A staff member responded, "We'll have to answer them."[20]

Most of these questions Creekers answer with foundational arguments. There are two basic branches of foundational apologetics: historical and philosophical arguments. Willow Creek affirms both of these. Mittelberg explains that both can be useful depending on the context, and that "there is not necessarily a 'right' approach." While philosophical arguments provide an interesting sideline, historical arguments are Willow Creek's principal source of foundational apologetics.[21]

Historical Arguments

Unchurched Harrys often ask, "How do you know you can trust the Bible?" Hybels's response is to provide historical evidence. Hybels doesn't immediately quote the Bible, as "unchurched people don't give the Bible a fraction of the weight we believers do." Hybels says that many Harrys view the Bible as "an occasionally useful collection of helpful suggestions, something like the *Farmer's Almanac*." Hybels believes, "If you just start out by saying 'Thus sayeth God's Word,' they say, 'So what?'"[22]

Strobel concluded at the end of his investigation of Christianity, "Historical evidence clearly supports the claims of Christ beyond any reasonable doubt." What is this historical evidence? Hybels, defending the Scriptures, argues that the historical record confirms the Bible, the New Testament has a greater amount and quality of manuscripts than other ancient documents, and the New Testament was written when eyewitnesses still remembered and could have repudiated the authors' testimony.[23]

Jesus' resurrection is the focus of Willow Creek's historical argument. Hybels teaches that "the whole of the Christian faith rests on the resurrection of Jesus Christ" and contends that Jesus held his resurrection as a proof of his claims:

> Jesus kept announcing that, yes, he would die, but in three days he would rise. And he never backed off that position or that prediction. He said that his resurrection would prove his identity as God's son, once and for all. . . .
>
> He said that his resurrection would serve notice on the human race, that Christianity is true, that it's rooted in history, and that it is substantiated by a supernatural event for which there is evidence for all people to see.

Strobel explains how he began his investigation into Jesus' resurrection as a skeptical newspaper reporter:

> I did the first thing that any reporter does in checking something out. And that's to ask the very simple question, How many eyeballs are there? . . . That's slang for how many eyewitnesses do you have? Because we all know that eyewitness testimony is very, very influential.

Strobel was shocked upon investigating that there were many eyewitnesses. After reviewing the fact that thousands of individuals began following Jesus soon after his death and resurrection, Strobel was stumped.[24]

Strobel's problem was multiplied when he realized that many disciples died a martyr's death for their new faith. Strobel says that this fact was very convincing for him: "Nobody will die for a religious belief, if they know the belief is false." Strobel realized, "The whole Christian faith hinges on whether or not Jesus returned from the dead." The question comes down to the believability of the disciples. Strobel concluded that they were credible witnesses:

> These disciples were in a position to know the truth, because they are the ones who said that they saw Jesus after he rose from the dead. . . . If they were lying do you think they would have willingly been tortured to death for a lie?

Jesus' life and death also fulfill Old Testament prophecy. Hybels argues that the Bible "made bold predictions of events that would happen in following centuries." Many of these prophecies concerned the life of Jesus:

> These prophecies were incredibly detailed. . . . what lineage he would be born from, what city he would be born in, his manner of birth, what his ministry would be like, how he would live, how he would die, and how he would rise again.

Hybels preaches, "How could anyone account for these prophecies being fulfilled to the letter, hundreds of years later, apart from admitting that God must have played a part in authoring those written prophecies?" For Strobel these fulfilled prophecies were tremendously influential: "In my opinion, fulfilled prophecies by themselves prove Christianity beyond a reasonable doubt."

If Jesus wasn't raised from the dead, what other explanation does justice to the facts? Hybels and Strobel review alternative theories and argue that they have numerous logical holes. Strobel concluded at the end of his search, "The only possible answer to me that makes sense is that they [disciples] were telling the truth."

Appeal for Honesty

The last element of Hybels's apologetic is an appeal for honesty. Hostile Harrys are challenged to be intellectually honest in examining Christianity. Curious Harrys are jarred from neutrality to consider Christianity's truthfulness. Sincere Harrys are urged to make Christianity's truthfulness a "front-burner issue" and take advantage of the church's programs and resources.

Hybels challenges unchurched Harrys to be honest about the person of Jesus Christ. He questions whether Harry is really being honest about the evidence for the resurrection: "I really wonder if you're being intellectually honest if you just blow off everything that you just heard." Hybels genuinely believes that the evidence for Christianity is so strong that there is no reasonable doubt.

Hybels argues that visiting Harrys often have vested interests in not being honest about Christianity:

> I suspect that many people know just enough about the Bible to have developed a vested interest in steering clear of it, or even berating it, because they know if they read it, it's gonna speak accurately, truthfully about their condition. It's gonna call them into account.

He suggests that many Harrys who stubbornly refuse to acknowledge Christianity have a bias against God: "You're coming into the debate with a nonrational bias against anything supernatural, and that's going to prevent you from objectively analyzing the evidence that we talk about tonight."

The definition of a seeker is one who sets aside his preconceptions and studies Christianity to see if it is really true. Hybels describes a seeker as one who is "gonna actively investigate the claims of Jesus Christ." Strobel argues that sincere seekers have several responsibilities:

> Come here regularly to hear the Word of God.
> Go down to the bookstore and . . . say, "Sell me books that can help me out here."
> Come to our Foundations class and learn about basic Christianity.
> Ask questions.
> Be serious seekers.

This is a constant and unchanging challenge at Willow Creek—to become a serious seeker. Harrys who are considering becoming seekers have the example of Strobel constantly lifted before them:

> At the outset, I promised myself three things. First thing I said—*I'm going to make this a front-burner issue of my life*. Second thing is, *I'm going to keep an open mind, I'm going to seek with sincerity.* And the third thing is, when the evidence is finally in, I told myself, *I would respond to it.*

Hybels and his fellow speakers argue that Christianity is true. Many unchurched Harrys are finding this argument credible and are converting. What they are converting to is explained in the next chapter.

13

Willow Creek's Gospel

Hybels has a message. And at this point in the process of persuasion, Harry is more open to hearing it.

Everything else we have reviewed so far is merely preface. The program has prepared Harry to listen. Hybels has identified with Harry, taught that Christianity is relevant, and argued that Christianity is true. Harry is now willing to listen to the solution Hybels offers, the main course, the reason for all the previous work and effort—the gospel.

Hybels is not unique in his emphasis on the gospel. The gospel is at the heart of the evangelical movement. The word *gospel* means "good news." The gospel or good news is that God became man in Jesus and has accomplished in his death and resurrection the means of salvation. As individuals understand this message, and respond by trusting Christ, they receive eternal salvation. It is this message that evangelicals are so motivated to preach at every opportunity.

Hybels and Willow Creek strongly affirm this historic evangelical commitment. Bilezikian, the Willow Creek theologian, teaches that "the appointed task of the church is to change men . . . by conversion." Hybels teaches that "there is no greater cause than the cause that helps people find a personal relationship with God and an eternity in heaven. No greater cause." The rest of this chapter is a summary of Willow Creek's gospel.[1]

Evangelism director Mittelberg teaches that unchurched Harry, if he is to become a believer, must understand and respond to certain truths: "He needs to understand—he needs a rational grasp of what it is that we're saying." This message or set of truths is what evangelicals call the gospel.

Some evangelicals regularly attack Hybels for not always explaining all of these truths at each weekend meeting. "I get bitterly, bitterly attacked from the fundamentalist side for not preaching a salvation message every time we have a seeker service." Some confront Hybels after a service, "You know, the blood of every seeker is on your hands" or "How can you have two thousand or three thousand seekers there and not give a full-blown message?" Hybels answers, "Because we're here every week."

Hybels is very committed to communicating the gospel. In fact, he thinks that his strategy of a persuasive process is a more effective means of communicating the gospel. This strategy takes a significant amount of time. A typical unchurched Harry doesn't quickly understand the gospel. As Mittelberg explains, "It involves putting together a jigsaw puzzle of content, of information . . . and that generally takes time to understand and put those pieces together." In the year I studied, it was only rarely that Hybels or another speaker would proclaim the whole gospel during one message.

Thousands of Creekers have been trained in how to share their faith at the church's Impact seminars. Evangelism director Mark Mittelberg summarizes the gospel at these seminars using four "handles," or categories: God, man, Christ, and response. These four principles are a summary of Willow Creek's understanding of the gospel.[2]

God

The first handle of the gospel, according to the Impact evangelism seminar, is understanding who God is. Willow Creek staff believe that Harry has a distorted view of God. "We feel like God is very misunderstood." Hybels and his staff believe that if they can help Harry see who God really is, Harry will be more likely to respond positively.

They don't believe this change will come easily or quickly for most people. Cousins comments, "We decided that our overall thrust in evangelism would be gradually to change unbelievers' concepts of God." The word *God* was used more often (1,882 times) than any other proper noun during the weekend messages (34.85 times each talk). Who is God? According to the gospel outline taught in the Impact seminars, God is loving, holy, and just.[3]

God Is Loving

According to the Impact seminar, the first trait of God is that he is loving. The first verse that Creekers are taught in the seminar is 1 John 4:16: "God is love." This is a constant message at Willow Creek. The word *love* was used a total of 489 times during the year I studied. Hybels teaches that God's love is shown through his kindness and grace.

God's Kindness

Strobel quotes Nehemiah 9:17, "But you are a forgiving God, gracious and compassionate, slow to anger and abounding in love," and explains that God "looks at us with a tender heart." The word *kind* was used 448 times over the course of the year I studied.

Verses that emphasize God's kindness are regularly quoted during messages. One example is 1 Peter 5:7, "Cast all your anxiety on him because he cares for you." One speaker paraphrases Jesus as saying, "I'm gentle, I'm humble in my heart, I have no desire to hurt you. And you shall find rest for your souls, for my yoke is easy and my load is light."

God's Grace

Hybels teaches that God is eager to forgive: "He's anxious to forgive us; in fact, his instinctive response is to be forgiving toward us." Hybels describes the gospel as the means God has provided to forgive his children: "The good news is you matter to him so much that he has provided a means by which your sins can be forgiven." This merciful love is held back only because individuals aren't willing to receive it. Hybels contrasts the "accusing, haughty, self-righteous eyes of the Pharisees" with the "forgiving, caring, restoring eyes of Jesus."[4]

God Is Holy

The second trait of God that is articulated in the Impact evangelism training class is that he is holy. The church staff teach that it is essential for unchurched Harry to know that God is loving, holy, and just. Without any one of these truths, they argue, Harry's understanding of God is distorted. For example, Mittelberg believes that many unchurched Harrys only like the idea that God is loving:

> They say God is love and that's it—end of story. . . . They make him into sort of a benevolent jellybean in the sky that just exudes some kind of warm, fuzzy happiness—you know, and warm, loving feelings.

Hybels asserts that most unchurched Harrys don't understand God's holiness. Some Harrys claim, "I don't have a reason in the world to worry about standing before a holy God come judgment day." Numerous Harrys often ask, "How can a loving God send such wonderful people to hell?" Other

Harrys think that God is "screaming" at them "in relentless anger—'you despicable sinners!'"[5]

Hybels believes that if Harry understands God's holiness, he realizes why he and others are responsible, and why God isn't screaming at him. Hybels paraphrases Romans 1:

> The apostle Paul said in Romans, chapter 1, that the entire human race could be cut into two groups. The first group would be those that tell the truth to themselves about the holiness and majesty of God.
>
> And when they tell the truth to themselves about that reality, people in that first camp submit themselves, humble themselves, and honor the majestic, holy God of their lives.

Hybels argues that the second group "see the holiness of God" but "lie in their spirits and turn away from the reality of the holiness and the majesty of God." The first group Hybels describes are those who have become Christians. In response to seeing the mirror of God's face, they see themselves and admit their sinfulness.[6]

God Is Just

The third characteristic of God taught in the Impact evangelism training class is that he is just. Mittelberg explains that this is "probably the least popular these days" of God's characteristics. He suggests that a way to understand this characteristic is that God "is a good judge," and "a good judge doesn't let lawbreakers off the hook."

Many Harrys ask why God can't just wave a wand and forgive them. Hybels and his Creekers respond that it's because God is a fair and just God and he "has to uphold the law." They often use an illustration of a judge to get across this idea:

> A girl was convicted of some sort of law breaking and stood in front of the judge and pleaded guilty to the crime. The judge, because he was a good judge, couldn't just let her off. . . .
>
> He's a good judge and he has to prescribe the penalty that the law demands. And so as a good judge he gave her the penalty . . . a penalty she couldn't afford to pay. . . .
>
> But then he did something very unusual. He stood up and took off his robe and laid it over the bench, and then he walked down from the bench, . . . came down next to her, . . . took out his own wallet, . . . took out the money, . . . handed it to her, and paid it for her. The reason he did that was because he was her father.

Hybels and his colleagues use this parable as a picture of what Christ has done in paying the penalty for mankind's sin. It emphasizes how God is both just and loving.

Nancy Beach explains that God's justice is one of the two consistent emphases of the weekend programming: "There has to be a balance between the grace and compassion and love of God . . . with the justice of God or the demands of God." The flip side of God's justice is that people who don't repent will one day be judged.

Man

The second category of the Impact evangelism training seminar is a regular topic of Hybels's messages. In fact, after *God,* the word *people* was the noun used most often (1,357 times) during the weekend services I studied. This is the purpose of Hybels's gospel: explaining how people relate to God.

According to the Impact seminar, there are three necessary elements to the gospel message about man: man is sinful, man deserves death, and man is spiritually helpless. We will review what Hybels teaches in the messages about each of these. Yet before we review these elements, we need to name a fourth characteristic of man that Hybels regularly teaches on the weekend that is not on the Impact list.

Man Is Valuable

Hybels regularly describes how human beings are valuable because they are "made in the image of God." Strobel asserts that unchurched Harry's evolutionary view of human nature "affects your view of people's worth. Because in that case we really don't have any intrinsic value. We're just animals." Hybels and his colleagues teach that the biblical view of people as made in the image of God makes them valuable.

The second reason people are valuable is that God loves them. Hybels preaches, "You matter to God, and you matter to God more than you know." The very motto of the church, "You matter to God," is an expression of how God loves people and thus assigns them value.

Man Is Sinful

The Impact evangelism seminar's first principle explaining who human beings are is that they are "sinful" or "rebellious toward God." "Sin" words were used 4.87 times each message in Willow Creek's weekend services during the year I studied.[7]

Yet staff members told me that many Harrys don't easily understand the idea of sin. One staff member described meeting a couple who were living together but couldn't understand why it was wrong: "Increasingly, we are running into people who don't even have a moral concept that that is sin, and that it's rebellion to a holy God." Thus it wasn't unusual for Hybels to use other terms to communicate the idea of sin, terms such as "dark side," "shadow side," "selfish," "sin nature," "evil thoughts," "cosmic treason," and having "not made the grade."

Cousins explains the idea of a sin nature using his children as illustrations: "I've got a two-and-a-half-year-old and an eleven-month-old. I never taught my two-and-a-half-year-old how to be selfish, and yet it's incredible how easily he can say 'Mine!'" Hybels regularly attempts to hold a mirror up to help Harry see that "all of us rebel against God shamefully."[8]

Hybels does add a unique, pragmatic twist to the idea of sin. Instead of only portraying sin as selfishness and a rebellion against God, Hybels also describes it as a flawed strategy to gain fulfillment. He describes the Bible as saying, "You have a faulty, self-destructive force at work in your life, and it's called sin." Hybels asserts, "If you don't do something about it, this force will plague you and wreak havoc in you in this life."

Man Deserves Death

The next part to understanding man is that human beings "deserve death." Mittelberg explains that death means "spiritual separation from God in eternity" and quotes Romans 6:23: "The wages of sin is death."

Hybels argues that this spiritual separation between God and a person will continue into eternity if that person doesn't respond to him. Hybels teaches that judgment day is not so much a condemnation as God affirming the decision that individuals have already made: "God doesn't slam dunk on judgment day. He just observes your yearnings and says, 'Have it your way.'" Hybels adds:

> For unbelievers whose greatest yearning on earth was to distance themselves from God, the church, the Bible, and other Christians, God grants an expanded capacity for distance from him in hell forever.

Man Is Spiritually Helpless

The last teaching about humans in the Impact evangelism seminar is that they are spiritually helpless. Mittelberg explains, "We're sinful; we deserve death, and there's not a thing we can do about it." Another phrase that is used to describe this condition is "morally bankrupt." Mittelberg asserts that "there's nothing in our moral bank account to pay back God the debt that we've incurred through our sin and rebellion."

Mittelberg underlines that so far the "good news" is actually rather "bad news": "It's important for people to understand the bad news. It's important for people to understand the predicament that we're all in apart from Christ."

Christ

During the weekend messages, Jesus is a constant focus as the solution for the "bad news." In fact, references to Jesus and Christ totaled 1,421 times over the course of the year I studied. Thus the three most common nouns during the weekend messages were *God, people,* and *Jesus Christ.* This in a nutshell is Hybels's gospel: explaining how Jesus has enabled people to have a relationship with God. Mittelberg articulates three subpoints under Christ.

God Became Man

Mittelberg repeats the question he constantly hears from unchurched Harrys: "It doesn't make sense that Jesus would have to die on the cross for our sins. I mean, why would he have to die?" Why is Jesus the solution for the human dilemma? Mittelberg argues that the incarnation is vital to the gospel. God isn't using Jesus as a sort of cosmic whipping boy; Christ is God incarnate and he chose to sacrifice himself. "God paid it himself. Christ is God in human form. He had both the nature of deity and the nature of humanity." This enabled him to provide something that no mere man could do: "The one we sinned against has to pay the price of forgiveness."

The incarnation is spelled out in the church's statement of faith: "Jesus Christ is the eternal Person of the Trinity who was united forever with a true human nature." Hybels occasionally teaches how Christ's divine and human nature has provided the means of salvation: "Jesus Christ, who was fully God and fully man, stepped in and was willingly executed in our place for the sins that we committed, so that we could be reconciled with God." This reality, Hybels argues, is what makes Christ's actions so astounding and loving.

He Died as Our Substitute

Hybels says that whenever someone truly forgives, he or she genuinely pays. If an owner of a lamp forgives another for breaking it, then the owner has to pay for the cost of a new lamp. Forgiveness costs.

Hybels emphasizes the cost:

> Now, get this part, because if you miss it you'll never understand Christianity. . . . While Christ was dying on the cross an amazing thing happened. God arranged for the shortcomings and the sins of the whole world, including yours and mine, to be transferred from our shoulders to Jesus' shoulders, and in Jesus' death, he assumed full responsibility for all of it.

Jesus was mankind's substitute. Strobel says, "Why in the world was he willing to endure the degradation and the humiliation and the pain of death like that? So you and I can be forgiven." This substitution was the only payment that could satisfy human guilt. Strobel explains, "In order for us to be reconciled with God, somebody has to pay the penalty for all this wrongdoing that we got ourselves involved in." Christ, as God incarnate, is the only one who could pay it.

He Offers Forgiveness as a Free Gift

Mittelberg notes that Christ's "gift is free, but it's very expensive." This gift is free to people because Jesus paid for it.

Hybels explains that this gift is the heart of the gospel's good news: "The good news is you matter to him so much that he has provided a means by which your sins can be forgiven." Hybels contends that biblical Christianity is distinguished from religion because of Christ's free offer of forgiveness. "Religion is spelled *D-O*. It's based on What can I do? How much do I have to do to please God, to earn his favor, to get to heaven?" In contrast, Hybels asserts:

> Christianity is not merely a religion. Christianity is spelled differently. It's spelled *D-O-N-E*. The reason it's the word *done* is because Christ has done for us what we could not do for ourselves.

Response

Mittelberg teaches that an appropriate commitment involves a personal choice of receiving Christ as forgiver and leader.

A Personal Choice

Mittelberg asserts that there are "many people who understand to some degree about God and his love and justice, and about us and our sin, and Christ paying the price," but don't understand the need for response. He preaches, "It's not enough to hear it. It's not enough to understand it. It's not even enough to believe it intellectually. A personal response has to be made."

The message that a decision has to be made in response to the gospel is regularly repeated in the weekend services. The words *decisions, committed, commit, commitment, choice, decision,* and *decide* were used a total of 502 times over the year I studied (an average of 9.3 times each message). Hybels tries to get across this idea by using a variety of pictures and explanations. During one talk he described Jesus as the great "wedge" who pushes people in one direction or another: "What is it about him that forces people into one camp or the other?" Hybels asserts that it is impossible to remain neutral about Jesus. One needs to decide for Jesus, or one has—by neglect—rejected him.

As is noted above, Hybels argues that if individuals don't choose to receive God's forgiveness and love, God allows them to walk away. This teaching strongly emphasizes human freedom of the will. Hybels argues that God doesn't force people to receive his forgiveness: "If you begin to put that kind of pressure on a human being, he won't be a human being anymore. He'll be kind of an automaton. He'll be kind of a puppet moving on the strings."

Hybels repeatedly underlines the opportunity people have to receive God's forgiveness, in his words, "by saying what sounds like a recording" in Willow Creek: "Friends, you have a choice to make. You have a choice to make."

Receiving Christ as Forgiver and Master

Mittelberg teaches in the Impact seminar, "We receive him as forgiver. He takes away our sins. . . . But that's half the story. The other half is, 'Now, control my life. Lead me.'"

Hybels clearly teaches that individuals need to confess that they are sinners and ask for Christ's forgiveness. This self-understanding comes as a result of clearly seeing God, and results in being able to say, "Oh God, I see who I am. I see your holiness and I know I've fallen short. I repent, Lord; on my knees I repent."[9]

The second emphasis of this decision is receiving Jesus as leader. The word *repentance* is especially crucial in understanding the idea of leadership. Hybels uses the biblical word *repentance,* because there is no adequate substitute:

> *Repentance* isn't a word that we use much anymore, is it? I mean it's not a word that's used in everyday conversation very much. It sounds very outdated.

> The original word used in the Bible was actually the combination of two words, words that mean change and the word that means mind: change and mind.
>
> It means that we need to acknowledge that we are spiritual rebels, that we've ignored God, that we've broken his laws. And then we need to literally change our minds.

Repentance includes a commitment to follow Jesus in a new way of life. During a baptism service one of the ministers asked a new convert for a confession of faith:

> Jeff, let me ask you a question. Have you admitted your sinfulness to a holy God? Have you received forgiveness and grace through Jesus Christ through his death on the cross? And you're committed to being his disciple for all your days?

These questions summarize the elements of this decision: (1) a confession of sin and request for forgiveness, and (2) a commitment to follow and obey Jesus in the future.

Challenge to Receive Christ

For the majority of his messages, Hybels emphasizes his own experience and what he shares in common with Harry. Yet to move people, Hybels has to challenge them. And to challenge them, he switches from intimacy and identifying to confronting them with a "you." Hybels used "you" 6,152 times during the year I studied. By so doing, Hybels points a verbal finger at visiting Harry and emotionally confronts Harry to be honest and make a choice.

Hybels first encourages unchurched Harry and identifies with him by saying, "God promises to relieve the burden of the guilt that many of us are feeling." But he clarifies that there is a foundational step that is necessary for this to happen. He challenges nonbelievers to get honest with themselves:

> Before *we* can be cleansed, first *we* have to come clean with God by admitting *our* own shortcomings.
>
> *You* know, if you try to take a shower with *your* clothes on, *you're* not gonna get very clean. And *you're* not gonna be cleansed until *you* can strip away *your* rationalizations, and *your* excuses, and *your* phony justifications and *your* sleek facade, and *you* come clean with God so that he can cleanse *you* [emphasis added].

To say that Hybels challenges unchurched Harry to trust Christ is not entirely accurate. He actually coaxes, suggests, pleads with, requests, and confronts unchurched Harry. Hybels intuitively chooses which skill of challenging is most effective in a particular situation.

In one situation, Hybels identifies with Harry by including himself in a description: "We must be just humble enough and trusting enough to pour our hearts out to him and then allow him to love us and minister to us." Hybels coaxes Harry to accept a description that Hybels is willing to apply to himself.

Hybels often makes suggestions to Harry. "Let me offer a few suggestions" is a common phrase in Hybels's messages. Don Cousins mildly encourages Harry, "The only suggestion I can offer for a troubled conscience is God's forgiveness through his Son, Jesus Christ." At times, Hybels offers as only a possibility something that he strongly believes: "If this book is God's Word . . . if it is God's message to you and the world, you had better find out what he's trying to communicate to you." Hybels believes that Harry will be more open to accepting his advice if the proposal comes packaged as a suggestion.

Hybels sometimes emotionally pleads with Harry: "I'm pleading with you, friends, as your pastor, as a brother, don't cop out on this." On another occasion, Hybels cried out, "Once again, I beg all of you to listen to what God says in the Bible." Hybels is trying to shake Harry up to the eternal seriousness of what he is saying: "I plead with you to turn to Christ. Delay no longer. Turn to Christ!"

Lastly Hybels occasionally confronts Harry with unambiguous decisiveness. Hybels challenged the large Christmas crowd, "Your choice this Christmas is simple, it's just simple. You can just stand and watch another Christmas go by, or you can fall on your knees in repentance." On other occasions, Hybels bluntly stated, "I want to challenge you without embarrassment or apology; I'll ask you straight on—when did you sign up? When did you sign up? Are you sure you have?"

Depending on the situation in his argument, Hybels applies a different kind of challenge. With these tools Hybels is urging Harry to make a decision.

As is obvious from the examples I have quoted, Hybels's challenges to unchurched Harry are often very emotional. By becoming emotional, Hybels is able to seize Harry's attention and spur him to decide to trust Christ for salvation.

Hybels and his fellow speakers often use emotional descriptions to emphasize their point. For example:

"His question haunted me for months and months."

"As he described his feelings of defeat, I found myself starting to choke back tears."

"If the companionship of God were ever removed from my life for even a day, I'd lose hope and give up, because my future looks bleak and lonely."

"I got three or four weeks into my summer study break—I felt like my insides were coming out."

Harry isn't hearing a dry-as-bones history of Christianity but is seeing an emotional, flesh-and-blood drama with his own eyes. This kind of emotional description makes Christianity appear vivid and a live option for Harry.

Hybels regularly tells emotional stories as a part of his gospel message. When he describes his own or another's pain, Harry and Mary listen to both his description of the problem—and his proposed solution. Harry and Mary often see themselves and their own pain in Hybels's stories. Through identifying with the pain of those in the story, Harry and Mary become open to Hybels's solution of a relationship with Christ.

Like any excellent orator, Hybels is able to express emotions with his voice. Hybels's voice is like a finely tuned instrument in its ability to carry emotions. As a result, he is very persuasive. One seminary student who was attending Willow Creek told me how he would sometimes choose not to be moved by Hybels's message before going into the weekend service: "I decided that he wasn't going to get to me that week." And yet week after week, against his will, he would still be moved. Emotion becomes the pry bar that Hybels uses to jar unchurched Harry out of spiritual inertia.[10]

On rare occasions, Hybels asks individuals to raise hands to show their commitment:

> If it would help you to kind of make a physical symbol of this, to make sure that you know that you mean business about it, if you want to change camps from the wrong camp, to the camp of Christ today by trusting in him, put your hand up real high.[11]

As Strobel explains, "We'll sometimes eventually ask for a show of hands . . . and people come across the line."

Part 2

Evaluating the Willow Creek Way of Doing Church

14

Learning from Willow Creek

I have tried to investigate and describe Willow Creek in a careful and impartial way. The Golden Rule, "do unto others, as you would have them do unto you," is a pretty good sociological guideline at this point. I have attempted to represent Willow Creek as fairly and accurately as I would like to be treated.

The description you have just read could have been written by any sociologist. At the analytical and evaluative stage, however, the author's perspective unavoidably becomes an element of the discussion. Evaluation assumes that one is writing from a particular outlook. Because I am an evangelical, my assessment of Willow Creek comes from this perspective. While the first two-thirds of this book is relatively straightforward sociology, the last third combines sociological analysis with theological evaluation. As such I will be writing it especially to my fellow evangelicals, as a sort of family discussion. I hope, however, that any interested observers will find it thought provoking and helpful.[1]

This background is important because it highlights my final evaluation of Willow Creek. I ultimately discovered that I do not fit on either side of the marketing controversy within evangelicalism. An evangelical critic of Willow Creek rejects their overall strategy as an unavoidable compromise of biblical faith. I do not. A Willow Creek advocate defends the church's strategy as it now stands. I do not. As a result of this in-depth study, I have become a critical advocate of the Willow Creek strategy to reach the unchurched.

A critical advocate, like myself, affirms the basic mission and yet has some fundamental questions about how Willow Creek is seeking to accomplish it. The rest of this book is an unpacking of this conclusion. This chapter is a critical exposition of what I believe can be learned from Willow Creek. The following six chapters explain five questions or critiques at greater length.

I believe that there are two major principles that can be learned from the Willow Creek seeker service. First, the idea of a "church" for the unchurched is a creative innovation that has great potential for the communication of the gospel. Second, Willow Creek's basic model of communication is a clarification of a useful model of persuasion.

A Church for the Unchurched

We see in the Scriptures that Jesus regularly taught many people who were not yet his disciples. A good deal of his ministry was public teaching on hillsides and at street corners. Only after listening to Jesus in these public settings, asking questions, and seeing the reality of his life, did individuals choose to become his disciples.

Likewise the apostle Paul regularly interacted with nonbelieving Jews and Greeks in whatever public forum was available. Acts 17:17 records that Paul "reasoned in the synagogue with the Jews and the God-fearing Greeks, as well as in the marketplace day by day with those who happened to be there." In Ephesus, Paul had daily discussions in a public lecture hall for two years with the effect that "all the Jews and Greeks who lived in the province of Asia heard the word of the Lord." Paul used a variety of public settings to proclaim and explain the gospel to his audiences.[2]

We see throughout church history this same willingness to use a variety of public settings to communicate the gospel. George Whitefield and John Wesley initiated open-air preaching in the eighteenth century as a useful public forum to communicate the gospel. Many individuals criticized them for this shocking method of preaching outside of churches. As Wesley explains, "I submitted to be more vile, and proclaimed in the highways the glad tidings of salvation." This innovation proved to be very fruitful as tens of thousands came to hear and respond to the gospel.[3]

In contemporary American culture, open-air preaching is generally not a fruitful method to attract a crowd and persuade them about the truthfulness of Christianity. Few persons are interested in a wandering evangelist in a local forest preserve, or the street corner preacher. Many Americans feel as if their invisible cocoon of anonymity has been violated in these settings. There is currently no neutral and socially accepted public forum that can be used to persuade individuals about the truth concerning Jesus.

Understood from a biblical and historical point of view, the idea of a seeker service is a modern adaptation of Wesley's open-air meetings, Paul's discussions in the Ephesus lecture hall, or Jesus' hillside parables. I believe that even the harshest of Willow Creek critics should concede this point. Even if people totally disagree with *how* Willow Creek goes about presenting the gospel, the concept of creating a public forum to present the gospel is a wonderful idea.

Different methods are useful to deliver the truth at different points in history and in different cultures. Because the apostle Paul proclaimed the gospel in a marketplace does not mean that we should climb on a crate in the vegetable section of our local grocery store. Instead of meeting on a hillside, a marketplace, or highway, Willow Creek's evangelistic meetings occur in a modern auditorium.[4]

I believe that the idea of a church service for the unchurched can be adapted in many places around the world. In many countries, however, such a service may not be useful. It would probably be more valuable in cultures that are secularized, modern, and urbanized. Individuals in such a culture are socially uneasy outside of the webs of their daily relationships; a seeker service provides a safe public environment for them in which the gospel can be presented and explained. This leads to the second major principle of creative persuasion.

Creative Persuasion

Evangelicals are willing, and often eager, to tell others the "good news" about Jesus—that he is the Son of God and gave his life as a sacrifice for others' sins. The extent to which someone believes in the uniqueness of the gospel and is motivated to tell others about this belief and related experiences is a barometer of that person's evangelical commitment.

Historically, a part of this process of communicating the gospel has been creative persuasion. The history of the Christian church is partially a history of how different Christian individuals and groups have sought to convince non-Christians about the truthfulness of Christianity. Yet modern evangelicals have emphasized proclamation and diminished, or denied altogether, the importance of persuasion.[5]

Many evangelicals feel that seeking to persuade non-believers is somehow wrong. In contrast, I would argue that a robust commitment to persuade others is a sign of a healthy biblical Christianity. The life of Augustine of Hippo (354–430) exemplifies the importance of persuasion.

Augustine, as a former professor of rhetoric, was not naive concerning the possible misuse of persuasive tools. Augustine described principles of persuasion as "the rules of eloquence" and noted, "They can be used in connection with true principles as well as with false, they are not themselves culpable, but the perversity of ill using them is culpable." Augustine argues that although the art of persuasive communication can be used toward false ends and with wrong motivations, Christians should not discard these tools.[6]

Augustine himself used persuasion to fight for orthodoxy and against various heretical movements. At different times over the course of his life, Augustine fought the Manicheans, Donatists, Pelagians, and Neo-pagans. We see in Augustine an activist whose theology was white hot and hammered strong in the heat of theological controversy. He was an intellectual boxer who adjusted his tactics and arguments depending on his opponent.

Creative persuasion is central to the Christian gospel. The apostle Paul is the premier biblical exemplar of an evangelist. He did not merely go to each different city, repeat the same rote message, and walk on. The New Testament chronicles an evangelist who sought to proclaim, explain, and defend the gospel (persuade) in a way that made sense in each separate context. At the Athens Areopagus, Paul affirmed his pagan audience's belief in an "unknown God," quoted a pagan poet, and then began to explain the gospel (Acts 17:16–34). In contrast, when Paul entered the synagogue in Thessalonica, "on three Sabbath days he reasoned with them from the Scriptures, explaining and proving that the Christ had to suffer and rise from the dead" (Acts 17:1–3). Paul sought to persuade each audience creatively using references and language that they could understand.

Willow Creek's weekend service recovers the importance of creative persuasion. Why do people make commitments to Christ at Willow Creek? I believe that the Holy Spirit is using this persuasive process to convince nonbelievers. The result? Thousands of unchurched Harrys and Marys made commitments to Christ at Willow Creek during the years of my research and writing.[7]

I would critically affirm much of the Willow Creek seeker service, but I need to underline the word *critically.* I believe that the central ideas of understanding, credibility, identifying, and so on can be affirmed as part of a biblical strategy of persuasion, but much of the content of these ideas needs to be examined. The rest of this chapter is a critical exposition of each of these ideas with cautions and criticisms attached.

Sociology has the ability to map out the intended consequences of social organizations. The two intended consequences of Willow Creek's seeker service are (1) the creation of an attractive setting to communicate the gospel and (2) a persuasion process to help the unchurched become believers. As we have noted, Willow Creek is successful with both of these fundamental goals.

Yet sociology's specialty is to delve beneath the surface of social reality to detect and analyze various latent consequences to social behavior that are neither known nor intended. These intended and latent functions could be compared to ocean tides and the resulting undertows they create. Like the high tide on any beach, intended functions can be seen and measured rather easily. Latent functions are like the hidden subterranean currents and undertows that these tidal forces create. There are a series of latent functions or unintended consequences of the Willow Creek seeker service in each element of persuasion.

Understanding

Understanding the people with whom one is seeking to communicate is the foundation of effective communication. There is a very good reason why missionaries study the culture, history, and language of the people they are trying to reach. They realize that effective communication requires an empathetic understanding of their audience. This principle is accepted by the best of preachers. Evangelical leader John Stott has depicted preaching as being "between two worlds," the Word and the world. He argues that preachers need to understand both.

We see this contextual understanding in Jesus' ministry. Jesus was communicating primarily to rural audiences. His parables reflect this agricultural background: Jesus taught about trees with good fruit or bad fruit, seeds that are fruitful or unfruitful, and trees that need to be pruned. Jesus understood his audience and employed images that they understood. As I noted above, the apostle Paul also sought to understand each of his different audiences and employed different strategies to reach them. Unless there is a conscious or intuitive grasp of one's audience, one cannot communicate successfully.

Willow Creek's goal of seeking to understand their unchurched audience is correct. Their aim is to understand unchurched Harry and Mary in order to help them comprehend the astonishing news that God has broken into history to reveal himself and has offered them an eternal relationship. I also believe that Creekers' motivation is biblical in that they truly love their unchurched friends and family and long for them to know Jesus as they do. A weakness of their strategy is found in their means of understanding Harry: marketing terminology and strategy.

Should we seek to understand our unchurched friends and family? Yes. Should we do a market analysis of unchurched Harry? I don't believe so. The topic of marketing is one of the most controversial elements of the Willow Creek seeker service. It is so difficult and complicated that it should not be summarized in a few paragraphs. I will discuss marketing in some depth in chapter 18.

Programming

Advocates of the Willow Creek approach believe that to reach unchurched individuals the church needs to speak the unchurched's language and use their methods. This is not only accurate in its depiction of how communication works, but it is also scriptural.

Those who totally reject Willow Creek's use of programming should reexamine the story of the prophet Nathan and King David in 2 Samuel 12:1–7. Following God's directions, Nathan told David a story of a rich man who had huge herds of sheep and cattle but stole and killed the pet prized lamb of a poor man. David in response "burned with anger." Nathan then rebuked David for stealing the lovely Bathsheba and killing her husband by sending him to fight in the front ranks against Israel's enemies.

The prophet Nathan created a drama to make a mirror for King David. David was leaning forward in anger as the story progressed and then fell down in remorse when Nathan pulled the rug out from beneath his feet. "I have sinned against the LORD," David concluded. This was a God-directed drama in which the moment of revelation showed David his sin. God obviously believes in creative communication and, in this case, drama.

We also see the importance in Scripture of the use of music in effecting spiritual change. When King Saul was tormented by an evil spirit, David was asked to play the harp. The result? "David would take his harp and play. Then relief would come to Saul; he would feel better, and the evil spirit would leave him" (1 Sam. 16:23). When David became king, over four thousand musicians were employed to sing in the temple in praise of God (1 Chron. 23:5). Music is a means to reorient human beings to a healthy relationship with God.

The Scripture also records that God and his spokesmen often communicated visually and creatively to get across God's point. For example, after Israel crossed the Jordan, God instructed Joshua to have twelve stones placed as a memorial of how God stopped the waters: "When your children ask you, 'What do these stones mean?' tell them that the flow of the Jordan was cut off before the ark of the covenant of the LORD" (Josh. 4:6–7). When God wanted Jeremiah to confront his people, he often gave him a physical symbol of the message he wanted him to take to Israel (Jer. 19:1–11).

Those who totally reject the use of the arts in Christian communication need to wrestle with these and many other similar Scripture passages. However, the arts should be used with some caution. The critics of Willow Creek's programming have some legitimate concerns.

The first potential problem of the use of the arts is that ultimately the method of how one communicates tends to shape the message. We see this clearly in modern communication as news reporting has been shaped by the medium of television. Robert MacNeil, coanchor of the *MacNeil-Lehrer News Hour,* reveals some important assumptions behind news shows: that "complexity must be avoided, that nuances are dispensable, that qualifications impede the simple message, that visual stimulation is a substitute for thought, and that verbal precision is an anachronism."[8]

Many of these same tendencies are also true of Willow Creek. Creekers generally seek to avoid complexity and they believe that "nuances are dispensable." Creekers often use "visual stimulation as a substitute for thought" and do not value verbal precision. Making Christianity more visual tends to make it less verbal. Simplicity is valued, and conceptual complexity is devalued. One church attender told me that when he leaves services, he feels "more 'liver shiver' than a clarity of direction." Creekers need to make a self-conscious effort to resist the dilution of their message.

The second possible problem in the use of the arts in Christian communication is the potential lack of willingness to upset or confront Harry. If a high priority is placed on providing entertainment rather than on communicating a message, the method will distort the message. The message will be shaped into a cheerful Christianity that is not true to the Scriptures. I do not believe this weakness is generally true of Willow Creek. Willow Creek's staff members leading the programming are aware of the temptation to get an extra laugh and compromise or soft-sell their message. They want their use of the arts to be "content driven" or "message driven."

The third potential problem in the use of the arts is their cultural adaptability. The arts can be used in other cultures, but there will probably have to be a great deal of cultural translation. Following American media, much of Willow Creek's programming leans toward being highly emotional. This style of communication will have difficulty being transplanted to many other cultural settings.

For example, at a pastors' conference in France, Willow Creek's international director said that "some of the criticism was that it could appear, on the surface, that the presentation of our program has a lot of glitz—that it was more style than substance." The director also questions the applicability of Willow Creek's American emphasis on emotional intimacy to the European context: "The whole idea of intimacy in relationships is another area that might be difficult to transfer. . . . When you go into the European cultural context . . . there is more of a formality to relationships." Staff members are aware of this problem and specifically warn other churches to not imitate Willow Creek's strategy but to crack their own unique "cultural code."[9]

The fourth weakness of the use of the arts is the temptation of image, which will be described in some depth in chapter 16.

All these potential weaknesses are not enough to discredit the arts, as they are an effective communication tool. We are seeing in the contemporary world the re-emergence of the importance and influence of visual forms of communication and to this extent a return to preliterate days. Before general public education, most individuals received information far more visually; thus the Christian use of images and ceremony was crucial. Christian beliefs were draped in the visual patterns that had been transmitted through history. I believe that Christians need to use modern, visual forms of communication cautiously and critically under the lordship of Christ.

Credibility

Hybels realizes that his credibility determines to a large extent his persuasive influence. Hybels seeks to be authentic and to communicate with integrity, intimacy, emotion, and affection. If Harry can come to trust and like Hybels as a person, Harry will be more open to his message.

There is no doubt that credibility is crucial in communication. This is why the Greeks described an authentic orator as "a good man skilled in speaking." Aristotle explained:

> Persuasion is achieved by the speaker's personal character when the speech is so spoken as to make us think him *credible*.
>
> We believe good men more fully and more readily than others: this is true generally whatever the question is, and absolutely true where exact certainty is impossible and opinions are divided [emphasis added].[10]

Overemphasizing credibility, however, can be dangerous. The first danger is the possibility that what one communicates could be shaped by the desire to be received well. Don Cousins argues that "in everything we do as a church . . . we make it clear that God and his followers are not backward or second-rate or dull." Implicit in this desire not to be "second-rate" is also a desire to be liked and admired.[11]

Hybels is aware that the effect of what he is saying can be greater if he emphasizes a certain point or exaggerates a little. He has admitted that consequently exaggeration is one of his weaknesses. Close friends sometimes confront him on his inclination to embellish the truth. Hybels reports how his small group once challenged him: "Bill, you're kidding yourself—you think you're obeying this, you're not. When you use that illustration about the seven-car pile-up, Bill. We were with you. There were only three cars in that pile-up."

Simply put, there is a danger in exaggeration or pretense. A speaker may become more aware of and concerned about how the audience sees him than how God sees him. Hybels's honesty in describing this temptation is commendable.

A second danger of credibility is that an emphasis is placed on how one communicates rather than on who one is. This is particularly true in our modern therapeutic culture, in which an emotional style of communication has become popular.

Willow Creek speakers often identify with unchurched Harry by confessing to various weaknesses. "You share victories in certain kinds of settings, and people start feeling second class, people start thinking, 'I could never do that—you're better than me.' But boy, you share losses and defeats, a totally different kind of thing."

In response to a speaker's confessions, Harry's emotions of envy and self pity are avoided and his feelings of compassion and affection are stimulated. As a speaker confesses his weaknesses, Harry feels intimate with, similar to, and thus compassionate toward him. Harry doesn't think the speaker is pointing a preachy finger at him. A speaker gains credibility with Harry in this confessional method of speaking.

This revelatory style of communication is a peculiar custom of modern American society. In the psychological recovery mindset, the first step to renewal is to admit that one has a problem. Hybels observes, "Thirty years ago, nobody had any problems. . . . Even if they did, for heaven's sake, they certainly wouldn't talk about it!" Today the modern psychological worldview has made raw emotional honesty a moral doctrine. Within this framework, to admit one's faults is not only acceptable and moral, but fashionable: One is not "in denial."

Thus a speaker's confessions resonate with unchurched Harry as a particular expression of the broader therapeutic culture. A speaker is able to identify with Harry, Harry in turn is able to identify with him, and the speaker's credibility is increased.

Yet, judging a leader to be credible primarily by how he communicates and what he says is a shallow understanding of biblical credibility. Understood biblically, credibility (respect or honor) is a consequence of integrity. If someone has proven by his deeds and maturity that he can be trusted and admired, he then should have credibility (respect or honor). Paul tells the Philippians to respect Epaphroditus: "Honor men like him." Why? Paul describes him as a "fellow worker" and "fellow soldier" who has a deep affection for the Philippians and nearly "died for the work of Christ"(see Phil. 2:25–30).

I need to be clear here. I believe that Willow Creek speakers are seeking to live with integrity and should be accorded respect and thus credibility. The point behind this discussion is to note the temptation of an emotional style of speaking.

The potential pitfalls of pursuing credibility do not invalidate its importance. But biblical credibility (respect or honor) cannot be achieved as a goal. Ironically, the more one focuses on gaining credibility, the less likely one will have it. Integrity should be one's goal, and credibility should be a consequence.

Identifying

Hybels and Willow Creek are not unique in their emphasis on identifying. Historian Peter Brown observed that Augustine's great ability as a preacher was partially rooted in his ability to identify with his audience:

> This is the secret of Augustine's enormous power as a preacher. . . . He could *identify* himself sufficiently with his congregation to provoke them to *identify* themselves completely with himself [emphasis added].[12]

The apostle Paul is the primary example of one who, in his efforts to communicate, identified with different audiences. In 1 Corinthians 9:19–22, Paul explains his reasoning:

> Though I am free and belong to no man, I make myself a slave to everyone, to win as many as possible. To the Jews I became as a Jew, to win the Jews. To

> those under the law I became like one under the law (though I myself am not under the law), so as to win those under the law.
>
> To those not having the law I became like one not having the law (though I am not free from God's law but am under Christ's law), so as to win those not having the law. To the weak I became weak, to win the weak. I have become all things to all men so that by all possible means I might save some.

Paul emphasized his similarities with each group he addressed. What is the result of this process of identifying? People listened to Paul. The message of Jesus Christ gained access to different groups as Paul moved as close to his audience as possible. As Henry Chadwick argues, "Paul's genius as an apologist is his astonishing ability to reduce to an apparent vanishing point the gulf between himself and his converts and yet to gain them for the Christian gospel."[13]

Hybels and Willow Creek have tried to model themselves after Paul's example. The broader church can learn from Hybels's ability to identify with his audience.[14]

Anyone seeking to persuade needs to use the audience's language. After Hungary shrugged off its Marxist past, a group of hip young politicians (FIDESZ) captured the attention and allegiance of a large portion of the populace. Why? Commentator Tina Rosenberg explains that they "used language everyone understood. . . . FIDESZ knew how to talk to Hungary." Other, older critics had been saying many of the same things for much longer, but were "so scathing and subtle in their analysis that no one else could understand them."[15]

An evangelical strength is the ability to adapt to and employ the language of the culture evangelicals are seeking to reach. Historian Nathan Hatch notes that evangelical speakers in the nineteenth-century revivals in America who were not theologically trained "could retain a deep empathy for their audience, what Philip Schaff called 'a decided aptness for popular discourse and exhortation.'" In contrast, Peter Brierly, the editor of *UK Christian Handbook,* argues that Anglo-Catholics in the United Kingdom are hampered in their outreach to the working class by their theological education: "It causes them to speak a different language from that of the working class." By using the common language of the people, evangelicals can more easily explain the Christian gospel.[16]

However, a danger in identifying with the audience is the temptation to compromise the gospel. The built-in weakness of evangelicalism's cultural flexibility is the temptation to compromise its basic message. There are certain biblical truths such as sin, God's holiness, repentance, and so on that cannot be easily translated into a cultural equivalent. As one seeks to translate the gospel message into the language of one's audience, there is the possibility of subtly changing the gospel in the process.[17]

The Bible's message could be paraphrased into terminology that does not accurately reflect the biblical message. For example, the *holiness* of God was regularly paraphrased by Creekers as *purity*. Lost in this casual depiction is the awesome magnificence of God's perfection that causes human beings to see their own sin. A vision of God's holiness caused Isaiah to cry out, "Woe to me! I am ruined! For I am a man of unclean lips!" (Isa. 6:5). Without an effort to understand biblical holiness, much of the gospel is clouded or garbled.

The language of the Scriptures needs to be translated to every unique culture, but to exchange these biblical truths with a cultural paraphrase may ultimately end up distorting them with a different cultural language. More work needs to be done by Willow Creek in understanding and explaining the unique language and worldview that the Bible teaches.

The second potential problem with identifying with the audience is the possibility of compromising one's ethics. Like the desire for credibility, the desire to move closer to one's audience can cause speakers or singers to emphasize something that is not true to who they are. Individuals can become more concerned with what their audience thinks of them than with what God thinks of them.

If these potential problems are acknowledged and successfully guarded against, the use of identifying can be a valuable part of a biblical process of persuasion.

Relevance

No aspect of Willow Creek's strategy is more controversial than the idea of relevance. Part of this problem is that people define "relevance" differently. Willow Creek advocate Barna teaches that relevance necessarily means meeting individuals' felt needs. Willow Creek critic MacArthur believes that relevance automatically causes compromise. We need to be careful here. One's definition of "relevance" determines one's opinion of it.[18]

Neither of these conceptions of relevance is adequate. On the one hand, Barna and Willow Creek's understanding of relevance unnecessarily stresses felt needs. This overemphasis comes from the marketing theory that guides their strategy and results in a theology that teaches that Christianity will bring fulfillment.

On the other hand, the concept of relevance need not be rejected, as MacArthur has done. Communicating relevantly does not necessarily imply that one has compromised the truth. The husk of felt needs can be discarded and the true seed within of biblical relevance can be salvaged.

Relevance, understood from a biblical viewpoint, refers to the ability that Jesus had to communicate to people where they were. Jesus taught the truth to people where they lived. His message was not a canned speech to be read to each new crowd that gathered. Rather we see in Jesus a flexibility that articulated a distinct word to each peculiar situation. When the scribes showed their lack of sincerity, Jesus responded by telling a parable that illustrated their hard hearts: "They knew he had spoken the parable against them" (Mark 12:12).[19]

Jesus taught people the truth, rather than the truth to people. The truth did not change, but the particular point of application did depending on the context or person that Jesus was addressing. This style of responsiveness was true for both his teaching and his evangelism. Walter Hollenweger explains:

> We find everywhere the same pattern: the starting point of Jesus' evangelism is mostly (although not always) a question, or the concrete situation of the people around him. . . . New Testament evangelism does not start from a proposition. It starts from a situation.[20]

Relevance, understood in this way, starts with people—but not necessarily with their felt needs. The ultimate goal of Jesus' ministry was to glorify his Father in heaven. To glorify means in part to reflect. Jesus reflected his Father's character and concerns in every situation he encountered. At times this meant he tenderly held the little children or gently healed a leper. In other words, Jesus occasionally met individuals' felt needs. But Jesus also had a ministry of confrontation and regularly rebuked those he came into contact with. One can hardly describe Jesus as having a ministry of only felt needs when he called some people "whitewashed sepulchers" or bellowed in rage and used a whip to clear the temple of the money changers.[21]

Following Jesus, our fundamental goal should be to glorify God in all that we do. This may sometimes mean reflecting God's love and compassion and meeting individuals' felt needs. At other times, it will mean reflecting his holiness and prophetic judgment to a stubborn and rebellious people. The criteria for our communication should be to glorify God by reflecting his character and concerns in each unique situation.

However, glorifying God does not mean that we should not communicate relevantly. To communicate relevantly, as I have defined it, means to understand the individuals one is addressing and communicate with them in a way that speaks to their unique situation. We see this same principle at work with the Gospel writers and the apostle Paul.

Why do we even have four different Gospels? Because the four separate authors had different audiences in mind and thus wrote books with different themes. The Gospel of Matthew is written for a Jewish audience, as it emphasizes how Jesus fulfilled the prophecies of the Old Testament. Does the truth concerning Jesus change? No. But the emphases of each Gospel are unique as each provides a different portrait of Jesus.

We see this same relevance with the apostle Paul's letters. When Paul writes the Philippians, he is seeking to reorient them as a church body. The church had been experiencing internal conflict and discord (4:2). Paul affirms them (1:1–11) and encourages them to concentrate on the gospel (1:12–26), be united (1:27–30), be humble (2:1–11), be obedient (2:12–30), be focused (3:1–11), be future oriented (3:12–4:1), and be thankful (4:2–23). In other words, without in any way compromising the content of the truth, Paul communicates relevantly by starting at the point where the Philippians were. He teaches them how to be united as a church family, because that was the problem they were dealing with. In contrast, Paul rebukes the Galatians for so "quickly deserting the one who called you" (Gal. 1:6). We see in the apostle Paul's letters to the various churches a profound understanding of each local situation and a relevant articulation of the truth.

Communication, if it is to be received, must take into account the situation of the hearer. Without this focus, communication is either easily dismissed or completely ignored.

It is true, however, that making the gospel relevant can easily compromise it. The unintended consequences of this approach are that Hybels incorporates large chunks of the American psychological worldview into his basic teaching and teaches that fulfillment is a consequence of the Christian life. There is a lack of critical evaluation to Willow Creek's approach to relevance. This felt-need approach to relevance ultimately distorts their Christianity.

A more biblical approach to the current American fixation with fulfillment is to call it the idolatry that it is. Jesus does not guarantee that to follow him will make one fulfilled. In fact, at several points, the direct opposite is communicated: "I have chosen you out of the world. That is why the world hates you" (John 15:19); "I did not come to bring peace but a sword" (Matt. 10:34); "If they persecuted me, they will persecute you also" (John 15:20). The temptation to say that Christianity will meet all one's felt needs and provide fulfillment is not true to biblical Christianity.

The second danger or weakness of making Christianity relevant is the possibility of manipulation. Any effective communicator can use an audience's felt needs as a tool of manipulation. Lenin, leading the Communist revolution in Russia, exclaimed, "The people need peace. The people need bread. The people need land. And they give you war, hunger, no bread. . . . We must fight for the social revolution!" Lenin connected his Marxist ideology with the poverty of the people and was able to manipulate the needy Russians to accomplish his revolutionary purposes.[22]

Both theological compromise and manipulation can be guarded against—if one's firm goal is to glorify God. If one is committed to glorifying God, communication takes on biblical substance and becomes theologically anchored. With this biblical relevance, one can start with an understanding of the audience but is directed by the nature and character of God. Thus Scripture—not the felt needs of the audience—dictates the substance of the message. In fact, a biblical commitment to glorifying God often requires confronting or rebuking one's audience rather than caring for their felt needs.

I am not arguing that needs should never be addressed. Rather I am suggesting that the appropriate way to evaluate how they are addressed is to ask what God's character and concerns are in response to each situation. The commitment to glorify God and reflect his character and concerns also guides the motivation and ethics of the speaker. If a speaker is reflecting God's concerns, he does not manipulate the audience, he structures the message so that the audience feels free to choose and not coerced to agree. By connecting the timeliness of relevance with the timelessness of glorifying God, a communicator can be both contemporary and faithful.

Christianity Is True

There is no aspect of the weekend service that I can as strongly advocate as Willow Creek's commitment to argue for Christianity's truthfulness. Many evangelicals have a negative attitude toward the whole idea of persuasion and often say, "You can't argue someone into heaven." Although true, this statement fails to acknowledge the importance the Bible places on the mind and obscures the centrality of truth. As John Stott writes, "The Holy Spirit is the spirit of truth. He persuades people through the truth, and not in spite of it."[23]

I believe the two elements of Willow Creek's apologetic strategy are clearly biblical. The apostle Paul used destabilizing arguments: "We demolish arguments and every pretension that sets itself up against the knowledge of God, and we take captive every thought to make it obedient to Christ" (2 Cor. 10:5). Peter describes foundational arguments' function of positive answers when he exhorts, "Always be prepared to give an answer to everyone who asks you to give the reason for the hope that you have" (1 Peter 3:15).

These two arguments fit together into one strategy. On the one hand, Hybels destabilizes Harry's current belief system or philosophy. Hybels identifies and takes apart any reasoning that keeps individuals from faith in Christ. By debunking Harry's beliefs and illusions, Hybels jars Harry loose from his neutrality and indifference. By putting pressure on Harry's understanding of the world, Hybels is seeking to push Harry toward nihilism. Harry feels an internal pressure to find a new and credible worldview.

This sets up an internal pressure or cognitive dissonance within visiting Harrys. Sociologist James Hunter explains that cognitive dissonance is "an experience of confusion and anxiety about the certainty of [one's] own understanding of reality." Harry begins to question the truthfulness of his worldview or philosophy and because of this disorientation more positively considers the gospel.[24]

Simultaneously Hybels seeks to demonstrate Christianity's intellectual credibility. The Christianity that Hybels and his colleagues present is plausible, and Hybels's arguments are very effective for the typical unchurched Harry.

As with the other principles of persuasive communication discussed above, the idea of plausibility is not new. "When dealing with the way to handle a popular audience," Aristotle comments, "we must use, as our modes of persuasion and argument, notions possessed by everybody." Hybels appeals to the common sense that he and unchurched Harrys hold in common.[25]

Hybels often argues that common sense confirms the biblical message: "Common sense, street smarts, business savvy, and biblical teaching would all agree." Instinctively, Hybels seeks to appeal to convictions that he shares with Harry to show that Christianity is credible.

By pitching his message and arguments to an unchurched Harry who is guided by his common sense, Hybels places a great deal of importance on Harry's using his own reasoning, rather than depending on the experts. The result? Hybels is effective in persuading unchurched Harrys. Why?

First, Hybels does not use a highly technical or academic vocabulary. He simplifies complex philosophical or theological reasoning and makes it palatable. His quick verbal sketches of various philosophical arguments evoke a sense that Christianity is true to the nature of reality.

Second, Hybels spotlights historical arguments in contrast to philosophical reasoning. Historical evidential arguments are more accessible to a popular audience than philosophical arguments and therefore appear more plausible. Hybels presents a popular historical apologetic for the common man.

Third, Hybels's arguments destabilizing Harry's philosophy and roadblocks to faith are very successful. Harry not only is encouraged to see Christianity as credible, but also has his present philosophy discredited before his eyes. As Harry's questions proliferate concerning his own worldview, he becomes correspondingly more open to the gospel.

Fourth, Hybels emphasizes the importance of each individual wrestling with the question of Christianity's truthfulness for himself or herself. The main criterion that Hybels urges Harry to use in judging the evidence is his own "common sense." Once again we find a remarkable parallel between Hybels's strategy and that in the nineteenth-century evangelical renewal. Hatch comments about one of the leading preachers then:

> Miller had no use for academic theology. . . . He invited common folk to . . . trust their own intellectual abilities rather than depending on answers that descended from colleges and seminaries.[26]

Finally, there are many examples at Willow Creek of individuals who are very similar to Harry, except for their commitment to Christ. This similarity makes the step of faith a live option.

This idea of individuals weighing the evidence for Christianity is reflected in Willow Creek testimonies. One man explained his conversion at a baptism service:

> I want to stress that this is a logical decision rather than an emotional one for me. I worked as an engineer, constantly pouring over drawings, test reports, and specifications. I am well accustomed with gathering data and making the most informed decision possible. To me, the utter logic and equality of God's plan for salvation is brilliant.[27]

Gospel

Willow Creek's gospel is not particularly persuasive—by itself. Its persuasive force comes first from the broader process, which I have outlined above. Harry at this point is willing and often eager to hear the four handles of the gospel (God, man, Christ, and response).

Comprehension is the next step of the persuasion process. Harry slowly comes to understand the four handles of the gospel. This step of comprehension, although obvious, needs to be stated. If a person is to accept Hybels's gospel, he or she must first understand it.

The next step of this persuasive process is for Harry to actually believe that the Christian gospel is true. At some point, the evidence for Christianity will be enough to make Christianity intellectually convincing. Simultaneously the message of a holy and loving God who has engineered a rescue operation in Christ's work on the cross becomes more compelling. The last step of this persuasive process is for Harry to make a response of faith.

The second reason why Willow Creek's gospel is persuasive is because of the distinct and clear teaching of how salvation can be appropriated. Most unchurched Harrys already affirm many orthodox Christian beliefs. Yet these Harrys often don't understand the gospel.

One group of Harrys makes the mistake of substance. These Harrys do not understand or believe one or more of the first three gospel handles. Over weeks and months of attending Willow Creek, many of these Harrys come to understand and accept the truth of these descriptions.

The second group of Harrys makes the mistake of method. They don't understand how to receive the free gift of salvation that God offers. In other words, they have either never heard or never responded to the fourth handle of receiving Christ as forgiver and Lord. As noted above, approximately 50 percent of Willow Creek's converts are former Roman Catholics. Many of these former Catholics believe that they need to do good works to gain salvation. It is the message of personally trusting Christ as Savior and Lord—without works—that Hybels emphasizes so clearly.

With the four simple handles, Hybels is presenting a clear and powerful worldview or paradigm for understanding life. Yet Hybels's message is more than a worldview: it is also a warm invitation to join. This is the powerful strength of Hybels's evangelical message: providing a simple summary of how people can begin a spiritual life. Hybels is offering individuals a paradigm shift into a relationship with God. Historian Hatch notes this same strength in the nineteenth-century evangelicals: "The evangelical message spread infectiously because it had redefined the most crucial step in the missionary endeavor: how to cross the threshold into the Christian church."[28]

In summary, I believe that the worldwide church can learn two basic lessons from Willow Creek's seeker service:

1. A church service that is directed at nonbelievers is an innovative creation and is potentially fruitful worldwide.
2. Willow Creek has developed a basic method of creative persuasion (with cautions attached) that also can be useful to the worldwide church.

This model of biblical persuasion could be summarized as follows:

Understanding. A compassionate understanding of the unchurched.
Programming. The use of the arts to help persuade the unchurched.

Credibility. The importance of a speaker and other participants who have personal integrity and thus credibility.

Identifying. Speakers and programs emphasizing the commonalities with their unchurched audiences.

Relevance. Beginning communication with the unchurched's situation.

Truth. Arguing for Christianity's intellectual credibility and against its alternatives.

Gospel. Presenting a clear, powerful statement of the gospel.

I would strongly affirm both the idea of a church service that is directed at the unchurched and this basic model of persuasion.

Bill Hybels and the Willow Creek staff and volunteers are to be commended for their dedicated efforts to communicate the gospel. They have sought to walk with integrity and faithfulness. The result of this twenty-year effort is that they have seen the Lord give them wonderful tools to communicate the gospel and many thousands of individuals have been rescued from an eternity in hell. We should honor them for their efforts and the resulting fruit of their labor. The Lord has used them and is using them.

But we also need to be honest concerning any weaknesses that are a part of this strategy. A tough-fibered realism is at the heart of a biblical worldview. We evangelicals have a higher authority over us than any human leader or movement. We have a commitment to honesty that is the result of our relationship with the Lord. Part of this honesty is a recognition that human beings are broken creatures. We all suffer from the fact that we live in a fallen world and have many character flaws. This is the nature of the human condition. Those who deny this reality are merely confessing their ignorance of their true nature. Every individual, organization, or movement has weaknesses. As we live in this world, we need to become accustomed to the here-and-not-yet quality of the kingdom of God. We need to be willing to see these weaknesses, if we are to honor the Lord.

Creekers are sincerely seeking to reach out in love to their family and friends. They have developed a systematic strategy of how to do this. Yet there are consequences to their strategy of which they are unaware.

15

The Christian Worldview and Culture

Before describing the unintended consequences of Willow Creek's method of communicating its gospel, the word *unintended* needs to be underlined. Hybels and his staff are seeking to be faithful to the Lord in their efforts to win the unchurched individuals from their community. In fact, they are sincere, dedicated, devout, and tireless in their efforts.

Yet in their labor to win unchurched individuals, Creekers use the tools of marketing, the language of psychology, and the communicative medium of modern media. In other words, Willow Creek uses elements of the broader culture in their efforts to see people converted to Christianity.

The problems of the Willow Creek seeker service are the mishaps of an inadequate Christian response to the American culture. To understand this, we need to clarify briefly two related concepts of a Christian worldview and culture.

A Christian worldview is a Christian understanding of reality. There are many synonyms for a Christian worldview including "thinking Christianly," "a Christian mind," "integration of faith and learning," and "a Christian view of culture." In classical terms, a Christian worldview means that an individual understands the world through a Christian theology. To have a Christian worldview is to see the world as it really is, by thinking God's thoughts after him. One who is thinking with a Christian worldview sees all of life from the framework of God's revealed truth. In essence then, a Christian worldview is Christ's view of the world.

Culture refers to the "whole way of life, material, intellectual, and spiritual of a given society." A culture includes the knowledge, art, laws, morals, methods, and customs of a particular people at a given time. Because cultures adapt and evolve over time, any specific culture is a particular social reality set within a broader historical process.[1]

We see in the contemporary evangelical movement in America a variety of responses or reactions to some aspect of culture. For example, James Dobson's "Focus on the Family" is an attempt to restore the American family in reaction to corrosive cultural forces. Likewise, Pat Robertson's "Christian Coalition" is an effort to influence the political structures of the culture.

These evangelical movements are not alone. All of church history could be understood as one long line of experiments in how to respond to one's culture. In his attempt to influence his contemporaries, Augustine began to use the cultural weapons of current philosophical and particularly platonic terminology:

> If those who are philosophers, especially the Platonists, have said things which are indeed true and are well accommodated to our faith, they should not be feared; rather what they have said should be taken from them as from unjust possessors and converted to our use.[2]

Augustine compared this borrowing of philosophical tools to Moses' Israelites taking the gold and silver from Egypt at God's command.

A similar thing could be said of virtually every period of the church. At different times various ideas, methods, and tools were influential in separate cultures. The Christian church has often adopted and used these ideas and tools in its work. The danger of this attempt is that the Christian church and message has often been profoundly shaped by this sort of cultural synthesis.

Willow Creek's unintended failures result from an uncritical use of various cultural tools and ideas. In particular, their mistakes are rooted in a superficial understanding of the American culture and an inadequate grasp of Christian theology. To understand the complexities of American culture takes an enormous amount of time and effort. Likewise, to understand the beauty and intricacy of the Christian worldview takes a tremendous amount of time and work. To frame a specifically Christian understanding of the American culture takes still further time and reflection.[3]

Willow Creekers, however, are people on the move. As various staff explained to me, "We are activists and pragmatists." They know what they are seeking to do (reach unchurched Harry with the gospel) and have developed an intuitive and pragmatic understanding of their culture to do this.

Their zeal and ingenuity in their efforts need to be applauded by the broader church. As I have already noted, I believe that the evangelical church has much to learn from Willow Creek. Yet the failure of Willow Creek is significant. The lack of a thoroughly Christian understanding of the dynamics of American culture results in several significant compromises.

Hybels and his staff approach the various aspects of culture as merely pragmatic tools to further the communication of the gospel. They do not understand that these cultural tools are double-edged swords and often cut those who wield them. What are the wounds, the unintended consequences of Willow Creek's seeker service?

1. Creekers use the methods of media to energize their message, creating the temptation of image.
2. Psychological categories and concepts are used to better identify with the unchurched and as a source of Hybels's Christianity 101. The use of psychology ultimately distorts the ethics of Willow Creek Christians.
3. Marketing tools are employed to better understand and communicate with unchurched neighbors. These marketing methods and ideas shape the Christianity that is presented.
4. Willow Creek seeks to be relevant in presenting Christianity to unchurched Harry. The result is that unchurched Harry's categories, language, and priorities shape the message of who God is.
5. As a result of Willow Creek's focus on pragmatic, measurable goals, the mind and education are not highly valued, which results in the loss of the centrality of truth.

To analyze any particular culture from a Christian worldview is not an easy process. Most individuals are often tone-deaf or color-blind to the sounds or hues of their own civilization. A way of cutting through this desensitivity is to ask, "What is Christ's view of this particular aspect of our culture?" The following five chapters ask this question about five aspects of Willow Creek's strategy.

16

The Temptation of Image

Because Hybels and his staff hope to persuade Harrys to become Christians they emphasize their similarities to them. As evangelism director Mittelberg asks, "How far can we move in their direction to best close the gap?" Their goal is to identify with Harry and Mary to facilitate communication so that they can ultimately become Christians.

Hybels and the programming team have been successful in identifying with unchurched Harrys and Marys and have seen them convert to Christianity. But there is an unintended consequence of this strategy of identifying. This strategy raises the question of image.

Hybels argues that image is a significant part of the Willow Creek strategy:

> In this community image is a real big deal. . . . When he (Harry) drives on the campus he is already assessing our corporate image and the effectiveness of our organization before the message has any bearing on his life.

Hybels believes that Harry places an "enormous emphasis on appearance." If image means this much to Harry, it should be no surprise that it has come to mean a lot to Hybels: "We say, 'Let's work really hard for the image sake.'"

Willow Creek's Efforts at Image Management

Hybels is very aware of how Harry views Willow Creek's grounds, buildings, and auditorium. Beach asserts that Harry is "assessing either positively or negatively the organization itself and the people on staff by the way this place looks."

Staff and volunteers work hundreds of hours each week to present the facilities in the best possible condition. We also see this concern for image in the stage design, those who appear on stage, and the overall program.

Stage

Beach explains that Harry is a "visual person." "The first thing that my team thinks about, the ten of us, is what the set is going to look like. What is he going to see on the stage?" The programming team develops a visual strategy to bring "color and light and interest" to the stage. It is not unusual for the weekend program to have stage props of some kind in order to enhance the program.

Performers

Those who appear on the stage are also scrutinized for image's sake. From the vantage point of an observer in the audience, I was surprised by the colorful variety of clothing worn by the singing team. This I learned was planned down to the last bright blue shirt. Mittelberg reports that identifying "relates to everything we do that communicates. It even comes down to the way that we dress."

Each singer has had his or her picture taken with every piece of clothing that he or she might wear onto the stage. One of the programming team members then selects which blouse, shirt, pants, or skirt each singer will wear. "We carefully prepare their attire, the style, the color, and the professional appearance," Beach says. The singers "dress like 90s' people dress."

Program

Last, and most important, every aspect of the program is a self-consciously chosen series of images. Nearly every moment is scripted. The programming and production crew know exactly what they want to do and how they want to do it. Nothing is left to chance. The production crew has a detailed list of cues to adjust the lighting at the right second.

Occasionally I sat in the auditorium during a rehearsal of a program. Each step and hand motion was scrutinized for effect. During one practice, the director told the singers to step forward "like you really mean it." A singer practiced his solo and rehearsed his hand motions and deep looks of sincerity to an empty auditorium.[1]

This is not to suggest that the programming team members are not sincere. The vocal team is taught to sing only when they can do so authentically. But there is a danger built into this method. Willow Creekers, in their efforts to identify with Harry, have developed a highly self-conscious method of performance. They seek to manage a series of impressions so Harry might feel and think certain things. The Creekers are aware of this distinction. Hybels exhorts other pastors to hire programming staff so "there will be the *perception* and later the *reality* of the fact that this is an exciting place to be" (emphasis added).

The distinction between perception and reality has become a part of the Willow Creek mindset. Hybels describes to a group of pastors that it is important to show their congregations that they are concerned about being responsible financially: "We do everything in our power to *posture ourselves* as being those who are concerned about these matters" (emphasis added). Such language as "perception," "reality," and "posture ourselves" reveals an awareness of the importance of image in a performance. There is a self-conscious choosing of appropriate impressions.

George Barna explicitly encourages churches to think of presenting their image to the unchurched: "You should be able to develop the image you want and more persuasively alert people to what you, as a church, are all about, and how they can benefit from what you offer." This pattern is a part of the modern image management in our culture.[2]

Image Management

The management of images is a large part of modern communication. People involved in entertainment, sales, and politics are professionals at managing the image they portray to their audience, buyers, and constituents.[3]

Entertainment

An article in the *Chicago Tribune* about an up-and-coming band comments: "In a volatile industry where packaging can make or break a group, image is everything." The article goes on to note that as a result, the band is very "careful about what they wear on stage." If the band wants to make it to the big time, they must be careful to develop the right image.

The National Football League (NFL) teaches its players in a media relations booklet to pay attention to their image: "A great deal of the impression you make in television interviews results from your personal style—

your body language." They warn players that their ability to manipulate their images will affect their bank book:

> Picture a player wearing sunglasses and a torn T-shirt, chewing gum, not smiling, slouching, and never looking at the reporter asking the questions.
>
> Picture another player smiling, standing up straight, speaking clearly, and showing enthusiasm. It doesn't take a genius to figure out which of these players has a better chance for endorsements and business opportunities.[4]

Sales

A new technique of home sales is to present the image of happy homes. The *Chicago Tribune* reports on a new housing development: "In the first house a 'husband' bakes chocolate cookies with the help of his 5-year-old 'child,' while his 'wife' plays backgammon with a 'friend.'" The problem with this image is that these people are actors who are paid to present a warm and friendly neighborhood to the visiting potential buyers. One actress "mother" explains, "We tell visitors about how we've just come back from a swim at the community center and the wonderful facilities in the area." Why is the company spending big money to present this elaborate image? A marketing manager expiains, "Where you have an empty street you don't get the same kind of warm, fuzzy feeling." The realty company knows that persuasion comes with warm and fuzzy feelings and hires professionals to present the right image that will spark these emotions.[5]

Politics

Creating an image is a politician's full-time job. Politicians are elected because of their ability to articulate the concerns of their constituents in a language they understand and to present an attractive image while doing so. They have developed sophisticated means to understand and then use the language and ideals of those they are seeking to influence. For example, the political organization Gopac sent the booklet "Language: A Key Mechanism of Control" to Republican candidates running in state-wide elections in 1990. It instructs:

> As you know, one of the key points in the Gopac tapes is that "language matters." . . . We believe that you can have significant impact on your campaign if we help a little. That is why we have created this list of words and phrases.[6]

The booklet goes on to instruct candidates to memorize and use these "optimistic positive governing words" in their speeches, letters, literature, and media info, and to avoid their opposites. Among these optimistic words are *common sense, courage, family, freedom, movement, passionate, pride, principle, truth,* and *vision.* They believe that these words resonate with the typical American voter at this point in history. The booklet argues that if the politicians use the "optimistic" words and avoid the "contrasting" words, they will be more successful. They will present a more attractive image.[7]

Entertainment, sales, and politics have the common elements of: (1) a self-conscious attempt to present an image and (2) a desire to achieve an external and measurable goal.

Image Management Is Self-Conscious

Entertainers, salespeople, and politicians who operate as outlined realize that they are presenting an image. They are choosing to adopt a certain persona for the sake of their audience. The word *persona* comes from the word for "mask" that actors used in Roman drama. In essence, these individuals are performing.

In December 1992, President-elect Clinton and his staff put together a summit conference on the economy. The economist John White, who had drafted the Ross Perot economic plan, had significant credibility in the eyes of the media. He was asked by Clinton staff to give "the hard message" to Clinton about some bad news about the economy. Staffers even provided White with the data and charts to illustrate the dilemma. In response to White's presentation, Clinton was attentive, teachable, raised good questions, and then summarized White's main points and asked, "Is that correct?"

But there is a problem with this picture. Although White and the audience didn't know it, Clinton had already heard all of this information before from his economic advisors. In fact, the very charts that White used were originally deployed in Clinton's earlier briefings. White was used and the audience was duped. This presentation was a pseudo-event, a performance, to get across information that Clinton wanted publicized and to show how open and teachable Clinton is. As a *Time* reporter commented:

> Assured that he had indeed accurately reflected what his staff had prompted White to say, the President-elect remarked, "Thank you very much. It was a terrific job." To those who knew what was going on, Clinton's smile seemed just a little wicked.[8]

There is a reason why politicians have a bad reputation: They are self-consciously attempting to craft images that put them in the best possible light. This creates the impression among most Americans that politicians can't be trusted.[9]

Schuller, Hybels's former church-growth mentor, has affirmed this goal of self-consciously creating the right image. He teaches pastors, "You must be an inspiring impression-maker." These images are self-consciously chosen with the goal of impressing the unchurched.

> The secret of winning unchurched people into the church is really quite simple. Find out what would impress the non-churched people in your community and find out who would impress them.

He instructs pastors to do what he did:

> Who are the heroes of your community? Who are the civic leaders, the writers, the actors, and other prominent personages that the unchurched people in your community admire?
>
> Grab hold of the coattails of these heroes. Invite them to your church. Use them unashamedly! Your job is to impress the non-churched people in your community.

Thus it should be no surprise to realize that Schuller depicts the preacher as a salesman: "Successful selling is nothing more than communicating to people a truth that they weren't aware of before."[10]

Hybels and Willow Creek do not follow Schuller's advice to use popular heroes to impress the audience but they have chosen a format for programming and speaking that requires constant self-conscious examination. The roles that people play are scripted down to the tears shed during a drama or a hand motion during an emotional song. I was interested in finding out if Hybels's messages were also identical in the different services. When I stayed to hear Hybels give the same message to a new audience, the similarities were startling—a virtual mirror image. Hybels not only used the same script and gestures, but even the pregnant emotional pauses were identical. His messages are scripted and honed to a razor edge of excellence.

Several individuals I interviewed commented that Hybels is a very "polished" speaker. One individual even remarked about Hybels, "He should be a politician." This was not a negative comment but rather a compliment on how adroitly Hybels was able to deal with the sensitive topic of homosexuality. One of the reporters I interviewed also commented on Hybels's politician-like smoothness:

> It's like a politician who is smart enough to use language to his advantage. He is not lying and he is not misrepresenting. He just wants to get his message across as effectively as possible.

Image Management Has a Measurable Goal

Entertainers, salespersons, and politicians have an external, measurable goal. Depending on the performer, this goal may be a ticket, a sale, or a vote. They are seeking to get their audience to be suitably impressed by their performance in order to achieve their goal.

Occasionally the stage curtain goes up and we can see the backstage reality. Jerry Markbreit, the former national sales manager at 3M, is also a leading referee in the NFL:

> I'm a salesman; I can sell anything. In order to sell billboard space, I have to be convincing and very positive.
>
> When I come across that way, the buyer has confidence in what I'm trying to sell. Officiating works the same way. A confident, crisp, positive attitude sells calls.[11]

Individuals in the image managing business realize that their image sells their product. If a certain behavior—a modification of one's image—increases one's sales, there is pressure to repeat this action. In other words, there is a sociological pressure to perform in such a way that one's external goal can be achieved.

Hybels and Creekers also have an external goal that the programming and message are designed to achieve: They are seeking to get unchurched Harry to become a believer. The strategy that I have described is a finely crafted product of hundreds of experiments with varying results. Intuitively, over time, Hybels and Willow Creek have become aware of what unchurched Harry responds to. They have developed a pragmatic expertise. Two temptations are embedded in the managing of images.

Manipulation

The first danger of managing images is manipulation. As I noted above the U.S. Army has prepared a manual on intelligence interrogation, which teaches interrogators how to interview captives. The manual teaches interrogators to "manipulate the emotions" of the captive. In the section of the manual titled "Establish and Develop Rapport" are the following methods by which one manipulates the captive:

- Feigning experience similar to those of the source.
- Showing concern for the prisoner through the use of voice vitality and body language.
- Helping the source to rationalize his guilt.

- Showing kindness and understanding toward the source's predicament.
- Exonerating the source from guilt.
- Flattering the source.[12]

These tools of manipulation can be used by any communicator. One Willow Creek staff member defined manipulation as "getting people to do what we want them to do without being honest about how we're going about doing that." One teacher acknowledged that every good speaker is tempted to manipulate: "If you know yourself well, you know how to turbo-boost whatever your strengths are to manipulate people. . . . I know how to use vulnerability to manipulate. I know how to do all sorts of junk to manipulate." In his attempts to identify with unchurched Harry, a speaker may act authentic or stress a similarity that is not true to who he is.

For example, a speaker or singer can spark an emotional intimacy with the audience. But this emotional closeness is actually devoid of a true relationship. A visiting Harry may actually know no one in the church and may even be sitting by himself. The emotional closeness is anonymous and can be manipulated to wrong ends.

I need to emphasize that the pressure I am identifying here is true of all who find themselves in this type of image-managing setting. If a particular behavior will increase the likelihood of achieving the desired results, the performer feels pressure to produce the image that will accomplish his goal. In the context of the high-powered world of Willow Creek, individuals feel a need to achieve and thus a pressure to perform and pretend.

Pretense

The second danger of image management is to operate merely on pretense. If a certain behavior increases the audience's response, it becomes a temptation to fake it. *Willow Creek* magazine describes how one Willow Creek leader in the early days began to perform externally:

> The pressure created internal changes. Swetman says that "he started playing the religion game again." For the sake of coping with the pressure of leadership, he retreated into his childhood world of "doing the external things right." He was always good at being what others wanted him to be.[13]

I asked Jim Dethmer, one of the teachers at Willow Creek, what effects he saw of the church's focus on image. He answered that the "potential effects are inauthenticity." He explained:

> It's a dangerous balance whenever you start working with exterior/interior. . . . It's all right for external things to interpret internals. But you want congruity. Where you have problems, is if you have incongruity.

Once this effort at communication becomes self-conscious and images are scrutinized for effect, the temptation to pretend grows ever stronger. Dethmer comments in this regard, "Once you get conscious about external communication and you start coaching it, or evaluating it, you've opened the door."

Dethmer's comments turned out to be prophetic. Two years later in the late summer of 1993, Jim Dethmer resigned. He had begun to shoulder a large amount of Hybels's teaching load for both the weekend and New Community services, and his resignation caused quite a stir within Willow Creek. In the midst of the swirling rumors, Dethmer wrote a letter to the church to clarify why he was leaving. He admitted that his "talents and gifts have created opportunities *to do* which exceeded" his "capacity *to be*. Such a discrepancy between doing and being is dangerous at best and destructive at worst, because it often leads to pretending." He told the congregation, "I am going to take steps to protect myself from pretense, that most subtle of hypocrisies." Dethmer took a courageous step away from pretense and resigned.

The important point is that this temptation of pretense is built into this model of doing church. The temptation to pretend is increased by the social pressure to produce. One's status in the organization is tied to the ability to perform and produce.

One of the major reasons that Willow Creek has been relatively stable is that Bill Hybels has been able to maintain a consistent presence with the Willow Creek audience. Hybels is an exceptionally gifted communicator, and he also seeks to be honest and authentic. These characteristics create emotional intimacy that is fresh and appealing.

Yet as I have shown, Hybels is intuitively aware of what is effective in communicating and realizes the benefits of confessing his faults. One regularly hears about Hybels's mistakes, failures, and confusion—but one hears at a distance. His intimacy from the platform is consciously processed.

Hybels came to describe himself as emotionally exhausted during the few months from November 1989 to March 1990. The first time I heard of this stressful time was at a pastor's conference in May 1990. Even though I was attending the church regularly during this stressful time and studied the transcripts of his talks, I could find no occasion during one of his messages when Hybels had referred to this most difficult of times. The audience heard about this experience, but at the safe distance of time and self-analysis.

A curious incident underlines this point. Lynne Hybels rarely speaks from the Willow Creek platform. She is not as polished a speaker as her husband and apparently does not even enjoy speaking. Yet occasionally she is asked to speak. Once at a pastor's conference she was giving a talk on lessons that she has learned over the years at the church. When she came to the present, she explained, "I really hesitated to talk about this today, because it's almost too fresh; it's a little bit too real; it's not finished yet." Lynne explained how she was asked to speak to a large women's group in the church:

> I wrote the best message that I could; it was a very personal message. And I got done and I read through it and I thought, *I cannot give this message. I mean you talk about laying yourself bare before the people, I mean, here I am doing it* [emphasis added].

In Lynne's talk, there was a level of real, intimate, and spontaneous honesty that seemed different somehow from the normal confession from the Willow Creek stage. Why?

In any setting of self-conscious image management, there is a sociological pressure to perform. This pressure creates a situation that at best lacks spontaneity and thus seems less real and at its worst creates pretense. Willow Creek is not unique in experiencing this pressure. Anyone in an image-management setting feels these social stresses.

The Ethics of Identifying

As I stated in chapter 7, in response to my questions of how to handle this dilemma, Creekers' answers were fuzzy and proverbial in nature. In answer to some of my probing about this area, Hybels admitted:

> I have not put a talk together on the eight boundary verses of the use of drama. It's prompting me as you're talking here to put some more thought to that and help our drama or music people.

From several staff members I did hear the common themes of truth, authenticity, and restraint.[14]

Truth. Mittelberg argues that Paul's principle of "becoming all things to all men" has limits:

> That's within parameters of what's biblically right and all that; it's also within, I think, some parameter of who I really am. Culturally, personality-wise, etc.

Thus there are two limits that truthfulness sets for identifying: biblical limits and personal limits.

> You don't have to wear the string bikini thing; that goes too far in order to relate to people. But you don't have to wear gunny sacks either. . . .
>
> I want to relate to people I want to reach, but I want to do it without compromise.

There are, in Willow Creek's view, clear biblical criteria that must not be compromised in their efforts to identify with Harrys. In Mittelberg's example, a woman wearing a string bikini would be moving too far toward Harry. There are also personal limits to identifying.

Authenticity. Beach explains that she is guided by the principle of authenticity with individuals who are involved with the programming. "We don't want any of them doing anything, first of all, that's not natural to who they are in any way." The first element of authenticity is not to act in a way that is inconsistent with one's personality. Mittelberg unpacks this idea:

> If I am a strong introvert and try to act like I'm the life-of-the-party kind of person in order to win the guy that really is. . . . I'm trying to force something that just isn't there.

Mittelberg explains that the limits of identifying are "the parameters of who God has designed me to be." The goal is:

> To move as far as I can toward relating to other people in a way that comes off with authenticity. But as soon as I move down that parameter it's going to come across non-authentic and do more damage than good.

Mittelberg summarizes, "We're trying to connect with people in our culture in a way that's true to who we are and who they are."[15]

The second crucial element of authenticity is one of motivation. One may "feign" showing kindness, or one may truly care. We noted earlier that Hybels emphasized that Harry can tell if a speaker doesn't like him. Hybels argues that it's not enough to emphasize one's similarities; one really needs to like and enjoy Harry.

I need to underline at this point that generally I found the staff to be genuinely concerned with truthfulness and authenticity. This emphasis comes from Hybels's commitment and personality. We have already noted above that Hybels's self-described speaking style is "transparent" and "authentic." Hybels genuinely believes in the importance of honesty and authenticity:

> Real spiritual vitality manifests itself in authenticity, where people can go to each other and resolve conflict without beating each other up first. . . .
>
> Or when pastors can stand in front of their congregations and say, "The truth of the matter is I had a terrible misunderstanding with my wife last night and I'm exhausted and defeated."

As Hybels explains, "the kinds of things where you're just more real."

Restraint. When I asked Lee Strobel about the possibility of emotional manipulation, he responded that Hybels trains the other speakers not to do "emotional turbocharging." The speakers are aware that they have an opportunity to manipulate listeners. They consciously restrain themselves.

Hybels defends himself against the charge that he is selling Jesus.

> People kid me and they say, "Oh, you're a salesman and your product is, you know, Jesus Christ," and this kind of stuff.
>
> I say, "You're dead wrong. You are dead wrong. I may be a communicator. I try very hard to communicate the powerful message of Jesus Christ, but I don't do sales jobs. I communicate and I pray. It's God's job to do the conversion."

Hybels tried to clarify the difference between sales and communicating. "I always give people an out. I'm not there to twist arms. I'm there to present the message." The difference between communicating and selling in Hybels's view seems to be this principle of "emotional turbocharging" and not "twisting arms." Hybels trains the other speakers to also avoid emotional manipulation.

Assessment

Like nearly all of the unintended consequences of Willow Creek's strategy, the temptation of image management has not been thought through. I have tried to be fair in piecing together the underlying principles that Creekers intuitively turn to when forced to think about this issue. But to honor the Lord, these fuzzy principles need further explication.

On reading this chapter Creekers argued, "We are trying to communicate what is real" and explained, "What we are trying to do is project what is already reality." I believe that this assertion of authenticity is true. After many interviews and conversations over my two-and-one-half years of study I believe that Willow Creek staff are sincerely seeking to honor the Lord.

Yet the method they have chosen to communicate (a self-conscious attempt to project images to get Harry to feel and think certain things) has certain built-in temptations. I have tried to outline these dangers or weaknesses. I need to clarify one principle that addresses this issue.

The Christian's Guidance System

In 1 Thessalonians 2:1–12, Paul outlines an understanding of integrity as a combination of proper motivation and action. Paul's central goal was to honor God: "We are not trying to please men but God." All that he did was with this fundamental goal in mind.

The danger of both trying to identify and trying to be credible to an audience is that they make one aware of the horizontal dimension in communication. The more one becomes aware of how one is being received, the greater the temptation to compromise one's message or manner to achieve the desired results. I need to emphasize that I am not rejecting these principles out of hand. I believe that both identifying and credibility are elements of a biblical model of persuasion. But isolated from the broader framework of the Christian worldview, these truths can easily be distorted into falsehoods.

The biblical principle of integrity provides a corrective vertical guidance to these principles. Instead of being primarily concerned with how he appeared or what others thought of him, Paul was concerned with pleasing God. Paul teaches that, like the North Star, this vertical axis of pleasing God provides direction regardless of the setting.

All else that Paul does flows from this one goal of pleasing God. Because of this goal Paul has a very clear sense of what he should do and how he should do it. There are two elements to Paul's understanding of integrity that flow from the goal of pleasing God, actions and motivations.

Paul specifically notes how his actions (he suffered, declared, spoke, worked, preached, exhorted, encouraged, and charged) came from his desire to please God and his love for the Thessalonians. Paul argues in this passage that his actions are justifiable because they are based on a clear understanding of what is true. In other words Paul had a focused ethical ideal to which he could appeal. Raymond Collins comments about this passage, "The God of whom he appeals is a moral God who wills that men's conduct should be worthy of the God who calls them."[16]

The second element of Paul's understanding of integrity is proper motivation. Paul in seeking to please God specifically denies the motivations of error, uncleanness, guile, pleasing men, flattery, greed, and seeking glory. In addition to the motivation of pleasing God, Paul claims the positive motivations of courage, gentleness, affection, and love. Commenting on this passage Howard Marshall says, "God is concerned not merely with the outward impression made by men but above all with the inward motives which dictate their conduct."[17]

Paul's integrity was a combination of conduct and attitude that had a vertical axis. Paul was not seeking to please man, but God. As a result of his integrity in his commitment to God, Paul sought to love and care for the Thessalonians.

The presence that comes from living this way is based in a knowledge-action-knowledge triangle. Like Paul we need to have clear convictions as to how the Lord wants us to live. Then we need to act in the power of the Spirit to seek to live out what we know. Then as a result of actions based on our convictions, we know that we are living consistently with our convictions. We are confident because we know, like Paul, that we are faithfully seeking to please God. Instead of being concerned primarily with how we appear or what others think of us (image), we need to be concerned with who we are (integrity).

Those individuals involved in speaking, singing, drama, and programming in seeker style (or other) churches need to examine their hearts before the cross and ask themselves, *Why am I doing this? Who do I want to please? Do I hunger and long that Jesus Christ be glorified?* Those who do not have the maturity and integrity in their commitments to please God should not be permitted to hold positions of leadership.

17

The Quagmire of Psychology

Hybels's desire to be relevant motivates him to move toward the language and priorities of popular culture. There is a major strength and weakness in this insistence on relevance. The strength of this strategy we have already described: Speaking with relevance communicates more effectively with a popular audience. Willow Creek's approach utilizes the language, categories, and priorities of the surrounding popular culture. It starts where people are.

Its weakness is that it often leaves them there. A lack of self-critical thinking impairs this approach to relevance. Without the correction of critical Christian thought, fuzzy thinking is maintained and encouraged. As a result, many ideas are accepted or adopted even though they may be inconsistent with some deeply held convictions.

Hybels's understanding of relevance, by definition, affirms the surrounding culture. This is a problem and is compounded by Hybels's commitment to identify with unchurched Harry, moving as close to him as possible. When one starts with Harry's language, categories, priorities, and felt needs, it becomes very difficult to be critical of the culture.

This process has profound consequences for Willow Creek. Willow Creek accommodates the culture in its theological message and adopts much of the American psychological worldview. Before we examine the specific influence of the psychological worldview on Willow Creek, a brief comment should be made about the broader evangelical community's response to the American psychological worldview.

Evangelicalism and the American Psychological Worldview

How has evangelicalism responded to the American psychological worldview? Peter Berger suggests that religion has "two basic options" in response to modern society's symbolic universe, "accommodation and resistance." Sociologist James Hunter explains:

> Religious organizations must choose either to accommodate their beliefs to cognitive standards external to their tradition or else defensively isolate themselves from those standards in order to remain theologically plausible.[1]

Resistance

The resistance to the psychological worldview has predictably come from the conservative, even fundamentalist, wing of evangelicalism. In *Our Sufficiency in Christ*, fundamentalist pastor John MacArthur rejects the use of psychology by evangelicals:

> Psychology is no more a science than the atheistic evolutionary theory upon which it is based. . . .
>
> Modern psychology and the Bible cannot be blended without serious compromise to or utter abandonment of the principle of Scripture's sufficiency.

MacArthur preaches that "'Christian psychology' as the term is used today is an oxymoron."[2]

The inherent strength of the resistance option is the ability to maintain a consistent worldview in the face of the broader culture. For those who are cultural resisters, there is willingness to defy cultural norms. With some groups, such rejection is seen as a badge of maturity.

Resistance can also challenge or confront the culture. Such resisters put most of their energy into maintaining their worldview and subculture rather than changing the culture. Ironically, this commitment retains seeds of potential renewal for the broader culture as resisters are fundamentally countercultural.

Sociologist Hunter suggests that a potential weakness of the resistance response is that it "leads to a boundary so rigid as to make religion irrelevant because of its withdrawal from the rest of life." A religious group that retreats completely from the surrounding culture and its dominant symbolic worldview finds it difficult to relate to or communicate with its cultural neighbors. Although a false caricature, the most popular stereotype of evangelicals is a Bible-banging, polyester-clad, red-faced, finger-pointing, sweating preacher. Viewed from the dominant culture, this figure and the evangelical faith he represents are irrelevant and unattractive.[3]

Accommodation

On the "accommodation" side we find the bulk of evangelicalism, including Willow Creek. Marshall Shelley, editor of the evangelical journal *Leadership,* describes how the psychological recovery movement has "swept over all of us like a tidal wave":

> You simply can't be a part of a church these days without having learned a new language about addictions, abuse, dependencies, co-dependencies, dysfunctional families, enablers, family of origin, re-parenting, unconditional acceptance, [and] adult children.[4]

The penetration of this psychological worldview has shaped evangelicalism profoundly. There are now recovery Bibles, twelve-step evangelical programs, psycho-evangelical best-sellers, and a burgeoning evangelical mental health industry. In short, the modern psychological worldview is molding evangelicalism in significant ways: Many evangelicals are thinking with its categories and priorities. There are both positive and negative consequences to psychology's influence on evangelicalism.[5]

When a principle of the broader psychological worldview fits the basic teaching of Christianity, psychology's contribution can be positive. Because the recovery movement so emphasizes honesty about one's failures, many evangelicals are finding it easier to follow the biblical injunction to confess their failings and weaknesses (James 5:16).

Without doubt, the use of psychological theory can provide insight into human personality, behavior, and relationships. Some people have carefully sought to integrate such insights within a biblical worldview. These kinds of patient efforts have yielded fruitful insights in Christian counseling and psychotherapy.

Another strength of the accommodation position is that individuals and churches in this position can effectively communicate with their cultural neighbors. Christians who are adapting to the culture are more willing to try to understand, identify, and communicate relevantly to individuals in the culture. These Christians can be a very powerful influence on those in the world.

A major weakness of this cultural accommodation is that the world can also be a very powerful influence on the church. What is most curious about the influence of the psychological worldview is that few evangelicals are alarmed by it or even aware of it. The majority of normally conservative evangelicals have welcomed this accommodation with open arms. If someone were to question Christ's deity, evangelicals would quickly reject such compromise. Yet the psychological worldview has flown by like a Stealth fighter under evangelicals' theological radar. *Christianity Today,* the flagship publication of evangelicalism, has generally baptized and defended this process with complimentary articles and editorials.[6]

The question, What are the consequences of the psychological worldview for evangelicalism? has yet to be answered. Thankfully, our question is more limited. What are the unintended consequences of Willow Creek's use of these psychological categories?

The Psychological Worldview at Willow Creek

Before I begin this analysis of the effect of psychology, I need to stress that I believe in the value of the social sciences. My Ph.D. training included graduate courses and doctoral exams in personality theory, social-psychology, and social science research methods and theories. The focus of my Ph.D. degree was "Religion in Personality and Society" and I am currently a member of a professional social science association. Even this book is in large part the fruit of careful social scientific research. I present here not the condemnation of a fundamentalist preacher, but the reservations of a professional in the field.

In chapter 11, I showed that psychological categories were a staple of weekend messages at Willow Creek. Attenders are aware that psychological categories are frequently used as a part of Hybels's teaching. Former NFL all-pro linebacker Mike Singletary, the best-known Willow Creek attender, writes about the church:

> There came a time when it seemed that the emphasis was more on positive mental attitude than on the Word of God, and I became concerned. . . .
>
> I worried because it seemed we were hearing more of a Robert Schuller or a Norman Vincent Peale type of an approach. . . .
>
> It bothered me a lot. I told Kim, "Something is going to have to happen soon, because I don't care where I am or how much I care for Bill Hybels, if I'm not hearing the Word of God, it's time to go."[7]

We also find the American psychological worldview in the psychological self-help books that are read by Willow Creek attenders and in the advocacy and use of professional psychotherapy.

Psychology Books

The American psychological worldview is taught in many of the books that are sold at the Willow Creek bookstore. During the year I studied, besides Hybels's books, the majority of the best-selling books were psychological self-help books. The book store staff realize this and have stocked the store accordingly. In the bookstore there are three racks of books on the topic of psychology, one rack of books on recovery, and only one rack on theology and church life. Yet when I examined the theology rack, I found hardly any theological titles. Most of the books on the theology rack are church-growth books.[8]

Part of the reason why these psychology books are best-sellers is because they are recommended by Hybels and other staff. Three of the most recommended, read, and influential books in the church are the psychological self-help books *Codependent No More, Please Understand Me,* and *When Your World Makes No Sense.* The first two are secular books that have proven to be very palatable for Willow Creek Christians. The last is a Christian psychological self-help book.[9]

Hybels exhorts the weekend audience, "Please buy Dr. Cloud's book entitled once again, *When Your World Makes No Sense,* because the section in that book on boundaries is the single best section on boundaries I've ever seen in print." The result of this kind of psychological testimonial was that during the course of my study, this book was being read by hundreds of Willow Creek attenders and staff. I was told by various staff members how this book was currently the most influential in their lives and in the church.

Cloud argues for a change in how Christians should approach life.

> Across the land, people are increasingly seeking the answers to emotional and psychological struggles, and even Christians find that their "spiritual" answers sometimes leave them less than whole.

Cloud explains how he came to write this book:

> I tried the "standard" Christian answers for myself and others, and I came to the same conclusions that Job reached: they are worthless medicine.
>
> I also tried to "baptize" psychological insights so that they would somehow feel "Christian" enough to allow me to think that my "theological" answers and training were the real key to healing. Somehow that never worked, either.[10]

Cloud's solution in this book is to use psychological ideas as his fundamental guidelines for living life.

It isn't that Cloud doesn't use Scripture. Scripture is laced throughout the book. But the primary grid that Cloud uses to interpret the Bible are four psychological ideas: "(1) bonding, (2) boundaries, (3) resolving problems of good and bad, and (4) establishing authority." Cloud even teaches that these principles are "four aspects of His [God's] personality." The consequence of this approach is an amalgamation of Bible stories and verses into a psychological matrix. The result? Psychological terms like "boundaries" become the primary ethical categories that are used to describe how individuals should live.[11]

Psychotherapy

During the year's weekend messages that I studied, there were at least twenty-one occasions when Hybels, or another speaker, encouraged the audience to consider therapy. Hybels exhorts:

> We have a counseling center. Maybe some of you needed to be prompted this morning to leave the shame and the shadows you've been walking in. No one's gonna feel any less about you if you come out for help. You'll be respected more.

The result of this emphasis on therapy is that many people do seek psychotherapy. Approximately one thousand people went to Willow Creek's counseling center during a single year of my study. About two-thirds of these individuals were then referred to over ninety counseling centers throughout the Chicago area. Many of these centers are not Christian counseling centers. One counselor estimated that if individuals at the church believed that they would be counseled at the church—and not sent to another counseling center—the number seeking therapy would jump to two thousand or three thousand.[12]

Over the course of a few years, thousands of Willow Creek participants receive therapy. These thousands of individuals in turn influence their families and friends within Willow Creek with their new analytical categories. These psychological terms become the ethical categories of how Creekers live their lives.

Willow Creek's dependence on therapy and its psychological worldview is also visible in the great number of staff who receive therapy. An estimated 50 percent of Willow Creek staff received therapy at the counseling center while I was doing my study. The church so believes in therapy that it allocates four hundred dollars per year for each staff member to use for therapy at the counseling center.

Therapy and its psychological framework is accepted as a necessary tool in Willow Creek's understanding of ministry. Yet there is no accepted model of integrating psychology and theology at the Willow Creek counseling center. The counseling director isn't concerned if counselors use a behaviorist, analytical, family system, or cognitive approach. Thus, a hodgepodge of various psychological ideas are employed with no consistent theological critique or guidance.[13]

What is the result of this penetration of the psychological worldview on Willow Creek's teaching and practice? Psychological categories are not neutral medical terms. They shape how people perceive and therefore live.

Social Scientific Theory

Social science is grounded in the philosophy of science, which makes a clear distinction between theory and empirical data. Theory in this view is used to analyze and interpret empirical data. Social scientific theory, whether psychological or sociological, is designed to help explain human behavior.

Social scientific theory has several purposes. It suggests issues that are important to investigate. It helps one understand research conclusions by putting them in a broader context. It reveals the importance of the empirical evidence. It relates the conclusion of an individual study to the broader scientific community. In short, theory serves as a hermeneutical lens to interpret human phenomena. Thus, to use social scientific theory properly, one must distinguish between theory and the empirical data, and use it as a lens to help bring specific empirical data into perspective.

This use of psychological theory is not what is presently occurring at Willow Creek. Rather, psychological categories have become a part of the very worldview of how individuals see reality. Instead of the scientific use of psychological theory as a hermeneutical lens to help analyze empirical data, individuals naively use theory as a part of their worldview. People identify themselves as "codependent" and argue that others violated their "boundaries." Instead of using psychological theory as a theoretical microscope to help understand specific empirical data, many Creekers, in effect, have lashed this psychological microscope to their heads. Many Creekers not only view everything and everyone with these categories, but they also are unable to refrain from using them.

In this way, psychological theory is being used as an instrument of meaning. This is why psychologist Paul Vitz argues that psychology has come to serve as a major meaning system—a religion—for modern man. Individuals are understanding and therefore guiding their lives with this psychological worldview. This is a crucial shift—because one's worldview provides the framework for one's ethics. The Oxford English Dictionary defines *ethics* as "the moral principles by which a person is guided." One's worldview gives the basic categories and priorities for one's ethics. An example is necessary to explain this dynamic. Sometimes by looking back in Christian history we can see a similar pattern that helps us see ourselves.[14]

Augustine's Neoplatonism

In the fourth century A.D., Augustine of Hippo introduced a new interpretation of the Christian worldview. In the Greco-Roman world, Christians understood themselves as being in a spiritual conflict. The enemy was pictured to be external, the "world" or "Satan." Augustine, without denying these enemies, argued that "the flesh" was a central source of conflict in the Christian life. "The Devil is not to be blamed for everything: there are times when a man is his own devil."[15]

The result of Augustine's new interpretation of the Christian worldview was an entirely different ethic. Before Augustine, Christians perceived the spiritual battle as external and fought against outward enemies. Augustine turned this inside out and explained the Christian life as a battle against oneself. As historian Dennis Groh explains, Augustine became convinced that the human body "enshrines a resistance to its very creator."[16]

The goal of Augustine's ethic was changed because of this new understanding of human nature. While many of the Christians of his day argued that the goal of the Christian life was perfection, Augustine argued that the goal of the Christian life was humility. Augustine believed that the goal of perfection for a Christian was both wrong and dangerous. At every level, Augustine's new understanding of the Christian worldview shaped a different understanding of ethics—how Christians should live.[17]

On the surface, this shift appears to be a helpful move toward a more biblical understanding of the Christian life. Yet underneath this new interpretation of the Christian worldview is Augustine's commitment to Neoplatonism. Before Augustine was converted to Christianity, he had embraced Neoplatonism. When Augustine became a Christian he carried many of these Neoplatonic ideas with him into his understanding of the Christian worldview.[18]

The split in Neoplatonism between the spiritual and the physical fundamentally skewed Augustine's ethics. Historian Peter Brown described Augustine as an "authentic follower of Plotinus" (the father of Neoplatonism) and explains that "the contours of Augustine's thought in his sermons are laid down by his deep attachment to Neoplatonism." I will briefly note two major distortions in Augustine's ethics from this influence.[19]

The first Neoplatonic influence in Augustine's ethics lies in his primary ethical question. Historian John Burnaby explains, "The starting point was the question posed by a pagan ethic; namely, 'what is the Good for man?'" Augustine, for a large part of his life, viewed life as a giant quest to gain happiness. Burnaby comments that "it was not easy, on such principles, to save . . . ethics from egocentrism."[20]

The second Neoplatonic influence in Augustine's ethics is Augustine's downplaying, even denigration, of the body and its senses: "God alone is to be loved: all this world, that is to say, the whole world of sense, is to be despised—to be used only for this life's necessities." This devaluation should come as no surprise when Augustine's Neoplatonic mentor is described as one who "seemed ashamed of being in the body." Brown writes that Augustine as a Neoplatonist "could seriously expect them [his congregation] to love the sexuality of their wives and the physical bonds of their families only as a Christian must love his enemies."[21]

When Augustine introduced a new interpretation of the Christian worldview, it had a profound effect on the ethics that he proposed. On the surface the ethics he taught seemed to be a helpful contribution. Yet upon closer examination we find that the alien philosophy of Neoplatonism penetrated Augustine's worldview and in turn skewed his ethics.

We see a similar process occurring as Creekers naively use psychological theory as part of their worldview. The modern American psychological worldview is a kind of modern Neoplatonism. Like Augustine's Neoplatonism, this new worldview seems to provide helpful categories that can be useful for Christians. Yet like the ancient Neoplatonism, this alien philosophy has momentous consequences on Christian ethics.

The psychological categories that Willow Creek's teaching, books, and therapy employ become the categories that Creekers use to understand themselves, their relationships, and life in general. These psychological categories become the principles that Creekers use to make decisions about their lives. In short, psychological categories penetrate Creekers' worldview and then shape their ethics—"the moral principles by which a person is guided."

Psychology and Willow Creek's Ethics

We see in Willow Creek's ethics a reflection of many of the central priorities of the American psychological worldview. Individuals who are committed to the psychological worldview described above accept an ethical commitment to clarify their psychological identity, structure their relationships according to psychological categories, and pursue personal fulfillment. We will look at the first two points in this chapter and the third in chapter 18.

Psychological Identities

Sociologist Hunter observes that Americans' preoccupation with identity is the result of a social dislocation. "The question [who am I?] is only comprehensible in a society in which identity has become deinstitutionalized." It is not coincidental that people have become more psychological as identity has become deinstitutionalized. As people have lost the relationships, roles, and institutions that once provided a sense of self, identity has become a central problem for modern man.[22]

Thus psychological categories are providing Americans generally, and evangelicals specifically, with the means of self-understanding. Evangelicals have accommodated the trend of modern society toward subjectivity with this preoccupation with psychological self-identity. Hunter explains how evangelicals seek to justify the use of these psychological categories:

> At the highest level, there is the synthesis of biblicism and humanistic or Freudian psychology. Here, the language of this perspective (e.g., awareness, assessment, self-actualization) is provided a biblical basis and given a spiritual relevance. . . . What they all share is a psychological Christocentrism.[23]

This same use of psychological language is apparent at Willow Creek. Hybels attempts to help individuals clarify their psychological "identity" by teaching about topics such as temperament, family history, emotions, and addiction patterns. Hybels had a five-week series entitled "Discovering the Way God Wired You Up." During another year, the recovery movement's twelve-step program was summarized over three months of weekend messages. A major theme of Willow Creek's teaching in the weekend service is to provide this self-understanding.

It was not unusual for me to hear testimonies of how a particular psychological insight was helpful, even life-changing, in someone's life. A management team member explained how Hybels's psychological teaching has been profoundly influential in his life:

> All those things help me deal with the past and prepare for the future. You know? All those psychological perspectives. . . . I'm going to parenthood now having dealt with my past, prepared to care for my kids in an appropriate fashion.

This psychological self-understanding is so important that it is a criterion for whom the church hires on staff. Hybels explains:

> We're looking for self-aware individuals who are coming to grips with their pain and their woundedness. . . .
>
> People on the journey toward health generally can answer yes to two important questions: (1) Will you admit that you have baggage from your past? and (2) Will you do honest work on it so it doesn't distort your relationships and work around here?[24]

Yet the fact that identity is a primary question for Americans is not the central issue. Because of the social processes of American culture the problem of identity is, and will be, a significant problem for many Americans. The difficulty comes when one understands the source of Willow Creek's answer to this question. Classical evangelical thought has often emphasized the importance of self-understanding. John Calvin wrote, "Nearly all the wisdom we possess, that is to say, true and sound wisdom, consists of two parts: the knowledge of God and of ourselves." Yet classical evangelical thought has presented self-understanding as the result of understanding God: "It is certain that man never achieves a clear knowledge of himself unless he has first looked upon God's face, and then descends from contemplating him to scrutinize himself."[25]

In contrast to this God-centered self-understanding, Willow Creek is often providing a psychological self-understanding. Instead of looking at God's face, this teaching suggests that individuals look in the distorted mirror of modern psychology. One couple was depicted in the *Willow Creek* magazine as a model of how individuals need to grow in Christian maturity. Yet when they were described, they sounded very similar to recovering alcoholics at an AA meeting:

> As they worked through the ministries, they learned about issues such as co-dependency, repressed anger in children, learned destructive behavior, addictions, [and] poor self-esteem.
>
> As one staff member explained, "they got in touch with their baggage."[26]

The reporter didn't use biblical language to describe this couple's maturity—(e.g., fruit of the Spirit, love, holiness, maturity, godliness)—but resorted to a psychological code of sanctification.

Willow Creek's use of psychological categories is an innocent attempt to describe empirical reality. However, an innocent use of psychological categories to describe empirical reality ends up providing both an understanding of what is, and the ethics of what should be. In other words, psychological categories frame issues in such a way that they give direction for how one should live. A large part of how one should live, according to this psychological ethic, is an internal psychological search for self-identity.[27]

Philosopher Robert Roberts explains the effect of psychological ideas on human behavior:

> We are verbivorous beings, the words we chew, swallow, and digest will determine how we see the world, what we take to be important, how our behavior, our character and our very life are shaped.[28]

When someone starts using psychological categories as basic elements of self-perception, he or she has also accepted a psychological ethic. Individuals feel a moral pressure not to be "codependent" nor to violate others' "boundaries." This terminology, instead of encouraging Creekers to know and love God, encourages them to know and accept themselves and develop a strong self-esteem. The goals and means of one's ethics change from a God-centered to a human-centered orientation.

Roberts sketches the result of this psychological molding:

> The various psychotherapies and personality theories that are influential today are not just neutral medical technologies or scientific theories; they are philosophies of life that endorse particular virtues, character traits, or features of personality.
>
> These are the traits a person would have if the therapist succeeded in making him or her into a fully functioning and mature person—mature, that is, by that therapist's reckoning. And they are traits the therapy is designed to foster.[29]

Willow Creek Christians have accepted the psychological framework as foundational to their self-understanding and as a trustworthy guide for daily living. The result of these psychological categories are psychological identities. Roberts explains, "Those who seriously interpret themselves in Christian terms will tend to have Christian selves; those who seriously interpret themselves in Rogerian or Jungian terms will tend to have Rogerian or Jungian selves."[30]

For example, one Creeker I interviewed told me about how he had read a pop-psychology book that listed five needs that spouses have in marriage. He then explained, "I meet all five of Susie's needs, but she doesn't meet any of mine." He told me how he was tempted to have an affair with his secretary as a result. Starting with the category of his "needs," he had a weak moral framework to resist his temptation.

Once again I need to emphasize that I am not rejecting social science—either psychology or sociology. But I am rejecting a naive or improper use of social science and in this case psychology. Secular psychological personality theories provide alternative and rival understandings to the Christian view of the person. Christianity has the strongest claims to have a true "psychology," or a study of the soul. For two thousand years, Christians have been in the business of "curing souls." Yet until Christians consistently teach the biblical conception of human nature in relation to a true understanding of God, a shallow psychological framework will continue to shape how Christians think and act.

Psychological Relationships

Willow Creek's weekend teaching addresses attenders' relationships in psychological terms such as "boundaries," "codependency," "control" issues, "conflict resolution," and others. An example of psychology giving direction in relationships is Melody Beattie's *Codependent No More*. This book is one of the best-selling texts of pop-psychology and one of the most influential books at Willow Creek. As the book begins, Beattie discusses real situations of pain and disappointment. Many readers who have been bruised by life can identify with these descriptions of pain and believe that Beattie has described their problems.

Beattie begins her solution with the second section of her book, "The Basics of Self Care," in a chapter entitled "Detachment." Beattie explains why she put detachment first: "I selected it because it is an underlying concept." She argues that the first step in resolving relational problems is to detach from the people one has the problem with:

> Frequently when I suggest to people that they detach from a person or problem, they recoil in horror. "Oh, no!" they say. "I could never do that. I love him, or her, too much. I care too much to do *that*. This problem or person is too important to me. I have to stay attached."
>
> My answer to that is, "WHO SAYS YOU HAVE TO?" I've got news—good news. We don't "have to." There's a better way. It's called detachment.[31]

Beattie is teaching ethics—pure and simple. She tries to justify detachment, saying it is actually a means to better relationships. Yet in practice, this theory easily justifies how individuals can and should leave difficult or painful situations. Beattie is teaching readers to follow their emotional desires for peace and fulfillment. As another chapter title puts it, "Have a Love Affair With Yourself." Should we be surprised to read Beattie's book dedication?—"This book is dedicated to me."[32]

Those who naively accept Beattie's or other psychological formulations are also accepting an ethic of how to live. I found acceptance of these psychological theories by both lay participants and leaders at Willow Creek. From the pulpit Hybels endorsed "codependency" theory as a fundamental contribution of the 1980s. A Willow Creek counselor told me that Beattie's book had been the most influential book at the church for the previous few years. People in my interviews regularly announced that they were "codependent" and explained how they dealt with relational problems from this perspective.

Individuals who use psychological theory to structure their relationships are not using biblical principles. Instead of describing relational responsibilities with the biblical concepts of love, humility, compassion, forgiveness, reconciliation, perseverance, and patience, they use psychological ideas like "boundaries" and "detachment." The result of this shift is profound. Because one thinks with different categories, one acts in different ways. Two illustrations may help to enflesh the consequences of this approach to relational ethics.

Hybels has commented in public meetings that hundreds of Willow Creek marriages have broken up over the years. "Detachment" is used as a justification for why individuals at Willow Creek separated from and divorced their spouses. In fact, Willow Creek's official divorce policy allows individuals to divorce their spouses if "their spouse is unwilling to be a viable marriage partner." The psychological code that legitimizes "detachment" from troubled relationships has shaped Willow Creek's theology at this point. The fact that two thousand years of Christian teaching is set aside with this guideline is astounding. Our Lord's command, "They are no longer two, but one. Therefore what God has joined together, let man not separate" (Matt. 19:6) was never mentioned in the church's eight-week seminar on divorce. This is a startling development and a profound compromise.[33]

The second example of their psychological ethics is the astounding results of Barna's survey of Willow Creek's weekend participants. Among the Willow Creek survey participants, 91 percent stated that their "highest value" was "having a deep personal relationship to God." Yet of this same group 25 percent of singles, 38 percent of single parents, and 41 percent of divorced individuals "admitted having illicit sexual relationships in the last six months." Their psychological ethics did not restrain the sexual desires of at least this significant portion of the congregation.

What is the result of their psychological ethics? Willow Creek's psychological relational ethics have helped to create psychology-oriented

Christians who affirm a commitment to an intimate relationship with God, yet indulge in "illicit sexual relationships." It is very difficult to justify sacrifice and obedience when one's ethics provide no reins to control selfish desires.[34]

The Accommodation of Evangelical Faith

Willow Creek's accommodation to the psychological worldview is unintended. Hybels and his staff are attempting to make Christianity relevant to the unchurched. They want to see Harry come to faith. They are using psychological categories to help show how Christianity works, in order to help prepare Harry for the gospel.

Willow Creek is not unique in the area of teaching a psychological Christian ethic. Sadly, many evangelicals understand themselves and live their lives with a psychological worldview. The problem comes when believers naively accept the built-in ethics that such psychological theory provides.

It would be a misunderstanding of my argument to think that psychology is an evil that should always be fought. As I explained earlier, a judicious use of various psychological theories is occasionally helpful for understanding human behavior. Such understanding can help people identify patterns that perpetuate sin. At this point, a shift in interpretation needs to take place. Without reframing the problem in biblical terms, the built-in ethics are psychological rather than biblical. Psychological theory may occasionally help us to understand human behavior, but it should not provide us our ethics.[35]

What is Christ's view of this psychological accommodation? Creekers and other evangelicals who have accepted this worldview often have good intentions. Many of these individuals are trying either to help others or to find healing in their own lives. These desires and goals are not wrong. The Lord is compassionate toward both those in need and those seeking to help others:

> We do not have a high priest who is unable to sympathize with our weaknesses. . . . Let us then approach the throne of grace with confidence, so that we may receive mercy and find grace to help us in our time of need.
>
> Hebrews 4:15–16

Yet, the Lord is harsh toward those who compromise his truth. Revelation 2:13–16 records his response to the church in Pergamum:

> You remain true to my name. You did not renounce your faith in me. . . . Nevertheless I have a few things against you: You have people there who hold to the teaching of Balaam, who taught Balak to entice the Israelites to sin by eating food sacrificed to idols and by committing sexual immorality. Likewise you also have those who hold to the teaching of the Nicolaitans. Repent therefore! Otherwise, I will soon come to you and will fight against them with the sword of my mouth.

The Nicolaitans were "a group in the early Church who sought to work out a compromise with paganism, to enable Christians to take part without embarrassment in some of the social and religious activities of the close-knit society in which they found themselves." Christians are always tempted to synthesize their Christianity with prevalent cultural ideas and practices. The Lord is very clear that compromise of his truth should be confronted. He called the church in Pergamum to repent for permitting this teaching (and advocates of it) to remain in the church.[36]

There are profound consequences to teaching the principles of this psychological worldview. Curiously, this is most clear with the Christians who are attending Willow Creek. Willow Creek staff have estimated that as many as one-third of the weekend attenders are visitors. Thus of the 14,000 individuals attending a weekend service, in this estimate, over 4,600 would be unchurched.

This estimate seems to me to be too high. A full 91 percent of those surveyed at a Willow Creek weekend service listed their "highest value" as "having a deep personal relationship to God." It is unlikely that an unchurched visitor would list a relationship with God as his or her highest priority, especially when only 31 percent of unchurched individuals say that religion is "very important" in their lives.[37]

Following these figures, I would estimate the unchurched in attendance at any one weekend service is between 10 and 20 percent. The point is, Hybels's primary message is directed to a relatively small percent of the audience. Probably 80 to 90 percent of the audience already have made a commitment to Christ.

The psychological categories Hybels teaches, however, become fundamental categories for how Willow Creek Christians view themselves, their relationships, and life in general. Ironically, while Hybels is evangelizing those in the world toward Christianity, he is also evangelizing Christians toward the world. As the unchurched Harrys in the audience (10 percent) move closer to Christianity, the Christians in the audience (90 percent) are often becoming more psychological and worldly.

This tendency to compromise Christian truth is built into this model of the church. An unintended consequence of this approach to doing church is the latent temptation to water down the biblical message with the culture's categories.

At times, Hybels has become aware of this dilution of his message. I noted above how *Willow Creek* magazine recorded that in the early days of the church, the word *sin* was rarely used at the church. In 1979, Hybels repented from this watery gospel and began to teach about the holiness of God.

Yet eventually the problem reemerged. After his 1988 summer vacation and study break, Hybels told both the staff and the weekend audience that he had been convicted that his messages had been too helpful and not sufficiently biblical. Mike Singletary recalls Hybels's confession to the weekend audience:

> He said the Lord had been convicting him about his sermons. He said from now on he would be preaching straight from the Bible, that it was the only honest thing he could do before God, regardless of how it went over with everybody.[38]

Hybels devoted that ministry year to the theme "Being a Fully Devoted Follower of Christ."

However, the use of psychology in his messages quickly returned. My year of study of the weekend messages started only nine months after Hybels's confession and commitment to teach only from the Bible. In other words, all of the evidence I have reviewed about the amount of psychological content in the messages, the psychology books, and psychotherapy at Willow Creek came only a few months after Hybels made his commitment to preach "straight from the Bible."

Creekers have sought to use the compass of psychological categories to guide their journey through American culture. The result of this strategy is that they have fallen into a quagmire of psychology again and again. They periodically realize their predicament and attempt to climb to firmer ground. They have yet to realize that the very compass of the psychological worldview that they are using to escape the quagmire is repeatedly leading them back to it.

The effect of this penetration of the psychological worldview on Willow Creek's teaching is profound. This sort of accommodation "leads to a disappearing boundary between religious beliefs and other beliefs, thus rendering religion irrelevant because they are indistinguishable from a secular viewpoint." In the effort to be relevant, Willow Creek ironically is in danger of becoming irrelevant.[39]

18

The Allure of Marketing

Marketing Christianity is one of the most controversial issues in evangelicalism today. Many pastors and Christian leaders are instinctive critics of marketing methodologies and condemn any attempt to market the church. Other Christian leaders, in their attempts to be faithful stewards, find marketing methods helpful and react defensively to criticism. Both groups need the same thing—a careful analysis of the dynamics of marketing.

Assessing Marketing

Marketing is a central feature of the market economy that is sweeping the globe in the aftermath of the fall of communism. The issue of Christianity and marketing is controversial because evangelicals have widely divergent opinions of how they should respond to their culture.

On the one hand, advocates like George Barna praise marketing enthusiastically and believe that the gospel can be communicated more effectively using these tools. No one should question their zeal and ethical motivation. The Christian advocates of marketing are willing to interact with the modern world to understand and use its resources in their Christian goals and strategies.

On the other hand, critics of marketing have rejected any use of marketing for Christianity. Critic John MacArthur bluntly states that "the simple reality is that one *cannot* follow a market-driven strategy and remain faithful to Scripture." The critics of marketing are concerned that the truth of the gospel is being compromised with this use of modern methods. Their admirable goal is to defend the truth. Like the advocates, the critics are seeking to be faithful to the Lord and his Word. No one should question their zeal and ethical motivation.[1]

How are we to understand this puzzle? Both sides are seeking to be faithful. Why the disagreement?

Seen from the perspective of modern business, marketing is the science and art of understanding customers and markets and creating or adapting products to meet their needs. Successful modern businesses require effective marketing. Thus marketing is an integral part of the American culture and increasingly that of the world generally.

Creekers argue that they are in the business of God's work. They believe that like any business, if their business is going to be successful they need to understand their customers (and their needs), clarify a target market profile, and develop or package products to meet these needs. Hybels says, "Businesses, if they're going to be successful for the long haul, must pull their attention off of themselves and refocus their energies on their only reason for existence—to serve their customers."[2]

There is a need for a little historical perspective at this point. Historical studies of Christianity in America have noted that America provided a more open market for the gospel than found in the state-supported Christianity of Europe. America's open-ended environment provided considerable latitude in entrepreneurial Christianity. The Methodists and Baptists were particularly skilled in proclaiming the gospel across the American frontier and planting thousands of new churches.[3]

An entrepreneurial Christianity that creatively communicates the gospel and charismatically leads new movements is not what I am describing in Willow Creek's use of market strategy. Although Willow Creek certainly fits within this historical pattern, it has also adopted the terminology and methods of the modern business discipline of marketing. Willow Creek's strategy of "target audience profile," "felt needs," and "product" is distinctly different from, for example, the methods of evangelism and revival practiced by Methodists in the early nineteenth century. Willow Creek understands itself as operating within a marketplace and is using modern marketing categories to strategize in how to do this. What is the effect of this method?

The Logic of Christian Marketing

The application of marketing strategy to Christianity provides a new way to understand the ends and means of the Christian life. This prism of interpretation identifies several elements of Christianity as high priorities. Several of the ideas that marketing emphasizes can be carefully and productively used by the broader church.

Vision. Creekers rightfully argue that the American church has lost its outward vision. Many churches have become what sociologist Robert Bellah has called "lifestyle enclaves," which are similar to country clubs. These churches satisfy social needs but have little spiritual or moral effect. The marketing strategy criticizes American churches' loss of vision and tries to reestablish the importance of the local church's mission. This directional focus can help the broader church.[4]

Stewardship. Hybels and his followers argue that the church needs to take responsibility for its resources and be faithful stewards. This biblical principle has often been neglected by much of the evangelical church, and this reminder is both helpful and necessary.

Strategy. The root of *strategy* comes from the Greek word *(stratiotes)* for soldier. The Scriptures describe believers as soldiers in Christ's army (2 Tim. 2:3). Adopting this biblical theme, Creekers have portrayed the church as God's army. As God's army Creekers believe that the church needs to establish effective strategies. For example, one Willow Creek strategy is the creation of a church service for the unchurched. As I argued above, many unchurched individuals will attend a seeker service who would not consider attending a traditional church.

Persuasive Communication. Willow Creek's marketing strategy has probably helped them create the persuasive process of their seeker service. The seeker service (with cautions and criticisms attached) is an effective process of leading nonbelievers to Christ. For example, a central element of Willow Creek's use of marketing is a commitment to understand the unchurched.

To a greater or lesser extent, all of the above principles have been emphasized at Willow Creek in part because of their marketing strategy. To the extent that marketing has clarified these ideas, the marketing framework has been helpful. However, these ideas are actually biblical at root. For example, the principles of stewardship and strategy are not marketing innovations. At most, marketing has helped to highlight or emphasize certain biblical ideas.[5]

On the flip side, the danger in using marketing tools is the temptation to let them shape Christianity. Willow Creek's use of marketing language and reasoning has been adopted wholesale from the marketplace. The problem is that the marketing perspective of needs, research, target markets, market share, target-audience profile, and product inevitably modifies any human endeavor to which it is applied.

Many of the advocates of marketing the church are unaware of the effect of marketing ideas and methods. George Barna enthusiastically describes the gospel with marketing categories:

> Don't underestimate the marketing lessons Jesus taught. He understood *His product* thoroughly, developed an unparalleled *distribution system*, advanced a method of *promotion* that has penetrated every continent, and offered His *product* at a *price* that is within the grasp of every consumer [emphasis added].[6]

This is a dangerous distortion of the Christian gospel. Thinking in marketing categories shapes the method of Christian evangelism. Marketing distorts how Christians view nonbelievers and the process of telling others the gospel. In fact, if followed consistently, marketing strategy even distorts the Christian gospel itself.

The way an issue is formulated is like the launching of a missile. At first glance, the use of marketing terminology seems to affect the Christian message only slightly. But the consequences are as catastrophic as when a seemingly small adjustment causes a missile to veer off target and crash.

Earl Shorris has worked for most of his life as a high-profile marketing specialist. He recently wrote a sort of marketing confession in which he described Proctor & Gamble's takeover of Folger's, a quality coffee bean company:

> When Proctor & Gamble took over the company, a group of humorless men was sent from P & G Cincinnati headquarters to take charge of the marketing of Folger's coffee in the West. These were the Jesuits of marketing; rigorous thinkers, examiners, cold men, driven by the rules of marketing logic to question every aspect of the operation.
>
> They put the business to the rack, the thumbscrew, and the boot of the salesman religion. . . . They had the power, they were on the side of the lord of business, they were the marketers.[7]

Where before Folger's had put its money in acquiring high-quality coffee beans grown in high-altitude volcanic soil, now the money went toward a high-powered television advertising budget. The logic was ruthless: "The marginal return on a dollar spent for sales and advertising was greater than the marginal return on a dollar spent for high-quality beans." Sales took off as the marketers created that shaman of coffee beans, Mrs. Olsen.

Marketing shapes how one views the world. People become "consumers" and "target audiences." These consumers have "felt needs," which "research" discovers in order to modify the "product" to meet these needs. Marketing shapes both the communicative process and eventually the product itself. In the case of Folger's coffee, the marketing logic dictated a change in the product: "the ratcheting downward of the quality and character of the product was not only possible but profitable."[8]

Marketing is not a neutral set of ideas and methods that can be adopted without consequences. Christians who are currently utilizing marketing do not realize that marketing shapes the processes and content of communication. Christians should not market the church, nor market the gospel. Put through the meat grinder of market analysis, the gospel becomes a "product," the unchurched become "consumers," Christians become "salesmen," and the "needs" of the unchurched become a potential tool of manipulation. What are the distorting effects of marketing strategy?

The temptation of image, the quagmire of psychology, the dilution of a biblical view of God, and the loss of the centrality of truth are the direct consequences of a marketing method. If marketing principles are followed consistently, one ends up with a Schullerian style of Christianity that emphasizes performance and psychology and presents a sub-biblical understanding of God and man. The entire assessment section of this book is an attempt to sift the wheat from the chaff in the Willow Creek seeker service strategy. The chaff that should be collected and discarded is the marketing terminology, strategy, and mindset. The wheat that should be collected and saved is a biblical model of persuasion.

There are several additional consequences of a marketing method.

The Allure of Success

As I noted in chapter 4, most Americans' dominant goal is their own personal fulfillment. Similarly, a close second to the pursuit of happiness is Americans' search for success. Noted sociologist Robert Bellah describes a typical American who is focused on being a success: "He defines his work by his corporate position, quantified in terms of gross revenue, profit margin, staff size, and span of control." The goal of success is the ever upward and onward push for achievement, accomplishment, status, and prestige.[9]

The final goal of the marketing strategy is the bottom line of success—numbers. Marketing is not ultimately concerned with the quality of the product, the beauty of the arts used to communicate, or the customer's concerns. The ultimate focus of marketing is the growth of numbers. If a particular marketing program increases the volume of sales, it is successful. If it does not increase sales, it fails. All other criteria are set aside in the quest for the bottom line.

Marketer Shorris remembers creating a television advertisement for Spare Tire, an aerosol can filled with latex designed to inflate a flat tire:

> In the commercial a man walked into his garage, saw that a tire was flat, took a can of Spare Tire from the glove compartment of his car, sealed and reinflated his tire, got into his car, and drove off. As I recall, there was one line that went something like: "One flat tire, one minute, one can of Spare Tire."

The commercial won many prizes, the product sold very well, and customers were pleased with it—as long as the can remained in the glove compartment. The product did not work. When people used the can, the latex tended to spill out of the puncture. Before creating this ad, Shorris had never seen the product demonstrated and confesses: "I believed the manufacturer's claims, which makes me both a fool and an accomplice." Yet the marketing was successful, even award winning, because of the sales.[10]

If a particular product or service does not produce a profit, its future is limited. As the chairman of Prefect International explains, "There's got to be measurable results—that's the corporate approach."[11]

Not surprisingly, those Christians who have explicitly applied marketing criteria to the church are aggressively focused on "measurable results"—numbers. Robert Schuller, Hybels's church-growth mentor, describes the central principle of his Institute on Successful Church Leadership, "The growth of the church is the only thing that matters." George Barna, the cheerleader for Willow Creek's use of marketing methods and tools, says, "For the local church to be a successful business, it must impact a growing share of its market area." The goal of marketing Christianity is numerical growth.[12]

As shown in chapters 3 and 4, the use of a marketing framework and methods are basic to Willow Creek's strategy. However, when Creekers read these chapters, they became uneasy. Hybels and his staff, in response to growing criticism, have sought to downplay their use of marketing categories. For example, one article in *Willow Creek* magazine described Willow Creek's choice of a "target audience." The magazine staff soon received a memo from Hybels informing them that the term "target audience" should be used only in-house. Willow Creek uses marketing terminology and yet feels a little queasy about it. This is reflected in their attitude toward numbers.

On the one hand, Hybels has become aware that numbers dominate the modern search for success. He described how a pastors' lunch he attended was dominated by the questions, "*How many* people attend your church? *How big* is your budget? *How large* is your staff?" He wryly commented, "We measure each other by counting carefully" (author's emphasis).[13]

On the other hand, I found Willow Creek staff members constantly referring to numbers to justify their work or ministries: "We have over three hundred small-group leaders"; "We baptized nearly one thousand individuals last year"; "We counseled nearly one thousand individuals last year"; "Over five hundred individuals meet each week in our self-help groups"; "We receive over one thousand eight hundred phone calls every day"; "We had forty-three thousand people go through the building during the anniversary week"; "five thousand individuals have been through our seminar."

Since success is so revered in America and numbers are considered to measure success, people are attracted to numerical growth. As a Creeker explained, "When I tell people about the church, they are respectful and impressed that there must be something working here." As Barna bluntly puts it, Americans "do not want to associate with a 'loser,' whether it is a person or an organization." A key Willow Creek leader concisely explained to me, "There is nothing that dispels doubt faster than success." That is, the visible success of numbers.[14]

This is the world of marketing shaping the life of the spirit. In the guise of spiritual growth, the purpose of the church can become numbers, success, and achievement rather than honoring or glorifying God. Increasing influence becomes the elixir of life and increasing statistics the sign of the Holy Spirit.

Again I need to underline that I believe Willow Creek staff want to honor God. Yet built into their strategy of the church is a preoccupation with success and thus numbers. Willow Creek and other churches in the midst of this American idolatry of success need to be wary of marketing terminology and strategy that easily shape and distort the best of intentions.

A church may be completely devoid of spiritual life and still be increasing in numbers and influence. Marketing techniques may be employed without integrity or spiritual maturity. Numbers are not necessarily a sign of God's presence. We would do well to remember Paul's warning:

> The time will come when men will not put up with sound doctrine. Instead, to suit their own desires, they will gather around them a great number of teachers to say what their itching ears want to hear.
>
> 2 Timothy 4:3

The Temptation of Manipulation

Marketers are savvy and skillful in exploiting their target audience. The hook of a sale is baited with the felt needs of the typical target audience individual. This dynamic raises the possibility of a manipulation that seeks to identify and manage the felt needs of the target audience. These needs become the pry bars that the marketer uses to jar the targeted individual into action.

When Interval Research Company began planning to have a booth at Lollapalooza (a traveling rock and cultural festival), they commissioned a marketing study. The report listed several characteristics of the typical concert attender and then suggested various strategies.

1. Their common preoccupation is the question of personal identity. . . . They are likely to be interested in exhibits that allow them to control the various elements of personal identity.
2. They feel marginal to mainstream society. . . . The tent and all the elements in it should reflect a countercultural aesthetic.
3. Shocking parents, family, friends, and community is often a part of this group's self-definition process. They will want a record of the most socially unacceptable image of themselves to freak out their parents.
4. They don't want to fail, especially in public. Thus we need to set them up for success. Exhibits must be designed and tested to limit the frustration factor.
5. The majority of them will be drunk, stoned, tripping, or otherwise chemically altered. . . . They need a constructive outlet for expressions of emotion, especially rage and grief.[15]

The cleverness of the marketing method is visible in each of these comments. The marketers are able to profile the target audience of stoned cyberpunks and graph how best to steer them to achieve their organization's goals. Marketing provides this sort of managerial manipulation.

The ability to identify and massage the target audience's emotions is a large part of the market strategy. Marketer Shorris notes the essential characteristics of a successful salesman:

> They're able to present their case in such a way that they convince the customer that, number one, he needs the product and number two, that this product is a good value. But more, the thing is that now is the time to make the decision.[16]

There is something hard and ruthlessly cold about a true marketing method. We see how this process sometimes works in the funeral home business. Individuals who are coming in to make arrangements for their loved ones are feeling particularly vulnerable. They often feel guilty that they have not shown enough love and concern for the dear departed one. An acquaintance of mine in the business described how some funeral directors use this emotion to spur relatives to buy the more deluxe caskets at as much as 1000 percent higher cost than a simpler casket. Some of these caskets are even waterproof and guaranteed for a long life—as if that mattered. The felt need of the guilt of neglect is twisted to manipulate relatives into a more expensive purchase.

When I questioned a Willow Creek staff member about marketing manipulation, he responded, "I guess what I'm saying is add the Holy Spirit to the equation of pure, simple, human marketing." He acted as if merely mentioning the Holy Spirit made the process more spiritual. The problem with this reasoning is that the Holy Spirit calls us to worship (and evangelize) in spirit and truth. The truth of the matter is that marketers often manipulate their audience by hooking their felt needs. We cannot "add the Holy Spirit" to a corrupt method. We need to reject this marketing method and any superficial reasoning that would support it.

There is a business logic in marketing analysis that reduces everything to a utilitarian purpose. We see this in Barna's summary of the marketing approach to Christianity: "This is what marketing the church is all about: providing our product (relationships) as a solution to people's needs."[17]

We must reject this crass characterization of the apostles as those who "opened 'franchises' (local churches) to further spread the product." The gospel is not a Big Mac, and Jesus did not die as the first step in a marketing plan. Lost in this marketing mindset is the compassion and love of Jesus who wept over Jerusalem. God's love is obscured in the machination of a global marketing plan. It is a modern mutation of the gospel.[18]

The marketing approach also warps the evangelist's motivation. The gospel is God's revelation to the world that he loves us. Those of us who have received this wonderful message have the joy of sharing this message and God's heart of love to others. Yet without this motivation of thankfulness and compassion, the gospel becomes a means to heavenly brownie points for a spiritual salesman. The marketing perspective connects a believer's value to his ability to convert spiritual customers. The result is that such a marketer is tempted to view a nonbeliever as an opportunity to add another spiritual notch to his Bible.

This marketing perspective is a subtle but deadly shift in Christianity. To love someone in order to communicate the gospel distorts the very gospel we communicate. Our love is not genuine if we use it to engender openness in our prospective spiritual targets. We need to love others because God has loved us and also loves them. And because we love them, we share the good news about Jesus. Manipulation is a failure to have compassionate respect for the individuals addressed.

Creekers are becoming aware of the temptation of this marketing manipulation. I found them desiring to honor God in how they communicate the life-changing message of the gospel. They specifically teach participants at their personal evangelism seminar to love and respect the unchurched.

Yet Creekers—who I believe generally have a biblical aim and motivation—occasionally slip into terminology that reflects this utilitarian motivation. This attitude is subtly apparent in the seminar that trains church attenders how to share their faith. Creekers are encouraged to make a list of friends and family whom they want to tell about Jesus. There is a flavor of a utilitarian mindset in what seminar teachers call this roster—a "hit list." People become spiritual targets as a result of this marketing method.

Biblical communication requires a compassionate respect for one's audience. This compassionate respect provides a brake to prevent communication from sliding into manipulation. Without compassionate respect, the communicator becomes a spiritual truck that is looking to dump his or her message on the nearest target. Should we seek to understand the unchurched? Yes. Should we market the gospel? No.

A Fulfillment Theology

My primary criticism of Willow Creek's use of marketing rests on the distortion of the gospel that necessarily results from its fixation with the audience's felt needs. Marketing makes the audience sovereign as it shapes or creates products to satisfy the audience's felt needs and desires.

One commentator observes that most American advertising is focused on "the hard sell: Buy because it tastes good or because it works better." Advertising uses these basic themes with Americans because they work. Americans want to be happy and are willing to buy products that promise happiness.[19]

An example of this focus on audience happiness is the test marketing that the major film studios require before releasing a new movie. Typical audiences are recruited for test screenings in suburban shopping malls. At the close of the movie, the audiences are asked: "Was the ending good for you? Which characters were too distasteful? Did any scenes offend? Would you recommend the film to a friend?" Paula Silver, the president of marketing for Columbia Pictures, explains, "It's the same thing you do with a product. You sample it: Is it too sweet? Is it too hot?" If needed, the studios then disappear back into the editing kitchen to flavor a more pleasurable taste experience for the audience.[20]

This marketing-based shaping of the product is mirrored in television evangelist Robert Schuller's concern for the audience: "I'm terribly sensitive to people out there. I don't want to insult them or embarrass them."

Schuller argues that if he makes Christianity useful to the visiting unchurched they will be willing to come back. Satisfying the felt needs of the unchurched is a central feature of Schuller's marketing method. Schuller argues that the need for self-esteem is the crucial felt need that will interest nonbelievers in the gospel: "Can I find a button to push so that I can reach them? I think their desire for self-esteem is that button."[21]

Hybels inherited from his mentor Schuller this emphasis on the value of Christianity for daily life. Following Schuller, Hybels emphasized self-esteem in the early years of Willow Creek:

> Early in my ministry I realized the importance of self-esteem. . . . It was tremendously exciting for me to see people developing a healthy self-esteem as I and other members of our church staff began to teach about the love of God and the value of man. We knew that this was the key to their personal satisfaction and productivity.[22]

After the 1979 "train wreck" Hybels kept Schuller's idea of connecting to the felt needs of the unchurched but changed the theme. Hybels came to believe that unchurched Harry's most important concern is his personal fulfillment. Hybels is more sociologically accurate concerning what is the greatest priority to the typical unchurched Harry (fulfillment), and thus has a more attractive message than Schuller.

When I have raised this concern to Willow Creek staff, they quickly denied any attempt to alter or change the gospel. It is certainly true that one doesn't find the blatant theological modification at Willow Creek that Schuller advocates. The shift that I am describing starts very subtly. But like the nose of a camel entering a tent, there are huge consequences following the marketing method. By Willow Creek's using the marketing approach adopted from Schuller, their understanding of unchurched Harry necessarily highlights his felt needs. As illustrated in chapters 10 and 11, Hybels teaches that Christianity will satisfy Harry's felt needs and provide fulfillment.

Hybels argues that Harry's felt needs can be met only when he begins a relationship with God and grows in it. He questions the audience, "I wonder how many really believe that soul satisfaction is only found in a vital relationship with God." Hybels and the other speakers do not condemn the search for fulfillment. Rather they argue that Harry has not searched in the right place. The question remains the same, but the answer has been changed. Harry asks, "How can I be happy?" "Accept Jesus," answers Hybels.[23]

As I showed in chapter 11 Willow Creek's canon within the canon is how Christianity brings fulfillment. At Willow Creek, Christianity is presented as the answer to anxiety, pain, meaning, identity, self-esteem, loneliness, marriage, sex, parenting, and work. Hybels motivates Harry by promising that there will be a positive benefit from a life of faith and warns against negative consequences if individuals reject his message.

As Willow Creek markets Christianity, marketing shapes Willow Creek's Christianity. Marketing logic does not leave the product alone. In fact, changing the product is one of the crucial elements of a consistent marketing method. The difficult or unpopular elements of the Christian message get shaved off by a marketing method. As the gospel is processed, packaged, and priced, the gospel assumes the image of the marketer's target audience.

The felt-need orientation of marketing fits hand-in-glove with the psychological worldview that Hybels regularly uses in his talks. As I noted in chapter 17, the third element of the psychological worldview is the pursuit of fulfillment. Philip Rieff explains, "Religious man was born to be saved, psychological man is born to be pleased." Willow Creek's weekend messages combine the marketing emphasis on satisfying felt needs with the psychological ethics of seeking fulfillment. Willow Creek's fulfillment theology also resonates with a long American tradition of Christianity being presented as a means to success and happiness.[24]

American Self-Interest

Hybels's message touches a deep chord in American character. Alexis de Tocqueville in the 1830s wrote an insightful analysis of American character and culture. De Tocqueville argued that Americans' "self-interest" was an "irresistible force" and profoundly shaped how Christianity was presented.[25]

De Tocqueville reported that pastors had lost all hope of contradicting Americans' basic self-interest. Picture Americans' self-interest as a swiftly flowing river. Instead of trying to row upstream, pastors decided to guide the boat downstream.

> They turn all their thoughts to the direction of it [self-interest]. They therefore do not deny that every man may follow his own interest, but they endeavor to prove that it is in the interest of every man to be virtuous.[26]

Pastors taught Americans that for their own good they should choose Christianity's virtuous path. Thus, Americans understood their own self-interest as leading them to morality, not as pulling them away from it.

De Tocqueville said that as a result, most Americans were convinced that being committed to Christianity and its morality was the best means of happiness: "Self-interest is the principal means that religions themselves employ to govern man." De Tocqueville understood this as a whole new approach to morality. Classic morality, he argued, was to do the good for good's sake, or for the appreciation of the beauty of virtue. Self-interest morality was seeing self-interest as the very means of motivating man to virtue.[27]

Seen from this perspective, Hybels's communication makes perfect sense as a modern update of what de Tocqueville observed pastors doing. Americans are still committed to their own self-interest. In the present context, this self-interest involves a search for fulfillment and satisfying their felt needs. If Hybels can convince Harry that Christianity is the best means to do this, he will get on board. Hybels has not sought to redirect the river of self-interest, but like the preachers of de Tocqueville's era, argued that he has the fastest boat.[28]

Assessing Fulfillment Theology

Hybels attempts to convince unchurched Harrys that a relationship with Christ will enable them to have their felt needs met and the end result will be personal fulfillment. How are we to respond to this fulfillment theology? Like Augustine, Hybels is answering the pagan ethical question, What is the good for man? It might be helpful to review how Augustine responded to this issue over the course of his life.

Augustine's Search for Fulfillment

Augustine was fascinated with happiness throughout his life: "Is not the happy life the thing that all men desire, literally every single man without exception?" Even before his conversion he was caught up in a search for happiness. Through Cicero he became convinced that truth and wisdom were the path to happiness. When Augustine became an eager young convert to Christianity, he attempted to map out how he and others should live. In one of his first books, *The Happy Life*, Augustine argued that happiness consists in true learning and religion: "What else is it to live happily but to possess an eternal object through knowing it?" Since Augustine understood the source of happiness as knowing an eternal object, he concluded that happiness comes from a perfect knowledge of God.[29]

Two years later, Augustine said that people can be happy only when they are good. He believed that adoption of the classical virtues would help him achieve happiness: "The function of this virtue is to restrain and still the passions which cause us to crave things that turn us away from the laws of

God and the enjoyment of His goodness, that is to say, from the happy life." Augustine believed that if individuals could grow in virtue, they would restrain their passions and thus become fulfilled.[30]

Augustine also asserted that love was crucial to achieving happiness: "The happy life may be found—when that which is best for man is both loved and possessed." He believed that no man can be happy "who lacks what he loves." Augustine concluded that God is most valuable and should be loved. This idea is later summarized in the best-known line of *The Confessions:* "You have made us for yourself and our hearts are restless until they can find peace in you." Augustine makes this idea more blatant, writing, "When I seek you, my God, I am seeking the happy life" and "This is the happy life—to rejoice—to rejoice in you, and to you, and because of you."[31]

Yet as the zealous young convert became the seasoned older bishop, the search for happiness had lost its rosy glow. Augustine realized that many of the areas in which he had sought his happiness were ultimately unsatisfying. Although prizing relationships, he sighed, "All human relationships are fraught with such misunderstanding. . . . All history is a tale of 'slights and fights and spirits vexed,' and we must expect such unpleasantness as an assured thing." This frustration, he said, is even true in one's relationship with God: "The Apostle hopes for a perfect knowledge of God, the greatest that man can have, in the life to come, for that alone should be called a happy life."[32]

As Augustine matured as a believer, he began recognizing that his previous preoccupation with fulfillment was not biblically grounded. As he became aware of the distortions of the platonic concepts in his earlier writings, he was willing to discard these ideas. One of these misguided ideas was his portrayal of the Christian life as the path to fulfillment.

The Biblical View of Fulfillment

To be fair to Willow Creek there is substantial biblical teaching that emphasizes that the life of faith is often one of wholesome satisfaction. The wisdom literature of the Old Testament regularly lists the positive effects of a life of faithfulness and the dire consequences to those who reject the Lord's guidance:

> Whoever finds me finds life
>   and receives favor from the LORD.
> But whoever fails to find me harms himself;
>   all who hate me love death.
>
> Proverbs 8:35

Many Scripture texts emphasize the joy of the Christian life, how Jesus will make his disciples' burdens light, and the importance of celebration.

Is it wrong to be fulfilled as believers? No. It has been a failure of the church at times to consider sacrifice and pain as innately more spiritual somehow than joy and happiness. It was no mistake that the Lord's first miracle was the creation of wine at a wedding party. Celebration, joy, and peace are elements of the Christian life. There will be seasons of particular joy and happiness. We should receive these times with thankfulness to our gracious Lord. There is a wholesomeness to God's way of life: "The path of the righteous is like the first gleam of dawn, shining ever brighter till the full light of day" (Prov. 4:18).

What is the result of this righteous way of life? Evidence exists that Americans who are "highly spiritually committed" tend to be more satisfied with their lives than their counterparts. George Gallup Jr. summarizes the evidence of his surveys:

> A total of 68 percent of the highly spiritually committed say that they are "very happy," compared to 46 percent of the moderately spiritually committed, 39 percent of the moderately uncommitted, and 30 percent of the highly uncommitted.[33]

David Larson, formerly researcher of the National Institute of Mental Health, has argued that psychiatric studies actually show great benefits to religious commitment: "What the data showed was that religion was highly beneficial—beneficial in more that 80 percent of the cases found in the psychiatric research." It makes sense that other things being equal, individuals seeking to live as they were made to live as God's children will on average be more satisfied.[34]

Yet this psychological evidence is often used as justification for the teaching that Christianity necessarily brings fulfillment. This is a faulty way of doing theology. Is Willow Creek correct in their teaching that a relationship with Christ will provide a life of fulfillment? In a word, no.

Willow Creek's fulfillment theology is a sort of American liberation theology flipped on its head. Liberation theology is a Latin American teaching popular in the 1970s and 1980s that combined theology and Marxism. It inspired the political mobilization of the poor to achieve social justice. The leading work of liberation theology is Gustavo Gutierrez's *A Theology of Liberation*. Gutierrez argues that salvation is the political liberation of the socially oppressed. He asserts that the focus of Christian life should not be the spiritual afterlife but the fight for political justice in the here and now.

The problem with liberation theology is that the Bible is approached as a collection of proof texts to illustrate and prove prior assumptions. The result of this method appears in the index of Bible texts, where the bulk of Gutierrez's references to the Bible are from Exodus, Isaiah, and Luke. The Exodus references are used as justification for political liberation for God's people. Isaiah, especially Isaiah 40 (which Gutierrez emphasizes), speaks of the pain and suffering of God's anointed and of God's judgment, justice, and grace. Luke is used as the portrait of Jesus that most clearly demonstrates Jesus' concern for social justice and teaching about the poor.

Latin American liberation theology justifies revolution and uses Christianity as a political means. This theology effectively communicates with the poor of Latin America because it supports their political aspirations and condemns their opponents. The central problem with liberation theology is that it does not do justice to the whole of Scripture. If one approaches the Bible with a set of basic beliefs, it is very easy to select verses that teach—or seem to teach—one's prior assumptions. Gutierrez selects those verses and themes that fit the goal of political mobilization.

But this gerrymandering method will always distort the resulting theology. Scripture is a God-inspired, complex collection of different types of literature. A biblical systematic theology is the careful teaching of the whole of Scripture, not this kind of picking and choosing verses that support one's current lifestyle or political aspirations. From the North American perspective, it is easier to see the shallow rationalization of such a Latin American politicized Christianity.

Likewise, Creekers (and many other evangelicals) in the lap of American luxury are faced with a different temptation—the idolatry of personal fulfillment. Personal fulfillment is the dominant goal of the vast majority of Americans. In this context it is a great temptation for American evangelicals to argue that Christianity is a means of a more fulfilling life. In this environment the gospel becomes a means to fulfillment and the church becomes another place that promises to satisfy emotional desires. This same biased method that liberation theology uses of picking verses to support one's aspirations is just as faulty if employed by Americans seeking to prove that God's children are promised fulfillment in this life. It is the same shallow cultural hermeneutics, but this time practiced from the perspective of North American abundance.[35]

Like Gutierrez's goal of political mobilization this focus on psychological well-being distorts one's theology. Seeking to use Christianity to achieve any goal (whether political or emotional) distorts the resulting theology. Christianity is not an ideology to be used for some pragmatic end. Christian truth evaluates and judges all human systems.

To argue for Christianity primarily by pointing to its usefulness in satisfying felt needs is to ultimately undercut it. To teach Christianity as a means eventually teaches that it is superfluous. If someone is able to satisfy their felt needs without Christ, the message of Christianity can be discarded. Evangelism would be only to the neurotic or emotionally damaged, and agnostic and atheistic intellectuals would be impervious to the gospel's challenge. The bottom line why individuals should repent and worship God is because God deserves it.

Fulfillment theology does not reflect the teaching of the Bible. We find in Scripture vast evidence that Christianity is often not "fulfilling." Jesus promises his disciples that "in this world you will have trouble" (John 16:33). Paul tells Timothy, "Everyone who wants to live a godly life in Christ Jesus will be persecuted" (2 Tim. 3:12). The writer of Hebrews tells us that many have been faithful to God and yet suffered torture, flogging, stoning, were sawed in two, and went about "destitute, persecuted and mistreated" (Heb. 11:35–39). Paul recalls how he was beaten, stoned, and shipwrecked and confesses that in one difficult spot he "despaired even of life" (2 Cor. 1:8).

The Lord's message to the church at Smyrna is a stunning warning of approaching pain:

> Do not be afraid of what you are about to suffer. I tell you, the devil will put some of you in prison to test you, and you will suffer persecution for ten days. Be faithful, even to the point of death, and I will give you the crown of life.
>
> Revelation 2:10

The Lord did not promise fulfillment, or even relief, in this world, but only the next. In the Garden of Gethsemane, even our Lord himself called out, "My soul is overwhelmed with sorrow to the point of death" (Matt. 26:38). Fulfillment is not a spiritual birthright of Christians.[36]

The goal of a Christian's life is faithfulness, not fulfillment. It is not wrong to desire happiness. The question is, how does this desire for happiness shape or influence your life? Does it distort how you make decisions? Does it shape how you present the gospel to nonbelievers? From a biblical perspective fulfillment is a gift, not a goal.

Fulfillment theology has an inadequate understanding of the biblical truth about the fallenness of the world and the role of suffering in the Christian's life. The Scripture teaches us that we live in a fallen creation that sin has marred in several ways. Brokenness exists in man's relationship with God, man's relationship with creation, man's relationship with man, and man within himself. As Paul writes, "the whole creation has been groaning as in the pains of childbirth" (Rom. 8:22). Until the Lord returns, this brokenness will never be completely mended. Suffering is a regular companion in this life. To argue that Christians should be fulfilled is to add the lash of spirituality to the burden of affliction.

Does God promise fulfillment in this life? Tell that to the thousands of martyrs and their loved ones who have died for the faith in this century alone. On the very day that I write these words, I have read reports of new martyrs in North Africa who are literally being crucified like our Lord, and their wives and children are being sold into slavery. Are they fulfilled?

God does not promise that the end of the Christian life on this earth will result in fulfillment. That sort of teaching is an American distortion of biblical teaching.

Marketing brings modern tools of communication that are basic elements of American, and increasingly world, culture. Creekers have borrowed these methods in their efforts to reach their unchurched friends and family. Although their intentions are good, the methods have tended to warp the content of the Christian gospel. As they seek to market the gospel, the gospel itself has been distorted.

19

The Mirror of God's Face

Hybels and his staff are seeking to present the biblical gospel. In fact, if asked, they quickly affirm that their message is the unchangeable gospel and condemn any attempt to modify it. Lee Strobel underscores this point:

> Let me emphatically add that I'm not suggesting anybody alter the gospel to make it artificially attractive to unchurched people. Watering it down or eliminating the difficult elements of sin or repentance is totally unacceptable.[1]

Few evangelicals would have serious problems with the understanding of the gospel that I summarized in chapter 13. Yet upon examining the emphases of Willow Creek's gospel, we find that the substance of their message has subtly been altered. Willow Creekers themselves have not been aware of how their method of communicating the gospel is shaping the message. Understanding the effect of this strategy requires summarizing a basic duality in Christian theology.

Christian theology teaches a fundamental duality of God's immanence and his transcendence. These characteristics refer to God's relationship to creation.

God's immanence means that he is present and active in the world. It is displayed in his love and kindness. It is fully demonstrated in Christ's incarnation and the active presence of the Holy Spirit.

In contrast, God's transcendence refers to God's separateness from the world. He is omnipotent, omniscient, holy, and righteous and transcends time and space. Theologian Millard Erickson explains the importance of clearly teaching both of these truths of God's nature: "Where either is overemphasized at the expense of the other, the orthodox theistic conception is lost."[2]

We will better understand Willow's gospel when we comprehend what they teach about God's immanent love and his transcendent holiness.

God's Immanent Love

Hybels constantly emphasized God's love to the weekend crowd the year I studied. Thirty-eight out of the fifty-four talks (more than 70 percent) had a strong emphasis on God's immanent love and its effects in people's lives. In a typical month, three out of the four weekend messages were about God's compassionate love. This theme of God's love is summarized in the church's motto, "You matter to God" and another popular Willow Creek slogan, "What a wonderful God we have!" A song that Hybels described as "crucial" in understanding Willow Creek emphasizes God's love:

> In heaven's eyes, there are no losers;
> In heaven's eyes, no hopeless cause;
> Only people like you, with feelings like me;
> Amazed, amazed by the grace we can find, in heaven's arms.[3]

When Hybels prays at the end of each talk, he invariably calls God a loving "Father," as in this prayer:

> Father, I pray that seekers right now who are standing with clenched fists or hands stuck in their pockets—I hope they'll realize that even if they can't trust you yet, they still matter to you and your eye is fixed on them, and your love is focused their way.[4]

Hybels often describes God as this compassionate father who has deep feelings of love toward the visiting unchurched Harry and Mary. In fact, one of the unique emphases of Hybels's teaching is the idea that God is very emotional: "God has feelings too; God has feelings too. And they can be wounded and ruptured just like yours can and just like mine can." Hybels argues that God's most powerful emotion is love: "God's deepest feeling for all of his people and for the world is love."[5]

Hybels emphasizes how God's love meets human needs. We can see this depiction of God in the table of contents of Hybels's book *Seven Wonders of the Spiritual World:*

1. You Matter to God
2. God Loves Me
3. God Can Be Trusted

4. God Forgives Me
5. God Transforms Me
6. God Guides Me
7. God Uses Me
8. God Satisfies Me
9. Now What?[6]

It should be no surprise at this point to see the word *Me* in the majority of the chapter titles. Hybels emphasizes God's immanent love and its value for human beings.

Sociologist Robert Wuthnow suggests that in contemporary America, God has been molded to satisfy people's needs:

> God has, in a sense, become "subjectivized" rather than existing as a metaphysical, transcendent, or omnipotent being. . . .
>
> God is relevant to contemporary Americans mainly because the sense of God's presence is subjectively comforting; that is, religion solves personal problems rather than addressing broader questions.[7]

This subjective, immanent understanding of God is apparent in Hybels's description of how God seeks to meet people's needs and make them happy:

> God satisfies.
> He does things for us and in us that we can't do for ourselves.
> God meets inner needs.
> He quiets restlessness and turmoil.
> He ministers to longings.
> He soothes wounds.
> He calms fears.
> He satisfies our souls.[8]

Hybels's sanguine portrayal of God to unchurched Harry could be summarized, "God loves you and will meet you where you are, forgive you, and meet your felt needs and make you fulfilled."

Unchurched Harry and Mary are attracted by this optimistic affirmation of God's lovingkindness. As one Willow Creek participant explained, "What attracted me most was its upbeat message." This positive message of God's love strikes a resonant chord in Americans. A full eight out of nine Americans "feel that God loves them." Eighty percent of Americans feel that God is close to them. Even many evangelists of the psychological worldview assert that God is loving. Codependency writer Melody Beattie proclaims, "God hasn't abandoned us. . . . He's there and he cares." The understanding of God as a loving Father also resonates with 84 percent of Americans, who believe God is a "heavenly father, who can be reached by prayers." Hybels's college-educated audience is particularly receptive to stories about Jesus' loving compassion.[9]

Yet even normally optimistic pollster George Gallup Jr. observes that Americans' strong belief in God's loving immanence is not all that it appears:

> When we use measurements to probe the depth of religious conviction, we become less impressed with the sincerity of our faith. We believe in God, but this God is often only an affirming one, not a demanding one.[10]

God's Transcendent Holiness

In contrast to this emphasis on God's love, the weekend messages did not emphasize God's holiness. The words *holy* or *holiness* were used only 145 times during the year's messages; *love* or *kind,* however, were used 928 times. While Hybels taught about God's holiness, he put the spotlight on God's love and compassion.[11]

Seventy-nine of the 145 weekend uses of *holy* or *holiness* were in only one talk. Only 66 uses of *holy* or *holiness* occurred in all the other 53 talks. I found only four messages in which God's holiness was presented clearly over the course of the year. This amounts to about 7 percent of the messages, in contrast to 70 percent of the messages emphasizing God's love. For every message that stressed God's holiness, there were about ten messages that emphasized God's love.

In fact, the words *holy* or *holiness* were often used in reference to the benefits available to people from God's holiness: "When God's *holiness* expresses itself in the issuing of a set of *holy*, moral standards for humans to obey, I benefit from that and so do you." Hybels argues that God's "*holiness* has established a clear sense of what is fair and wrong in this world." Hybels says that people should thank God for his holiness, because they are not trapped by relativism, and for laws that protect them and their family. These statements emphasize the usefulness of God's holiness. We also see Hybels's lack of emphasis on God's transcendent holiness in that he did not regularly teach God's moral law in the weekend messages.[12]

God's Moral Law

Central to the Protestant Reformation was the tenet that law precedes gospel. Classical Protestant theologians have emphasized passages like Romans 3:20: "Through the law comes knowledge of sin." They have argued that one was not teaching the biblical gospel if one did not emphasize how God's transcendent moral law calls one into account.

Martin Luther believed that salvation through faith is only possible if individuals see themselves clearly. He asserted that God's law is the means of this self-revelation:

> God wants to teach man to know himself through the Law. He wants him to see how false and unjust his heart is, how far he still is from God, and how entirely impotent his nature is. . . .
>
> Thus man is to be humbled, to creep to the cross, to sigh for Christ, to long for His grace, to despair of himself, and to base all his confidence on Christ.[13]

Luther argued that the law provides a transcendent mirror for the individual to see himself and especially his sin.

Luther also depicted God's law as a hammer that powerfully humbled unrepentant sinners:

> In no other way than by the use of the Law can God soften and humble a man to cause him to acknowledge his misery and damnation. For the Law is the hammer of death, the thundering of hell, and the lightning of God's wrath, crushing the hardened and insensate hypocrites.[14]

Luther said that God's means to humble people was for them to hear preachers proclaim the transcendent, holy truth of God's moral law.

John Calvin also argued that God's law is a preparation for the gospel: "By comparing the righteousness of the law with our life, we learn how far we are from conforming to God's will." Thus, God's moral law serves as a means of condemnation in that it reveals who we really are:

> However remarkable an opinion of his powers he formerly held, he soon feels that they are panting under so heavy a weight as to stagger and totter, and finally even to fall down and faint away. Thus man, schooled in the law, sloughs off the arrogance that previously blinded him. . . .
>
> The law is like a mirror. In it we contemplate our weakness, then the iniquity arising from this, and finally the curse coming from both—just as a mirror shows us the spots on our face.[15]

Calvin explains that "the severity of the law takes away from us all self-deception" and by its "accusing moves us to seek grace."[16]

John Wesley also clearly taught the importance of God's moral law in faithfully preaching the biblical gospel. Wesley explained how he preached law as a central element of the Christian message:

> I think the right method of preaching is this. At our first beginning to preach at any place—after a general declaration of the love of God to sinners and his willingness that they should be saved—to preach the law in the strongest, the closest, the most searching manner possible, only intermixing the gospel here and there and showing it, as it were, afar off.[17]

Wesley was convinced that the emphasis on God's grace in the gospel should "not be done too hastily" and taught "it is only in private converse with a thoroughly convinced sinner that we should preach nothing but the Gospel."[18]

Wesley, Luther, and Calvin argued that central to the biblical gospel is the self-revelation that comes from being confronted with God's holy law. As J. I. Packer writes, "Nobody can see what sin is till he has learned what God is."[19]

The law provides this dual vision of God's holiness and human sinfulness. The law reveals the cellar of our souls and is designed to show us that we cannot live according to its requirements. The law shows our corrupt motives and selfishness and the rationalizations of our reasoning.

The point behind this brief comparison between God's love and God's holiness, and the excursus about God's moral law, is that Willow Creek's gospel, as summarized in chapter 13, is not the whole story. Hybels's relevant teaching that God wants to meet individuals' needs and make them fulfilled unduly shapes his gospel message. The holiness of God and the convicting nature of God's moral law are obscured. Hybels's overall message on the weekend is a rather optimistic approach to Christianity. It is not that Hybels does not speak of God's holiness and the need to repent, it is merely that the message of God's transcendent holiness is flooded by the broader emphasis on God's immanent compassionate love.

After reading this chapter, a Willow Creek staff member argued that Willow Creek's audience comes from backgrounds that emphasize that God is holy and transcending: "We're emphasizing those parts of the gospel that tend to be lacking and left out of the background of many of the people we're trying to reach." He asserted that Willow Creek is spotlighting the part of God's nature (immanent love) that the audience doesn't understand yet. It is true that there may be certain individuals who need to understand elements of the gospel such as God's love, yet this argument ignores all the evidence indicating that the majority of Americans believe in God's love. He is suggesting that Willow Creek's audience is somehow different from most Americans. This is the direct opposite of what all my research indicates. All the seekers or weekend attenders I interviewed were convinced that God loves them. They held this belief before coming to Willow Creek, and the belief was confirmed by the weekend teaching. The problem is that they were not receiving strong teaching about God's holiness.

We can see the result of this teaching in several examples. Eighteenth-century theologian Jonathan Edwards, in his famous sermon "Sinners in the Hands of an Angry God," depicts the anger of God against man's rebellious sin. He pictures humans as spiders dangling before the fire of God's wrath. During the year's messages I studied the harsh news of God's anger against mankind's defiant sin was virtually never heard. This idea of God's anger at mankind's rebellion is so far away from the Willow Creek teaching, that during the Impact Evangelism Training seminar, one of the speakers made a joke about Edwards's picture of God's anger against sin.

We also see this sanguine attitude after a church-wide survey when Hybels broke the news that large percentages of the congregation in the previous six months had lied (33 percent), stolen (18 percent), committed adultery (12.5 percent), and its men had viewed pornography (27 percent). After describing how Creekers had failed, Hybels's response was not to rebuke the congregation, but to compliment them:

> Put your chest out a little bit—we are acknowledging our unrighteousness and we are exposing it to grace and truth. And we are banding together learning how we can have it forgiven and learning how the Holy Spirit can help us walk a little differently next week and next month and next year.

Yet the audience had not repented. They had not confessed their sin. They had merely noted on a survey form that they had committed adultery, viewed pornography, and so on.

The next week Hybels noted that large percentages of the singles (25 percent of singles, 38 percent of single parents, and 41 percent of divorced individuals) "admitted having illicit sexual relationships in the last six months." Again Hybels did not call the congregation to repent for their rebellion against a holy God. Instead he emphasized God's compassionate love:

> We are a love-starved people, with broken parts that need the kind of repair that only he can give long-term. We need to bring our brokenness out into the light of his grace and truth.

Hybels did not teach about God's moral law or warn his listeners to examine themselves to see if they were truly in the faith (2 Cor. 13:5; 2 Peter

1:10). This is a subtle process of emphasizing the truth of God's loving compassion and willingness to forgive, which has distorted the truth about God's holiness.

Willow Creek's View of Jesus

I have already shown that Willow Creek clearly affirms an orthodox understanding of Christ: Jesus was fully God and fully man. Yet as each historical age has sought to describe who Jesus was, it has also attempted to validate itself. Historian of Christian thought Jaroslav Pelikan notes that "it has been characteristic of each age of history to depict Jesus in accordance with its own character." If Willow Creek is being influenced by the American psychological worldview, we should not be surprised if their view of Jesus were characterized by therapeutic categories.[20]

Hybels teaches:

> Jesus, by all indications, was a picture of emotional and relational and psychological health. . . .
>
> His relationships were strong and secure. He was steady in adversity, calm in a crisis. He showed absolutely no propensity for any kind of erratic or psychotic behavior. . . .
>
> There is no basis on which to assess Jesus as being anything less than a healthy, whole, integrated person deserving respect and even admiration.

This Jesus sounds very similar to a well-balanced, mature Rogerian therapist. In fact, Willow Creek's descriptions of God the Father could often be that of a helpful therapist: "I can almost hear God saying, 'I'm rooting for your wholeness, for your growth, for your health—I really am.'" This is a theology that emphasizes elements of the gospel that are appealing to the typical unchurched Harry (immanent love) and a corresponding lack of emphasis on those elements that are not as attractive (transcendent holiness). We can understand this shift when we realize that Willow Creek, as evangelicals, is a cognitive minority in society.

Cognitive Minority

Peter Berger suggests that any group that is a cognitive minority in society finds itself in a difficult position:

> The status of cognitive minority is . . . invariably an uncomfortable one—not necessarily because the majority is repressive or intolerant, but simply because it refuses to accept the minority's definitions of reality as "knowledge."[21]

A cognitive minority often adopts one of three different responses to the broader culture's symbolic universe: cognitive defiance, cognitive surrender, and cognitive bargaining.

Cognitive Defiance

Cognitive defiance is the choice of the theological conservative. The theological conservative rejects the fundamental truth claims of the broader society. A theological conservative often retreats from the society and creates his or her own social settings to provide social settings for fellow cognitive dissidents. The theological conservative has rebelled against the world, and says in effect:

> The rest of you go climb a tree; we believe this, we know this, and we are going to stick to it. And if this is irrelevant to the rest of you, well, that is just too bad.[22]

Cognitive Surrender

Cognitive surrender is the choice of the theological liberal. Berger argues that for the theological liberal, "the cognitive authority and superiority" of the dominant symbolic universe "is conceded with few if any reservations. . . . Modernity is swallowed hook, line, and sinker, and the repast is accompanied by a sense of awe worthy of Holy Communion." The theological liberal's central concern is to adjust Christianity's theology to modernity's worldview. The result of this process is "the progressive dismantling of the supernaturalist scaffolding of the Christian tradition."[23]

The beginning of this sort of "cognitive surrender" is apparent in Robert Schuller's gospel. Schuller preaches that theology should reflect the insights and priorities of psychology and that the church needs to reframe the Christian life in psychological categories of self-esteem. Schuller has laid aside the idea of the moral law preceding the gospel. The concept of a holy God who is angry about man's rebellious sin has disappeared from Schuller's message. Schuller has created a positive-mental-attitude Christianity and urges fellow pastors:

> *Let every message stimulate the positive emotions of the listeners.* Positive emotions are: love, joy, kindness, gentleness, goodness, faith, hope, humor, aspiration, trust, respect, self-confidence, enthusiasm, ambition, courage, optimism.
>
> Never play the negative emotions—fear, suspicion, anger, prejudice, sorrow, despair, self-hate, pessimism etc. [author's emphasis].[24]

The artificial grin of this cheerful Christianity strains out any negative emotion—and much of the historic Christian message.

Cognitive Bargaining

Cognitive bargaining occurs when "there are two conflicting views of the world and they start to negotiate with each other." The goal of this strategy is to "arrive at a cognitive compromise." Willow Creek has followed this strategy of cognitive bargaining.[25]

What we are talking about here is not the "cognitive surrender" of a Robert Schuller. In the early years of Willow Creek, Hybels and his staff did adopt Schuller's strategy and thus diluted their message. In 1979 Hybels repented of this "cognitive surrender" and began to teach a clear evangelical gospel. We see in the summary of the weekend's gospel that Hybels has clearly departed from his former mentor Schuller.

In cognitive bargaining we find something much more subtle than cognitive surrender. Cognitive bargaining is visible in a sort of evangelical civility. Sociologist Hunter explains:

> Civility is most noticeable when those who have already accepted the Evangelical message interact with those being introduced to it.
>
> The civilizing process entails a deemphasis of Evangelicalism's more offensive aspects: the notions of inherent evil, sinful conduct and lifestyles, the wrath of a righteous and jealous God, and eternal agony and death in hell.
>
> The deemphasis has been more quantitative than qualitative. The offensive elements are, in the main, neither substantively devalued nor glossed over as unimportant. They are simply not referred to as much as they have been in the past.[26]

This evangelical civility is what we find at Willow Creek. Few evangelicals would have difficulties with Willow Creek's gospel that I have summarized. The problem is that Willow Creek does not teach the elements of their gospel very consistently.

This stems partially from Hybels's method of teaching topically. I noted above that all of the talks on the weekend are topical messages and not exegetical. As a result, Scripture does not provide the outline and content of the talks. In fact, Scripture is often only used as an illustration. By referring to Scripture topically, Hybels is guided in his choices of Scripture by the broader argument of his talks. Thus, as chapter 11 notes, Hybels often referred to those verses that affirm his message that Christianity is the most fulfilling way to live.

Willow Creek cognitively bargains by unintentionally emphasizing those elements of Christianity that fit in the broader methodology of the weekend service. By focusing on the relevance of Christianity and how it provides fulfillment, Willow Creek obscures the biblical message of a holy God who is angry at sin. The moral law is rarely presented in this context. One staff member who was beginning to see this problem in Willow Creek's strategy explained:

> It's not works that save you. It's not devotion, it's not information that saves you. It's really, from the Sermon on the Mount, *being poor in spirit.* But that's not a real popular message for this weekend crowd . . . [emphasis added].

This lack of teaching God's holiness and the moral law helps create "the churched Larry problem."

The Churched Larry Problem

An average of 13,220 individuals attended each weekend during the year that I studied. Children attending "Promiseland" comprised 2,074 of this number. Thus, an average of 11,146 adults attended each weekend service. Over the course of this same year, an average of 3,828 adults attended the weekday New Community service. Only one-third of those who attended on the weekends also went to New Community. The gap between these two totals is a huge 7,318 adults who attended weekend services but did not attend weekday services.

The bulk of this two-thirds majority is what I would call "churched Larrys," since 91 percent of those attending the weekend service state that their highest value is a "deep relationship with God." Even if one expands the total of remaining unchurched Harrys to 15 percent of the weekend attendance (a total of 1,672 individuals), we still would have a huge group (5,646) of churched Larrys.[27]

Churched Larrys have understood and responded to the gospel. But these Larrys are only superficially "churched." One former Willow Creek counselor was frustrated that week after week, he saw twenty to thirty of these immature Larrys and merely gave them temporary bandaids for deep spiritual wounds. Looking back on his work, he commented, "Willow Creek is a mile wide and one-half inch deep." This group of churched Larrys affirm that their deepest commitment is to God, and yet they do not attend the weekday services, substantially give of their finances, volunteer their time in serving at the church, or have strong relationships at the church.

The director of finances told me that only 1,500 to 2,000 people tithe to the church. The total number of volunteers in the church is 4,461. Although this is a significant number, we need to note again that it is approximately only one-third of the weekend attenders.[28]

Among all the churched Larrys that I interviewed, I did not find any who had any relationships with other church attenders. One churched Larry I interviewed, "Steve," had attended the church for more than nine years and had no involvement other than weekend services. Steve's longest conversation, and best personal contact with a fellow church attender during this nine-year period, was the one hour-long interview that I had with him.

The problem of churched Larrys who attend on the weekend but do little else is even larger if what many of the staff say is true. During my interviews, church leaders asserted that there are approximately twenty thousand church attenders, many of whom do not attend every week, but like Steve, come on average one to three times during a month. If this figure is accurate, then the total number of churched Larrys is much higher than calculated—perhaps as many as ten thousand to twelve thousand individuals. Instead of 20 percent of the church attenders tithing, it would be less than 10 percent. Instead of one of three church attenders volunteering, it would be one of five. The point is this: Even in the most optimistic scenario, there are thousands of churched Larrys who attend only during the weekend services.

"Ben," a staff member, explains how the weekend service itself hampers these churched Larrys from growing in the Christian life:

> The philosophy of the church in some ways hinders that. . . . It's the danger side of reaching out to unchurched Harry and holding him and encompassing him and meeting some of his needs and making him feel comfortable and all that, and even letting him continue to be anonymous.

Ben explains that this approach of "let's help them out and lure them into having an interest in Christ" often creates a situation where churched Larrys are given only milk and remain spiritual babies. Ben is arguing that churched Larrys are stuck in spiritual inertia partially because by attending only the weekend service they are missing many of the key elements for spiritual growth.

The Biblical Balance

I have attempted to outline Willow Creek's teaching against the broader canvas of Christian history, showing Willow Creek's lack of emphasis on God's holiness in contrast to the historic Protestant emphasis on God's holiness and the moral law. Yet it is not enough to merely restate the understanding of Wesley, Calvin, or Luther. To be evangelical means a commitment to return to the Scripture to clarify the truth. The question of how much God's love or holiness should be emphasized is a theological question. What is the biblical balance between God's transcendent holiness and his immanent love?

A brief review of biblical material reveals that the twin messages of God's holiness and his love are intertwined throughout the Scripture. Jesus describes John the Baptist as God's foretold "voice in the wilderness" who laid the foundation for his ministry: "This is the one about whom it is written: 'I will send my messenger ahead of you, who will prepare your way before you'" (Luke 7:27).

John the Baptist had a message of blunt words of confrontation to Israel. He presented God's holy law and called on them to repent and be baptized. God's preparation for Jesus' good news message of love and forgiveness was one bellowed, "You brood of vipers! Who warned you to flee from the coming wrath? Produce fruit in keeping with your deeds" (Luke 3:7–8). The message of God's holiness preceded his offer of forgiveness.

When the apostle Peter preached the first sermon at Pentecost, he clearly put the responsibility of Jesus' death on those who were listening: "You, with the help of wicked men, put him to death by nailing him to the cross" (Acts 2:23). The result of this blunt confrontation was a deep repentance: "When the people heard this, they were cut to the heart and said to Peter and the other apostles, 'Brothers, what shall we do?'" (v. 37).

The apostle Paul also emphasizes the twin themes of God's love and holiness. Paul uses the word *holy* in reference to both God's holiness and the need for God's people to be holy. Paul clearly states that the holiness of God's law brings people to a consciousness of their sin: "No one will be declared righteous in his sight by observing the law; rather, through the law we become conscious of sin" (Rom. 3:20). Paul also regularly teaches about God's love and mercy. To emphasize either at the expense of the other is to distort the biblical understanding of who God is.[29]

In the New Testament, whenever the Lord's transcendent holiness was revealed, people fell down in response. When the Father spoke to Peter, James, and John at Jesus' transfiguration, the disciples "fell facedown to the ground, terrified" (Matt. 17:6). When the resurrected Jesus confronted Saul on the road to Damascus, Saul "fell to the ground" (Acts 9:4). When John saw the Lord, he "fell at his feet as though dead" (Rev. 1:17). To truly see the glorified Jesus one must fall at his feet. Philippians 2:10–11 records that one day "at the name of Jesus every knee should bow, in heaven and on earth and under the earth, and every tongue confess that Jesus Christ is Lord."

Whenever individuals in the Bible glimpsed a vision of God they became aware of their own sin. As Hebrews 12:21 records, "The sight was so terrifying that Moses said, 'I am trembling with fear.'" As individuals glimpsed God's glory they knelt with deep inward pain and confessed their failings and frailties. Isaiah records after his vision of God, "'Woe to me!' I cried. 'I am ruined! For I am a man of unclean lips . . . and my eyes have seen the King, the LORD Almighty'" (Isa. 6:5). A deep humility is our response to seeing the holiness of God.

Biblical humility results in forgiveness and confidence. Yet there is no shortcut. We must see him clearly and feel the pain of our sin. For in seeing Jesus clearly, we are able to see ourselves. Jesus' face provides a true and certain mirror for self-understanding. As we see Jesus, we become aware of both our brokenness and our great value as his children, and our heads are lifted in joy and thankfulness: "How great is the love the Father has lavished on us, that we should be called children of God!" (1 John 3:1).

Willow Creek is not alone in the problem I have depicted. The American evangelical church generally has lost a vision of the Lord's holiness. In our pragmatic age and culture, we are tempted to see God only as a means to the Christian life. We will be called to judgment if we compromise the Lord's holiness. God explains that Moses was not permitted to enter the Promised Land "because you did not uphold my holiness among the Israelites" (Deut. 32:51). Are we upholding God's holiness among the Americans? If we are going to gain a clearer grasp of the nature and character of God and of the way of life that he has for us to live, we need to develop a Christian mind.

20

The Loss of Truth

All of the weaknesses in Willow Creek's strategy have one root cause: Hybels and his team have not thoroughly evaluated the American culture from a Christian perspective. In short, Creekers generally do not think with a consistent Christian worldview.

We have seen illustrations of this deficiency in the preceding four chapters. I discussed Augustine's Neoplatonism, the tension between God's transcendent holiness and his immanent love, the improper use of social-scientific theory, the moral law as a precursor to the gospel, and liberation theology. These are difficult topics for those unfamiliar with them. But to formulate a biblical response to Willow Creek's interaction with American culture, it is necessary to deal with these concepts.

And this is the very problem. I cannot imagine having an in-depth conversation with a Willow Creek staff member about Augustine's Neoplatonism. This is a great tragedy. The effect of the modern psychological worldview on Willow Creek cannot be understood without this sort of historical window from which to view the present. Unless this kind of critical reflection is brought to bear, popular American categories and mores will continue to shape Willow Creek's thought and practice.

A serious critique of American culture from a Christian perspective is generally absent at Willow Creek. The fundamental reason for this failure is that Creekers do not think critically with the categories and content of Christian theology. For example, not only do Creekers not read Augustine's works, but the majority of the staff would not even know who he was and what he taught. That the most influential Christian thinker since the apostle Paul is ignored at Willow Creek is an illustration of this serious problem. I found many volumes of business management and pop-psychology on staff members' bookcases, but I never found a volume of classical theology. The vast reservoir of two thousand years of Christian wisdom is virtually untapped at Willow Creek.

The mind that results from this approach quickly uses the latest management or psychological tool but resists serious or sustained study. As one staff member explained why he enjoyed working at Willow Creek, "My fellow staff members don't think like 'ministers,' they approach Christian work as marketplace people."

During the first few days of my study, I was confronted by a startling example of the loss of the importance of Christian truth. One of the first staff members I spoke with proudly told me how more than five hundred individuals met at the church each week in various self-help groups (e.g., Alchoholics Anonymous, Emotions Anonymous, Sexual Anonymous). Upon investigation, I discovered that these programs were not actually the church's. Although many church attenders were participating in the programs, the actual meetings were being run according to outside organizations' policies. One of the requirements of these organizations was that individuals could not evangelize or otherwise teach other participants about God. One official code of instruction explains:

> The Steps suggest a belief in a Power greater than ourselves, "God as we understand Him." The Program does not attempt to tell us what our Higher Power must be.
>
> It can be whatever we choose, for example, human love, a force for good, the group itself, nature, the universe, or the traditional God (Deity).

The code instructs, "We never discuss religion."[1]

Even church members could not talk about Christian truth in these meetings at Willow Creek. Although the programs give lip service to a "Higher Power," they function as practical atheism, teaching the categories of the contemporary psychological worldview. Yet the lack of theological content did not stop the church from advertising these programs each week during the weekend and weekday services. That Willow Creek would sponsor and advertise these programs illustrates the church's lack of priority for educating its members in Christian truth.

The Lack of Theological Education

There is no theological education requirement for Willow Creek staff members. I regularly found former real estate brokers, house painters, and salesmen who were directly hired into staff positions. Their only training (and main prerequisite) had been participation in the Willow Creek program for some time. No theological training was necessary, even if a staff member's position involved teaching—even for central teachers at the church.[2]

During the year of my study, none of the three teaching pastors had graduated from seminary. They conceded in interviews that the weekend messages drew heavily on psychological principles and categories. Their lack of education, however, resulted in an inadequate critical analysis of the American psychological worldview. They tended to describe psychological categories as biblical principles. Lee Strobel explained that "there are times when as long as there's a biblical basis for it, that some psychological terms and concepts are used." Strobel gave "boundaries" as an example: "So, in other words, the idea of boundaries. You can find that in Scripture." Likewise, Don Cousins also acknowledged that psychological categories are used, but sought to argue that this was just "the principles of Scripture which could be illustrated in a number of ways."[3]

Willow Creek teachers have accepted and internalized these psychological categories as basic elements of their worldview. Yet one searches the Bible in vain for "boundaries" or "codependence." Without serious biblical training, the teachers at Willow Creek did not have the resources to evaluate critically the American psychological worldview.

The pastors' lack of theological education is especially dangerous when we realize that the vast majority of Willow Creek talks are topical in nature, rather than exegetical messages rooted in a detailed analysis of particular Scripture passages. When an evangelical preacher is speaking topically, he is summarizing what he believes the whole of the Bible is saying on a particular topic. Yet without a substantial theological education and training, it is unrealistic to expect a teacher to summarize a balanced understanding of the whole of biblical teaching. It is asking a pastor to give an oral systematic theology even though he has never seriously studied systematic theology.

This lack of emphasis on theology was particularly visible in a two-week series on Roman Catholicism. Hybels believed that there was a need to build a bridge of charity between Willow Creek and a local Catholic church. With this admirable goal in mind, he invited the local priest over to have a discussion one week on "What Protestants Can Learn from Catholics" and followed this the next week by speaking on "What Catholics Can Learn from Protestants."

The first week, Hybels introduced the Catholic priest and commented that they "agreed on the need for a personal relationship with Jesus Christ." Yet what they actually believed was shown to be clearly different later in the discussion. Hybels asked the priest to explain how he was born again, and the priest commented, "I think we need to be born and reborn in Christianity. We're born and raised, but I think we need to be born and reborn again and again. Not just once, but again and again." The priest was not teaching the evangelical gospel of the need for all people to be "born again" but transformed this idea into an ongoing spiritual renewal. When the priest prayed at the end of the meeting, he called God, "Mother of us all" and said, "Only one in twenty babies born as children or as adults will ever be baptized. The other nineteen will never come to know Christ." The priest identified baptism with coming to know Christ and implied a baptismal regeneration.

These are profound differences. Central to evangelical faith is a commitment to the gospel, which provides an opportunity for individuals to be born again and justified through faith. Yet Hybels, during this week and the following week's message, never critiqued the priest's comments. I was told by staff members that Hybels received more criticism for this series than any before in the history of the church. There is a good reason for this. Many of Willow Creek's members are former Roman Catholics who realized that the priest had affirmed a different understanding of how to receive salvation. Yet Hybels never sought to challenge the priest's teaching. In Hybels's charity, the truth was obscured.

The Loss of Biblical Truth

Willow Creek affirms a conservative evangelical theology. Yet these beliefs somehow do not get communicated consistently on the weekend. Why?

Hybels's gift of evangelism dominates the church's weekend meetings. Hybels wants to persuade the unchurched to become believers and uses his considerable talents accordingly, teaching a simple theology on the weekend. In a purely evangelistic setting, this strategy of simplifying Christian theology is appropriate. Most nonbelievers need to understand the pure milk of the gospel rather than meaty messages of Christian truth. Yet the majority of Willow Creek weekend attenders are churched Larrys who have already made a commitment to Christ. They do not attend the weekday worship services, so the only theological teaching they receive is the weekend's user-friendly Christianity 101 and the basic salvation message. These churched Larrys are not receiving enough biblical feeding on the weekend to grow to spiritual maturity.

The theme during the year I studied was "Becoming a Fully Informed Follower of Christ." Hybels argued at the beginning of this year that there was a block of knowledge that Christians needed to know if they were going to be fully devoted followers of Christ. True enough. But the subjects and content of this year's weekend messages could hardly be described as the foundation for a fully devoted follower of Christ. Rather, the primary goal of these weekend services was evangelistic. There were series on apologetics, satanism, marriage, decision making, modern philosophies, anger, and how Christianity makes common sense.

This is not to suggest that Hybels does not challenge the weekend crowd. On one occasion Hybels insisted, "Ninety-five percent devotion to Christ is 5 percent short. It makes a mockery of the cross. It makes a mockery of the death of Christ on our behalf." Hybels really does want believers to be fully devoted to Christ.

During another series Hybels bluntly confronted the congregation:

> Far too many people call themselves Christians. It's patently obvious they only have a skin-deep faith. They're cosmetic Christians. There's a thin veneer of spirituality covering over an inside that is basically unconverted and still self-seeking. . . .
>
> It's almost as though large segments of the Christian community have decided to lighten up and loosen up with respect to the definition of who a Christian is and how a Christian ought to live his life.

This two-week series on Cosmetic Christianity was a powerful challenge for nonbelievers to actually receive the gospel and believers to begin obeying God. The problem with this kind of challenge is that this exhortation does not make up for the lack of weekly biblical feeding for churched Larrys.[4]

Hybels and his colleagues affirm an evangelical theology. It would not be accurate or fair to depict them as theologically liberal. Liberal Christianity denies central Christian truth claims. However, there is a lack of emphasis on Christian truth at Willow Creek. Willow Creek does not teach substantial biblical truth consistently on the weekend.

As discussed in chapter 19, Willow Creek's gospel emphasizes the loving immanence of God and deemphasizes his transcendent holiness. One of the few theologically trained staff members commented on the difficulty of emphasizing God's holiness and man's sinfulness in the seeker services:

> We need to be aware of our sin in such a way that we're really broken over it—I mean really broken over it. More than emotional and more than circumstan-

> tially. I mean really broken. *But see, how do you get that into the weekend philosophy?* [emphasis added].[5]

Darrel Schultz, the former senior pastor of a Willow Creek style church, comments about the theological dilution that results from this strategy:

> For the preacher who wants to be seeker-sensitive, the list of potential topics goes up and list of usable Bible passages goes down. It is more than likely that many of the areas a church needs to hear about (for example . . . sin, repentance, and God's judgment) will fall victim to the preacher's inner censorship board which evaluates all seeker-service events on the criterion of sensitivity to non-churched Harry.

Schultz argues that when his church attempted to follow the Willow Creek model, the natural result was to move many of the elements necessary for spiritual growth for believers to the weekday service:

> These elements that had done so much to build the body of believers in other churches were moved to the Wednesday night worship service which attracted a whopping third of the normal morning attendance.[6]

Although a third of the Willow Creek congregation also receives more in-depth teaching during the week, the majority of Willow Creek weekend attenders do not.

There is also a possibility that the weekend teaching inadequately prepares nonbelievers to follow Jesus. After one summer study break, Hybels returned with this thought:

> I was still basking in the blessing of having just witnessed the baptism of nearly four hundred adults from this church on the last Sunday in June. But the basking came to an abrupt end when I asked myself the sobering question: "I wonder how many of those four hundred who were just baptized will still be faithfully following God, and growing in him, and bearing fruit for him upon my return in eight short weeks?"

Hybels had to acknowledge to himself that many Willow Creek conversions did not last:

> The honest answers were terribly painful for me to admit. Over the course of thirteen years in this church, thousands of people have proven to be rocky-soiled people, thorny-soiled people whose faith has faded.

One staff member even argued that many individuals who have been baptized and have been around the church for years are not even believers:

> I don't think Bill [Hybels] really understands that there are as many unsaved people—who think they're saved—around here as there are. . . .
>
> I have worked with a number of those people who have been baptized here . . . and I could develop the safety and freedom with them to say, "Now, really, for eternity's sake, where is your heart, really with God? Has it changed or is it still pretty much the same old heart that there really isn't any change? . . ."
>
> Consistently I have people sit in that chair and receive Christ after they've attended Willow Creek for five, eight, ten years.

Hybels has admitted this need to make the gospel clearer. After his 1988 study break, Hybels confessed to his staff, "We've been too helpful to people." One staff member said this tendency at Willow Creek produced "numbers but not disciples." Another staff member admitted that many church attenders have never made "a very humble cry for God's mercy, founded on the faith that Christ died for our sins and then asking or pleading and trusting for him to come in and change my heart such that I can be presented before him as a regenerate person." What is the source of this neglect of Christian truth and the mind? The answer is found in Willow Creek's pragmatism and dualistic theology.[7]

Willow Creek's Pragmatism

Willow Creek does not have the fundamentalist's rejection of the broader intellectual world. On the contrary, Hybels is the ultimate pragmatist who is willing to use any aspect of academia—if it helps further his agenda. During my analysis of the weekend messages, I discovered Hybels repeatedly returning to three academic disciplines: psychology, apologetics, and business management.

Hybels's use of psychology could be summarized by the phrase, "It works." Hybels is willing to use psychological theory that helps to show how Christianity works. He is attempting to convince Harry that Christianity is the best means to satisfy his felt needs and provide fulfillment. He even refers to psychologists to argue that Jesus lived a wholesome life.

Hybels's use of apologetics could be summarized by the phrase, "It's true." Hybels used quotes from philosophers, historians, and archaeologists to argue that Christianity fits with the facts and is true. Hybels quotes these experts to underline how Christianity has intellectual credibility.

Hybels's use of business management could be summarized by the phrase, "It's useful." Hybels tries to show Harry that Christianity will not only make him happy, but will be useful for his work. Harry heard references to management gurus and business professionals as a part of an argument for the usefulness of Christian principles in the workplace.

These disciplines that help show that Christianity works, is true, and is useful are regularly used. Yet beneath Hybels's pragmatic use of academic experts in each of these categories is an underlying ambivalence toward and even disdain for education itself. One staff member described to me how he was converted at Willow Creek and then decided to go to seminary: "I applied to seminary, because I figured that was the route to go . . . until I realized that ain't the route to go." Willow Creek staff discouraged him not to waste his time on seminary.

Over the course of my research, I observed that staff would often assert that they did not want to be "academic." In their view, "academic" means dry, abstract, archaic, and useless. Pragmatic common sense in contrast is real, down-to-earth, relevant, and practical. This preference for action moves Hybels and the other Willow Creek staff away from academia.[8]

The root of this pragmatic approach to knowledge and the mind, like most things at Willow Creek, is found in Hybels. Don Cousins explains:

> The whole seminary curriculum—three years of studying God's Word, Hebrew, Greek—see, that holds no appeal for a Bill Hybels. . . . Why? Because we're not book people in the sense that we're activists. We're people people. We're leaders. We want to make things happen.

The result of this neglect of education is that few staff members have substantial Christian knowledge.

I believe that there is a legitimate frustration built into Willow Creek's criticism of academia. In fact, a deep skepticism exists in the general evangelical community about the effect of graduate theological education. Seminaries have acquired the reputation that eager, vibrant young Christians often enter their front doors, only to exit prideful and ineffectual eggheads out the back door. The evangelical jest about preachers graduating from a cemetery has a biting truth.[9]

Willow Creek's pragmatic impulse is a reaction to this sort of evangelical academic egghead. This pragmatism is the source of flexible innovativeness that is a great strength of Willow Creek. During my study I discovered a fundamental weakness in the Willow Creek strategy. Individuals were supposed to move from step 3—attending New Community—to step 4—joining a small group. In contrast, I discovered that the majority of individuals skipped joining a small group to begin step 5—attending the Network seminar. At Network they were trained to understand their spiritual gifts in order to serve in the church. Yet approximately 50 percent of those attending Network had never had an extended conversation with a Willow Creek staff member or volunteer. Unknowingly, Network was being used as the major point of assimilation for the church. While only a few hundred people joined small groups during a year, more than 2,000 individuals attended Network every year.

A second problem was related to this. While Hybels taught about the importance of relationships, only a tiny 10 percent of the lay individuals I interviewed had regular accountable relationships.

The leaders were just becoming aware of these problems while I was doing my study. They realized that they needed to provide small groups where attenders could develop relationships with other believers. They also were just becoming aware that their strategy was functioning as a funnel that was wide at the top but extremely narrow at the bottom where so few were joining small groups. Thousands of individuals were attending the weekend services but were eventually spilling out and leaving the church because they were not finding a place to connect with others.

In response, the leadership initiated a new strategy of community small groups. I have been told that, as a result, Willow Creek now has more than 1,100 small groups with 9,000 participants. The flexibility and innovation that are evident with this new strategy are found in their pragmatism. This is the bright side of pragmatism.

The dark side of pragmatism is seen in Willow Creek's attitude toward education. Hybels teaches a pragmatism that devalues education per se. "I'm a pragmatist," Hybels comments, "and I measure things by whether or not they work." Hybels's pragmatic bias against academia has intellectually impoverished Willow Creek. Topics, books, and scholars that fit within the parameter of what is useful for Willow Creek's purpose gain wide circulation. Those outside this parameter are neglected.[10]

This is ironic. Although pragmatically arguing that Christianity is true, Willow Creek has devalued the place of the mind in the Christian life. When academic disciplines are approached only as an intellectual smorgasbord of useful tools, the value of the mind is tied to its pragmatic usefulness. No great scholar will come from Willow Creek. A subject is studied only if there is the possibility of immediate results.

This position has developed partially from Hybels's concept of the church as a business and his pragmatic view of knowledge. Hybels's mentors in running the church have been management gurus interested in the bottom line. One management expert, Tom Peters, reflects the bias that pragmatic business people often have toward academia: "We're often hard on the academics."[11]

Learning that does not immediately show results in the bottom line is not considered worthwhile at Willow Creek. As one staff member told me, "Education for education to me is not helpful." He explained that Creekers are not interested in education: "They need to know *how*. . . . they need to know *what* they need to do" (emphasis added).

One of the few theologically educated staff members was aware of this negative view of education: "Willow Creek is not sociologically fundamentalist, but there tends to be an anti-intellectual skew. . . . It's not rooted in a fear of liberalism, it's rooted in pragmatism." He described this as a "ruthless pragmatism which says, If I can't use this information today, it's of no value to me."

Another theologically educated staff member complained to me that the church does not sufficiently value learning and the mind. He then curiously argued that the church needs "to have some credentialed people who can produce." He believed that the only way that academic training could gain credibility within this system was to appeal to the pragmatic ideal of results—"people who can produce."

Willow Creek evaluates people's gifts by their results. Individuals prove themselves by the standard of productivity. Another of the few staff members who have received theological training described how when he joined the church staff Creekers didn't trust him—because he was theologically educated. He had to prove that he could still produce a Willow Creek style ministry even though he was educated. In this narrow system of immediate usefulness, the cultivation of the mind has little value.

Various movements in church history reflect similar strengths and weaknesses from a focus on pragmatism. The nineteenth-century revivalist Charles Finney "called for a Copernican revolution to make religious life audience centered." While Presbyterians emphasized theological training and precision, Finney argued for the "language of common life."[12]

The basic strength of this pragmatic approach is the ability to communicate to a popular audience. The weakness is that this style of Christianity does not have much staying power. Without intellectual roots, within a generation or two, much of this Christianity was swept away by the flood of late nineteenth-century liberalism and its intellectual challenges. Pragmatic Christianity, which focuses on what works in the immediate context, in the end does not work.

Christian education for a robust mind does not have the immediate "so what" factor that pragmatism demands. There is no quick turnaround for investing in individuals' understanding. The energy it would take to develop individuals' understanding is directed to programs with practical goals that can be achieved more easily. Willow Creek—like most of evangelicalism—is shortsighted. Like a business that delays long-term investment in order to show dividends in quarterly statements, Willow Creek wants immediate success. Like fast-growing ivy, Willow Creek (and evangelicalism) is able to spread rapidly over the landscape. Yet like ivy, it can easily be ripped up because of its shallow roots. There are no deep roots or deep minds to stabilize the movement (or individual) when the storms come. The pragmatic impulse ultimately drains the vitality of any movement.

Willow Creek's Dualistic Theology

A primary source of this lack of respect for learning and the mind in general comes from Hybels's basic theology. Deeply embedded in Hybels's theology is the idea that the true purpose of the Christian life is evangelism. Although Willow Creek's statement of faith affirms exhortation, exaltation, and extension as aspects of the purpose of the church, the central and driving function of the church is evangelism. Willow Creek theologian Bilezikian writes, "The appointed task of the Church is to change men and therefore affect society through spiritual means—not by force but by persuasion, not by coercion but by conversion."[13]

Hybels, echoing Bilezikian, teaches the believers at New Community:

> There's something far more important than catching fish and bringing them to market. And that is capturing the attention of sinful men and women and bringing them to the cross of Christ.
>
> There is no higher calling in life. There is no greater challenge; there is no more significant task that you can be committed to.

This is a consistent message at Willow Creek: The most important activity in life is evangelism.

This commitment to evangelism is powered by the conviction that the physical world is one day going to be destroyed. Immediately after asserting that evangelism is the priority of the Christian's life, Hybels elaborated:

> I read a verse in 2 Peter 3:10 that just wiped me out. It simply says, "There's coming a time when every single thing on this planet will melt with a fervent heat. It will all be consumed." . . .
>
> I was totally preoccupied with fishing, not being a fisher of men. And it dawned on me. Every single thing I'm working for is gonna go up in smoke!

The result of Hybels's revelation was a new vision of the world. He now had a new set of labels to apply to everything he saw.

> So what am I doing being preoccupied with all this stuff that's gonna get all burned up? How come I'm not preoccupied with people?
>
> I started thinking, You know, I ought to go around and put a little red tag on every thing that is so important to me in this life. And the red tag ought to have a big word on it that just says *temporal, temporal, temporal, temporal.*
>
> And then I ought to go around and mentally put a green tag on people which says *eternal, eternal, eternal.*

The lesson from this insight is that Bill and his Creekers should be committed to do the eternal things and abstain from the temporal. This dualism between the "temporal" and "eternal" motivates and guides Hybels. Hybels clarifies this idea:

> Every other earthly activity pales in comparison with the significance of helping an individual man, woman, boy, or girl come into a saving, liberating relationship with the God of the universe through Jesus Christ.

This is a sort of platonic dualism where a horizontal line is drawn across one's worldview. Those things labeled "eternal" are placed in the upper spiritual level, the remainder in the "temporal" lower level. Eternal activities become valuable and temporal activities are considered wasteful. This theology skews how one views and lives life. There are two problems with this theology: It does not work, and it is not true to the Scripture.

Like all pragmatic philosophies, this dualistic theology fails the test of implementation. In practice, if the purpose of the church is only evangelism and the salvation of souls, there is no logical justification for any vocation or activity that is not directly or indirectly connected to these evangelistic activities. All nondirective activity is wasted energy.

Emotional burnout is a likely possibility—even probability—in this theological system. Hybels had an emotional burnout in the winter of 1989–90. He concluded a few months later:

> I was filling my life chock full of eternal opportunities. What's wrong with that? Besides the emotional drain, I realized two other hidden costs of such a ministry-centered lifestyle. First, if you are concerned only with spiritual activities, you tend to lose sight of the hopelessness of people apart from Christ. You're never in the world. Second, you lose your wonder of the church, of salvation, and of being part of the work of God. You can overload on eternal tasks to the point that you no longer appreciate their glories.[14]

Hybels became freshly committed to temporal activities because he believed that this would enable him to perform his eternal activities more effectively. Temporal activities in dualistic thinking are viewed only as a pragmatic mechanism to greater achievement of the eternal. Recreation can only be justified as a means of recuperation so more evangelism can be accomplished.

We also see the painful result of this eternal-vision theology in two articles by Lynne Hybels. In one she described observing some playful geese on a pond. She struggled with trying to justify this non-purposive behavior:

> We perceive watching as an unnecessary leisure-time activity, or worse, as something entirely frivolous. As such, it violates our work ethic. Why waste time observing when we can be doing?[15]

In Willow Creek's theology, there is no justification for slowing down to enjoy a peaceful moment. This moment can be rationalized in Willow Creek's theology only if the pleasant moment gives one more energy for the great spiritual war.

The constant life-and-death struggle of this dualistic theology wore Lynne down. She confessed, "The natural tendency that allowed me to embrace the dream so wholeheartedly nearly proved to be my undoing." She began to think about the possibility of getting a puppy as a means of recreation. Yet she questioned whether she should spend the seemingly wasteful time and energy that go into having a puppy: "Yes, I know Christianity is a life-and-death issue, but I'm tired of being serious all the time, tired of everything mattering so much." Within the theological system of her husband, there was no logical justification for the supposed frivolity of watching geese or playing with a puppy.[16]

This experience of burnout is not unusual at Willow Creek. Highly committed volunteers and staff regularly burn out after years of faithful effort. One nearby chiropractor reportedly commented to a staff member, "I see dozens of your staff members; what are you doing to people over there?!" A pastor from the area described to me how many committed Creekers regularly end up joining his more traditional, Bible-teaching church after years of running on the Willow Creek treadmill. A constant stream of individuals is attracted through Willow Creek's front door to the excitement of their program. But many of these same participants eventually feel the overwhelming pressure of its dualistic theology and slip out the back door.

Second, Willow Creek's dualistic theology is an inadequate understanding of the Christian's purpose. Human beings were made to know and love God as his children and to reflect his character and concerns to the world as his representatives. This biblical purpose includes both loving God as his beloved children and loving other human beings as precious and made in his image. One undeniably important way of displaying this love to nonbelievers is communicating the gospel's life-saving message. But evangelism is only a part of the biblical purpose, not its entirety. The Great Commission is not the great commandment.

We are also called to reflect God's character and concerns to the world as his people. This includes learning how to live the truth and growing in holiness and understanding, using our gifts in serving his people, and faithfully being salt and light in our various vocations and callings. We are called to reflect God's character and concerns in every situation in which God places us.

We are also called to love God with our minds. Willow Creek's dualistic theology ultimately skews this biblical understanding of life. The logical result of dualistic theology is to devalue the doctrines of creation and redemption. If the only "eternal" or valuable activity is evangelism, the biblical mandate to care for God's creation (Gen. 1:29–31) is inadequately appreciated. Willow Creek's narrow understanding of the Christian's purpose also distorts the biblical understanding of redemption. God's redemption is to involve the restoration of the entirety of his creation. If you dismiss all of creation as ultimately burnable and disposable, you misunderstand and discard many of the vocations that God wants us to be involved in.

This theological perspective devalues the very idea of education in general and theology in particular. Why spend time studying a topic for years—a lower-level, temporal activity—if the only valuable activity is evangelism? In a curious way, this is a sort of theological suicide. If one allows dualistic theology to shape one's purpose, one loses the value for temporal activities—including theology. The concept of vocation the Reformers carved out—that a shoemaker can cobble, or an academic can study, to the glory of God—has been lost in this dualism.

One result of Willow Creek's dualism is that the vast majority of Willow Creek staff have never been theologically trained. Only a handful of over two hundred staff members had the basic M.Div. degree. They have been educated in the Willow Creek way of doing things, and they believe that is all they need. As one former staff member explained, Willow Creek leaders "want staff members to be blank slates." Leaders expect to train staff in what to do and how to do it, and thus staff need no formal education. Very few staff appreciate the importance of theology, serious study, or the mind.

As a result, these staff members do not understand the wisdom of church history and the beauty of the Word. In these pages, I have discussed Neoplatonic influences on Augustine's ethics and Luther, Calvin, and Wesley's use of the moral law in the gospel. The great majority of Willow Creek staffers would not be interested in these topics. They would consider them as too intellectual and not relevant. Yet these topics are crucial in helping us understand the very heart of Willow Creek.

This devaluation of Christian thinking has helped to create a church where the majority of church attenders are passive observers. Weekend listeners are rarely confronted with God's moral law or challenged strongly to grow in their understanding. Only rarely did Willow Creek insiders see the weaknesses of Willow Creek's attitude toward education and theology. One of the few theologically trained staff complained to me:

> There's not enough biblical fund of knowledge for people to learn to feed themselves. And there's not enough doctrine taught so they have a structure from which to evaluate the truth. And that to me is one of the greatest weaknesses in the church.

This staff member argued that many Willow Creek Christians emphasize unduly, "This is how I relate to God, this is what God does for me," and the focus is always on their "experience." He asserted that Creekers needed to begin living based on their understanding of Christian truth.

This lack of emphasis on spiritual meat creates an environment where churched Larrys feel very comfortable with a minimal commitment. A staff member explained that many churched Larrys do not hear much of biblical substance: "They just know they come to a nice weekend service that sounds good and helps them. And therefore they must be Christians." This staff member believes that one of the best things that Hybels could do is "teach on evidences of salvation, teach straight through 1 John . . . certain evidences that can only be seen over time and experienced over time." He continued:

> Why did Paul at the end of 2 Corinthians say, "Test yourselves to see if you are of the faith"? Here he wrote two whole letters to a church full of Christians. You know? He's addressing Christians in the letters to the Corinthians, but he says, "Test yourselves to see if you are of the faith."

He answered his own question: "I think he's [Paul] saying it is possible for people not to be saved and not know it—think in fact that they are, not know that they need to test that."

Bill Hybels and his colleagues are sincerely reaching out in love to unchurched Harry and Mary. I am describing problems and tensions that are the unintended consequences of the strategy that Willow Creek has chosen and implemented.

Creekers argue that their contribution is the use of new methods to communicate the age-old gospel. They contrast themselves with theological liberals who have changed the message of Christianity. There is truth in this perspective. Creekers really do want to maintain the message and be creative with Christianity's methods. What they don't realize is that fundamentally altering the methods of communication potentially alters the message of what is communicated.

It is difficult to raise these sorts of painful questions to earnest believers who are seeking to honor the Lord. I do not take pleasure in noting their weaknesses or mistakes. Scrutinizing my life and ministry (or yours) in this level of detail would also reveal mistakes, failures, and tensions. When we read or write about others' weaknesses we need to remain humbly aware of our own frailties and shortcomings. Yet our responsibility lies in telling the truth. Hiding it helps no one.

Imagine Hybels and his team attempting to save someone being swept down a swiftly moving river. Hybels reaches out to try to catch the unfortunate soul before he or she is swept away. Hybels is using the tools of our culture to reach out to the unchurched Harrys being swept away to their judgment. Yet in attempting to reach out to others in the fast-flowing river of our culture, Hybels and his followers also sometimes fall in.

Creekers' intentions are correct and their effort should be applauded. Yet we should help so that Hybels and the other would-be-rescuers do not fall in. A biblical framework is needed to protect them and their ministries from the culture's treacherous waters.

Central to the Protestant Reformation was the importance of biblical teaching. When the Reformation swept over Roman Catholic Northern Europe, many European Catholic cathedrals became Protestant churches. In many of these long, narrow Protestant churches you find an odd arrangement where the pulpit and the church's Bible have been moved to the center of the church. This symbolic positioning reveals the commitment of the Reformation pastors to teach the people the truth and the closeness of the Scriptures to the people. The evangelical church needs a new reformation that is grounded in the powerful truth of God's Word.

It is very easy to dismiss lessons from the past. As the old maxim warns, "Those who do not learn from history are doomed to repeat it." We would do well to remember that this problem is not new, nor its solution. The apostle Paul, after writing a densely intellectual epistle, warns the Romans, "Do not conform any longer to the pattern of this world, but be transformed by the renewing of your mind" (Rom. 12:2). Without the renewal of our minds in consistent, sometimes difficult Christian thought, we will unknowingly continue to be shaped profoundly by popular American culture.

Afterword

I have attempted to accurately describe and analyze Willow Creek's new way of doing church. The response to this two-pronged strategy has been curious. Those individuals skeptical or critical of the Willow Creek strategy tended to be impatient with the descriptive first two-thirds of this book. They were eager to hear the analysis and critique. In contrast, most of the advocates of Willow Creek liked the description and felt I was fair and accurate.

The response to the analysis portion of the book was reversed. Skeptics appreciated my attempt to evaluate the strengths and weaknesses of Willow Creek's strategy, but seeker church advocates often sharply disagreed with my conclusions.

In other words, I didn't make either side happy. I believe the fact that neither side feels completely comfortable with this work is a good sign. The broader church has a responsibility to understand and evaluate this new way of doing church. If we are going to honor the Lord we must be honest.

The appropriate response to this analysis for critics of the seeker service is not to point the finger of judgment at Willow Creek. If I were to study any church (including your church or my church) as closely as I have studied Willow Creek, I would find many frailties and flaws. This is the nature of the fallen human condition. The appropriate response to this type of study is to acknowledge our fellow humanity and humbly thank God that he still uses any of us in his purposes. I hope that critics will respect advocates of the seeker church strategy, even if they disagree with them.

For advocates, being honest means a willingness to see and acknowledge disturbing consequences of the present Willow Creek strategy. I have serious concerns about the seeker service strategy. I believe that there are fatal flaws that—unless corrected—will eventually cripple the seeker church movement. I have tried to be as frank as possible to underline these issues.

At this point I need to explain one element of my method. Any close reader noticed that I regularly used Augustine of Hippo as a mirror to help analyze Willow Creek. The reason for this choice is that Augustine and Willow Creek have several similarities. As we understand Augustine we can see a reflection of Willow's potential and problems.

Augustine was a professor of rhetoric who had finely crafted tools of persuasion. Willow has similarly shaped a powerful method of persuasion and evangelism. Augustine plundered the thinkers of his day to shape useful tools for Christian thought and practice. Likewise Willow has sought to creatively use the tools and methods of modern culture to effectively communicate. A great virtue of both is their insights into how to communicate and persuade.

The vices of both Augustine and Willow are also similar. As we have seen, in Augustine's attempt to use Neoplatonic ideas he fundamentally skewed Christian ethics with an alien ideology. In other words, Augustine's very methods of thinking and communication had built-in weaknesses.

Toward the end of his life Augustine was beginning to recognize some of these problems. He dedicated one of his last works, *Retractions,* to correct these flaws. He was ruthlessly honest and attempted to strip away his faulty ideas by applying critical Christian thinking. He said that someone who asserted that he "never uttered a word which he would wish to recall" was "more applicable to a complete ass than to a genuinely wise man." Augustine combined a brutal honesty with a deep and disciplined Christian mind.[1]

As Augustine matured as a Christian leader he thought more scripturally. While his early works were filled with Neoplatonic and philosophical categories, his mature writing became more biblically rooted. He was committed to developing a deep biblical mind.

The modern seeker church movement is in need of Augustine's virtues of honesty and a mature Christian mind. If seeker churches are willing to see the built-in weakness of their chosen method of communication, I have a great hope for their potential for the kingdom. If they flinch from the painful task of examining themselves in the mirror of God's truth I fear for their future. This sort of maturing Christian mind will provide the corrective guidance that is so needed with these young seeker churches.

Because we human beings are fractured in our sin, we all tend to respond to our brokenness with pride. Sometimes this means pride in our accomplishments and other times it spurs a self-righteous criticism of others. Yet pride, biblically understood, is a defensive reaction to an awareness of our sinfulness. The biblical solution to both types of pride is humility.

Biblical humility is not some self-induced groveling or hang-dog attitude. Biblical humility is seeing ourselves as we are. Humility is a response to beholding the holiness of God. Revelation 1:17–18 depicts how John, in response to seeing the Lord Jesus in his glory, falls on his face in humility.

> When I saw him, I fell at his feet as though dead. Then he placed his right hand on me and said: "Do not be afraid. I am the First and the Last. I am the Living One; I was dead, and behold I am alive for ever and ever! And I hold the keys of death and Hades."

It can be a cutting and painful experience to see Jesus clearly. He is not merely the Good Shepherd, but the risen holy Lord. If we truly see Jesus and his holiness, we—like his good friend John—will fall on our faces. And it is only then that he will kneel down, touch us, raise us up, and tell us not to fear. God's response to our awareness and repentance of our sin is to touch, heal, and comfort us.

I long that I might daily see the face of the Lord and kneel in worship in his presence. I also long that the advocates and critics of the seeker church see the merciful and holy God and kneel in humility in his presence. He will then tell us, "Do not be afraid," and will tenderly lift us up. From this place of true self-understanding, we need to continue the discussion of how we can best honor him and be involved in his work.

Notes

Note: Bold type in the notes is used to identify material when there is more than one reference in a single paragraph.

Willow Creek's in-house materials, talks, and interviews are not referenced in the notes. If the reader would like detailed information on these, he or she may request a copy of the dissertation. Please see page 333 for details.

Introduction

1. Michael G. Maudlin and Edward Gilbreath, "Selling Out the House of God?" *Christianity Today,* July 18, 1994, 25.

2. Ibid., 21.

3. **for growth with balance:** Advertisement in *Christianity Today,* July 18, 1994, 15.

Ministering to the Unchurched: This is the Willow Creek Association's self-description.

4. See Bruce Bugbee, *Network* (Pasadena, Calif.: Charles E. Fuller Institute of Evangelism and Church Growth, 1989).

5. See Willow Creek's Director of Finance and Development Richard Towner's letter to financial supporters, October 14, 1993.

6. Ken Kantzer, "The Doctrine Wars," *Christianity Today,* Oct. 5, 1992, 32.

7. George Brushaber, "Marketing the Jesus Franchise," *Christianity Today,* June 22, 1992, 17.

8. This is not to suggest that I, as a researcher, had no biases. A large part of good research is clarifying one's biases and leaning against them in order to be accurate and fair. I describe one bias in some depth in chapter 14, "Learning from Willow Creek." For more background, refer to my dissertation. See page 333.

9. **the church made available to me:** In general, the church was fairly open to my research. But three quantitative studies were not made available to me. The church did an internal survey of weekend attenders in the 1980s and then commissioned George Barna to do a study of the weekend audience in 1991 and David Schmidt and associates to do a study of the New Community audience in 1993. I was told that the 1980s study had been misplaced and that the Barna and Schmidt studies were only in-house studies and outside researchers were not permitted access to them.

that year of messages: Although other information is used to help analyze this information, the content analysis itself is limited to this twelve-month period. When a description is made of Willow Creek's messages it is a summary of this data.

10. The one exception to this positive feedback to the description was Bill Hybels. Hybels reacted very negatively at several points. I will include his (or his staff's) response where appropriate in either the text or footnotes.

A specific limitation of this study needs to be noted. One of the unique problems of social research is that those being studied sometimes change. It is focused on a moving target. This is particularly true of Willow Creek, which tries to make significant changes fairly often. Any examination needs to be qualified as a specific study at a particular time. In this case, the study was conducted primarily from 1989–92.

11. Nancy Tatom Ammerman, "Fundamentalist World View: Ideology and Social Structure in an Independent Fundamental Church," Ph.D. diss., Yale University, 1983, 12.

12. A brief note about the format of the book is necessary. Although the research was precise and careful, the presentation in this book will be a bit different. For example, the description of the methods and strategy of the research that I covered in a few paragraphs above took almost one hundred pages in my dissertation. To make the smallest of points academically one often has to

use three or four documented references. My resulting dissertation was an eight-hundred-page tome with over nineteen hundred footnotes.

In this book all references to published materials (books, articles, etc.) have endnotes, but all of the church's in-house materials, tapes, etc., and my interviews do not. Many issues exhaustively described and analyzed in the dissertation are barely even mentioned here. This popularizing of the material was necessary because the topic is of interest to thousands of church leaders, church attenders, and interested observers. (Individuals who want to study this topic further can order the dissertation. Ordering information can be found on p. 333.)

Chapter 1: *A New Way of Doing Church*

1. Willow Creek is leading a new way of how to even think about church. Elmer Towns writes, "Formerly, a doctrinal statement represented the reason for a denomination's existence. Today, methodology is the glue that holds churches together. A statement of ministry defines them and their denominational existence." Elmer Towns, *An Inside Look at 10 of Today's Most Innovative Churches* (Ventura, Calif.: Regal, 1990), 249.

2. Lee Strobel argues that without a committed effort, Christians will only have relationships with fellow believers. "Within two years of becoming a Christian, the average person has already lost the significant relationships he once had with people outside the faith." Lee Strobel, *Inside the Mind of Unchurched Harry and Mary: How to Reach Friends and Family Who Avoid Church and the Church* (Grand Rapids: Zondervan, 1993), 15 (hereafter cited as *Inside the Mind*).

3. The Impact evangelism course is now called "The Contagious Christian" course.

4. This step of the strategy has changed since I did my study of the church. Formerly, the seventh step was Harry reaching out in friendship to a new unchurched individual. There were actually only six steps then, because step seven was merely Harry beginning the process over with a new individual. During my research several management team members told me that the church's finances were problematic. Since then, as a result of this difficulty, the church has instituted several new programs and even changed the seventh step of their strategy to stewardship.

5. After reading this section, Lee Strobel observed, "A frequent comment of [leadership] conference participants is how WCCC is so much *more* than just a seeker service." This comment is probably fair. However, it is also reasonable to note that Willow Creek's distinctive is the service for the unchurched. Other aspects of the Willow Creek program have not had the influence the seeker service has had.

6. Hybels regularly teaches on Luke 15, enough so that he could tell the one thousand pastors who were visiting, "Most of you have probably heard the message that I give on this text."

7. Willow Creek's official purpose is broader than just evangelism. The church's statement of faith also lists exultation, exhortation, and extension (social action) as elements of the church's purpose.

As a part of my study, I was able to clarify exactly how many Willow Creek volunteers were currently serving and in what capacities. The weekend services used the highest numbers of volunteer and staff work hours.

Chapter 2: *Willow Creek's History*

1. Recently Bill and Lynne Hybels wrote *Rediscovering Church: The Story and Vision of Willow Creek Community Church* (Grand Rapids: Zondervan, 1995). The first half of the book is an honest attempt to tell an inside history of Willow.

theologically conservative Protestantism: James Hunter, *Evangelicalism: The Coming Generation* (Chicago: University of Chicago Press, 1987), 3.

fifty million Americans: James Hunter, *American Evangelicalism: Conservative Religion and the Quandary of Modernity* (New Brunswick: Rutgers University Press, 1983), 3–4. This is close to the forty-four million Marsden quoted in 1980 in *Fundamentalism and American Culture: The Shaping of Twentieth-Century Evangelicalism 1870–1925* (New York: Oxford University Press, 1980), 291. Depending on how *evangelical* is defined, this figure has varied between the *Christianity Today* poll of thirty million and the Gallup Poll of sixty-six million.

2. Randall Balmer, *Mine Eyes Have Seen the Glory: A Journey into the Evangelical Subculture of America* (New York: Oxford University Press, 1989). Balmer depicts the vast differences among some evangelical groups.

3. Alan Merridew, "Religion with a Beat: Son City Spectacular," *Chicago Tribune,* 12 June, 1974.

4. "The Theater Days," *Willow Creek,* Special Anniversary Issue, 29.

5. For background on Son City, see Don Cousins's short booklet *Tomorrow's Church . . . Today* (South Barrington, Ill.: Willow Creek Publications, 1979).

6. **"Son City" was begun:** There continued to be a smaller Bible study group called "Son Village."

answered God's call: Cousins, *Tomorrow's Church . . . Today,* 1ff.

7. For a list of some of these leaders in the church see "The Theater Days," *Willow Creek,* Special Anniversary Issue, 29.

8. James Mellado, "Willow Creek Community Church" (case study, Harvard Business School, 1991), 15.

9. **a management team:** Staff members told me that the number of management team members changes fairly regularly.

Two of these three: The third member of this management team is highly gifted and before being hired by Willow Creek was the director of an international Christian organization. He is responsible for beginning the Willow Creek Association. His work is primarily outside the church, while his colleagues supervise the church.

10. Hybels, *Seven Wonders of the Spiritual World* (Dallas: Word, 1988), 16–17.

11. Ibid., 21.

12. **bearded rebel:** See Steven M. Tipton, *Getting Saved from the Sixties* (Los Angeles: University of California Press, 1982).

We were young people: Lynne Hybels, "Full Circle," *Willow Creek,* Special Anniversary Issue, 11.

13. Gilbert Bilezikian, "A Vision for the Church," *Willow Creek,* September/October 1990, 21.

14. "Into the Stratosphere," *Willow Creek,* Special Anniversary Issue, 23, 25.

15. Hybels states in *Seven Wonders* that he was aware of the importance of spiritual gifts when he first began teaching the youth group (14).

16. Ted Johnson, "It's a Sin to Bore Kids with the Gospel," *Relationships: The Young Life Ministry in Action,* Spring 1993, 3.

17. On another occasion the Chicago Orchestra's hall was rented for a concert by the Son Company band. Lynne Hybels writes, "Yes, we were trying to reach the lost. But we were also having a riot." See "Full Circle," *Willow Creek,* Special Anniversary Issue, 24.

18. "Laying the Foundations," *Willow Creek,* Special Anniversary Issue, 14–21.

19. Ibid., 14–15.

20. Ibid.

21. **He started Son Company:** Holmbo laughs, "Compared to what we are doing now—believe me, it was much more traditional than we thought. 'Contemporary' or 'informal' are very relative terms."

Holmbo fondly remembers: Holmbo explains, "Actually where Bill and I met was part of the ministry of Lance Latham . . . [Latham] was the pastor of a church in Chicago called the Northside Gospel Center. That's a very fundamentalist church (and still is). They owned a summer camp up in Wisconsin. Both Bill and I went to the camp and were both students of Lance Latham (Doc). We . . . became friends. . . . We would stay at each other's home. . . . We just got to be really good friends."

He was a hack: "Laying the Foundations," 17.

22. "Into the Stratosphere," *Willow Creek,* Special Anniversary Issue, 20.

23. Ibid.

24. Many of the following quotes come from the article, "The Theater Days," *Willow Creek,* Special Anniversary Issue, 35–43.

25. Holmbo was eventually divorced. His wife moved away to another state for a time. She eventually returned to Willow Creek and has become an important staff member in the church. Holmbo has remarried and is currently the programming director of a seeker church in Maryland.

26. I was told in several interviews that Hybels studied with and was deeply influenced by evangelical theologian R. C. Sproul during this time. There is some evidence of this in Hybels's writings: "R. C.'s tapes on 'The Holiness of God' impacted me more than any tapes I've ever listened to" (Hybels, *Honest to God: Becoming an Authentic Christian* [Grand Rapids: Zondervan, 1990], 112–14).

27. Kenneth Blanchard et al., *Leadership and the One Minute Manager* (New York: William Morrow and Co., 1985).

28. A staffer admitted that loyalty "can be the sign of a very sick organization." He then suggested that loyalty can also be the sign of a healthy organization.

29. This was the only time during hundreds of conversations that I heard a staff member make this negative a comment. She was frustrated with the church. To even describe the church as "they," she had moved herself out of the loyal inner circle. She left her staff position during the next year.

30. Bilezikian's parents were Armenian immigrants from the Ottoman Empire (present-day Turkey) who moved to France to escape the Islamic persecution.

This summary is taken primarily from a personal interview and the following two articles: Gilbert Bilezikian, "A Vision for the Church," *Willow Creek,* September/October 1990, 20–21; and Rob Wilkins, "The Spark of Vision," *Willow Creek,* September/October 1990), 18–19.

31. Bilezikian, "A Vision for the Church," 21. Bilezikian is a French expatriate. This individual who was such a powerful influence on the young Hybels had an entirely different cultural background. The reason in part why Bilezikian felt like an outsider to the American church may be that he was an outsider.

32. Ibid.

33. Hybels, *Seven Wonders,* 9.

34. Bilezikian prefaced this acknowledgment of his influence: "I don't want to assume too much responsibility here. It's not just a question of humility, it's a question of historical accuracy." The summary of his theology can be found in his *Christianity 101* (Grand Rapids: Zondervan, 1993).

35. Calvinism basically follows the theological system of John Calvin, which emphasizes God's sovereignty. In contrast, Arminianism (named for Jacob Arminius) grew up as a protest movement to Calvinism and emphasized human freedom and responsibility. Probably the most influential Arminian theologian has been John Wesley. For background information see "Calvinism" and "Arminianism" in Elwell's *Evangelical Dictionary of Theology* (Grand Rapids: Baker, 1984). This division is not a new feature of Protestantism but a historic tension. See the extended discussion and American examples in Nathan Hatch, *The Democratization of American Christianity* (New Haven: Yale University Press, 1989), 162–92, 227–43.

36. Dirk Jellema, "Dort, Synod of," in *The New International Dictionary of the Christian Church,* ed. J. D. Douglas (Grand Rapids: Zondervan, 1974), 309–10.

37. Several of the following references come from Bill Hybels, *Too Busy Not to Pray: Slowing Down to Be with God* (Downers Grove, Ill.: InterVarsity Press, 1988), 142–43.

38. Pietism began as a renewal movement in the seventeenth century that emphasized the importance of personal holiness and experience in relation to God. Through Moravian missionaries it led Wesley toward his strange heart warming. It then came to the United States. See "Pietism" in Elwell's *Evangelical Dictionary of Theology,* 855–58.

39. Bilezikian explains in "A Vision for the Church" how his understanding of the primacy of the church shapes the rest of his thinking: "Once I had acquired this perspective on the primacy of the church, the implications became clear for the conduct of our lives as Christians, for the use of our gifts and resources, for evangelism and outreach, and for the building up and energizing of the local church" (21). Bilezikian revealed in our interview that he was deeply influenced in his theological understanding by New Testament scholars George Ladd and Oscar Cullmann.

40. Bilezikian taught Hybels about "the preeminence of the church in God's purposes" ("A Vision for the Church," 21).

41. The counterculture ideals of intimacy and authenticity in the late 1960s and early 1970s were very influential on both the youth group and the church.

42. Friends of the Hybels family described to me how Hybels's father was continually frustrated in his efforts to initiate change in his church.

43. Bilezikian, "A Vision for the Church," 21.

44. "Into the Stratosphere," 20.

45. This discussion is taken from a personal interview with Robert Schuller and from Robert Schuller, *Your Church Has Real Possibilities* (Glendale, Calif.: Regal Books, 1975). "Unlimited potential" is a description by *Willow Creek* magazine of the message that Hybels had received from Schuller ("The Theater Days," 28.)

46. The Schuller connection is avoided in an article by Lorna McNeill, "10 Years, But Who's Counting?" *Willow Creek,* September/October 1991, 8. The article is about the tenth anniversary of Dan Webster as student ministries director. It records how Webster originally came into contact with Hybels: "He first met Senior Pastor Bill Hybels in 1975 at a conference in Garden Grove, California."

What the article doesn't reveal is that Hybels and Webster were in Garden Grove attending Robert Schuller's conference on church leadership; that the conference was being held at Schuller's church, the Crystal Cathedral; that Webster served on the staff of Schuller's church; or that Hybels built a relationship with Webster when Schuller asked Hybels to serve as a consultant with Garden Grove.

47. Schuller also acknowledged that he was intuitively following the model of his uncle who was a Reformed church missionary in China. "That's what established the paradigm for what later would be 'Schuller philosophy of marketing the church,'" he says.

48. Most individuals in the church-growth field claim that missiologist Donald McGavran is the founding father. See McGavran's influential textbook of church growth, *Understanding Church Growth* (Grand Rapids: Eerdmans, 1970). The constitution of the Academy for American Church Growth records, "Church growth strives to combine the eternal theological principles of God's Word concerning the expansion of the church with the best insights of con-

temporary social and behavioral sciences, *employing as its initial frame of reference, the foundational work done by Donald McGavran*" (emphasis added). See C. Peter Wagner, *Church Growth and the Whole Gospel* (San Francisco: Harper and Row, 1981), 75.

Yet there is no doubt that Schuller has been a, if not the, central figure in actually implementing church-growth principles in the U.S., as Peter Wagner states in Schuller, *Your Church Has Real Possibilities:* "North American interest in church growth is in no small measure due to the efforts of Dr. Robert Schuller" (iv).

49. Schuller, in *Your Church Has Real Possibilities,* calls "possibility thinking" another principle of successful marketing: "What is possibility thinking? It's having the right value system, asking the right questions and making the right decisions" (13, 25, 28).

50. **The secret of winning:** Schuller, *Your Church Has Real Possibilities,* 128.

extravagance: Robert H. Schuller, *Self Esteem: The New Reformation* (Waco, Tex.: Word Books, 1982), 12.

51. C. Peter Wagner, *Your Church Can Grow* (Glendale, Calif.: Regal Books, 1976), 95.

52. C. Peter Wagner describes in *Church Growth and the Whole Gospel* how Schuller has created a variety of ministries within his church: "He has encouraged the formation of between twenty and thirty local mission structures which are separate from the congregation itself, with their own leadership, programs and budget" (74, 189). This development of various sub-ministries is another example of Schuller's influence on Hybels.

53. The short biography on the cover of his book *Self Esteem* claims that his "television program 'The Hour of Power' was the most widely watched broadcast of all televised church services." See Robert H. Schuller, *Self Esteem.*

54. **possibility thinking:** When I asked, Schuller acknowledged that Peale was a strong influence: "But the difference between us is he never thought in a logical form—he didn't have the logical thinking that a John Calvin had. And I got that from studying John Calvin."

fibre of your being: Schuller, *Your Church Has Real Possibilities,* 134.

55. Schuller, *Self Esteem,* 12.

56. **failure in mission:** Ibid. Schuller explains, "Would you give an expository sermon on the Bible? No. Because most of those people don't even believe it's a holy book at this point."

their human hurts: Schuller writes in *Self Esteem,* "For decades now we have watched the church in Western Europe and in America decline in power, membership, and influence. I believe that this decline is the result of our placing the theocentric communications above the meeting of the deeper emotional and spiritual needs of humanity" (12).

57. **felt by human beings:** Ibid.

both negative and positive: Schuller makes his argument that the basic human need is self-esteem in the introduction to *Self Esteem,* 15.

self-esteem: Schuller, *Self Esteem,* 14.

58. **you're a sinner:** This explanation came when I asked Schuller why it was not more widely known that he was so influential on Hybels and Willow Creek. He defends his discarding of historic evangelical language, however, saying, "Jesus didn't do it. Believe me, I'm following the strategy of Jesus. Paul had a different strategy. His strategy wasn't the same as Jesus'. They don't contradict but they're different. You can have two different strategies and there is a place for each." Schuller gave one other reason why his reputation has been hurt in the evangelical community: "I'm a television pastor and that hasn't helped my reputation."

swallowed up theology: Schuller admits that he has received a lot of criticism from the Christian community: "It was a painful thing to build the Crystal Cathedral. . . . Christians made fun of me. I wouldn't be surprised if people in this room criticized me. Do you think I like to be criticized?" See Robert Schuller, "Possibility Thinking and the Growth of the Church in Japan," *Japan Christian Quarterly,* Spring 1988, 89.

condescension: Schuller argues, "I don't have a problem today with Calvin's *Institutes,* but I do disagree with Calvinists." See "Hard Questions for Robert Schuller about Sin and Self-esteem" and Kenneth Kantzer, "A Theologian Looks at Schuller" in *Christianity Today,* August 10, 1984, 14–20, 22–24. Kantzer, kindly and incisively, writes, "Robert Schuller is an evangelist—first, last and always. I admire his zeal to reach the ear of twentieth-century Americans and to win them to Christ and the gospel. But I am never quite certain what gospel they are being won to" (22).

his influence: Schuller received opposition for his positive-thinking message even within his own church. Garden Grove had a staff member who Schuller reports in *Your Church Has Real Possibilities,* "challenged the congregation to 'beware of a man who only preaches positive thinking and doesn't preach the full gospel of Jesus Christ'" (107).

59. **in 1979:** "The Theater Days," 33.

the church campus: Hybels imitated Schuller in how he named Willow Creek. Schuller named his church Garden Grove Community Church after the community it was in because he wanted it to be the community's church: "I didn't think the name 'Reformed' would bring the *unchurched* people in" (author's emphasis, *Your Church Has Real Possibilities,* 160). Hybels likewise named his church Willow Creek Community Church after the Willow Creek theater where they originally held the weekend services and because he also wanted it to be the community's church.

student ministry: McNeill, "10 Years, but Who's Counting?" 8.

Successful Church Leadership: Schuller eventually realized that Hybels was gifted in management and asked him to serve as a consultant at his church. Holmbo recalls, "Bill was employed by Bob for a year as a consultant to Garden Grove Community Church. . . . Once a month Bill would fly out to Garden Grove for a weekend and meet with Bob or different ministry leaders that they had out there."

60. It should be noted that not all of these influences from Schuller to Hybels are exclusive. For example, it is logical to suggest that Schuller's emphasis on entertainment in reaching the unchurched affected Hybels and Willow Creek. Yet Hybels had already incorporated a strong emphasis on entertainment in his youth work. It would be incorrect to see many of these influences as simple causal relationships. Rather, Schuller can be best understood as one among several influences. "The Theater Days," 28.

61. Willow Creek did not even have a collection during the weekend services for the first nine months of the church. *Willow Creek* magazine commented that the word *sin* was "almost never heard in the early days of the church" (Special Anniversary Issue, 38).

62. Schuller, *Self Esteem,* 13.

63. **"inventory" of his community:** Schuller, *Your Church Has Real Possibilities,* 3.

your community: Ibid., 78. As Schuller's audience expanded through the use of television, he continued to try to understand them. He hired the Gallup organization to survey the beliefs of the unchurched individuals in America. George Gallup Jr. summarizes the results of this survey in "Religion in America" in *The Annals: The American Academy of Political and Social Science* (Beverly Hills: Sage Publications, July 1985).

His new mentor: The fact that Hybels was inspired to do the survey by his mentor Schuller is in no official history of Willow Creek or any of Hybels's descriptions of the survey that I heard.

64. Schuller's interest in psychology has been active for most of his ministry. One of his majors in college was psychology, and he attended the World Psychiatric Congress in 1967. He also was strongly influenced by Victor Frankel, who had developed Logos Therapy. See Schuller, *Self Esteem,* 21–22.

twentieth-century psychologists: Schuller, *Self Esteem,* 27.

theology of self-esteem: Sociologist James Davison Hunter calls this syncretism a "psychological Christocentrism" in *American Evangelicalism,* 95. Hunter believes Schuller's emphasis, although more blatant than most, is characteristic of much of evangelicalism. See Hunter, *Evangelicalism: The Coming Generation,* 71.

65. **Theological content:** Schuller claims that Hybels and Willow Creek have been faithful to his model of a positive, attractive message. "They caught that, and they are doing a fabulous job of keeping it positive."

joyous experiences: Cousins, *Tomorrow's Church . . . Today,* 67.

66. Hybels, *Seven Wonders,* 75–76.

67. Schuller, *Your Church Has Real Possibilities,* 6, 179.

Chapter 3: *Understanding Unchurched Harry*

1. Hybels, *Seven Wonders,* 17.

2. Mark Mittelberg, "A Critical Analysis of the Epistemological Starting Points in Presuppositional Apologetics" (master's thesis, Trinity Evangelical Divinity Seminary, 1988), 104 (hereafter cited as "A Critical Analysis").

3. **book of all time:** Thomas J. Peters and Robert H. Waterman Jr., *In Search of Excellence: Lessons from America's Best-Run Companies* (New York: Harper and Row, 1982).

their findings concerning marketing: Philip Kotler, *Marketing Management: Analysis, Planning, Implementation, and Control,* 6th ed. (Englewood Cliffs, N.J.: Prentice Hall, 1988), 1.

4. Ibid., xvii.

5. **church's guru of growth:** Steve Rabey, "Will Change Undo the Church?" *Christianity Today*, October 26, 1992, 82.

market-driven environment: George Barna, *Marketing the Church: What They Never Taught You about Church Growth* (Colorado Springs: Navpress, 1988), 23.

6. Ibid., 7–8.

7. These include *User Friendly Churches; The Power of Vision; The Frog in the Kettle; What Americans Believe; Church Marketing: Breaking Ground for the Harvest; The Barna Report 92–93; Not Willing to Settle: A Portrait of the Baby Bust Generation.* Two of these books even use Willow Creek terms—"user friendly" and "vision"—in their titles.

8. The original Willow Creek survey and other of its methods are being discussed in England as useful tools for other churches. See Martin Robinson, *A World Apart: Creating a Church for the Unchurched* (Tunbridge Wells, England: Monarch, 1992), 167.

9. James Mellado, "Willow Creek Community Church," 1. Willow Creek sells this case study in its bookstore.

10. **Wall Street Journal:** Thomas Stewart, "Turning Around the Lord's Business," *Fortune*, September 25, 1989, 116–17, 120, 124, 128. Peter Drucker, "Marketing 101 for a Fast-Changing Decade," *The Wall Street Journal,* November 20, 1990.

should know them: Drucker, "Marketing 101."

11. **afternoon of recreation:** Robinson, *A World Apart,* 60.

among the Gentiles: Maudlin and Gilbreath, "Selling Out the House of God?" 24.

Other ministries at Willow Creek are also guided by the idea of isolating a target audience. The director of evangelism argued that all believers should evangelistically "have their own *target audience* just as we need to have that as a church." Interns are trained to "program events designed to reach *target markets* similar to those they will be trying to reach during their church planting." A Willow Creek *team* is those individuals who agree with who the *target audience* is and the *strategy* of how to reach that audience.

12. Kotler, *Marketing Management*, 49.

13. **scream for attention:** Barna, *Marketing the Church*, 54–55.

we have to offer: Ibid., 54–55. In the book that had such a powerful influence on Hybels, *Your Church Has Real Possibilities,* Schuller advises pastors to begin "calling door-to-door in the immediate vicinity of your church" (80).

14. Kotler, *Marketing Management*, 107.

15. Dennis Farney, "Inside Hallmark's Love Machine," *The Wall Street Journal,* February 14, 1990, B1.

16. **Composite of Sales-Force Opinions:** Kotler, *Marketing Management*, 272.

park district team: Bill Hybels, *Mastering Contemporary Preaching* (Portland, Ore.: Multnomah Press, 1989), 29.

17. Hybels listens to his fellow researchers. On one retreat, the topic of anger repeatedly came to the table from different sources. Although Hybels himself didn't see anger as a crucial issue, the others encouraged him to include it. He did, and it was a successful series in the following year.

18. Another example of this commitment to research is that the audio-visual department subscribes to over thirty magazines that the department believes will help its members sharpen their skills and understanding.

19. **changing environment:** Kotler, *Marketing Management*, 271.

accurate information: Barna, *Marketing the Church*, 30.

attitudes and behavior: Ibid.

20. George Barna, *The Frog in the Kettle: What Christians Need to Know about Life in the Year 2000* (Ventura, Calif.: Regal Books, 1990), back cover.

21. Besides the Barna report on the church, the church has had detailed research done on their small groups' effectiveness and has used the Network data bank. Strobel, *Inside the Mind,* 44.

22. After reading this section on research, Strobel underlined the importance of the intuitive response: "The norm is that Barna's studies confirm and add statistics to observations and decisions we've already made. I've never been in any meeting where we've looked at Barna's research and said, 'Based on this, we need to take action.'"

Chapter 4: *Profile of Unchurched Harry*

1. Barna, *Marketing the Church,* 42.

2. Strobel himself is a former unchurched Harry and serves as the church's classic example of a non-Christian. His book *Inside the Mind* sketches the thinking and behavior of a typical unchurched Harry.

3. Strobel argues that Willow Creek's strategy would be different if they chose as their target audience baby busters—those born between 1965 and 1983. See Strobel, *Inside the Mind,* 163, 45.

4. This is extremely high compared to the national average of individuals who have a college education, which is 21.4 percent. See Bureau of the Census, *Statistical Abstract of the United States,* Table 220 (Washington, D.C., 1992), 144.

5. According to Network's study, a total of 55.4 percent of Willow Creek attenders live in the following neighborhoods from 1 to 10 (1 having the highest number of attenders): Palatine, Schaumburg, Hoffman Estates, Elgin, Arlington Heights, Barrington, Crystal Lake, Rolling Meadows, Mount Prospect, and Des Plaines. Willow Creek is located in the center of jobs and new housing that have exploded over the last twenty years. For example, Schaumburg is the second largest "edge city" in the United States, with over 190,000 employed individuals. See Sue Ellen Christian, "Jobs Help Schaumburg Hit the Big Time among Cities," *Chicago Tribune,* January 14, 1994, 1.

6. Kotler, *Marketing Management,* 17.

7. Evangelism director Mark Mittelberg asserts that the emphasis on responding to unchurched Harry's felt needs doesn't come from marketing, but from Scripture: "It comes from God and the Bible. If it happens to parallel some marketing ideas that's fine."

Kotler details this process in *Marketing Management:* "People satisfy their needs and wants with products. We will define products broadly to cover anything that can be offered to someone to satisfy a need or want" (30, 4).

8. **product solutions:** Kotler, *Marketing Management,* 405.

prospects in mind: "Improve Your Relationship Skills," *Lifelines,* November 1989, 2.

9. Barna agrees that marketing "revolves around satisfying the needs of the consumer" (*Marketing the Church,* 51).

10. Ibid., 17. The seed form of these ideas is Robert Schuller's. He believes that his church has "a program and service designed to meet almost every conceivable need that an unchurched person might seek and expect from a church" (Schuller, *Your Church Has Real Possibilities,* 29).

11. Strobel, *Inside the Mind,* 214.

12. Kotler, *Marketing Management,* 175.

13. Robinson, *A World Apart,* 6.

14. Daniel Yankelovich, *New Rules: Searching for Self-Fulfillment in a World Turned Upside Down* (New York: Random House, 1981), 3.

15. Ibid., 5.

16. Joseph Veroff, Elizabeth Douvan, and Richard A. Kulka, *The Inner American: A Self Portrait from 1957 to 1976* (New York: Basic Books, 1981), 141.

17. **essential person:** Ibid.

their own lives: Ibid., 532.

18. George Gallup Jr. and Jim Castelli, *The People's Religion: American Faith in the 90's* (New York: Macmillan, 1989), 253.

19. Barna, *Marketing the Church,* 51.

20. **means of integration:** Veroff, Douvan, and Kulka, *The Inner American,* 141.

personal fulfillment: Ibid.

21. **moral training:** Strobel, *Inside the Mind,* 72.

religious training: Ibid. The source of this information is the article "Here Come the Baby Boomers," *Emerging Trends,* June 1991, 5.

22. Barna, *The Frog in the Kettle,* 157. The result of this frantic pace is a desire for convenience. Barna concludes in *The Frog in the Kettle,* "Businesses which save us time and make life convenient will prosper" (39). Willow Creek is attempting to meet this need with their seeker service, which is a convenient one-hour event with efficient arrival and departure.

23. For example, see Robert N. Bellah, William M. Sullivan, Ann Swidler, and Steven M. Tipton, *Habits of the Heart: Individualism and Commitment in American Life* (Berkeley, Calif.: University of California Press, 1985), 297–307, and Peter Berger, *The Sacred Canopy: Elements of a Sociological Theory of Religion* (Garden City, N.Y.: Anchor Books, 1969), 81–101. Berger writes, "Religion has been one of the most effective bulwarks against anomy throughout human history" (87).

24. Strobel, *Inside the Mind,* 48.

25. **can connect with:** Ibid., 69.

biblical leadership: Ibid., 65.

26. **ultimate consumers:** Hybels, *Mastering Contemporary Preaching,* 27.

the same reason: Cindy York, "Gimme That New-Time Religion," *U.S.A. Today Weekend,* April 13–15, 1990, 4.

Harry is king: After reading this chapter, Strobel responded, "God is king; we won't compromise his message to placate Harry." My point is that the choice of Harry as the target audience guides Willow Creek's strategy of how to reach him. In this sense it is still appropriate to use the marketing proverb "The customer is king."

27. Strobel, *Inside the Mind,* 201. The study Strobel is referring to was James Patterson and Peter Kim's *The Day America Told the Truth* (New York: Prentice Hall, 1991), 143.

28. George Gallup Jr., ed., *Religion in America 1990* (Princeton: Religion Research Center), 53.

29. **belief in God:** Gallup, *The People's Religion,* 45.

daily life: Gallup, *Religion in America 1990,* 48.

30. Strobel, *Inside the Mind,* 17.

31. Valeo, "Why Do 12,000 People Listen to This Man Each Week?" *Daily Herald* (May 18, 1988), sec. 2, p. 2.

32. Strobel, *Inside The Mind,* 26.

33. Ibid., 45.

34. Ibid., 46.

35. Ibid., 56.

36. Strobel echoes this idea in *Inside the Mind:* "Once a person sincerely begins to check out Christianity, it's only a matter of time before he'll discover the truth about God. The Bible says, 'You will seek me and find me when you seek me with all your heart'" (56).

There is a philosophical and theological principle behind this idea of sincere seekers. Mittelberg argues that people have the ability to "aim, with relative success, at the ideal of rational objectivity." This emphasis on free choice and the ability of human beings to discover the truth is an example of Willow Creek's optimistic

Arminian theology. See Mark Mittelberg, "A Critical Analysis," 125.

37. This placing of responsibility on unchurched individuals to honestly investigate Christianity is not new. Historian Nathan Hatch explains in *The Democratization of American Christianity* how nineteenth-century evangelist Lorenzo Dow "was able to depict his times as an 'Age of Inquiry,' in which individuals had to think for themselves and take matters into their own hands" (37).

38. The stages of spiritual interest have been developed in some detail by marketer James Engel. It has been described in mission circles as the "Engel scale." Willow Creekers do believe that this process is led by the Holy Spirit. As Strobel writes in *Inside the Mind,* "It's important to realize that the seeking process itself is a response to the Holy Spirit's work" (43).

39. Altogether the staff assert that the total of hostile, curious, and sincere Harrys who attend the weekend service is about one-third of the weekend attendance. Yet the internal Willow study revealed that 91 percent of the weekend attenders assert that a close relationship with God is their highest value. This would seem to indicate a much smaller percentage of the weekend audience are unchurched Harrys. See Robinson, *A World Apart,* 81.

40. **with Scripture:** Barbara Dolan, "Full House at Willow Creek," *Time,* March 6, 1989, 60.

programming plans: Hybels, *Seven Wonders,* 59.

41. Barna, *Marketing the Church,* 42.

42. **target audience:** "Willow Creek's International Ministries," *Update,* August 1989.

of Willow Creek: Robinson, *A World Apart,* 76.

43. Strobel, *Inside the Mind,* 213.

Chapter 5: *Weekend Service Programming*

1. Hybels explains, "It's better to hire the guy that can sow seed so you can get seed flying around and falling on the ground and eventually have at least something to work with come harvest time."

2. The church turned him down. See "You've Got Nice Curves," *Willow Creek,* January/February 1991, 10.

3. Anthony B. Robinson, "Learning from Willow Creek Church," *Christian Century,* January 1991, 68.

4. **doesn't it?:** Schuller argues that a church needs to be designed to impress and relax nonchurched people: "To convert them, first you need to relax them so they will listen to you. I wanted to create a place where secular cynical, untrusting people would come. We have no stained glass windows, but lots of water and natural plantings" ("Hard Questions for Robert Schuller about Sin and Self-esteem," 14).

unchurched people: Evangelism director Mittelberg clarified this point: "It's a safe environment in which they can come and hear a message which is going to challenge them to do things which are very uncomfortable, like repent of their sins and follow Jesus Christ."

5. If unchurched visitors have children, they may take them to Promiseland, the weekend ministry to all children from infancy to fifth grade. It is structured much like the seeker service, with music, drama, and a message on the same theme as the adult message. There are approximately two thousand children who attend Promiseland each week. See *Willow Creek,* January/February 1990, 8.

6. Before joining the programming team, the singers also go through what Beach describes as a "vigorous personal interview."

7. One sees historical parallels in the nineteenth century, as popular music dominated the renewal movement and eventually emerged as American gospel music. See Hatch, *The Democratization of American Christianity,* 146ff. Beach explains, "The reason that we don't have a choir . . . [is] because we want the music to be similar to what nonchurched Harry is exposed to on the radio." Strobel, *Inside the Mind,* 180.

8. This is the only time during the service besides the prelude when the band plays instrumental music.

Chapter 6: *The Use of the Arts*

1. Hybels, *Caution: Christians Under Construction* (Wheaton, Ill.: Scripture Press, 1978), 12.

2. Dolan, "Full House at Willow Creek," 60.

3. Strobel, *Inside the Mind,* 182.

4. Neil Postman, *Amusing Ourselves to Death* (New York: Penguin, 1985), 63.

5. **images over ideas:** *Harper's* magazine brought Neil Postman and Camille Paglia together to debate television's role in American culture. Although both scholars had different interpretations on the value of television, they agreed on its importance. As Paglia asserts, television "is the culture." Neil Postman and Camille Paglia, "She Wants Her TV! He Wants His Book!" *Harper's,* March 1991, 44.

and movement: quoted in Postman, *Amusing Ourselves to Death,* 105.

6. David Wells, *Turning to God* (Grand Rapids: Baker, 1989), 140.

7. Strobel, *Inside the Mind,* 182.

8. Although both multi-media and drama are utilized by Willow Creek, drama is normally used. I will describe the use of drama in the following examples, but the discussion applies to the use of multi-media as well.

9. For statistics on television viewing see William Bennett, *The Index of Leading Cultural Indicators* (Washington: The Heritage Foundation, 1993), 21. This image orientation has certain built-in problems. Postman's *Amusing Ourselves to Death* is a popular description of some of these dangers.

10. Drama director Steve Pederson reveals the purpose of the drama: "We want to raise questions, not answer them." See Steve Burdan, "Willow Creek Plays Up Drama to the 'Seekers,'" *Worship Leader,* February/March 1992, 11.

11. This process follows marketing strategy. Marketers have determined that the stages in the buying decision process are (1) problem recognition, (2) information search, (3) evaluation of alternatives, (4) purchase decision, and (5) post-purchase behavior. Drama is used in the Willow Creek program to clarify an initial problem. This often leads to discussion of the problem of how individuals relate to God. See Kotler, *Marketing Management,* 194.

12. Strobel, *Inside the Mind,* 184.

13. Robert T. Oliver, *The Psychology of Persuasive Speech* (New York: Longmans, Green and Co., 1942), 169.

14. Strobel, *Inside the Mind,* 183.

15. Robinson, *A World Apart,* 78.

16. John MacArthur, *Ashamed of the Gospel: When the Church Becomes Like the World* (Wheaton, Ill.: Crossway Books, 1993), xii. MacArthur never directly refers to Hybels or Willow Creek by name. Yet he does quote "a leading pastor in the movement" that is actually a published comment by Hybels and from articles that are describing Willow Creek (126, 50). MacArthur wholeheartedly condemns Hybels's approach: "It would be hard to imagine a ministry philosophy more at odds with the Word of God than that" (126). I describe MacArthur as a fundamentalist because he is a member of the Independent Fundamental Churches of America.

17. **place of proclamation:** Robinson, *A World Apart,* 65.

on the planet: Maudlin and Gilbreath, "Selling Out the House of God?" 20–25.

18. **meant by "entertainment":** This disagreement is also a rhetorical, as well as substantive, one. Many evangelicals don't believe the church should be a place of "entertainment." This earmark partly explains Robert Schuller's lack of credibility among many evangelicals. As Ken Kantzer characterizes Schuller's Sunday morning service: "It's strictly 'Show-Biz.'" See Kantzer, "A Theologian Looks at Schuller," 24. In any political conflict, rhetoric is the first stage of the battle. The categories one uses to describe the issues, and one's opponents, help to determine the outcome. If Willow Creek were to just allow others to label them as Christian entertainers, they would lose credibility in many evangelicals' minds.

for an audience: *The Compact Edition of the Oxford English Dictionary*, vol. 1 (New York: Oxford University Press, 1971), 214.

19. Cousins explains in *Tomorrow's Church . . . Today* how this philosophy worked in Son City: "The non-Christian student . . . is made to feel comfortable with the team scores, 'jam,' music, drama, and media. Each of these steps is not only painless, but quite enjoyable for the student" (48).

20. Entertainment used as a powerful tool in attaining other ends is also true in politics. Roger Ailes, the Republican media consultant, has made a career out of teaching politicians how to use television. In 1968, when Richard Nixon grumbled about having to use the gimmick of television in politics, Ailes reportedly replied, "If you believe that, Mr. Nixon, you're going to lose—again." Nixon hired Ailes to handle his media campaign. *Success* magazine reports that Ailes has "taught political leaders that *entertainment is necessary to succeed at politics*" (emphasis added). "The Power of Personality," *Success,* January/February 1994, 37.

21. Some clearly advocate the use of entertainment. Robert Schuller coaches in *Your Church Has Real Possibilities,* "Let your Sunday morning services aim at inspiration, *entertainment* and a basic commitment to Jesus Christ. . . . There is a great deal of therapeutic and spiritual value in wholesome *entertainment*" (135–36, emphasis added). Likewise, Barna preaches in *The Frog in the Kettle,* "Church programs should include more *entertainment*-related activities" (93, emphasis added).

Chapter 7: *The Programming Principles of Persuasion*

1. Strobel, *Inside the Mind,* 73. As Barna puts it, in *The Frog in the Kettle,* "We must recognize that we are in a competitive environment. If we hope to include people in the life of the Church, we must provide appealing and high quality activities that can successfully compete for people's time, attention and resources" (93).

2. In over two years of attending the weekend and weekday service I saw only one small pro-

duction mistake: On June 20, 1990, the singers on the stage were singing one set of lyrics, while the audio-visual people were displaying a slightly different version on the video screens.

3. Sociologists have observed a pattern of modern life toward increased anonymity. As individuals have moved from farms and small towns to cities (urbanization), anonymity has grown. Individuals in a modern urban or suburban setting are used to anonymity in the public sphere. Thus, it should not be a surprise to see that Willow Creek has tried to imitate this pattern in its seeker services. See Hunter, *Making Sense of Modern Times: Peter L. Berger and the Vision of Interpretive Sociology,* 97ff.

4. **what is expected of him:** Lee Strobel explains in *Inside the Mind,* "Most Christians underestimate the tension and anxiety that Unchurched Harry and Mary experience when they walk through the church door" (171).

the first time: Ibid., 170.

inadvertent gaffe: Ibid., 171.

5. Tom Valeo, "The Drama of Willow Creek," *Daily Herald* (May 19, 1988), 9.

6. Strobel, *Inside the Mind,* 172.

7. "Size Wise," *Willow Creek,* January/February 1991, 6.

8. Strobel, *Inside the Mind,* 173.

9. **your eternity:** Hybels, *Mastering Contemporary Preaching,* 39.

quick decision to follow Christ: Don Cousins found helpers in the children's ministry who were inviting children each week to accept Christ. He told them, "We appreciate your heart's desire, but we hold that it's more important to week by week build a relationship with the child and to sow seeds in them, and then to periodically give opportunities. But not to beat kids over the head with the gospel."

10. Valeo, "The Drama of Willow Creek."

11. The phrase "pre-evangelism" was used by only a few staff members that I spoke with. Generally the terminology used to explain this pre-evangelism included "process," "spiritual journey," "spiritual seeker," "roadblocks," and "re-understanding God."

12. Aristotle, *The Basic Works of Aristotle,* ed. Richard McKeon (New York: Random House, 1941), 1327, 1329–30.

13. **logic and emotion:** Gerald R. Miller, ed., *Persuasion: New Directions in Theory and Research* (Beverly Hills: Sage Publications, 1980), 15.

cognitive means of persuasion: Affect means of persuasion were more effective than cognitive means when dealing with affect-based attitudes and equal when dealing with cognitive-based attitudes. Kari Edwards, "The Interplay of Affect and Cognition in Attitude Formation and Change," *Journal of Personality and Social Psychology* 59, no. 2 (1990): 202–16.

14. Margot Hornblower, "Advertising Spoken Here," *Time,* July 15, 1991, 71.

15. Richard Corliss, "Peter Pan Speaks," *Time,* February 22, 1993, 67.

16. *Time,* August 5, 1991, 17.

17. See Veroff, Douvan, and Kulka, *The Inner American,* and Philip Rieff, *The Feeling Intellect* (Chicago: University of Chicago Press, 1990).

18. **stressful society:** Hybels, *Honest to God,* 9.

Bill Clinton: Steve Daley, in his article " '93 Proves that Eloquence and Wit Remain Part of U.S. Political Dialogue," quoted a January 25, 1993, *Newsweek* profile of Clinton: "There's no doubting that the nation is about to be led by its first sensitive male chief executive. He's the first president to have attended both Lamaze classes and family therapy. . . . He can speak in the rhythms and rhetoric of pop psychology and self actualization" (*Chicago Tribune,* December 26, 1993, sec. 4, p. 4).

19. Ken Briggs, "How Does God Speak to People Today?" *Emerging Trends* 9, no. 2 : 1. It should be noted that Willow Creek is not unique in trying to influence the emotions of possible converts. For generations, evangelicals have attempted to influence their audiences' emotions in their efforts to convert them. Historian Nathan Hatch reports that popular preaching in the nineteenth century "was personal rather than abstract. Sermons were most effective which expressed a preacher's deepest personal feelings. Frequently preachers overcome by emotion would weep and cry aloud. A hearer found it difficult to keep this kind of sermon at arm's length." In fact, preachers often sought to "trigger deep emotional reactions in their hearers" (Hatch, *The Democratization of American Christianity,* 137, 105).

Music also has been used in these efforts to persuade individuals to convert. D. L. Moody did not even appear on the stage of his campaigns until his fellow workers had prepared the crowd. Historian David Wells writes in *Turning to God,* "The people were warmed up emotionally by popular songs with a plain gospel message until their expectation of the main preacher had reached its summit" (93).

20. Hybels said at one point that "moments" are "not something that you can manipulate or fabricate." Creekers seem to believe that the moments are crafted by the programming team but completed by the Holy Spirit. The staff sometimes say that at times they didn't even know that a moment was going to occur. Yet the programming team is seeking to create these emotional

moments. One drama writer clarifies the goal of the programming: "We make no bones about what we're doing. We want to create this moment. We're really shooting for what we call the 'moment,' the moment of feeling."

21. Strobel, *Inside the Mind,* 59.

22. **reinforced positions:** The famous military strategist Sun-Tzu advises, "Resort to assaulting walled cities only when there is no other choice." See Roger Ames, ed., *Sun-Tzu: The Art of Warfare* (New York: Ballantine Books, 1993), 111.

much lower: After reading this chapter, Nancy Beach wrote that this quote "sounds so manipulative." She emphasized that the programming team doesn't ever want to "take away a person's God-given freedom to choose."

23. Oliver, *The Psychology of Persuasive Speech,* 170.

24. Ibid.

25. Department of the Army, Headquarters, *Intelligence Interrogation* (approved for public release: distribution is unlimited), FM 34–52.

Chapter 8: *The Credibility of the Speaker*

1. Hybels lists "effective preaching" as the second transferable concept of Willow Creek's leadership conference.

2. Oliver, *The Psychology of Persuasive Speech*, 215.

3. Hybels tells in *Christians in the Marketplace* how this credibility can be created in the workplace: "What are the various threads that must be woven together to create the fabric of credibility? In the next few pages I want to discuss four elements that I believe are basic and necessary to the establishment of a God-honoring level of credibility: a proper attitude toward authority, a willingness to show initiative, a commitment to excellence, and a good, old-fashioned honesty" (21).

Hybels seems to have been influenced in the importance of credibility by the business world's emphasis on credibility. An article on the executive life in *Fortune* magazine reports that when baby-boomer managers were asked, "'What's the worst thing that could happen to you in business?' The most common response: 'Losing my credibility.'" See Walter Kiechel, "The Workaholic Generation," *Fortune*, April 10, 1989, 58.

4. Oskamp, *Attitudes and Opinions*, 2d ed. (Englewood Cliffs, N.J.: Prentice Hall, 1977), 217. Robert Oliver argues in *The Psychology of Persuasive Speech,* "If an audience has such a high opinion of a speaker that it wants to accept what he says, his persuasive battle is more than half won" (91).

5. Oskamp, *Attitudes and Opinions*, 217.

6. Oliver, *The Psychology of Persuasive Speech*, underlines the importance of authenticity in persuasive speech: "Unless they [emotional appeals] are a sincere expression of the speaker's own feelings, they will not ring true" (91).

7. Strobel, *Inside the Mind,* 184.

8. Attenders are also encouraged by the fact that Hybels doesn't live on another spiritual level. Hybels explains, "A good leader ought to be able to say to his people, 'Wrestle with this truth like I'm wrestling with it.' . . . I let the people see my failures enough because I've learned that people are greatly blessed when they see that their pastor has sinned."

9. **through our preaching:** Hybels, *Mastering Contemporary Preaching,* 30.

friend of sinners: Hybels, *Christians in a Sex-Crazed Culture*, 121.

10. Hybels, *Mastering Contemporary Preaching,* 30.

11. Ibid.

12. **Bible text:** For example, I interviewed one individual who heard Hybels speak on three different occasions before he began attending Willow Creek. On each of these occasions, Hybels used Luke 15 as his text. Hybels paraphrases Jesus' message in Luke 15: "Go after the lost people. Go after them. Don't shy away from them, don't think you're a white hat and they're a black hat; they matter to God. They ought to matter to us."

against them: Hybels, *Mastering Contemporary Preaching,* 30.

Chapter 9: *Identifying with Harry*

1. Oliver, *The Psychology of Persuasive Speech,* 173. See Oskamp, *Attitudes and Opinions,* 214ff.

Hybels believes that he is following Jesus' example in identifying with those he is trying to love. He describes Jesus' ministry as "divine love, outrageous love that turns over every stone and exhausts every opportunity to communicate affection to us by demonstrating a total willingness to *identify* with us at every point in our experience" (emphasis added).

2. Steve Burdan, unpublished paper, "Resources for the Christian Year," 1.

3. Other examples of verbal identification are *we're* (480 times) and *we've* (122 times). Obviously, Hybels in some cases is referring to himself and his staff, family, friends, etc.

4. Strobel explains in *Inside the Mind* his perspective as an unchurched Harry: "My mental

caricature of pastors was that they were academic bookworms who lived in ivory towers far removed from the real world" (217).

5. On past occasions Hybels has joked about typical seminarians or pastors. He describes the guys in his college who were planning to go to seminary: "They still wore their shiny black polyesters. . . . Naturally I began to get the idea if a person was going to be a serious Christian, he had to be a real 'loser.'" See Hybels, *Caution: Christians Under Construction,* 11.

6. Ibid., 12. One Creeker explained, "Willow Creek has shown me that Christianity doesn't belong to another world. In so many churches, you accept Christ and then drop out of reality. You become residents of another world. But, at Willow Creek, the message is that God fits into the real world" (Russ Daughtry, "Serious Rock 'n' Roll," *Willow Creek,* January/February 1990, 31).

7. Peter Berger, "Consciousness Raising: To Whom—By Whom?" *Social Policy,* September/October 1974, 38–42.

8. Cousins, *Tomorrow's Church . . . Today,* 67.

9. Ibid.

10. Strobel, *Inside the Mind,* 216.

11. Ibid., 217.

12. Computer concordance. The infrequency of use of the words *gospel* and *evangelism* is contrasted with the popular use of *spiritual* (198 times over the course of the year).

13. **modern culture:** This is found on the 1989–90 Willow Creek form describing the leadership conferences.

everyday words: Strobel, *Inside the Mind,* 218.

14. Strobel asserts in *Inside the Mind* that "Christians today must strategically think through how to present the Gospel in an environment that will attract those who are in need of it." He argues that "Christians can't speak the language of the people they're trying to reach until they know who their target audience is going to be" (161, 162).

Creekers report finding individuals with little knowledge of Christianity. Mittelberg recalls some of his conversations with Harrys: "I would nonchalantly say, 'I'm sure you know John 3:16,' and in some cases they would look at me kind of cross-eyed, and they'd think, *What's that? Is that some code? What are you talking about?* I'd say, 'John—that's a Book in the Bible. He was one of the disciples, and three is the chapter.'"

15. Mittelberg, echoing Hybels, believes it necessary to "strip ourselves of Christian clichés, even when they may be biblical and dear to us."

16. Cousins says, "Harry needs to hear the story of the prodigal son in a way that he says: 'I understand.'"

17. The use of theological language was *eschatological* (the study of the future) on three occasions, *theology* on two occasions, *omniscient* (all-knowing) on six occasions, *omnipresent* (all-present) on one occasion, and *omnipotent* (all-powerful) on four occasions during the year studied. After reading a draft of this chapter, Mittelberg commented, "We don't water down theological truths—we just teach them at a basic level, in terms understandable to beginners."

18. **Millard Erickson:** Strobel, *Inside the Mind,* 161, 234. This is one of the few references to a theologian I heard during my study.

one language to another: Millard Erickson, *Christian Theology,* (Grand Rapids: Baker, 1983), 113.

twentieth-century America: Strobel, *Inside the Mind,* 162.

19. Hatch, *The Democratization of American Christianity,* 133.

20. The editor of *Willow Creek* magazine details, "We, as Christians, tend to complicate our faith. We use words like 'sanctification' when we mean 'growing' or 'substitutionary atonement' instead of 'Christ died for us'" (Rob Wilkins, "The Profound Simplicity of Love," *Willow Creek,* January/February 1991, 3).

21. Strobel, *Inside the Mind,* 218.

22. J. I. Packer, "Humor Is a Funny Thing," *Christianity Today,* October 22, 1990, 15.

23. This statement is actually Wuthnow's summary of McLuhan's basic argument. See Wuthnow, *The Struggle for America's Soul: Evangelicals, Liberals, and Secularism* (Grand Rapids: Eerdmans, 1989), 137.

24. Richard Zoglin, "And What a Reign It Was," *Time,* March 16, 1992, 64.

25. Interview with Bonnie Angelo and Jordan Bonfante, "Thanks for the Memory," *Time,* June 11, 1990, 10.

26. Ronald Reagan was the great communicator as president in part because of his ability to joke about himself. He joked about his age: "When I go in for a physical, they no longer ask how old I am. They just carbon date me." Even Reagan's political opponents were seduced by his charm. After his presidency, a collection of jokes from his speeches sold tens of thousands of video tapes. Somehow people are attracted to, and identify with, leaders who don't take themselves too seriously. See "Reagan Video Is Prime Ribbing," *Chicago Sun Times,* March 22, 1989, 20.

The knack to make light of one's abilities seems to be a component of many successful leaders. *Time* magazine reported that "connoisseurs of corporate entertainment eagerly await" the annual report written by Warren Buffet. Why? Super-investor Buffet has the ability of "mocking his own financial acumen": "Your Chairman displayed exquisite timing, I plunged into the business [USAir] at almost the exact moment that it ran into severe problems," he once reported. See "The Best of Buffet," *Time,* April 15, 1991, 45.

27. McKeon, *The Basic Works of Aristotle,* 1329–30.

Chapter 10: *Christianity Is Relevant*

1. Hybels, *Mastering Contemporary Preaching*, 32.

2. Ibid., 31.

3. **his needs will be met:** Strobel, *Inside the Mind,* 66.

directly to those needs: Barna, *The Frog in the Kettle*, 146.

4. A part of this difference in attendance is also due to who was speaking.

5. Hybels often spends hours on just the title of a talk or series in order to attract and keep his audience. Hybels explains in *Mastering Contemporary Preaching* how a large audience attended a series of talks on "What Makes a Man a Man?" and "What Makes a Woman a Woman?" When he followed these with a series on "A Portrait of Jesus" the audience dropped off (31). Again Hybels is following his mentor Robert Schuller, who says, "The secret of a growing church is so simple—find the hurt and heal it!" Schuller makes the argument in *Your Church Has Real Possibilities,* that weekend messages should be helpful and inspirational and not controversial (4, 130).

6. The actual number of occurrences of the words are *need*—386, *needs*—66, *feel*—246, *feelings*—63, *problem*—85, *feeling*—75, *wanted*—103, *pain*—128, *broken*—29, *disappointment*—26, and *hope*—64 times.

7. Hybels's "Fit to Be Tied" series on relationships averaged 13,618 individuals in attendance, while Hybels's series on Satanism, immediately preceding "Fit to Be Tied," only averaged 12,467. Lee Strobel gives an example of an important worldwide trend that has no relevance for an audience in Chicago's northwest suburbs: "You can look at the statistics worldwide and see that Islam is growing very fast. And so therefore, maybe we should address that as an issue. In our area, the choice people are making is not between Christianity and Islam, it's between Christianity and moralism or Christianity and adventurism." In other words, Islam is not relevant.

8. Barna, *The Frog in the Kettle,* 156. Barna reports, "As a nation we believe that the more different experiences we have, the more likely we will be to find fulfillment" (85).

9. Strobel, *Inside the Mind,* 50.

10. The bulletin announcement for the following week's topic read, "The music, drama and message by Bill Hybels will focus on the *fulfillment* that can be had in a personal relationship with Jesus Christ" (emphasis added).

11. I discovered this theme of personal fulfillment at all levels of Willow Creek. The church's welcome brochure for newcomers describes the church's counseling ministry: "The Counseling Center is available for those who feel that conflict, emotional pain or unresolved issues are hindering them from experiencing the freedom and *fulfillment* that Christ has offered" (emphasis added).

12. Bill Hybels, "The Changing American Dream," talk given April 29, 1989. Published in "A Day in the Life," *Willow Creek,* Special Anniversary Issue, 21.

13. **fulfilled and happy:** Hybels, *Caution,* 55.

Hybels's product: Studies in public persuasion have noted the power of linking new issues with deeply held personal desires or values. Gerald Miller describes in *Persuasion: New Directions in Theory and Research* (Beverly Hills: SAGE Publications, 1980) how individuals involved in a public relations battle over a nuclear power plant will try to connect their agenda with the audience's values: "Thus, an anti-nuclear power spokesperson may assert, 'The existence of nuclear power plants, such as Three Mile Island, poses a *threat to the safety of your family,*' while an advocate of increased development of nuclear power facilities may contend, 'Only by expanded use of nuclear power can you hope to retain the *many comforts and conveniences you now enjoy*' (18, emphasis added). Hybels is likewise linking Christianity with Harry's deep desire for personal fulfillment.

14. Hybels, *Caution,* 7.

15. Ibid., 5.

16. "A Day in the Life," 7.

17. Hybels also argues this same point: "They fear he [Christ] wants to break into their lives and rob them of the joy of living. They are sure he wants to limit their freedom and make them live in confinement. They suspect he wants to take away fulfillment, put an end to adventure." See Bill Hybels, *Who You Are When No One's Looking: Choosing Consistency, Resisting Compromise* (Downers Grove, Ill.: InterVarsity, 1987), 104.

18. As one Willow Creek convert explained, "I discovered new fulfillment, new contentment, and a sense of adventure that eclipsed everything that I've ever experienced before." Willow Creek

uses the phrase "The thrill that fulfills" to encapsulate the idea of Christianity as a fulfilling adventure.

19. **means of fulfillment:** Hybels's emphasis on fulfillment through service came partly from his relationship with Gilbert Bilezikian. Hybels recalls, "The first to give me this radical information was one of my college professors. 'Fulfillment,' he would say in a thick French accent, 'will never come through self-gratification. . . . If you really want to live, then give yourself to God and others.'" See Bill Hybels and Rob Wilkins, *Descending into Greatness* (Grand Rapids: Zondervan, 1993), 98.

with disastrous effect: Cousins says, "Too many of us have bought into a very different counsel that says, Take your paycheck, spend it on yourself, buy that which you want, and you'll be happy. And then we discover after living out that counsel that we don't end up happy; instead we end up lonely and even more unhappy."

20. Hybels explains to visitors what Willow Creek is all about: "We're learning how to get beyond our own self-centeredness and learn what our gifts are, so that we can serve others. We should find fulfillment in that."

21. **after fruitfulness:** Hybels exhorts the listeners to get involved and begin serving in the church: "The people who do that are the ones who receive back from God a multiple kind of blessing."

begins to take place: Strobel gives an example of a doctor who began serving people: "This doctor's life is so much more fulfilling and fuller, now that he sees these patients not as statistics but he sees them as people who are worthy of care and compassion because of the compassion that God has poured out on him. And so we benefit greatly when God fuels us with his compassion."

22. In my dissertation I review in more than fifty pages what Hybels teaches about each of these felt needs.

Chapter 11: *Christianity 101*

1. **Christianity does work:** Strobel, *Inside the Mind,* 56–57.

for my life: Tom Valeo, "Why Do 12,000 People Listen?" 4.

2. Kotler, *Marketing Management,* 5.

3. Cousins, *Mastering Church Management,* 79.

4. Eph. 4:26, "Do not let the sun go down while you are still angry," was used four times in the series that Hybels did on anger.

5. John 8:11 actually says, "'Woman, where are they? Has no one condemned you?' 'No one, sir,' she said. 'Then neither do I condemn you,' Jesus declared. 'Go now and leave your life of sin.'"

6. Hybels, *Mastering Contemporary Preaching,* 36. There also was a mode of preaching in the nineteenth century that was crowded with illustrations. Hatch writes, in *The Democratization of American Christianity,* "This was an age of communication entrepreneurs who stripped the sermon of its doctrinal spine and its rhetorical dress and opened it to a wide spectrum of fresh idioms: true to life passion, simplicity of structure, and dramatic creativity. Most noticeable were the uses of storytelling and overt humour" (138).

7. Elizabeth Taylor, "Taking Care of Herself," *Time,* December 10, 1990, 106. I should note that this psychological worldview is not monolithic and static. Rather it is a hodgepodge of often conflicting and competing ideas and methods.

8. For background see Robert Wuthnow, *Meaning and Moral Order: Explorations in Cultural Analysis* (Berkeley: University of California Press, 1987), 195–202.

9. Midway through the popular 1980s *Cheers* comedy show, a psychiatrist joined the cast. Eventually this psychiatrist was so popular that a new hit television show was spun off. Psychology is not only Americans' common language, it has come to be a significant source of American drama and humor. Americans like to watch, and occasionally laugh at, pompous teachers of psychological moral principle who cannot handle their own lives.

10. **vocabulary of Americans:** See Bellah et al., *Habits of the Heart,* 113ff.

a Higher Power: Richard Brookhiser, "Does Familiarity Breed Contentment?" *Time,* December 7, 1992. Clinton repeatedly called on the American people to have "the courage to change." This quote is from the Alcoholics Anonymous "Serenity Prayer."

11. Elizabeth Taylor, "Al's O.K., You're O.K.," *Time,* October 12, 1992, 60.

12. One of the major goals of the original Son City group was to "build a positive self-image" for the students. See Don Cousins, *Tomorrow's Church . . . Today,* 22.

Chapter 12: *Christianity Is True*

1. Strobel, *Inside the Mind,* 57–58.

2. Ibid., 58.

3. Ibid., 56.

4. Allan Bloom, *The Closing of the American Mind* (New York: Simon and Schuster, 1987), 25.

5. Evangelism director Mittelberg explains in "A Critical Analysis," "The task in Christian apologetics is to argue on the basis of shared pre-

suppositions and beliefs in a way that supports biblical teachings and challenges anti-Christian conclusions and theories" (126).

6. **understanding of apologetics:** Alvin Plantinga, one of the leading philosophers of religion, defines apologetics as "the attempt to defend Christianity (or more broadly, theism) against the various sorts of attacks brought against it" (Kelly James Clark, *Philosophers Who Believe: The Spiritual Journeys of 11 Leading Thinkers* [Downer's Grove, Ill.: InterVarsity Press, 1993], 69). Strobel, *Inside the Mind,* also defines apologetics as "using evidence and reasoning to defend the faith" (43).

Although this understanding of apologetics as a defense for the faith is popular, it is not entirely accurate. From Augustine's arguments against resurgent paganism in *The City of God* to evangelical Francis Schaeffer's *The God Who Is There*, Christians have often used arguments to destabilize non-Christians' worldviews. Apologetics can better be understood as the study of the process and elements of Christian persuasion. Os Guinness has sought to develop an understanding of Christian apologetics as persuasion by utilizing Peter Berger's sociology of knowledge theory. See Guinness, "Towards a Reappraisal."

for rejecting Christ: Mittelberg, "A Critical Analysis," 127.

7. Ibid., 91.

Foundational is a word that is used by Creekers to describe their apologetics, but *destabilizing* is not. Like many apologists for Christianity, Hybels is operating at an intuitive level. Although the church's specialist in evangelism and apologetics, Mark Mittelberg, was aware of this process of "destabilization," it was never discussed in depth or given a label.

8. Ibid.

9. Peter Berger and Hansfried Kellner, *Sociology Reinterpreted: An Essay on Method and Vocation* (Garden City, N.Y.: Anchor Press, 1981), 148.

Mittelberg explains in "A Critical Analysis," "An unbeliever's ruling theory against the existence of God might be broken successfully by either approach, depending on his personality, the strength of his desire to resist God, and the wisdom and skill of the apologist" (93).

10. Gallup reports in *The People's Religion* that 44 percent of the unchurched report having made a commitment to Christ, 72 percent say that Jesus is God or the Son of God, and 63 percent believe that the Bible is the inspired Word of God (140–41).

11. **religions or worldviews:** Strobel states in *Inside the Mind* that "Harry doesn't understand Christianity, but he's also ignorant about what he claims to believe in" (51).

attention and commitment: As George Barna writes in *Marketing the Church,* "The church, like it or not, is in a competitive environment" (28). Destabilization follows marketing strategy. Kotler writes in *Marketing Management* that a major part of the marketing process is to identify and "attack" various competitors (250–51).

questions of life: It has been noted in research studies that persuasive presentations are often more compelling if they first present the opposing point of view and then argue against it. One leading researcher reports, "In general, this 'two-sided' presentation was found to be more effective, especially with intelligent audiences" (Oskamp, *Attitudes and Opinions,* 215).

12. Peter Berger and Thomas Luckman, *The Social Construction of Reality* (Garden City, N.Y.: Doubleday, 1986), 102.

13. Mittelberg, "A Critical Analysis," 126.

14. **track toward God:** Strobel, *Inside the Mind,* 104.

adopting Christianity: Mittelberg, "A Critical Analysis," 126.

15. Strobel, *Inside the Mind,* 96.

16. Ibid., 51.

17. Apologetics served as a distinguished branch of Christian thought for two millennia (see Avery Dulles, *A History of Apologetics* [Philadelphia: Westminster Press, 1971]). However, in the modern era, the Christian discipline of apologetics has come into disrepute. Karl Barth, one of the most influential theologians of the twentieth century, fundamentally rejected apologetics as an exercise in bad faith. Many others, influenced by modern relativism, consider apologetics a provincial and futile endeavor. It is evangelicals, having a strong commitment to the idea that Christianity is true, who have continued to have a robust interest in apologetics. Evangelical apologetics is divided between presuppositionalists and evidentialists. Theologian Harold O. J. Brown explains that presuppositionalists "take the view that one's conclusions about the trustworthiness of Christian assertions depend largely if not entirely on one's presuppositions and that the validity of Christianity's truth claims cannot be established apart from personal conversion."

Evidentialists in contrast maintain, "There is good and sufficient evidence for the trustworthiness of many of the most important assertions of Christianity, foremost among them being the historicity of the resurrection" (Harold O. J. Brown, "The Shroud Still Mysterious," *The Religion and Society Report,* October 1990, 6). Although presuppositionalism has a large and growing following among evangelical scholars, evidentialism has proven to be more popular with rank and file evangelicals. Josh McDowell, the leading popularizer of evidential apologetics, has sold millions of copies of his books to the evangelical public (see his popular books *Evidence That Demands a Verdict* [San Bernardino, Calif.: Campus Crusade for Christ, 1972] and *More than a Carpenter* [Wheaton, Ill.: Living Books, 1977]). Willow Creek comes down firmly on the side of evidential apologetics (see Mittelberg's "A Critical Analysis").

18. Hybels argues that "the roots that will sustain your faith have a lot more to do with your mind than with your feelings. The roots that will sustain your faith through the scorching heat of the afternoon sun will be the roots of rationality."

19. Strobel described this false understanding of faith: "It's like the little girl in Sunday School who was asked one time to define faith. And she said, Well, faith is believing in something even though you know in your heart it can't be true."

20. Strobel, *Inside the Mind,* 54.

21. Mittelberg, "A Critical Analysis," 93. One gets the impression from some staff that all that is required for conversion is a skillful apologist. Yet when asked, the staff always affirm that the Holy Spirit has to do the actual conviction and conversion. Strobel explains, "I think one thing that the Holy Spirit uses in drawing people to Christ are people who are gifted in apologetics."

22. **trust the Bible:** Strobel, *Inside the Mind,* 96.

we believers do: Hybels, *Mastering Contemporary Preaching,* 34.

the Farmer's Almanac: Ibid.

Hybels says in *Mastering Contemporary Preaching,* "Some day they won't have to ask all the *why* questions but will be able to say to themselves, *Because it's in the Book; that's why.* . . . Almost every time I preach, I'm trying to build up the reliability of Scripture and increase their respect for it" (36).

23. Strobel, *Inside the Mind,* 41. Strobel acknowledges elsewhere in *Inside the Mind* the source of much of this reasoning: "I was greatly influenced by Josh McDowell, whose books *More Than a Carpenter* and *Evidence that Demands a Verdict* first opened my eyes to the possibility that a person could have an intellectually defensible faith" (30).

24. Strobel explains, "I had to ask myself, would this thing called Christianity, this phenomenon, have taken root if these men were going around proclaiming things that their audience knew were false or exaggerated?"

Chapter 13: *Willow Creek's Gospel*

1. Bilezikian, "The Great Shutout."

2. Evangelicalism summarizes the gospel in a variety of ways. There have been differences since the Reformation in how Protestants have formally defined the gospel. (See Wells, *Turning to God,* 88–89.) For example, J. I. Packer argues in *A Quest for Godliness* (Wheaton, Ill.: Crossway Books, 1990) that the Puritans defined the gospel as "the whole doctrine of the covenant of grace. . . . to preach the gospel meant to them nothing less than declaring the entire economy of redemption" (16). The value of using the Impact seminar's outline is that it is church approved. This is the outline that they teach their members and that they are seeking to communicate on the weekends to unchurched Harry. It is a list of their beliefs.

3. Cousins, *Mastering Church Management,* 80.

4. After reading this passage, Mittelberg commented, "This seems oversimplified. People are held back by their preoccupation with and ensnarement in sin, their spiritual blindness and confusion, the negative influences of peer pressure and secular culture, their pride, and through the work of Satan. But ultimately God will clear the way for them, if they'll respond to the Holy Spirit's pull and seek him and his truth."

5. Hybels, *Christians in the Marketplace* (Wheaton, Ill.: Scripture Press, 1982), 9.

6. Hybels argues that "the concept of God's holiness is the single best argument against the notion that human beings just made up the idea of there being a God. Human beings might well conjure up the notion of there being a loving deity somewhere in the universe. . . . But mistake-prone human beings would certainly stop well short of inventing an absolutely holy God who would hold them accountable to his exacting standards of holiness."

7. *Sin*—145 times, *sins*—49 times, *sinner*—40 times, *sinful*—29 times.

8. During his teaching at the New Community service, Hybels strongly affirms an evangelical doctrine of sin: "For years I have kept beating the drum around here that I really don't think a person can become truly saved, I don't think a person can really come to Christ, until he's broken by his sinfulness. Until he's staggered by it, until he looks at the holiness of God and it sucks the breath out of him and he says, I am in trouble. I cannot measure up to that standard.'"

9. Hybels used several different words in the year I studied to explain the nature of this commitment: *believe* (190 times), *faith* (198 times), *trust* (113 times), *admit* (69 times), *confess* (19

times), *repent* (26 times), and *repentance* (29 times).

10. Mark Mittelberg responded to this analysis: "He is expressing real emotions and doing it effectively as a communicator but not in a way where he is pretending to care or feel things that he really doesn't." I think this is probably true.

11. When Harrys aren't ready to make a commitment, Hybels gives them alternatives. They are invited to visit with Hybels in the "bull pen" (the front right part of the auditorium) after the service; go to the "hospitality room" to ask questions about Christianity; attend the Foundations class on the truthfulness of Christianity; go to the New Believers class, which reviews the gospel and basics about the Christian life; or buy applicable books or tapes.

Chapter 14: *Learning from Willow Creek*

1. A brief word concerning how I approached this study is necessary at this point. I began this study primarily as a researcher, but a researcher who had some initial skeptical attitudes. I realized that in order to be fair, I needed to grow in my empathy towards and understanding of Willow Creek. I sought to structure my study to listen carefully to the staff and participants. As noted in the introduction, staff and other participants have generally found my descriptions to be honest and accurate.

This is important because the analogy I have used of a sociological microscope breaks down at this point. Researchers are not emotionless computers that process information and antiseptically deduce conclusions. They have experiences, beliefs, feelings, and preferences (biases), which can influence their research.

The best way for a good researcher to deal with biases is to identify them so that their influence on the study can be reduced. I had one major bias that should be detailed at this point.

As noted in chapter 1, I first heard of Willow Creek after I moved to the Chicago area in the fall of 1983. After attending my first seeker service, I was stunned. As the service was concluding, I had the distinct impression that I had just experienced a Christian Johnny Carson show: a comedic monologue, a drama skit, musical performers, and a back-up band. Frankly I was not impressed. I did not return to Willow Creek for several years.

During the next three years, while taking classes at an evangelical seminary in the area, I occasionally heard comments about this fast-growing Willow Creek and I would respond with my unfavorable impressions (Christian Johnny Carson show, etc). With more contact with individuals involved at Willow Creek, this negative impression became somewhat modified. In 1986 my roommates and I attended Willow Creek for approximately one month. My experience was more positive than before, but I was still not attracted to the format.

In 1989 my fiancée and I wanted to attend a church together for a few months before being married. We didn't know where we were going to live after our marriage and felt we couldn't choose a permanent church home, so we decided to attend Willow Creek for a few months. We were there when I needed to find a dissertation topic.

This background is important because it helps to describe the context from which I began my study and gives perspective as to why I chose to study Willow Creek as I did. It also underlines my final assessment as a critical advocate of Willow Creek.

For further perspective on my research methodology, see the thirty-seven-page section in my dissertation. For a general background on qualitative research methodology see Steven J. Taylor and Robert Bogdan, *Introduction to Qualitative Research Methods: The Search for Meanings,* 2nd ed. (New York: John Wiley & Sons, 1984).

2. See Acts 14:1; 17:1–3; 18:4, 28; and 19:8–10.

3. Maldwyn Edwards, *John Wesley and the Eighteenth Century* (London: George Allen, 1933), 92.

4. Willow Creek staff are seeking to have not a "church service" on the weekend but primarily an evangelistic meeting.

5. Avery Dulles explains that the history of Christian apologetics is "the story of the various ways in which thoughtful Christians, in different ages and cultures, have striven to 'give a reason for the hope that was in them.'" See Dulles, *A History of Apologetics*, xvi.

The movement away from Christian persuasion has been influenced by Western culture's disinterest in the discipline of rhetoric since the early seventeenth century. When modern science (beginning with Isaac Newton) and modern philosophy (beginning with Descartes) came into prominence, Western rationality deemphasized oral rhetoric; "formal logic was in, rhetoric was out" (Stephen Toulmin, *Cosmopolis: The Hidden Agenda of Modernity* [New York: The Free Press], 31).

6. Augustine, *On Christian Doctrine,* trans. D. W. Robertson (New York: The Liberal Arts Press, 1958), 73.

7. From a biblical point of view, individuals respond to the gospel because the Holy Spirit has led them to faith. The question is whether the Holy Spirit can use a persuasive process to do this. I believe that the biblical answer to this question is a resounding yes.

Hybels has crafted most of the Willow Creek persuasive strategy; many elements (credibility, identifying, etc.) are connected to Hybels's personality and gifts and are the result of Hybels's intuitive choices and responses. Hybels's personality has served as the emotional spark for many of those who eventually converted to Christianity at Willow Creek.

8. Neil Postman, *Amusing Ourselves to Death*, 105.

9. "The European Connection," *Willow Creek*, July/August 1990, 24–25.

10. **skilled in speaking:** James Graves, "Education and Community," *Chronicles*, September 1990, 26–27.

opinions are divided: McKeon, *The Basic Works of Aristotle*, 1329.

11. Cousins, *Mastering Church Management*, 81.

12. Peter Brown, *Augustine of Hippo* (Berkeley, Calif.: University of California Press, 1969), 251.

13. Henry Chadwick, *The Enigma of St. Paul* (London: Athlone Press, 1969), 275.

14. Sociologist David Martin argues that this ability to so identify with the different strata of society has given American Christianity its unique vitality, in contrast to the secularization of the European church: "Disassociate religion from social authority and high culture, let religion adapt to every status group through every variety of pulsating sectarianism. The result is that nobody feels ill at ease with his religion, that faith is distributed along the political spectrum, that church is never the axis of dispute." See David Martin, *A General Theory of Secularization* (Oxford: Blackwell, 1978), 30, 36.

15. Tina Rosenberg, "From Dissidents to MTV Democrats," *Harper's*, September 1992, 48.

16. **discourse and exhortation:** Hatch, *The Democratization of American Christianity*, 136, 104.

of the working class: "Counting England's Flock," *Christianity Today*, February 5, 1990, 29.

17. Protestantism's cultural sensitivity and flexibility also makes it more susceptible to cultural compromise. Protestantism lacks Roman Catholicism's or Orthodoxy's leadership hierarchy and historical gravity, and consequentially liberal theology was Protestantism's illegitimate offspring.

18. Barna, *Marketing the Church*, 33, 146. MacArthur writes in *Ashamed of the Gospel* "that those who desired to be embraced as 'relevant' by a changing world could not and would not long remain faithful to the unchanging Word of God" (135).

19. See Matt. 9:36–38; 11:28–30; Mark 8:11–12; 10:17–31; 13:1–6; Luke 10:25–37; 14:7–11; John 3:1–13; 4:5–28.

20. Walter Hollenweger, *Evangelism Today: Good News or Bone of Contention* (Belfast, Ireland: Christian Journals Ltd., 1976) 80, 82; quoted in Guinness's "Towards a Reappraisal," 310.

21. E. F. Harrison comments that "Christ is the effulgence of the divine glory (Heb. 1:3). By means of him the perfection of the nature of God is made known to men." See *Evangelical Dictionary of Theology*, ed. Walter Elwell (Grand Rapids: Baker, 1984), 443.

22. Otto Friedrich, "Headed for the Dustheap," *Time*, February 19, 1990, 37.

23. John Stott, "A Resurgence of Evangelical Scholarship," *Christianity Today*, October 5, 1992.

24. Hunter, *American Evangelicalism*, 13.

25. **plausibility is not new:** The concept of plausibility is distinct from credibility. Credibility addresses the objective truthfulness of an idea. Plausibility raises the question of its believability in a particular context. Sociological theory suggests that plausibility has a strong social component. For example, Roman Catholic Christianity appears more plausible in Catholic Ireland than in Islamic Mecca. The social context provides supports that make a particular belief more or less plausible or believable. In Berger's words, there are "plausibility structures" that support beliefs. Berger argues in *The Social Construction of Reality* that "subjective reality is thus always dependent upon specific plausibility structures, that is, the specific social base and social processes required for its maintenance" (154).

possessed by everybody: Aristotle, *The Basic Works of Aristotle*, 1328.

26. Hatch, *The Democratization of American Christianity*, 136.

27. Hybels's apologetics are not very persuasive for the typical academic. To one who has received graduate training in philosophy or history, Hybels's arguments appear rather thin.

This is not to suggest that the philosophical and historical arguments for Christianity are not credible in themselves. There is a growing movement within the broader academic community that historic Christianity is intellectually credible. See Kelly James Clark, *Philosophers Who Believe: The Spiritual Journeys of 11 Leading Thinkers* (Downers Grove, Ill.: InterVarsity Press,

1993), and Terry Miethe, *Did Jesus Rise from the Dead? The Resurrection Debate* (San Francisco: Harper and Row, 1987).

The fact that Hybels's arguments are plausible, but not academically credible, reflects a basic reality of modern life. Academic thinking could be considered an entirely different way of thinking from the commonsense thinking of the man on the street. Intellectuals are trained in modern research tools and analysis. Hybels's popular argument is not directed at this group but at the rank and file Harrys of the suburbs. Jonathan Alter comments in *Time* that one of the distinctive difficulties of modern communication "is to talk to intellectuals and the public at the same time" (Jonathan Alter, "The Intellectual Hula Hoop," *Time*, October 9, 1989, 39).

28. Hatch, *The Democratization of American Christianity*, 104.

Chapter 15: *The Christian Worldview and Culture*

1. Raymond Williams, "Culture and Civilization," *The Encyclopedia of Philosophy,* vol. 2 (New York: Macmillan, 1967), 273–76.

2. Augustine, *On Christian Doctrine,* 75.

3. See H. Richard Niebuhr's typology of various models in *Christ and Culture* (New York: Harper and Row, 1951).

Chapter 16: *The Temptation of Image*

1. Lee Strobel responded to this analysis: "Every moment is not scripted. . . . However, much of what takes place is planned out in advance. If you were going to stand in front of 5,000 people, you might want to have a game plan concerning what you are going to say and do. If you want to honor God with your service to him, you want to do the hard work of preparing. If people's eternities are at stake, you want to be as effective and clear as possible."

I would agree with Strobel's desire to be faithful. The point of my analysis is that Willow Creek has developed a new way of doing church that is a self-conscious performance designed to achieve external goals. My desire is to map out his new method and its potentially built-in weaknesses.

2. Barna, *Marketing the Church,* 34.

3. Erving Goffman develops the image management idea at some length in *The Presentation of Self in Everyday Life* (Garden City, N.J.: Doubleday, Anchor Books, 1959). See Dick Keyes' articles on "Image and Reality in Society" in *What in the World Is Real?* ed. Gregory A. Pritchard (Champaign, Ill.: Communication Institute, 1982), 71–101.

4. "Avoiding Fumbles," *Harper's,* January 1992, 28–29.

5. Ann-Liza Kozma, "Meet Your New Neighbors: The Imitations," *Chicago Tribune*, October 31, 1993, sec. 6, 5.

6. "Accentuate the Negative," *Harper's*, November 1990, 17–18.

7. The same trend is true of the democratic liberals. One leading liberal law professor argues, "Polling data suggest that, if the prochoice movement is to maintain its momentum, it cannot let the prolife side shift the debate to *why* a woman wants any given abortion. The movement's current popularity clearly depends on keeping the question focused on *who* will make the decision." Quoted in Mary Ann Glendon, "Intra-Tribal Warfare," *First Things,* August/ September 1990, 57.

8. Michael Kramer, "Moving In," *Time,* January 4, 1993, 33.

9. Leaders in a democratic environment often shape their image and message to their audience. Clinton is an excellent communicator. Part of his skill in communication is this ability to discern the central beliefs and attitudes of his audience. He is often able to present an image of how he is similar to his audience and is fighting for their concerns. Embedded in this maneuver is Clinton's deep desire to be liked. As one of Clinton's advisors explained, his "will to please is so strong that it is interfering with his effectiveness" (George J. Church, "His Seven Most Urgent Decisions," *Time,* January 25, 1993, 28).

10. Schuller, *Your Church Has Real Possibilities*, 125, 128, 127, 14.

11. Ron Berler, "Managing Crises, On-field and Off," *Chicago Sun Times,* November 25, 1990, 49.

12. *Intelligence Interrogation,* Headquarters, Department of the Army, FM34–52, 3–4.

13. *Willow Creek* Special Anniversary Issue, 32.

14. The speakers evidently had not given these principles a great deal of attention. Lee Strobel suggested that his role was that of a lawyer—to present evidence before a jury and to argue for the truthfulness of a case. When I raised the fact to him that lawyers pay for research to know which emotions to manipulate, he said that he had never thought of that.

15. Obviously those individuals who are involved in drama are seeking to project an image that is not true of who they are. The staff were referring to singers and speakers with these ethical principles.

16. Raymond Collins, *Studies on the First Letter to the Thessalonians* (Leuven, Belgium: Leuven University Press, 1984), 238.

17. Howard Marshall, *1 and 2 Thessalonians* (Grand Rapids: Eerdmans, 1983), 65.

Chapter 17: *The Quagmire of Psychology*

1. **accommodation and resistance:** Berger, *Sacred Canopy,* 156.

theologically plausible: Hunter, *Making Sense of Modern Times,* 151–52. Like much sociological theory, the categories of accommodation and resistance highlight certain facts and obscure others. While this division is helpful and groups do tend to fall on either side of this basic divide, this conflict could also be portrayed as a long continuum between a fully resisting fundamentalist like Bob Jones to a fully accommodating television evangelist like Robert Schuller.

2. MacArthur is one of the few fundamentalists who has a significant impact on the broader evangelical movement. Most other fundamentalists, following separatist doctrine, want nothing to do with evangelicals, whom they see as compromising the faith. This doctrine of separation from the world makes the fundamentalists combative toward the psychological worldview. See John MacArthur, *Our Sufficiency in Christ* (Dallas: Word, 1991), 66, 59.

3. Hunter, *Making Sense of Modern Times,* 151–52.

4. "Evangelicalism: An interview with Marshall Shelley," *Faith and Renewal,* July/August 1992, 11.

5. See "Recovery Books Turn Problems into Best Sellers," *Christianity Today,* September 16, 1991, 70; and "In Brief" news section, *Christianity Today,* March 7, 1994, 47. The best description and analysis of this influence is still Hunter's *American Evangelicalism* and *Evangelicalism: The Coming Generation.*

6. **aware of it:** Only a few evangelicals have written critically about psychology. See, for example, essays by Os Guinness and Paul Vitz in *No God But God: Breaking with the Idols of Our Age,* Os Guinness and John Seel eds. (Chicago: Moody Press, 1992); and essays by David Powlison and Edward Welch in *Power Religion: The Selling Out of the Evangelical Church,* Michael Scott Horton, ed. (Chicago: Moody Press, 1992).

articles and editorials: See Tim Stafford's complimentary articles in *Christianity Today,* "The Therapeutic Revolution," May 17, 1993, and "Franchising Hope," May 18, 1992; David Neff's article "Summer Camp for Troubled Adults," May 18, 1992; and the editorial by Stanton L. Jones defending psychology, "Demonizing the Head Doctors," *Christianity Today*, September 16, 1991, 21. *Christianity Today* over the last twenty years has increasingly become a popular magazine and less a source of substantial analysis. The very fact that *Christianity Today* would have a popular writer—rather than a sociologist, historian, or theologian—write about such a massive shift is an indication of how naively they approached the topic. This popular gullibility is also visible in the fact that they choose as an author one who is very optimistic about evangelical use of psychology and whose wife has an M.A. in psychology. This seems to be a clear example of intellectual nepotism: choosing a critic who is actually an advocate. Only rarely has *Christianity Today* published articles more critical of psychology, such as "Psychobabble" by Robert C. Roberts, May 16, 1994, 18–24.

7. Mike Singletary with Jerry Jenkins, *Singletary on Singletary* (Nashville: Thomas Nelson, 1991), 106.

8. See the best-seller report for the Willow Creek bookstore from May 1989 to May 1990. Many of these were evangelical psychological self-help books.

9. Melody Beattie, *Codependent No More* (San Francisco: Harper, 1987); David Keirsey and Marilyn Bates, *Please Understand Me: Character & Temperament Types* (Del Mar, Calif.: Prometheus Nemesis Book Company, 1984); Henry Cloud, *When Your World Makes No Sense* (Nashville: Thomas Nelson, 1990).

10. Cloud, *When Your World Makes No Sense,* 16–17.

11. Ibid., 17.

12. The counselor told me that the counseling center is normally a "short-term place—six months or under. . . . So if someone comes in with a long-term problem, that person will often be sent to someone outside." Since I completed my study I have heard that the church has restructured the counseling center.

13. One counselor explained to me, "I've made it my job to go to each of the ministries and do a lot of speaking and teaching and showing how therapy really could help people continue to grow spiritually and relationally."

I was told that therapists are required to have taken some courses in Bible and theology. Yet this training doesn't provide a clear theological framework that could provide control beliefs for psychological integration. This isn't to suggest that there is no theology held in common by the center's therapists. They would all affirm the church's statement of faith and are required not to teach against "the pulpit." Yet in practice, there is little guidance given concerning the validity of various psychological ideas. Therapists counsel individuals with whatever psychological categories they find useful.

14. Paul C. Vitz, *Psychology As Religion: The Cult of Self-Worship* (Grand Rapids: Eerdmans, 1977).

15. Brown, *Augustine of Hippo*, 245, 366.

16. Dennis Groh, *Augustine: Religion of the Heart* (Nashville: Graded Press, 1988), 32. One's understanding of human nature is a foundation stone for one's ethic.

17. As Brown describes in *Augustine of Hippo*, "Latin Christian piety could never be the same again" (245).

18. A full explanation of Neoplatonism and its influence on Augustine is beyond the purpose of this section. For more information see the brief bibliography in Augustine, *Eighty-three Different Questions*, trans. David Mosher, vol. 70 of *The Fathers of the Church* (Washington, D.C.: Catholic University of America Press, 1982), 30.

19. Brown, *Augustine of Hippo*, 245.

20. John Burnaby, ed., *Augustine: Later Works* (Philadelphia: Westminster Press, 1953), 255.

21. **life's necessities:** Burnaby, *Amor Dei: A Study of the Religion of St. Augustine* (London: Hodder and Stoughton, 1947), 43.

in the body: Brown, *Augustine of Hippo*, 245.

love his enemies: Ibid., 142. By the end of his life, Augustine had become aware of the effect of his Neoplatonic ideas on his teaching and tried to recant from them.

"I have rightly been displeased, too, with the praise with which I extolled Plato or the Platonists, or the Academic philosophers beyond what was proper for such irreligious men, especially those against whose great errors Christian teaching must be defended." See Augustine, *The Retractions*, trans. Sister Mary Inez Brogan, vol. 60 of *The Fathers of the Church* (Washington, D.C.: Catholic University of America Press, 1968), 10.

Yet Augustine was not able to untangle all of the elements of Neoplatonic ideas from his theology. Even in his last days, while his city was under siege, his biographer writes how he "was comforted by the words of a certain wise man"—Plotinus, his Neoplatonic tutor (Brown, *Augustine of Hippo*, 425–26. See also 26–27).

22. Hunter, *American Evangelicalism*, 94.

23. Ibid., 95.

24. *Leadership*, Winter 1993, 21.

25. John Calvin, *Institutes of the Christian Religion*, ed. John T. McNeil (Philadelphia: Westminster Press, 1960), 35, 37. A modern attempt to respond more biblically to the problem of identity is Dick Keyes, *Beyond Identity: Finding Your Self in the Image and Character of God* (Ann Arbor, Mich.: Servant Books, 1984).

26. Rob Wilkins, "The Second Chance of a Lifetime," *Willow Creek*, March/April 1991, 20.

27. Some elements of psychological theory are more useful and less dangerous to a biblical ethic. For example, the use of psychological theory in the Network seminar is more integrated into a broader biblical understanding of human nature. Although the seminar could be significantly improved, it is markedly better than the general use of psychological theory in the church. The four-week Network seminar—that more than five thousand Creekers have attended—is structured to help individuals understand their spiritual gifts, their passions, and their temperament. Individuals generally find this seminar very valuable in providing a basic framework for self-understanding.

28. Roberts, "Psychobabble," 22.

29. Ibid., 23.

30. Ibid., 22–23.

31. Beattie, *Codependent No More*, 51.

32. The psychological worldview also provides powerful analytical tools to condemn those who we perceive have hurt or offended us (Beattie, *Codependent No More*, iii, 109).

33. The complete summary statement reads: "A spouse is free from a broken marriage covenant if, in the discernment of those to whom they are spiritually accountable, this spouse has a soft heart and their spouse is unwilling to be a viable marriage partner." Biblical language is set aside in this policy in favor of the psychological terminology "soft heart" and "viable marriage partner."

34. It should be noted that it is not possible with the above evidence to prove a causal relationship between Willow Creek's weekend attenders' psychological ethics and their illicit sexual activity. There are probably several causes of this phenomenon. For example, a contributing cause of this problem is probably the lack of substantial relationships with fellow Christians among the majority of the attenders. I found that less than 10 percent of the lay people I interviewed had accountable relationships with others at Willow Creek. However, to argue that there is no relationship between Creekers' psychological worldview and their sexual behavior ignores this conspicuous data.

35. Part of the problem is that at present there are few resources that provide a more biblical model and tools of spiritual, psychological, and relational growth. For an example of a more judicious integration of psychological theory within a biblical worldview, see Richard Winter, *The Roots of Sorrow: Reflections on Depression and*

Hope (Westchester, Ill.: Crossway Books, 1986). There is a great need for further publications of a biblically rooted framework and methods for spiritual, relational, and emotional growth.

36. E. M. Blaiklock, *New Bible Dictionary* (Grand Rapids: Eerdmans, 1979), 886.

37. Gallup, *The People's Religion*, 141.

38. **sufficiently biblical:** I was also told that Hybels again retreated from this tendency in 1993. In the fall of 1993, instead of following his normal pattern of teaching topically, Hybels decided to teach through the Gospel of Matthew.

it went over with everybody: Singletary, *Singletary on Singletary*, 106.

39. Hunter, *Making Sense of Modern Times*, 151–52.

Chapter 18: *The Allure of Marketing*

1. MacArthur, *Ashamed of the Gospel*, 121.

2. Bill Hybels and Mark Mittelberg, *Becoming a Contagious Christian* (Grand Rapids: Zondervan, 1994), 14–15.

3. See Nathan Hatch, *The Democratization of American Religion;* and Jon Butler, *Awash in a Sea of Faith: Christianizing the American People* (Cambridge, Mass.: Harvard University Press, 1990). Recent sociology of religion studies have also begun to emphasize that the context of American religions is a marketplace. Stephen Warner argues that a "new paradigm" is beginning to emerge that presents "the idea that religious institutions in the United States operate within an open market." See Warner's overview of the general field of the sociology of religion and apologia for this new paradigm (R. Stephen Warner, "Work in Progress toward a New Paradigm for the Sociological Study of Religion in the United States," *American Journal of Sociology* 98, no. 5 [March 1993]: 1044–93).

4. Bellah, *Habits of the Heart*, 71–75.

5. This illustrates the influence of cultural background on one's view of Scripture. Sometimes one's culture helps one see certain truths of Scripture more clearly. At the same time, one's culture often tends to distort how one understands and explains the whole of Scripture.

6. Barna, *Marketing the Church*, 50.

7. Earl Shorris, "A Nation of Salesmen," *Harper's*, October 1994, 46.

8. Ibid.

9. Bellah, *Habits of the Heart*, 71–75.

10. Shorris, "A Nation of Salesmen," 41.

11. *The Wall Street Journal*, special report on education, February 9, 1990, R25.

12. **only thing that matters:** Schuller argues, in *Your Church Has Real Possibilities*, "One thing is certain: *a church must never stop growing.* When it ceases to grow, it will start to die" (125, author's emphasis).

its market area: Barna, *Marketing the Church*, 14.

13. Hybels, *Descending into Greatness*, 116.

14. Barna, *The Frog in the Kettle*, 138.

15. "Targeting the Stoned Cyberpunk," *Harper's*, December 1994, 24, 26.

16. Shorris, "A Nation of Salesmen," 43.

17. Barna, *Marketing the Church*, 51.

18. Ibid., 33.

19. Hornblower, "Advertising Spoken Here," 71.

20. Lewis Lapham, "Notebook," *Harper's*, September 1992, 9.

21. Schuller, "Hard Questions for Robert Schuller about Sin and Self-Esteem," 19–20.

22. Hybels, *Christians in the Marketplace*, 98.

23. In one of Hybels's more recent books is the statement, "Curiously, Christianity, in its purest form, is not bent on human fulfillment" (*Descending into Greatness*, 204). I was puzzled by this departure from Willow Creek's fulfillment theology and so interviewed Hybels's co-author Rob Wilkins. Wilkins admitted that although he used many of Hybels's transcripts, he was the primary author of the book and only met with Hybels on a few occasions to discuss the book. Wilkins emphasized that while much of the content came from Hybels, this particular idea was probably his contribution.

24. Philip Rieff quoted in Guinness, *No God But God*, 130.

25. Alexis de Tocqueville, *Democracy in America* (New York: Vintage Books, 1945), 130.

26. Ibid.

27. Ibid., 134.

28. This self-orientation was visible in Creekers' descriptions of their involvement in the church. At times individuals explained their serving in the church as if it were merely an act of selfishness. One volunteer explains why he volunteers to repair vacuum cleaners: "Let's just say it's a little bit selfish. I get satisfaction out of it, and it makes pleasant companionship" (John Bollow, "Serving God in a Vacuum," *Willow Creek*, January/February 1991, 9). *Willow Creek* magazine explains why another volunteer helps to repair cars: "It's kind of selfish motivation, really. . . . [He] has come to grips with the fact that self-fulfillment comes through self-abandonment" (Rob Wilkins, "Covert Operation," *Willow Creek*, September/October 1990, 16). I do not believe that this kind of service is merely selfishness. But the fact that individuals resorted to using this kind of language to describe their service shows how deeply this mindset is a part of Willow Creek.

29. **without exception:** Augustine, *The City of God,* trans. Gerald Walsh, S. J., and Daniel Honan, vol. 8 of *Fathers of the Church* (New York: Fathers of the Church, Inc., 1954), 230.

through knowing it: *Eighty-three Different Questions,* trans. Mosher, 66.

30. Augustine, *The Catholic and Manichaean Ways of Life,* trans. Donald Gallagher and Idella Gallagher, vol. 56 of *The Fathers of the Church* (Washington, D.C.: The Catholic University of America Press, 1966), 6.

31. **what he loves:** Ibid., 5–6.

because of you: Augustine, *The Confessions of St. Augustine,* trans. Rex Warner (New York: New American Library of World Literature, 1951), 229, 232.

32. **an assured thing:** Augustine, *The City of God,* vol. 7, 202.

a happy life: Augustine, *The Retractions,* 12. See Burnaby's *Amor Dei,* 98–100.

33. George Gallup Jr., "Religion in America," *The Annals,* July 1985, 169.

34. David A. Hall's interview with David Larson, "Holy Health," *Christianity Today,* November 23, 1992, 19.

35. Gallup, *Religion in America 1990,* 7.

36. For an example of a more biblical response to the topic of fulfillment see John Calvin, *Institutes of the Christian Religion,* bk 2, 4, 6.

Chapter 19: *The Mirror of God's Face*

1. Strobel, *Inside the Mind*, 161.

2. Erickson, *Christian Theology*, 302.

3. This emphasis on God's love was present from the Son City youth group. Don Cousins explains in *Tomorrow's Church* that the central theme of the messages should be "communicating God's love" (23).

4. The word *father* was used 224 times during weekend messages.

5. If we don't receive God's love, Hybels argues, God becomes a frustrated and yet persistent lover: "Often we don't receive the love that God offers. And so this introduces God's second primary emotion—frustration" (Hybels, *Caution: Christians Under Construction*, 49–50). This emphasis on God's emotions seems to elicit some rather odd statements from Hybels: "After creating our world, God acknowledged that it was very good. . . . It appears to me that He had the *emotional vulnerability* to tell everyone who reads His Book that the labor of His hands brought Him tremendous pleasure (Hybels, *Christians in the Marketplace*, 16, emphasis added).

6. Hybels, *Seven Wonders*, 7.

The emphasis on a compassionate God was visible in the staff's descriptions of how God has related to them. One said, "I learned more about God's grace and his love and his friendliness and his kindness and his intimacy and his warmth."

7. Wuthnow, *The Restructuring of American Religion: Society and Faith Since World War II* (Princeton, N.J.: Princeton University Press, 1988), 300.

8. Hybels, *Seven Wonders,* 137.

9. **its upbeat message:** "The Theater Days," *Willow Creek*, Special Anniversary Issue, 34.

close to them: Wuthnow, *The Restructuring of American Religion*, 303.

he cares: Beattie, *Codependent No More*, 99.

reached by prayers: Gallup, *Religion in America 1990*, 21.

loving compassion: Wuthnow notes in *The Restructuring of American Religion*, "College graduates are about twice as likely as those without college education to be most impressed by Jesus' compassion and forgiveness" (300).

10. Gallup, *Religion in America 1990*, 7.

11. There were also 67 references to the Holy Spirit. Thus, although the word *holy* was used 67 times, it was used as a name and not in reference to God's holiness. Many of the uses of *holiness* refer to how God wants individuals to walk in holiness. Therefore, these references would not be referring to God's holiness. So a significant percentage of the total 145 references are not referring to God's holiness at all. It also should be noted that many of the times the words *love* and *kind* were used, they were also not referring to God's nature.

12. Hybels emphasized, "When's the last time we thanked him for writing down holy laws that serve as moral landmarks for those of us who float around on society's seas of relativism?"

13. Ewald M. Plass, comp., *What Luther Says*, vol. 2 (Saint Louis: Concordia, 1959), 757.

14. Ibid., 758.

15. Calvin, *Institutes of the Christian Religion*, 369.

16. Ibid., 355.

17. In the days immediately before his conversion, Wesley wrote to a friend and described how he was convicted by God's moral law: "I am under the same condemnation. I see that the whole law of God is holy, just and good [cf. Rom. 7:12]. I know every thought, every temper of my soul, ought to bear God's image and superscription. But how am I fallen from the glory of God! I feel that I am sold under sin [Rom. 7:14]. I know that I too deserve nothing but wrath, being full of all abominations; and having no good thing in me to atone for them, or to remove the wrath of God."

See Albert C. Outler, ed., *John Wesley* (New York: Oxford University Press, 1964), 60.

In his famous Aldersgate conversion, Wesley affirms, "I did trust in Christ, Christ alone for salvation; and an assurance was given me that he had taken away *my* sins, even *mine*, and saved *me* from the law of sin and death" (Ibid., 66, 232–33, author's emphasis).

18. Ibid., 233. All three theologians are using *law* as a synonym for God's law as seen in the Ten Commandments and the general corpus of Old Testament law.

19. J. I. Packer, *A Quest for Godliness,* 169.

20. Jaroslav Pelikan, *Jesus Through the Centuries* (New York: Harper and Row, 1985), 2.

21. Peter Berger, *A Rumor of Angels: Modern Society and the Rediscovery of the Supernatural* (New York: Anchor Books, 1981), 7.

22. Peter Berger quoted in David Singer, "The Unmodern Jew," *First Things*, June/July 1991, 20. Curiously, the conservative, in his attempt to affirm the historical truth of his tradition, often unconsciously baptizes cultural elements that have attached themselves to his tradition. By this uncritical affirmation, he is often preaching an older cultural adaption rather than a newer one.

23. **Holy Communion:** Berger, *A Rumor of Angels*, 19.

the Christian tradition: Ibid., 9–10.

24. Schuller, *Your Church Has Real Possibilities,* 137. Schuller continues, "See how many positive emotions you can identify. Now make an equally long list of negative emotions and vow never to let your message—or your pulpit announcements, or the words of the anthems, hymns, or prayers—be allowed if they send out and stimulate negative vibrations."

25. Peter Berger quoted by Singer in "The Unmodern Jew," 20.

26. Hunter, *American Evangelicalism*, 87.

27. Some individuals may attend New Community once or twice a month. My purpose is merely to note that the vast majority of weekend attenders do not attend the weekday services.

28. This is based on his questionable judgment that $30,000 is the average yearly income for church attenders. Since most of the participants own homes in the upscale northwest suburbs it is highly unlikely that they are making only $30,000.

29. For example, while Paul uses the adjective *hagios* (holy) 76 times and the verb *hagiazo* (holy) 9 times, he also uses the noun *agape* (love) 75 times and the verb *agapao* (love) 34 times. For brief definitions and the varied uses of these words see Walter Bauer, William Arndt, and F. Wilbur Gingrich, *A Greek-English Lexicon of the New Testament and Other Early Christian Literature* (Chicago: University of Chicago Press, 1958).

Chapter 20: *The Loss of Truth*

1. *Emotions Anonymous*, Emotions Anonymous International, St. Paul, Minn., 1978, 2.

2. This movement away from academic education is true of a growing circle of evangelical churches. See, for example, "Re-Engineering the Seminary," *Christianity Today,* October 24, 1994, 74–77.

3. In response to this section, Lee Strobel commented that Willow Creek's emphasis on psychology increased after hiring a theologically trained pastor. He noted that theological education is no guarantee that psychological categories won't be misused. His point is valid, as there certainly are theologically trained pastors who have become captivated by psychology. Yet, as a rule, those individuals who have spent years studying to understand the language, history, and theology of the Bible have more resources at hand with which to be critical of the culture's categories.

4. Hybels challenged the congregation, "I think we've got a lot of cosmetic worshipers here at Willow Creek—skin-deep exalters, superficial praise givers—whose lives do not have as a central theme this river of worship that's heading toward God." The result of this exhortation was that more than six hundred people were baptized in the following weeks.

5. It is very difficult for Americans to see themselves clearly. Sometimes the most insightful analysis of American evangelicals comes from outside our culture. Romanian Christian leader Josif Ton was repeatedly arrested by his Communist government before deportation to America in 1980. After living in America for more than ten years, he was awarded an honorary doctorate at Wheaton College. In his speech at this event, Ton commented on American evangelicals' understanding of Jesus: "Look at the Jesus most of your evangelists present to the masses. This is a Jesus that gives peace, that heals the wounds, that gives inner satisfaction, self-esteem, and especially prosperity. Brothers and sisters, this is not the Jesus of the New Testament.

"The Jesus presented in the New Testament is the King! He is the one who calls people on his terms, who calls them to surrender their own selves, to participate in his sufferings for a lost world, to self-sacrifice. I am afraid that these are lost concepts in most of the evangelical churches of the West today" (Josif Ton, "The Cornerstone at the Crossroads," *Wheaton Alumni*, August/September 1991, 8).

6. Darrel Schultz, "Second Thoughts on Swimming in 'Willow Creek,'" *Christian Week*, October 19, 1993, 9.

7. One staff member explained to me how Hybels read John MacArthur's book *The Gospel According to Jesus* in his 1988 study break and told the staff, "This is probably the single most influential book as it relates to the gospel that I have maybe ever read." Hybels confessed one Sunday morning, "Friends, I'm haunted often by the question of what's really going on in this church. How many of us have been vaccinated with a mild case of Christianity? How many among us have the real disease?"

8. There is a tendency of American leaders to not want to be identified as "academic." Melvin Maddocks reviewed George Bush's attempts to be a "Good Old Boy" and then commented, "For an American politician, the charge of being an intellectual is about as close to defamation of character as name-calling gets" (*World Monitor*, August 1990, 79). There is often a skepticism toward academics by the man on the street. As Robert Oliver explains in *The Psychology of Persuasive Speech*, "The thoroughgoing 'intellectual' is always regarded with distrust by the masses of the people" (175).

9. The education occurring at evangelical seminaries needs to be analyzed.

10. Hybels, *Caution: Christians under Construction*, 76.

11. Tom Peters and Nancy Austin, *A Passion for Excellence: The Leadership Difference* (New York: Random House, 1985).

12. Hatch, *The Democratization of American Christianity*, 197, 134–35.

13. Bilezikian, "The Great Shutout," 1.

14. Bill Hybels, "Reading Your Gauges," *Leadership*, 1991, 38.

15. Lynne Hybels, "Watching Lessons," *Willow Creek*, July/August 1990, 30.

16. For a critique of this theological system see Jerram Barrs and Ranald Macaulay, *Being Human* (Downers Grove, Ill.: InterVarsity Press, 1978).

Afterword

1. Brown, *Augustine of Hippo*, 353.

Bibliography

"Accentuate the Negative," *Harper's* (November 1990), 17–18.

"A Day in the Life," *Willow Creek* (September/October 1989), 4–33.

Alter, Jonathan. "The Intellectual Hula Hoop," *Time* (October 9, 1989), 39.

Ames, Roger, ed. *Sun-Tzu: The Art of Warfare*. New York: Ballantine Books, 1993.

Ammerman, Nancy Tatom. "Fundamentalist World View: Ideology and Social Structure in an Independent Fundamental Church." Ph.D. diss., Yale University, 1983.

Angelo, Bonnie, and Jordan Bonfante, "Thanks for the Memory," *Time* (June 11, 1990), 10.

Aristotle. *The Basic Works of Aristotle*. Ed. by Richard McKeon. New York: Random House, 1941.

Augustine. *The Catholic and Manichaean Ways of Life*. Vol. 56 in *The Fathers of the Church*. Trans. by Donald Gallagher and Idella Gallagher. Washington, D.C.: The Catholic University of America Press, 1966.

———. *Eighty-three Different Questions*. Vol. 70 in *The Fathers of the Church*. Trans. by David L. Mosher. Washington, D.C.: The Catholic University of America Press, 1982.

———. *Later Works*. Ed. by John Burnaby. Philadelphia: Westminster Press, 1953.

———. *On Christian Doctrine*. Trans. by D. W. Robertson. New York: The Free Press, 1958.

———. *The City of God*. Vol. 8 in *The Fathers of the Church*. Trans. by Gerald Walsh, S. J., and Daniel Honan. New York: The Catholic University of America Press, 1954.

———. *The Retractions*. Vol. 60 in *The Fathers of the Church*. Trans. by Sister Mary Inez Brogan. Washington, D.C.: The Catholic University of America Press, 1968.

———. *The Confessions of St. Augustine*. Trans. by Rex Warner. New York: New American Library of World Literature, 1963.

"Avoiding Fumbles," *Harper's* (January 1992), 28–29.

Balmer, Randall. *Mine Eyes Have Seen the Glory: A Journey into the Evangelical Subculture of America*. New York: Oxford University Press, 1989.

Barna, George. *The Frog in the Kettle*. Ventura, Calif.: Regal Books, 1990.

———. *Marketing the Church*. Colorado Springs: Navpress, 1988.

Barrs, Jerram, and Ranald Macaulay. *Being Human*. Downers Grove, Ill.: InterVarsity Press, 1978.

Beattie, Melody. *Codependent No More*. San Francisco: Harper and Hazelton, 1987.

Bellah, Robert N., Richard Madsen, William M. Sullivan, Ann Swidler, and Steven M. Tipton. *Habits of the Heart: Individualism and Commitment in American Life*. Berkeley, Calif.: University of California Press, 1985.

Bennett, William. *The Index of Leading Cultural Indicators*. Washington, D.C.: The Heritage Foundation, 1993.

Berger, Peter. "Consciousness Raising: To Whom—By Whom?" *Social Policy* (September/October 1974), 38–42.

———. *A Rumor of Angels: Modern Society and the Rediscovery of the Supernatural*. New York: Anchor Books, 1969.

———. *The Sacred Canopy: Elements of a Sociological Theory of Religion*. New York: Doubleday, 1969.

Berger, Peter, and Hansfried Kellner. *Sociology Reinterpreted: An Essay on Method and Vocation*. Garden City, N.Y.: Anchor Press, 1981.

Berger, Peter, and Thomas Luckman. *The Social Construction of Reality*. Garden City, N.Y.: Doubleday, 1986.

Berler, Ron. "Managing Crises, On-field and Off," *Chicago Sun Times* (November 25, 1990), 49.

"The Best of Buffet," *Time* (April 15, 1991), 45.

Bilezikian, Gilbert. *Christianity 101*. Grand Rapids: Zondervan, 1993.

———. "A Vision for the Church," *Willow Creek* (September/October 1990), 21.

Blanchard, Kenneth. *Leadership and the One Minute Manager.* New York: William Morrow and Co., 1985.

Bloom, Allan. *The Closing of the American Mind.* New York: Simon and Schuster, 1987.

Briggs, Ken. "How Does God Speak to People Today?" *Emerging Trends* 9, no 2, 1–2.

Brookhiser, Richard. "Does Familiarity Breed Contentment?" *Time* (December 7, 1992), 86.

Brown, Harold O. J. "The Shroud Still Mysterious," *The Religion and Society Report* (October 1990), 6.

Brown, Peter. *Augustine of Hippo.* Berkeley, Calif.: University of California Press, 1969.

Brushaber, George. "Marketing the Jesus Franchise," *Christianity Today* (June 22, 1992), 17.

Bugbee, Bruce. *Network.* Pasadena, Calif.: Charles E. Fuller Institute of Evangelism and Church Growth, 1989.

Burdan, Steve. "Resources for the Christian Year," unpublished paper.

———. "Willow Creek Plays Up Drama to the Seekers," *Worship Leader* (February/March 1992), 11.

Burnaby, John. *Amor Dei.* London: Hodder and Stoughton, 1947.

Butler, Jon. *Awash in a Sea of Faith: Christianizing the American People.* Cambridge, Mass.: Harvard University Press, 1990.

Calvin, John. *Institutes of the Christian Religion.* Ed. by John T. McNeil. Philadelphia: Westminster Press, 1960.

Chadwick, Henry. *The Enigma of St. Paul.* London: Athone Press, 1969.

Christian, Sue Ellen. "Jobs Help Schaumburg Hit the Big Time among Cities," *Chicago Tribune* (January 14, 1994), 1.

Church, George J. "His Seven Most Urgent Decisions," *Time* (January 25, 1993), 28.

Clark, Kelly James. *Philosophers Who Believe: The Spiritual Journeys of 11 Leading Thinkers.* Downers Grove, Ill.: InterVarsity Press, 1993.

Collins, Raymond. *Studies on the First Letter to the Thessalonians.* Leuven, Belgium: Leuven University Press, 1984.

Corliss, Richard. "Peter Pan Speaks," *Time* (February 22, 1993), 67.

"Counting England's Flock," *Christianity Today* (February 5, 1990), 29.

Cousins, Don. *Tomorrow's Church . . . Today.* South Barrington, Ill.: Willow Creek Publications, 1979.

Cousins, Don, Keith Anderson, and Arthur DeKruyter. *Mastering Church Management.* Portland, Ore.: Multnomah, 1990.

Daley, Steve. "93 Proves That Eloquence and Wit Remain Part of U.S. Political Dialogue," *Chicago Tribune* (December 26, 1993), sec. 4, p. 4.

Daughtry, Russ. "Serious Rock 'n' Roll," *Willow Creek* (January/February 1990), 31.

Department of the Army, *Intelligence Interrogation,* FM 34-52. Approved for public release: Distribution is unlimited.

DeTocqueville, Alexis. *Democracy in America.* Vols. 1 & 2. New York: Vintage Books, 1945.

Dolan, Barbara. "Full House at Willow Creek," *Time* (March 6, 1989), 60.

Drucker, Peter F. *The Effective Executive.* New York: Harper and Row, 1966.

———. "Marketing for a Fast-Changing Decade," *Wall Street Journal* (November 20, 1990), A20.

Dulles, Avery. *A History of Apologetics.* Philadelphia: Westminster Press, 1971.

Edwards, Kari. "The Interplay of Affect and Cognition in Attitude Formation and Change," *Journal of Personality and Social Psychology* 59, no. 2 (1990): 202-16.

Edwards, Maldwyn. *John Wesley and the Eighteenth Century.* London: George Allen, 1933.

Elwell, Walter A. *Evangelical Dictionary of Theology.* Grand Rapids: Baker, 1984.

Emotions Anonymous. St. Paul, Minn.: Emotions Anonymous International, 1978.

Erickson, Millard. *Christian Theology.* Grand Rapids: Baker, 1983.

"Evangelicalism: An Interview with Marshall Shelley," *Faith and Renewal* (July/August 1992), 11.

Farney, Dennis. "Inside Hallmark's Love Machine," *Wall Street Journal* (February 14, 1990), B1.

Friedrich, Otto. "Headed for the Dustheap," *Time* (February 19, 1990), 37.

Gallup, George Jr. *Religion in America 1990.* Princeton, N.J.: Princeton Religion Research Center, 1990.

———. "Religion in America," *The Annals: The American Academy of Political and Social Science.* Beverly Hills: Sage Publications (July 1985).

Gallup, George, and Jim Castelli. *The People's Religion: American Faith in the 90's.* New York: Macmillan, 1989.

Glendon, Mary Ann. "Intra-Tribal Warfare," *First Things* (August/September 1990), 57.

Goffman, Erving. *The Presentation of Self in Everyday Life*. Garden City, N.J.: Doubleday Anchor, 1959.

Graves, James. "Education and Community," *Chronicles* (September 1990), 26–27.

Groh, Dennis. *Augustine: Religion of the Heart*. Nashville: Graded Press, 1988.

Guinness, Os. "Towards a Reappraisal of Christian Apologetics: Peter L. Berger's Sociology of Knowledge as the Sociological Prolegomenon to Christian Apologetics." Ph.D. diss., Oxford University, 1981.

Guinness, Os, and John Seel, eds. *No God But God: Breaking with the Idols of Our Age*. Chicago: Moody Press, 1992.

"Hard Questions for Robert Schuller about Sin and Self-Esteem," *Christianity Today* (August 10, 1984), 14–20.

Hatch, Nathan O. *The Democratization of American Christianity*. New Haven, Conn.: Yale University Press, 1989.

Hollenweger, Walter. *Evangelism Today: Good News or Bone of Contention*. Belfast, Ireland: Christian Journals Ltd., 1976.

Hornblower, Margot. "Advertising Spoken Here," *Time* (July 15, 1991), 71.

Horton, Michael Scott, ed. *Power Religion: The Selling Out of the Evangelical Church*. Chicago: Moody Press, 1992.

Hunter, James D. *American Evangelicalism: Conservative Religion and the Quandary of Modernity*. New Brunswick, N.J.: Rutgers University Press, 1983.

———. *Evangelicalism: The Coming Generation*. Chicago: University of Chicago Press, 1987.

Hunter, James D., and Stephen C. Ainlay, eds. *Making Sense of Modern Times: Peter L. Berger and the Vision of Interpretive Sociology*. New York: Routledge & Kegan Paul, 1986.

Hybels, Bill. *Caution: Christians Under Construction*. Wheaton, Ill.: Scripture Press, 1978.

———. *Christians in the Marketplace*. Wheaton, Ill.: Scripture Press, 1982.

———. *Christians in a Sex Crazed Culture: A Frank Look at God's Good Gift*. Wheaton, Ill.: Scripture Press, 1989.

———. *Honest to God? Becoming an Authentic Christian*. Grand Rapids: Zondervan, 1990.

———. *Laws That Liberate: The Relevance of the Ten Commandments to Modern Living*. Wheaton, Ill.: Victor Books, 1985.

———. "Reading Your Gauges," *Leadership* (1991), 38.

———. *Seven Wonders of the Spiritual World*. Dallas: Word, 1988.

———. *Too Busy Not to Pray: Slowing Down to Be with God*. Downers Grove, Ill.: InterVarsity, 1988.

———. *Who You Are When No One's Looking: Choosing Consistency, Resisting Compromise*. Downers Grove, Ill.: InterVarsity, 1987.

Hybels, Bill, and Mark Mittelberg. *Becoming a Contagious Christian*. Grand Rapids: Zondervan, 1994.

Hybels, Bill, and Rob Wilkins. *Descending into Greatness*. Grand Rapids: Zondervan, 1993.

Hybels, Bill, Stuart Briscoe, and Haddon Robinson. *Mastering Contemporary Preaching*. Portland, Ore.: Multnomah, 1990.

Hybels, Lynne. "Full Circle," *Willow Creek*, special anniversary issue, 23, 25.

Hybels, Lynne. "Watching Lessons," *Willow Creek* (July/August 1990), 30.

"Into the Stratosphere," *Willow Creek*, special anniversary issue, 23, 25.

Jellema, Dirk. "Dort, Synod of," in *The New International Dictionary of the Christian Church*. Ed. by J. D. Douglas. Grand Rapids: Zondervan, 1974, 309–10.

Johnson, Ted. "It's a Sin to Bore a Kid with the Gospel," *Relationships: The Young Life Ministry in Action*, Spring, 1993.

Kantzer, Ken. "A Theologian Looks at Schuller," *Christianity Today* (August 10, 1984), 22–24.

———. "The Doctrine Wars," *Christianity Today* (October 5, 1992), 32.

Keirsey, David, and Marilyn Bates. *Please Understand Me: Character & Temperament Types*. Del Mar, Calif.: Prometheus Nemesis Book Company, 1984.

Keyes, Dick. "Image and Reality in Society," in *What in the World Is Real?* Ed. by Gregory A. Pritchard. Champaign, Ill.: Communication Institute, 1982, 71–101.

Kiechel, Walter. "The Workaholic Generation," *Fortune* (April 10, 1989), 58.

Klages, Karen E. "The $100,000 Men," *Chicago Tribune* (April 10, 1991), sec. 7, p. 18.

Kotler, Philip. *Marketing Management: Analysis, Planning, Implementation, and Control*. 6th ed. Englewood Cliffs, N.J.: Prentice Hall, 1988.

Kozma, Ann-Liza. "Meet Your New Neighbors: The Imitations," *Chicago Tribune* (October 31, 1993), sec. 6, p. 5.

Kramer, Michael. "Moving In," *Time* (January 4, 1993), 33.

"Laying the Foundations," *Willow Creek,* special anniversary issue, 14–21.

MacArthur, John. *Ashamed of the Gospel: When the Church Becomes Like the World.* Wheaton, Ill.: Crossway Books, 1993.

———. *Our Sufficiency in Christ.* Dallas: Word, 1991.

Marsden, George. *Fundamentalism and American Culture: The Shaping of Twentieth-Century Evangelicalism, 1870–1925.* New York: Oxford University Press, 1980.

Marshall, Howard. *1 and 2 Thessalonians.* Grand Rapids: Eerdmans, 1983.

Martin, David. *A General Theory of Secularization.* Oxford: Blackwell, 1978.

Maudlin, Michael G., and Edward Gilbreath, "Selling Out the House of God?" *Christianity Today* (July 18, 1994), 25.

McDowell, Josh. *Evidence That Demands a Verdict.* San Bernardino: Campus Crusade for Christ, 1972.

———. *More Than a Carpenter.* Wheaton, Ill.: Living Books, 1977.

McGavran, Donald. *Understanding Church Growth.* Grand Rapids: Eerdmans, 1970.

Mellado, James. *Willow Creek Community Church.* Cambridge, Mass.: Harvard Business School, 1991.

Merridew, Alan. "Religion with a Beat: Son City Spectacular," *Chicago Tribune* (June 12, 1974), sec. 3, p. 20.

Miethe, Terry. *Did Jesus Rise from the Dead? The Resurrection Debate.* San Francisco: Harper and Row, 1987.

Miller, Gerald R., ed. *Persuasion: New Directions in Theory and Research.* Beverly Hills: Sage Publications, 1980.

Mittelberg, Mark. "A Critical Analysis of the Epistemological Starting Points in Presuppositional Apologetics." Master's thesis, Trinity Evangelical Divinity Seminary, Deerfield, Ill., 1988.

Niebuhr, H. Richard. *Christ and Culture.* New York: Harper and Row, 1951.

Oliver, Robert T. *The Psychology of Persuasive Speech.* New York: Longmans, Green and Co., 1942.

Oskamp, Stuart. *Attitudes and Opinions.* 2d ed. Englewood Cliffs, N.J.: Prentice Hall, 1977.

Packer, J. I. "Humour Is a Funny Thing," *Christianity Today* (October 22, 1990), 15.

———. *A Quest for Godliness.* Wheaton, Ill.: Crossway Books, 1990.

Patterson, James, and Peter Kim. *The Day America Told the Truth.* New York: Prentice Hall, 1991.

Pelikan, Jaroslav. *Jesus through the Centuries.* New York: Harper and Row, 1985.

Peters, Thomas, and Robert H. Waterman Jr. *In Search of Excellence: Lessons from America's Best-Run Companies.* New York: Warner Books, 1982.

Peters, Tom, and Nancy Austin. *A Passion for Excellence: The Leadership Difference.* New York: Random House, 1985.

Plass, Ewald M., ed. *What Luther Says.* Saint Louis: Concordia, 1959.

Postman, Neil. *Amusing Ourselves to Death: Public Discourse in the Age of Show Business.* New York: Penguin Books, 1985.

Postman, Neil, and Camille Paglia, "She Wants Her TV! He Wants His Book!" *Harper's* (March 1991), 44.

"The Power of Personality," *Success* (January/February 1994), 37.

Rabey, Steve. "Will Change Undo the Church?" *Christianity Today* (October 26, 1992), 82.

"Reagan Video Is Prime Ribbing," *Chicago Sun Times* (March 22, 1989), 20.

"Re-Engineering the Seminary," *Christianity Today* (October 24, 1994), 74–78.

Rieff, Philip. *The Feeling Intellect.* Chicago: University of Chicago Press, 1990.

Roberts, Robert C. "Psychobabble," *Christianity Today* (May 16, 1994), 18–24.

Robinson, Anthony B. "Learning from Willow Creek Church," *Christian Century* (January 23, 1991), 68–70.

Robinson, Martin. *A World Apart: Creating a Church for the Unchurched.* Tunbridge, Wells, England: Monarch, 1992.

Rosenberg, Tina. "From Dissidents to MTV Democrats," *Harper's* (September 1992), 48.

Schuller, Robert. "Possibility Thinking and the Growth of the Church in Japan," *Japan Christian Quarterly* (Spring, 1988).

———. *Self Esteem: The New Reformation.* Waco: Word, 1982.

———. *Your Church Has Real Possibilities!* Glendale, Calif.: Regal, 1974.

Schultz, Darrel. "Second Thoughts on Swimming in 'Willow Creek,'" *Christian Week* (October 19, 1993), 9.

Shorris, Earl. "A Nation of Salesmen," *Harper's* (October 1994).

Singer, David. "The Unmodern Jew," *First Things* (June/July 1991).

Singletary, Mike, with Jerry Jenkins. *Singletary on Singletary.* Nashville: Thomas Nelson, 1991.

Stafford, Tim. "Franchising Hope," *Christianity Today* (May 18, 1992).

———. "The Therapeutic Revolution," *Christianity Today* (May 17, 1993).

Statistical Abstract of the United States. Table 220. Washington, D.C.: Bureau of the Census, 1992.

Stewart, Thomas A. "Turning Around the Lord's Business," *Fortune* (September 25, 1989), 166, 117, 120, 124.

Stott, John. "A Resurgence of Evangelical Scholarship," *Christianity Today* (October 5, 1992), 33.

Strobel, Lee. *Inside the Mind of Unchurched Harry and Mary: How to Reach Friends and Family Who Avoid Church and the Church.* Grand Rapids: Zondervan, 1993.

Taylor, Elizabeth. "Al's O.K., You're O.K.," *Time* (October 12, 1992), 60.

———. "Taking Care of Herself," *Time* (December 10, 1990), 106.

"The Theater Days," *Willow Creek,* special anniversary issue, 29.

Tipton, Steven. *Getting Saved from the Sixties.* Los Angeles: University of California Press, 1982.

Toulmin, Stephen. *Cosmopolis: The Hidden Agenda of Modernity.* New York: The Free Press, 1990.

Towns, Elmer. *An Inside Look at 10 of Today's Most Innovative Churches.* Ventura, Calif.: Regal, 1990.

Valeo, Tom. "Bill Hybels Knows How to Coax Folks Back to Church," *Daily Herald* (May 18, 1988), sec. 2, p. 4.

———. "The Drama of Willow Creek," *Daily Herald* (May 19, 1988), 9.

———. "Why Do 12,000 People Listen?" *Daily Herald* (May 18, 1988), sec. 2, p. 4.

Veroff, Joseph, Elizabeth Douvan, and Richard A. Kulka. *The Inner American: A Self Portrait from 1957 to 1976.* New York: Basic Books, 1981.

Vitz, Paul C. *Psychology As Religion: The Cult of Self-Worship.* Grand Rapids: Eerdmans, 1977.

Wagner, Peter. *Church Growth and the Whole Gospel.* San Francisco: Harper and Row, 1981.

———. *Your Church Can Grow.* Glendale, Calif.: Regal, 1976.

Wells, David F. *Turning to God: Biblical Conversion in the Modern World.* Grand Rapids: Baker, 1989.

Wesley, John. *John Wesley.* Ed. by Albert C. Outler. New York: Oxford University Press, 1964.

Wilkins, Rob. "The Profound Simplicity of Love," *Willow Creek* (January/February 1991), 3.

———. "The Spark of Vision," *Willow Creek* (September/October 1990), 18–19.

Williams, Raymond. "Culture and Civilization" in *The Encyclopedia of Philosophy.* Ed. by Paul Edwards. 8 vols. New York: Macmillan Publishing Co. & The Free Press, 1967.

Winter, Richard. *The Roots of Sorrow: Reflections on Depression and Hope.* Westchester, Ill.: Crossway Books, 1986.

Wuthnow, Robert. *Meaning and Moral Order: Explorations in Cultural Analysis.* Berkeley: University of California Press, 1987.

———. *The Restructuring of American Religion: Society and Faith Since World War II.* Princeton, N.J.: Princeton University Press, 1988.

———. *The Struggle for America's Soul: Evangelicals, Liberals, and Secularism.* Grand Rapids: Eerdmans, 1989.

York, Cindy. "Gimme That New-Time Religion," *U.S.A. Today Weekend* (April 13–15, 1990), 1, 4–6.

Yankelovich, Daniel. *New Rules: Searching for Self-Fulfillment in a World Turned Upside Down.* New York: Random House, 1981.

Zoglin, Richard. "And What a Reign It Was," *Time* (March 16, 1992), 64.

Acknowledgments

Many individuals have contributed in significant ways in the preparation of this book.

The first life of this project was as a Ph.D. dissertation at Northwestern University. Several of my academic teachers and colleagues provided insightful and wise comments. I want to particularly thank Alan Schnaiberg, Richard Tholin, and R. Stephen Warner.

Occasionally in the text I refer to the number of times a particular word was used during a year of Willow Creek's messages. I was able to create this computer concordance with the gracious effort of my good friend David Gorman.

In the metamorphosis of changing a dissertation into its second life as book, several friends and family members were particularly helpful. At different times the following readers provided astute and discerning observations: Eric Bobbitt, Os Guinness, Brian Heller, Bill Helm, Sandy Jaffe, Jay Pinney, and Skipp Pritchard. The book is much better because of their insights, and I want to thank them for their gracious help and friendship.

I also want to thank my wife, Lori, for her discernment and suggestions. Many of the ideas presented grew out of long discussions between us. Some of the best insights originally came from her comments and observations.

Although I borrowed many insights and suggestions from these individuals, this book is solely my responsibility.

Lastly, and most of all, I want to thank the Lord Jesus Christ. He has provided strength in weak times, light in dark times, and hope in bleak times. *Soli Deo gloria!*

Index

About the Author

Gregory A. Pritchard has an interdisciplinary background in sociology, history, and theology including a Ph.D. in Religion in Personality and Society from Northwestern University. He has lectured at various conferences, colleges, and universities and is the editor and contributing author of *What in the World Is Real?* and *Charting a Revolution.* Dr. Pritchard is a member of the Society for the Scientific Study of Religion, the Society of Christian Ethics, and the Evangelical Theological Society and has taught in graduate schools in the United States and Asia.

To contact the author write to:

Communication Institute
P. O. Box 213
Washington, IL 61571

Evaluation of G. A. Pritchard's dissertation "The Strategy of Willow Creek"

Greg Pritchard's dissertation is a detailed and judicious examination of Willow Creek Church and its strategy for reaching the world. His careful analysis and accessible prose make this scholarly treatment essential reading for all interested in the seeker-church movement.

James Davison Hunter
Professor of sociology
University of Virginia

I can offer the highest recommendations for Dr. Pritchard. He has completed a creative, multimethod study of one of the most dramatically different Protestant milieus, one which has now trained upwards of 35,000 participants. In our geographic area, Willow Creek is *the* best-known church today and has drawn the attention of both clerical and lay scholars. But none have the depth of research approaches that Greg is bringing to this project and none have produced the rich understanding of both the means and goals of Willow Creek that Greg achieved in his study. His thesis is really the equivalent of two or three of the sociological theses I normally supervise.

Alan Schnaiberg
Professor of sociology
Northwestern University

As the senior pastor of a seeker sensitive church, I hope this study receives a wide and careful reading. I don't agree with everything Dr. Pritchard has written; however, this study deserves to be read by any leader in the seeker movement willing to honestly examine the strengths and weaknesses of the seeker-church model. This kind of constructive and insightful evaluation will hopefully lead to healthy discussion and stronger local churches.

Peter Grant
Senior pastor
Buckhead Community Church
Atlanta, Georgia